CAMPUS STRATEGIES FOR LIBRARIES AND ELECTRONIC INFORMATION

EDUCOM Strategies Series on Information Technology

CAMPUS
STRATEGIES
for LIBRARIES *and*
ELECTRONIC
INFORMATION

Caroline Arms, Editor

E D U C O M
Strategies
Series
On Information
Technology

Digital Press **digital**™

Library of Congress Cataloging-in-Publication Data

Campus strategies for libraries and electronic
  information.

      (EDUCOM strategies series on information technology)
      Includes bibliographical references.
      1. Libraries, University and college--United States--
Automation. 2. Libraries and electronic publishing--
United States. 3. Library information networks--United
States. 4. Information technology--United States.
I. Arms, Caroline R. (Caroline Ruth) II. Series.
Z675.U5C16 1990   027.7'0973   89—16879
ISBN 1–55558–036–X   CIP

9 8 7 6 5 4 3 2 1

Order number EY-C185E-DP

A list of the trademarks mentioned in the text appears at the back of the book.

Jacket and interior design: Sandra Calef
Production coordination: Timothy Evans / Editorial Inc.
Composition: Editorial Inc.
Printing and binding: Hamilton Printing Company

Printed in the United States of America

Contents

Foreword

Kenneth M. King

Over the last few years, I have become conscious of a new and encouraging phenomenon. At an increasing number of institutions, library and computing professionals are working together with extraordinary harmony. These cooperative cross-cultural relationships, characterized by both good chemistry and compatibility, are creating varied and valuable services in support of scholarship and instruction. Out of these relationships, a shared vision of the future seems to be emerging. After discussions with a number of computer and library professionals, it appeared timely to produce a book in the EDUCOM Strategies Series on Information Technology devoted to trying to define this vision.

EDUCOM is a higher education membership organization with 600 colleges and universities as members and 125 corporate associates. A major goal of EDUCOM is to promote the rational and effective use of information technology in higher education. It attempts to accomplish this through publications, conferences, seminars, workshops, consulting services, and task forces directed toward achieving specific goals. The primary goal of the Strategies Series is to help colleges and universities plan. Everything begins with a good plan.

The first step in preparing a new volume in a series is to find an editor. Fortunately, Caroline Arms, who writes on technical issues with extraordinary clarity, was not only agreeable to editing this volume, but enthusiastic. This is the third volume in the series, and Caroline was also the editor of the second, *Campus Networking Strategies*. John W. McCredie, formerly president of EDUCOM and now at Digital Equipment Corporation, edited the first volume, called *Campus Computing Strategies*.

By tradition, the books in the series each comprise about ten chapters by authors from a range of higher educational institutions doing cutting-edge development work in the area covered by the book. Their task is to describe where they are, how they got there, and where they think they are going. Since these chapters provide potential recipes for other institutions to follow, these authors are also asked to describe the context in which they were able to succeed, necessary resources, lessons learned, pitfalls, and opportunities. We then seek some leading expert to write the introduction, and the editor provides chapters containing technical and background information. This is the formula, tried and true.

Having secured Caroline as the editor, the next challenge was to find authors. Caroline and I, in consultation with a small group of unindicted co-conspirators, prepared a list of potential contributors. On lists of this sort, there are sometimes a few evangelists. Signing up these people is easy because they are, in a sense, our natural prey. There may also be a few people who will kill you if you fail to ask them, and it is important not to miss any of them. But most of the people on these lists turn out to be too intelligent and too busy to be easily persuaded to get involved in an effort requiring a major unremunerated commitment of time, and that was the big problem with the people on our list. Persuading them to contribute required great skill, charm, and some begging.

Another major problem is that, because of the attempt to get balance among institutions representing a range of sizes, disciplines, and cultures, or through oversight, or through the mistaken conviction that the task of persuading some people to participate would be overwhelming, some institutions doing great work do not appear in this book. If your institution is one of these, please send me a note, and I will try to find another EDUCOM channel to get your story on the record.

Since the Online Computer Library Center and the Research Libraries Group provide an important element of the context in which library information systems in higher education evolve, we felt it was important to include their stories. The strategy in such circumstances is straightforward: simply tell each that you are sure the other is going to be represented.

Finally, we needed a leading expert to write the introduction. The obvious choice was Patricia Battin; in her distinguished career, she has worked in both computing and library circles. Pat is President of the Commission on Preservation and Access, a nonprofit organization that fosters collaboration among libraries and allied organizations to ensure the preservation of the published record and enhance access to our intellectual and cultural heritage. Before taking her current position, she was a vice president at Columbia University, with responsibility for both libraries and computing services. Fortunately, she was in a poor position to refuse our request. She was just completing a term on the EDUCOM board, where she had devoted a lot of time and energy to the issues covered in this book. Over time, she was moved from being willing to consider it, to probably being willing to do it, to agreeing to do it. With her commitment, the effort was launched, and the rest is history.

We are deeply grateful to the authors of this book. They took a lot of time from the process of creating the future to describe for us the journey. We are also grateful for the institutional support they received.

We are also indebted to Apple Computer, Inc., Digital Equipment Corporation, IBM Corporation, NeXT, Inc., and Sun Microsystems, Inc., whose financial support made this volume possible. These organizations are corporate associates of EDUCOM and continuing supporters of the goals of higher education.

The opinions expressed in this book are those of the individual authors and are not intended to represent policy statements of EDUCOM, the contributing universities and organizations, the supporting corporations, or Digital Press.

I believe that the institutions contributing chapters to this book prove that remarkable things can be accomplished through cooperation between computing and library professionals and that a common vision of the future is emerging: access to an array of information resources from the scholar's desktop. Librarians are stepping up to the challenge of taking responsibility for information in electronic format. It is also clear that some information, but not all, is more useful in electronic form than in print. Over the next decade, as gigabit-per-second networks connect institutions of higher education, as workstations with high-resolution graphics and sound become ubiquitous, and as an increasing body of knowledge is available in electronic form, some institutions will be ready to deliver information to their constituencies in whatever manner works best. How about your institution? Will it be ready?

Introduction

Patricia Battin

During the past thirty years, the rapidly accelerating use of technology in our universities has had a profound impact on higher education in the United States. The effects have been particularly visible and dramatic in the traditional disciplines of engineering, the sciences, and the social sciences, where computing technology transformed the labor-intensive number-crunching activities basic to research and instruction. Both the patterns and potential dimensions of scientific research changed rapidly as communications technologies combined with computing capacities to make possible high-speed networks capable of delivering enormous computing power, electronic imaging capabilities, and machine-readable data to individual workstations throughout the international scholarly community.

The visibility and glamour of the extraordinary dimensions of scientific research enabled by the new technologies—and the justifiable euphoria they inspired—overshadowed the recognition of even more revolutionary changes taking place in the central scholarly information system fundamental to research and instruction in higher education—the library. The chapters in this book reveal that, contrary to the conventional perceptions, those responsible for integrating technology and its products into the traditional library function have faced a series of enormous challenges made all the more difficult by the persuasive overlay of mythology and unexamined assumptions that surround the role of the library in academia. The understandable reluctance of the university community to reexamine time-honored traditions and services despite overwhelming evidence of their inadequacy in an environment of rapidly changing information requirements has further complicated the process. Introducing new services and opportunities such as computing and communications capabilities is far easier than replacing or even enhancing, in a financially straitened context, traditional services basic to scholarly research and instruction. Subjective perceptions of the destruction of that fundamental scholarly verity—the library—by the unwelcome invasion of technology continue to obscure the twin realities of disproportionately rising costs and the growing disjuncture between the strengths and capabilities of the traditional library and the changing information habits and demands of its clientele. The financial pressures arising from a steadily expanding commercialization of the scholarly publishing process, swollen by the expanding production of knowledge and a proliferation of new storage and dissemination technologies, pose a persistent and disquieting threat to the distinctive sine qua non of the university—the commitment to broad and equitable access to information regardless of the ability to pay.

The research library relies heavily upon labor-intensive internal operations to manage the printed materials that constitute the knowledge base and demands equally labor-intensive efforts from its users. Approximately 90 percent of the information needs of the academic and research programs depend on this essentially nineteenth-century information system. It coexists with an emerging twenty-first century information system that currently serves only 10 percent of those needs. The coexistence contributes to a frenetic schizophrenia among students and faculty, who expect the efficiency and convenience of electronic facilities from traditional library services and the comprehensive literature coverage of traditional library collections from electronic systems. That the technical potential to provide services that combine the best of both systems exists, in the abstract, creates unrealistic expectations. The problem is compounded since the bulk of scholarly literature still resides only in traditional print formats.

For the last several hundred years, the requirements for information support services in colleges and universities have been met by centralized library systems. During the past two decades, libraries have automated many of their technical operations, such as acquiring and cataloging materials, but this "library automation" was not designed to provide direct services to scholars and students and did little to revolutionize information habits. Now, microcomputers and sophisticated telecommunications systems are used widely by faculty and students. As a consequence, the requirements for library support in the modern university extend far beyond the automation of specific operational processes. Service requirements in the electronic university will be driven and shaped by this increasing use of technology by scholars and students and their demands for new and improved information services available at individual workstations regardless of the physical location of the knowledge base.

Perhaps the most critical issue facing university officers in the next decade is the change in the nature, character, and financing of information services brought about through the use of technology by scholars and students. If information is defined as a function rather than a format and if we assume the perspective of the "wired scholar"—the user at the workstation—then the task (as these essays illustrate) is to create a new information infrastructure for the electronic university. And, because the use of information is deeply embedded in the academic pursuits of the scholarly community, any change in the way it is acquired, stored, and delivered must be planned carefully. The revolution that began twenty years ago as the automation of specific internal processes now challenges our traditional, fundamental assumptions concerning basic disciplinary requirements, ownership of intellectual property, provision of equitable access to information, financing formulas, university organizational structures, and strategies for the interinstitutional support of networks, databanks, and machine-readable information resources.

The characteristics of one format—print—have over the years obscured the diverging uses of information by different disciplines. A key strategy—the departmental library—was developed in the early twentieth century to adapt the rigidities of the print format to disciplinary differences in information habits and research patterns. Even so, the specific information requirements and research methodologies of the scholarly community remained, in large part, subordinated to the information services available through large collections of printed materials. Technology has evolved to permit a greater decentralization of access and a broad range of format choices. An unprecedented flexibility in the hands of the user to define and satisfy individual requirements is rapidly replacing the traditionally accepted accommodation to the constraints of the provider. As a consequence, these disciplinary differences, heretofore suppressed in the monolithic context of print format, are reflected in a diversity of strategies for adapting the mission and enhancing the capability of an institution's information services. Nonetheless, as in networking and computing strategies, the capacity for customized access to and manipulation of information resources can only be fully and productively realized within a coordinated and managed infrastructure with standardized gateways, common access protocols, and compatible software systems.

The financial support of access to information resources proliferating in both volume and format can no longer be usefully accommodated by the traditional budgeting structures of academic institutions. The codex format of pages bound into volumes lent itself well to the concept of centrally supported institutional ownership of the knowledge base required to support the institution's academic programs. Equitable access within that context was assured by tuition payment or faculty appointment. A vast and reasonably responsive (for the preelectronic age) interlibrary loan network provided access to research resources not heavily used on the local campus. Since the library was viewed as the virtual core of most institutions, the budget was determined centrally, with the allocations based essentially on perceptions of the rate of publishing and the research domains of the early twentieth century. These formulas have long since become grossly inadequate to respond to the publication explosion, the increasing specialization of scientific and scholarly research, and the changing demands for information resources and services as technology influences the research and instructional patterns of faculty and students equipped with powerful workstations. Nonetheless, the traditional budget structures of most institutions continue to isolate the library budget in the unexamined straitjacket of the past. Fierce adherence to an undefined sense of "entitlement" to information services and resources by faculty and students (which grew out of the nineteenth-century concept of institutional ownership of the knowledge base) remains a serious deterrent to a rational and judicious analysis of both the costs and the appropriate proportion of institutional financial resources committed to information services.

This volume presents a microcosm of the broad themes of the past two decades—case studies of a range of extraordinarily successful, pioneering, and ingeniously financed applications of technology to library operations and services, applications that have begun to transform the manner in which scholarly information is acquired, stored, disseminated, and preserved. These achievements are made the more extraordinary by the fact that, in contrast to computing and communications applications, they have often been accomplished without significant infusions of external funds in environments where traditional services are being financed and provided as well.

The evolution from the initial objectives of "library automation" to new concepts of information delivery and services is depicted graphically in the historical accounts of the two large bibliographic networks, OCLC and RLIN. Though OCLC and RLIN are programmatically distinct in origin, primary mission, and targeted user clientele, both chapters reflect the passage from a somewhat narrowly conceived technical support system for conventional library operations to a broadly based supplier of information services and products to individuals as well as libraries. The differences in the ownership, governance, and primary services reflect the two organizations' basic missions and provide interesting contrasts as well as complementary functions. OCLC was organized to furnish a range of services to all libraries, while the primary objective of the Research Libraries Group, the parent of RLIN, is to serve the special programmatic needs of research libraries.

The two accounts illustrate the complex and interdependent relationship among the diversity of user requirements, new technical capacities, and the traditional knowledge base. The maturation of these organizations revolutionized the library environment and heavily influenced automation efforts in individual libraries. The existence of the large centralized databases of bibliographic records of the nation's libraries made possible the cost-effective automation of local library operations by eliminating the costly redundancy of cataloging each item independently. Increased demand by students and faculty for access to machine-readable information influenced the development of more sophisticated products and programs by the two organizations. The growth in campus networks led to a demand by newly networked users for remote, unmediated access to library catalogs and databases. The development of integrated systems for automating library operations, coupled with rising communications costs, spurred a renewed interest in stand-alone local systems that threaten the continuing viability of the large centralized database necessary for a variety of cooperative program activities.

The late 1960s and early 1970s spawned a large number of institutional efforts to build fully integrated online systems before the maturation of OCLC and RLIN services. All but a few failed; Northwestern University's NOTIS, however, has been successfully exported to many other institutions and eventually was developed by the university into a commercial product that has proved particularly popular with large academic libraries. Eloquent testimony to the complexity of library automation, the history of NOTIS by McGowan, Horny, and Baker traces how the initial goal of a fully integrated online system to support internal library operations evolved into the broader aim of a university information system supporting a range of academic information needs.

As the trend to automate library operations gained momentum, a distinct diseconomy of scale became apparent. Costs and technical complexities rise with the size, comprehensiveness, and age of the collection. Some large institutions may never complete the retrospective conversion of their bibliographic records. It is no coincidence that most of the libraries represented in this book, libraries that have moved beyond the stage of automating internal operations toward providing the users with a wider variety of information online, are medium-sized.

Alexander and Meyer present a model description of the complexity involved in the installation of the NOTIS system in a medium-sized library at Clemson University. As they point out, the ready access to the online catalog, combined with a networked campus, created a demand for online access to other databases, underscoring the need for coordinated and compatible gateways from the self-contained library system as new services generated newer demands. The demand for networked access to databases other than the catalog can be provided in two ways: by licensing or creating databases and mounting them locally or by providing links to permit direct access to remote databases. The Clemson experience points up the importance of the user's perspective—the library catalog as the entry or gateway to all other information resources, regardless of location or ownership.

The Illinois chapter describes the evolution of an early library automation project into a statewide information system. The project that began with the automation of labor-intensive circulation control systems to support a greatly expanded interlibrary loan capacity developed steadily into a fully operational statewide network of enhanced information access and document delivery—recapitulating on an interinstitutional level the history of computer applications in libraries. As do the other studies, this history reflects a set of common issues and the diversity of possible strategies as technical developments and user demands increasingly influenced the directions of library computing activities.

The chapters by Thomas and Drake illustrate the institutional capacity to develop information services that are tailored to a particular user community and demonstrate the importance of careful analysis of user requirements and educational mission before embarking on a major redesign of information services. From the Georgia Institute of Technology, Drake describes the strategies developed for a scientific and technical university based on a primary objective of access to information regardless of location rather than local collection strength. Interlibrary loan and document delivery are important components of the strategy. The model of the integrated library automation system was specifically rejected because of its high cost and irrelevance to the needs of the primary user group. This contrasts with the disciplinary needs of the law school population at Brigham Young University, as described by Thomas. The commercial legal databases, LEXIS and WESTLAW, are essential to contemporary legal instruction and research, but materials in print form are used heavily as well. An integrated library system's ability to supply information on the current status of local materials is therefore valuable to law students and faculty.

Although the two institutions have chosen different strategies for providing access to large, privately vended databases of machine-readable information to their faculty and students at individual workstations, both illustrate the serious dilemma facing universities as they seek to maintain equity of access in an increasingly commercialized information marketplace. Georgia Tech provides access through a licensing contract with commercial vendors to mount the databases on the institution's mainframe computers, thus eliminating telecommunications and external computer usage charges. Also under licensing arrangements, the BYU Law Library provides access to the off-site LEXIS and WESTLAW databases. In both instances, contractual conditions limit access to the immediate user community, a radical shift of ownership control from the university to the private vendor.

The concept of the planned teaching library described by Johnson, Lyman, and Tompkins reflects another facet of the library prism. State-of-the-art information services are being developed at the University of Southern California to respond to the curricular needs of undergraduates by integrating traditional classroom teaching and learning pedagogies with those inherent in a powerful information system.

The range of choices afforded by information technology in redesigning both the organizational structure of the library and its role in the university, evident in the models developed by the Mann Library of Cornell University and the Columbia University Libraries, reflects the influences of the second decade of library computing. The strategies of both institutions assume a networked campus and wired scholars. Columbia combined its libraries and academic computing facilities into a Scholarly Information Center, while the Mann Library provides a Scholarly Information System through cooperative mechanisms. The Columbia model met the demand for new technical skills in the library and new information skills in the computer center by coordinating existing talent; the Cornell solution was to add technically trained individuals to the library staff. Both examples amply illustrate the complexity of the challenge and the importance of developing strategies that capitalize on institutional strengths and styles.

Carnegie Mellon University's Project Mercury builds on the experiences of the past twenty years and the vastly increased technical capacities available on some campuses today. Project Mercury seeks to explore the feasibility of an electronic library that would provide both traditional and enhanced library services to the workstation in a dramatic revision of the traditional library. Such a concept depends on a fully networked campus and a computing environment capable of supporting very large amounts of online storage. The project structure of a demonstration component, a laboratory environment, and a working library for a single discipline underscores the complexity of integrating information technology into the traditional system of print formats. Changing user requirements, technological capacities, and cost implications must be explored before new services can fruitfully replace the traditional library function.

The strategy articulated by the Johns Hopkins Medical Institutions redefines the library's role in the scholarly communication process as bearing the primary responsibility for a knowledge management system. Access to a full range of information services, including clinical databases, full-text and bibliographic literature files, electronic textbooks, drug reference sources, and specialized research databases, will be managed by the library in its new role. In certain instances, the library will develop and maintain databases itself, in close cooperation with the faculty; in others, the library will participate in the international scientific community to ensure access for Johns Hopkins scholars. As has been reported by the other authors, each succeeding application of technology has placed new types of demand on libraries and librarians. The knowledge management environment will yet again alter the qualifications needed by the professional staff and require substantial changes to traditional library and university organizational structures if the new strategies are to succeed.

The imperative of new cooperative links, both within and outside the institution, recurs frequently in Arms's sampling of projects and progress at other libraries and universities. As the decentralization of technology continues, the demand for costly equipment, specialized technical talents, and disciplinary knowledge to create and maintain complex systems exposes the inadequacy of traditional organizational structures. The required talents are scattered across the university, and the costs are too great for one institution to develop systems and applications in isolation. As Arms notes, each new innovation brings a host of new complexities, further blurring the distinctions among the traditional roles of libraries, computer centers, and academic departments. Her discussion of the complex standards and sophisticated software required to support the unfettered exchange of scholarly information provides a useful summary of progress toward this goal. As she perceptively remarks in the final chapter, the shape of our technological future may well be determined, not by technology's endless capacities, but by the human ability to manage its potential in the interests of our intellectual and cultural values.

Not surprisingly, the question of financial strategies for the future forms the subtext of many chapters. It represents the essential challenge, and cannot be solved by the library operating within a tradition-bound budget based on a vanished historical context. Achieving the reality of the wired scholar, connected through a global network to his or her peers and to information resources, will require bold and unprecedented strategies. The creation of a new scholarly information infrastructure, appropriate to the educational mission of the particular institution, will occur only through the cooperative efforts of university officers, faculty, and librarians. New interinstitutional strategies will be required to ensure equitable access to scholarly information in an unprecedented global context of scholarly demands driven by new dimensions of knowledge and technology.

Much progress has been made during the past decade, but much more remains to be accomplished. The successful transition of our massive collective investment in print resources to an affordable, efficient, and effective information system for the electronic scholar will require a planned and sustained financial commitment over the next decade. As these studies indicate, changing the nature of information services raises a wide range of issues fundamental to the university's mission in our society. The nature of the library operation requires a consistent commitment, financial and intellectual, over a long period, if we are to preserve the knowledge of the past, serve the present, and plan for the future.

Chapter 1

The Technological Context

Caroline Arms

Academic libraries have functioned within a technological context of remarkable—and increasing—change during the last few decades. Campus computing organizations have lived with continuous change since their inception and have grown to expect it, although they hardly relish it when trying to provide service to users whose demands range from perpetual consistency to state-of-the-art facilities. Fifteen years ago, the campus computing service was based on large central time-sharing computers used primarily by scientists and engineers. By the early 1980s, departmental computers were common, and demand for time-sharing services had grown, as faculty, students, and administrators in all fields discovered the advantages of word processing. Just a few years later, personal computers are on desktops and in dormitory rooms all over campus. The academic computing organization now must redirect its focus from central computers to a campus network that will allow users with their own computers to communicate with one another and to share common resources. It struggles to satisfy a community of faculty and students whose expectations grow, not just with each new service offered on campus, but with each new product in the commercial marketplace.

This same community is the library's clientele, but, for libraries and librarians, the frenetic pace of change has not always come with the territory. Traditional patterns of library organization and operation have developed over centuries of experience with storing and disseminating information in printed form. Within this framework, libraries first used computers for "library automation"—that is, to automate traditional internal operations. The computers were kept in the back room, and academic libraries could choose not to automate or to automate gradually. Yet, as more and more faculty and students use personal computers for writing papers, sending electronic mail, and other routine tasks, they become aware of the computer's remarkable utility as a tool for retrieving and managing information. As a result, libraries are under increasing pressure to provide access to information in electronic form and to integrate their services with other aspects of academic life that take advantage of the same technology. This book describes the approaches of a number of institutions that responded to this pressure early or even foresaw it.

The libraries and library consortia contributing to this volume have moved beyond basic library automation and are taking steps toward providing an "electronic library." Nevertheless, the stories they tell are based on a common background—the early history of library automation and developments in computing technology. Although this book may be read most widely by librarians and computer professionals, it also is aimed at a more general audience—those interested in understanding the changes occurring in today's academic libraries. This chapter attempts both to establish a common ground of terminology and to set the stage for the case-study chapters.

The Development of Library Automation

A discussion of library automation is best begun with a brief introduction of the traditional library operations that have benefited from automation.

Traditional Library Operations

Library organizations traditionally have been divided into two areas: "public services," such as circulation, reference, and user assistance, that involve direct contact with users, and "technical services," the backroom operations such as acquisitions, cataloging, shelving, and binding. In the technical services department, a book is acquired, cataloged, and placed on the shelves. From this point on, staff in the public services department can help users locate relevant items in the catalog and check them out. In many ways, the catalog is the keystone that joins the two areas of technical and public services.

Once a decision has been made to acquire an item, the acquisitions process involves clerical tasks such as issuing a purchase order, checking the order status with the supplier, recording receipt, and generating information for the university departments responsible for paying invoices and accounting. An "on-order" file must be maintained to prevent duplicate purchases and to answer queries from users or other library staff. This is often combined with an "in-process" file, where staff keep track of the status of items that have been received but not yet cataloged and placed on the shelves.

Cataloging involves recording information about the item (title, author, date and place of publication, and so on) and assigning subject headings. The cataloger also will classify the book into a discipline by assigning it a "call number," a unique identifier that will indicate where it should be shelved. The information recorded by the cataloger is "bibliographic" information. Depending on the attitude of the speaker, whose emphasis may be on the collection itself or on helping people use it, cataloging may be described as providing "bibliographic control" for an item or "bibliographic access" to it. Parts of the process that require particular skill and experience are classification and the selection of subject headings. Subject headings must be used consistently throughout the collection. If one book is cataloged under "Data communication" and a comparable one under "Computer networks," users may fail to find all the material they need. To facilitate consistency, libraries have developed "authority files" of subject headings. There are also authority files or lists specifying the authoritative form and spelling, along with alternatives, for names of people and organizations.

During this century, most catalogs have been in the form of cards filed in drawers. For each item, cards are generated for filing by author, title, and subject. Another file often has been kept for use by library staff; this "shelflist" is sorted by call number and is usually the official record of holdings but sometimes has less complete information than the catalog records.

Periodicals and other serial publications need somewhat different treatment. The title need only be cataloged when a subscription is first taken out, but the receipt of each issue must be recorded, and, if the issue does not arrive as expected, the problem must be followed up. Later, when issues are bound into volumes, bindery activity must be tracked. "Serials control" or "serials management" usually is handled separately from the acquisitions process for monographs.

The technical operations described above take place behind the scenes. The library patron is only aware of the final result: a catalog or a list of serials holdings. Operations of which the user may be more aware, which hardly need an introduction, are circulation, interlibrary loan of items not held by the local library, and reference services. The last two functions require bibliographic access, not only to the library's own collection, through its catalog, but to other sources, such as collections at other libraries or, through indexing and abstracting services, to individual articles within periodicals.

Some library operations are not needed in every library. A university library usually provides a "reserves" system for faculty to reserve certain items in connection with a particular course, so that this material only can be used within the library or borrowed for a very short period. Manuscripts and archives require special treatment for cataloging, physical preparation, and storage.

Library Automation

Automation in libraries began before programmable computers were developed. In the late 1930s, punched-card equipment, which already had been used for some years in the business world for accounting, was applied to circulation and acquisitions functions in a few adventurous libraries. Ralph H. Parker and Frederick G. Kilgour, who later were to be instrumental in the founding of OCLC to provide shared automation facilities for libraries, were among the pioneers. In 1942, E. Carl Pratt commented, in an article describing the circulation system at the University of Florida, "Enough has probably been written on the principles of the punched card method and its application to library routines."[1] He cited four references! The prime advantage of automating circulation was that a single card (and a single procedure to prepare it) replaced the two or three records required in earlier systems: one to be sorted by call number, another by date due, and, in some libraries, a third by borrower. The same equipment could be used to prepare a card for each item returned late; these cards were processed through an electronic accounting machine in the registrar's office to prepare monthly invoices for unpaid fines. Apart from the cited projects, Pratt was aware of systems based on similar equipment at three other universities.

Twenty years later, in the spring of 1961, Alan Perlis reported that there were about a hundred computers in universities.[2] In 1962, the library at the University of California, San Diego, claimed that a new serials management system represented the first use of a computer in a university library operation. If the UCSD library was first, it was not so by much; many other university libraries soon were introducing similar batch-processing systems to automate individual operations. Computer jobs were prepared offline on punched cards and submitted for running one at a time. Time-sharing computers to support simultaneous interactive sessions were still on the drawing board, but the far-sighted had no doubts that automation would have some role in the library of the future. Among these was the administration of Northwestern University, where plans for a new library building included computing facilities.

In the spring of 1963, the Graduate School of Library Science at the University of Illinois sponsored a Clinic on Library Applications of Data Processing,[3] the first of a series that is still held annually. Burton W. Adkinson, head of the Office of Science Information Service at the National Science Foundation, introduced the clinic with a discussion of "Trends in Library Applications of Data Processing," based on a comprehensive bibliography of 135 items describing experiences in automating acquisitions, serials management, circulation, producing catalogs on cards and in book form, and interlibrary communication. Reaching back twenty-five years, most of these applications, and those described by the clinic participants, made use of equipment that processed punched cards or paper tape. The potential for following business practice and migrating to computers for faster, more flexible systems was discussed at the clinic. Then, as now, the National Library of Medicine was in the vanguard: the library reported that, after two years of planning, the first computer had just been installed. At the time, it was estimated that there would be twenty thousand computers in the United States by the end of 1963, but only a few were in academia.

Important Developments of the Mid-1960s

The mid-1960s brought technological developments that directed the path of library automation for the next two decades. Dartmouth College and the Massachusetts Institute of Technology introduced their pioneering time-sharing systems. These systems supported many users and many tasks simultaneously, and remote interactive access was possible over telephone lines, from across the campus or across the country. The first experiments with computer networks began. Smaller institutions could buy time on a computer at another institution or group together in a cooperative venture. Real-time online access opened up new possibilities for convenience and efficiency in library automation. It was clear that traditional practices and policies were not going to be able to handle the information explosion: libraries saw cooperative ventures based on computers as a way of sharing resources and expenses.

Equally important was a development more specific to the library community. In 1963, a survey by a team led by Gilbert King "was an enthusiastic endorsement of the benefits and feasibility of automation in the Library [of Congress]."[4] The following year, the Library of Congress acquired its first computer and commissioned a study to determine how machine-readable catalog records could be produced and used. Cataloging had long been recognized as an expensive operation, and, since 1901, the Library of Congress had been reproducing its catalog cards for use by other libraries; automation was expected to enhance this service. In 1966, sixteen American libraries joined an experimental project known as MARC (MAchine-Readable Cataloging) for distributing bibliographic records on magnetic tape. These records could be used to print catalog cards, to generate catalogs in book form, or for any other purpose, including distributing records to other libraries. Over a two-year period, the initial MARC format was revised, and an extended character set was developed to cover all the major languages using the Roman alphabet. The American National Standards Institute (ANSI) approved MARC II as a national standard in 1971, and an international equivalent was adopted by the International Standards Organization (ISO) in 1973.

It is hard to overemphasize the importance of the existence of the MARC II standard to the progress of library automation. Just as the card catalog had been the keystone of library services during the first two-thirds of the twentieth century, the automated version of the catalog, a database of bibliographic records, would be the keystone of automated library operations. Without an accepted standard for such records, each independent development might have been based on a different format; as it is, no library automation system is acceptable today unless it can import and generate MARC-compatible records.

Library Automation Takes Root (1967–75) . . .

The late 1960s and early 1970s saw much progress based on these developments. Cooperative projects were established to produce "union catalogs" that listed the combined holdings of a group of libraries. Such catalogs could serve as the basis for developing coordinated acquisition policies and also could be used to identify sources of material for interlibrary borrowing. Other cooperative projects put less emphasis on producing a printed product, focusing instead on the savings achievable through "shared cataloging." Ideally, one expert librarian would catalog the book from scratch ("original cataloging"), and any other library simply could locate and copy that record, a task that could be carried out by a clerical assistant (or student). The use of Library of Congress catalog cards was a primitive form of shared cataloging, but, without automation, there were long delays before cards for new publications were available, and it took time to establish whether cards were available for an item that needed cataloging.

Among the cooperative organizations founded at this time are OCLC, UTLAS, and WLN, all of which use computer systems to support shared cataloging, retrospective conversion of catalog records to machine-readable form, and interlibrary lending. Initially, they were based on batch-processing systems, but online services soon followed.

Although often grouped together under the term "bibliographic utility," the organizations are very different. OCLC has grown from a consortium to support shared cataloging for libraries in Ohio into a worldwide non-profit organization with eight thousand member libraries. UTLAS began as a project to develop a union catalog for five new universities in Ontario, Canada, developed into the University of Toronto Library Automation System with a mandate to support the Canadian library community in general, expanded to serve libraries in the United States and elsewhere, and, in 1985, was sold to the International Thomson Organization and became a for-profit corporation. WLN started life as the Washington Library Network and later became the Western Library Network; it is still a regional organization and provides a more limited range of services and products than OCLC or UTLAS.

A few years later, the Research Library Group (RLG) was formed specifically to cater to the needs of research libraries, becoming the fourth bibliographic utility in North America. Almost all academic libraries are affiliated with one or more of the bibliographic utilities; shared cataloging is now an economic necessity.

During this period, work also began on the interactive systems for library automation from which the systems in use today have evolved. The desirability of integrated systems that could support all library functions in a coherent fashion through a common set of data files had been recognized already. But, in libraries, as in many other areas, it was soon discovered that software projects always take longer than expected, the procedures to be automated are always more complex than anyone had thought, and introducing new systems always generates new problems in management and staffing. Library applications, however, differed from scientific or business applications for two important reasons. Firstly, it was essential for bibliographic databases to allow textual data fields of variable length and multiple occurrences of many data fields, such as authors, in the record for a single item. These features are not common, even today, in database systems designed to handle enormous quantities of data for business applications. Secondly, the early high-level programming languages, FORTRAN and COBOL, were not suitable for handling character strings of variable length. Even in projects where the final goal was an integrated system, the functions were usually automated one by one, often over many years.

In many libraries, circulation was seen as the area where the most was to be gained most easily from an online system. In many cases, these systems were based on short shelflist records that identified the circulating items, rather than on full bibliographic records. Most used punched cards or strips of reinforced paper tape to identify items and borrowers. Online terminals were teletypewriters. Early online circulation systems developed at Ohio State University and Virginia Polytechnic have been built on and used at other institutions, and circulation was the first function automated at Northwestern, in the system that was to become NOTIS. But not all projects survived, often because the expense of developing and maintaining complex software could not be justified for a single institution. (University libraries often could not take advantage of the commercial systems for circulation and other library processes that had begun to appear, because these products were aimed primarily at public libraries.)

Some libraries found ways to share the effort and expense. At Stanford University, the BALLOTS system (Bibliographic Automation of Large Library Operations using a Time-sharing System) was based on software developed for accessing and maintaining another bibliographic database; SPIRES was initially the Stanford Physics Information Retrieval

System, but "Physics" soon was changed to "public." BALLOTS supported the library's technical services and was based from the start on full bibliographic records in the MARC format.[5] It was thought that, by using a more general database management system, the library would be able to deliver information beyond that contained in the catalog. BALLOTS was the first system on the Stanford campus to make use of CRT display terminals. And, by the mid-1970s, when a circulation module was designed, labels with bar codes that could be read by a light pen were used to identify volumes. These technical developments were two more important steps toward effective library automation.

. . . And Flourishes (1975 on)

In the mid-1970s, shared cataloging, as a way of pooling resources, became accepted practice. The BALLOTS system at Stanford was extended to other libraries in California and later adopted as the underlying system for the Research Libraries Group's shared cataloging system. WLN introduced its online cataloging system and expanded to include the University of Alaska. OCLC expanded its services beyond Ohio and encouraged the formation of regional organizations to act as brokers of OCLC services to member libraries. By 1978, there were about ten such organizations, for example, SOLINET in the southeastern states, CLASS in California, and ILLINET in Illinois. Their function is to provide library support services to their members; these services may be based on computing or telecommunication facilities, but it is the higher-level services that are important. As well as acting as brokers for OCLC services, many now offer discount rates for supplies, software, and commercial information services.

By the late 1970s, minicomputers were well established. The National Library of Medicine was one of several institutions that began developing library automation systems to run on minicomputers. Several commercial circulation systems based on minicomputers also were launched. Since minicomputers required less space and environments less strictly controlled for temperature and humidity than did mainframes, they often could be installed in library buildings without excessive remodeling cost.

Remote online services also proliferated during the 1970s. Both the bibliographic utilities and commercial brokers began to offer online acquisitions systems that included direct ordering of books from cooperating distributors. Computerized systems to process requests for interlibrary loans were introduced by bibliographic utilities and regional organizations. Commercial systems for searching reference databases online also emerged: BRS/Information Technologies (then Bibliographic

Retrieval Services) and DIALOG (then known by the name of its parent company, Lockheed) were important participants in the market, then as now. Because of the costs and the training needed to use the systems efficiently, searches usually were—and still are—performed by librarians on behalf of library patrons.

Electronic information was first delivered directly to library users through online catalogs introduced in the early 1980s. Among the true pioneers in academic libraries were Northwestern, Penn State, and Ohio State, which expanded their existing library automation systems to include a public catalog with full bibliographic records. The University of California had moved already to create a machine-readable union catalog of the holdings of the nine campuses. In 1980, it had published a catalog on microfiche, but only as an interim measure.[6] Putting catalogs on microfiche or microfilm allowed them to be duplicated easily for distribution to other libraries, but it was felt that, in the long run, an online catalog would be cheaper to maintain, as well as much more convenient for users. The online catalog, known as MELVYL, was launched officially in August 1981. Dartmouth College chose not to develop its own system but licensed search software developed by BRS and added a friendly user interface tailored to the catalog. Some commercial vendors of circulation systems integrated online catalogs with their circulation systems.

Developing software that can run robustly in a variety of settings and is flexible enough to support local requirements demands considerably more effort than writing software for use in a single organization, but, finally, after years of planning and development, integrated library automation systems that could be acquired rather than developed became a reality. Northwestern had resisted for many years the pressure to make NOTIS available to other universities, but, in 1981, the University of Florida became its first customer. By 1984, several commercial systems that supported acquisitions, circulation, and online catalogs were available. OCLC and UTLAS now market integrated systems as part of their overall product range. A variety of systems are available, suitable for different types and sizes of library. Some, like NOTIS, use mainframes and can handle collections of several million items; others, like OCLC's LS/2000, use minicomputers and are more appropriate for medium-sized libraries; still others, particularly appropriate for multicampus installations, are designed to use several linked computers. As the distinction between large workstations and small minicomputers blurs, at least one vendor of integrated systems has plans to introduce a version that runs on one of the popular UNIX workstations. For very small libraries, there even are systems based on personal computers. Today, it is unlikely that an academic library would plan to develop its own system for automating traditional processes.

The Development of Online Information Services

While automation of library processes is now well established, the potential for computers to deliver the information traditionally stored in libraries directly to the scholar is only beginning to be realized. This is not for lack of vision. In 1945, Vannevar Bush urged scientists no longer dedicated to the war effort to turn their creativity to making knowledge more accessible.[7] The device he pictured, which he called a "memex," was a desk that incorporated a numerically controlled microfilm store, reader, and camera. The stored information would include both published works and personal records; several items would be visible simultaneously at high resolution; pages would be assigned unique numbers; and the scholar would be able to create connecting "trails" between items, using a system of small dots that would be interpreted by photocells as numeric addresses for cross-references. One application of such trails would be to annotate texts with personal notes. The computer had not yet escaped from the wartime cryptography departments when Bush described his scholar's workstation, but his vision is still a goal for the library of the future. He pointed the way for technological developments that have only recently emerged: displays that can show several documents at once; personal machines for creating and organizing notes and papers; and hypertext for systems for generating links between items of information.

Bush overestimated the acceptance of microfilm as a medium and probably underestimated the magnitude of the information explosion. Almost twenty years later, when MIT held a series of guest lectures to celebrate its centenary, John Kemeny described his vision for the library of 2000 A.D.[8] The library he pictured still was based on microform; however, it would be stored on a central computer, from which images of pages would be transmitted to a projecting terminal in the scholar's office. Kemeny also foresaw the need for a nationwide system for sharing resources using computer networks. In 1965, Project INTREX at the Massachusetts Institute of Technology set out to create a library system for 1975.[9] This ambitious project covered many aspects of library services and organization, but one component was a central store of images on microform that would be transmitted to receiver stations. Basic technical feasibility was established, but the equipment was expensive, unreliable, and unsuitable for large numbers of workstations or transactions. No technology had yet emerged for transmitting and displaying images at a speed and resolution acceptable for reading directly from the screen and at a cost that would allow widespread availability. It was too early for the library to store and deliver the primary information in its collection by electronic means.

However, progress had been made, at MIT and elsewhere, during the late 1950s and early 1960s in the area of secondary information, or "information about information." Bibliographic information, such as that held in catalog records, was recorded in databases, and procedures were developed for searching these files. As well as information about volumes, such systems could handle records for individual articles in periodicals and include short abstracts in addition to titles. Since academic journals are the main channel for disseminating the results of research in many disciplines, this type of service was of enormous potential value. Indexes to the literature in various disciplines had been produced manually and distributed in book form for many years. These indexing and abstracting publications, usually organized both by author and by subject, were the basis for many of the reference services of an academic library. The first computerized systems were developed to assist in preparing the printed indexes, but the databases also could be used for preparing individual bibliographies by request. In 1964, the National Library of Medicine, the publisher of *Index Medicus,* introduced its MEDLARS (Medical Literature Analysis and Retrieval System) service, indexing fourteen thousand issues of medical journals a year. Initially, such systems were based on batch processing: search requests from reference librarians were punched onto cards and batched together for input. The printed output was returned by mail. Turnaround time was often several weeks.

Online bibliographic search systems were demonstrated as prototypes in the early 1960s, and, by the end of the decade, effective software packages for online searching had emerged. Many were never used outside the institution where they had been developed, but others served as the basis for systems that have been used widely. Among these were the SPIRES system developed at Stanford University, DIALOG from Lockheed, and ORBIT from Systems Development Corporation. The two commercial systems were developed initially for government agencies (including NASA and the U.S. Air Force). At first, these systems were available only as packages for installation on a local computer system, and the related expense was too great for individual universities to justify. But, by the early 1970s, public online services were offered, and interactive online bibliographic searching became an option for the reference librarian in a general academic library, a time-saving alternative to wading through printed indexes. Remote online services based on

DIALOG and ORBIT were offered by Lockheed and SDC; the initial databases mounted were from government agencies, such as the ERIC (Educational Resources Information Center) database from the U.S. Office of Education. Nongovernment databases, such as the database for Psychological Abstracts (now known as PsycINFO), soon were added. In 1971, the National Library of Medicine launched MEDLINE, an online service accessing the MEDLARS database. In 1977, BRS launched an online service using software derived from STAIRS (Storage And Information Retrieval System), a product from IBM.

Since then, many other online services have appeared. Some provide a specific service, such as the Economic Bulletin Board, which holds releases by government agencies. Others, such as DIALOG and BRS, provide access to varied databases generated by a broad range of public and private organizations. Some services are aimed primarily at experienced users, among them, professional reference librarians; others provide more guidance (but perhaps less power) for novices or casual users. DIALOG and BRS now offer services at three levels: the full service, aimed at information specialists; a cheaper, more limited service, aimed at individual users; and easy-to-use services aimed at particular sectors, such as corporate finance or medicine. A few databases include the full text of material, but these usually are aimed primarily at the business or professional market. Several services provide access to the text of newspapers and industry newsletters. Two important full-text services (LEXIS and WESTLAW) serve the legal profession, providing access to state and federal statutes, judicial opinions, and the legal literature.

Charges for searches on remote services are based on several factors, usually including the amount of time that the searcher's terminal is connected to the remote computer, and vary widely among databases. Most academic libraries provide access to a few online services, usually for a fee, although faculty and students may be permitted a certain number of free searches. End users may be allowed to perform their own searches through the least expensive and simplest services or if they have proved their experience, but, in order to control costs, most remote online searching of commercial services from academic libraries is performed by reference librarians.

A Technological Transition

Three important applications of technology to libraries have been described so far: the bibliographic utilities to support shared cataloging; integrated systems to automate technical processes; and remote online services for information retrieval. Each of these developments was planned originally around a central computer system with access from terminals that simply accepted input from a keyboard and displayed the results of the central computer's processing. Fifteen years ago, one large computer system was a much better value than two small ones, and disk storage for online access was expensive enough that it made sense to store large databases only once. Computer "centers" running time-sharing systems were the primary source of computing power on campuses for the same reasons. But the economies of scale have vanished, and this change has altered fundamentally the technological structure in which computing and library services operate.

Decreasing Costs
The cost of computing power has been decreasing steadily by over 25 percent per year. Raw processing power is now available at less than one-hundredth of its cost fifteen years ago, and the trend is expected to continue. The personal computers on today's desktops are as powerful as the time-sharing systems that served whole universities fifteen years ago. And the advanced workstations that are becoming standard personal equipment for engineers and computer scientists would have served as departmental computers only five years ago. The cost of microcomputer power has been dropping faster than that of larger computers. One thousand personal computers at $2,000 each now provide ten times as much raw computing power as one $2 million mainframe.

The cost of conventional disk storage for computers of all sizes also continues to decrease rapidly. In 1983, an IBM mainframe disk storage device with a capacity of 2.5 gigabytes cost $100,000. In 1987, a new model in the same series cost $120,000 but held 7.5 gigabytes. With each new model, the speed at which information can be found and read from a disk increases, and the physical space required to store a fixed amount of information decreases. Around 1980, when the first Winchester hard disks for personal computers appeared, a 5-megabyte disk cost at least $2,000. Now a disk with four times the capacity costs a quarter of the price and takes up half the space. Until very recently, the cost per megabyte of storage was less on a mainframe than on a personal computer, but, in 1989, the cost is roughly the same. The economies of scale for storage capacity have disappeared, although the speed at which information can be read is still around ten times faster from a mainframe disk than from a personal computer's hard disk.

When large computers lost the advantage of economies of scale, the first effect on campuses was the proliferation of minicomputers. Academic departments began to use research funds to acquire their own minicomputers rather than pay computing charges to a central organization. For administrative tasks, it was often more economical to identify an existing software package and buy a minicomputer on which it could run than to write or modify software for an existing campus mainframe. This process made library automation feasible on campuses that ran computer services on hardware for which no library software was available. Decreasing costs also encouraged the commercial development of software by increasing the number of libraries for which automation was affordable.

Beyond the automation of library processes, the changing economics have brought about a second change in academic libraries. It is now feasible to acquire copies of databases for abstracting and indexing services that are used heavily, purchase information retrieval software, and mount the databases on a local computer. The most important advantage of a local information service over the remote commercial services is that faculty and students can be given unlimited access at no additional cost and without requiring reference librarians as intermediaries. Databases can be selected to serve the particular institution, and those generated locally can be mounted along with those acquired elsewhere.

The bibliographic utilities also have been affected by changing economies of scale. OCLC originally had plans for supporting all aspects of library operations through a centralized system and so developed central systems for handling acquisitions and serials. It now has become clear that libraries can perform these tasks more economically locally, since telecommunications costs have not fallen as dramatically as costs for processing power and storage. OCLC now supplies products for local, distributed use; its centralized services now focus on its massive database of nineteen million bibliographic records, which incorporates files acquired regularly from national library organizations around the world. Although storage costs have decreased, few libraries would be interested in replicating the maintenance effort. The other bibliographic utilities have made similar adjustments in their services.

Computers Are Everywhere

The drop in price has brought computing within the reach of everyone in the academic community. In 1983, a basic personal computer configuration was recommended for student purchase at the Amos Tuck School of Business Administration at Dartmouth College; it cost $2,500. In 1989, an equivalent computer costs under $700. Alternatively, $2,500 can buy a computer with twice the memory, a processor three times as fast, a 30-megabyte hard disk, and a color display with much higher resolution.

The number of faculty with personal computers in their offices and students with personal computers in their dormitory rooms is rising on every campus. At a few universities, such as the Stevens Institute of Technology, all undergraduates are required to have personal computers. At Dartmouth, students are strongly encouraged, but not required, to buy computers; 90 percent of the incoming class bought computers in the fall of 1988. Many universities have found that, even when they have made no concerted effort to encourage the use of computers in the curriculum, 30 percent of students have acquired them anyway for word processing. On almost all campuses, clusters of public machines assure that all students and faculty members have easy access to a computer.

For libraries, this universal access solves problems but creates pressures. When the concept of the electronic library first was proposed and in the early days of online catalogs, a major concern was the number and distribution of terminals. What were the advantages if you had to come to the library and line up for a terminal? That problem has disappeared on networked campuses. If most members of the community can check the catalog from their own offices, the demand for terminals within the library is usually manageable. However, this very ease of access creates pressures. Once students and researchers who use their computers every day can consult the catalog from their desks, they begin to recognize the potential for other conveniences. Can I have an item delivered, rather than going to the library? Can I download citations to my personal computer for inclusion in the paper I am writing? Can I create a personal bibliography with my own annotations? Can I forward an interesting citation to a colleague by electronic mail? Responding to these pressures requires not only reconsideration of existing library policies but extension of the librarian's traditional expertise and close cooperation with the organization that supports personal computer users.

Networks
For the electronic library to become a reality, cooperation with computing-service organizations is essential, since a prerequisite is a computer network that reaches the client community. Describing the context of computer networks on campuses and across the country could take a complete book—and has done, in the previous volume in this series, *Campus Networking Strategies*.[10] However, some important points are worth emphasizing.

The first campus computer networks developed in the days of centralized computing services, and their purpose was to connect terminals to central host computers. Many campuses developed such networks, starting in the 1970s, often to save the cost of leasing telephone lines. The networks originally established by OCLC and RLG to support their services were also of this type. These networks operate on the assumption that the host computer is in control of the communication session, allowing the user at a terminal to log on and invoke programs on the remote computer. The host computer is master to the slave terminals. Most terminal-to-host networks are designed for particular classes of terminals. OCLC and RLG used special terminals, but the most common class of terminals in use on campuses supports asynchronous communication using the ASCII codes for the characters on the keyboard.

When personal computers replaced terminals, the master-slave relationship changed slightly: the slave was promoted to servant. Since a personal computer has processing power and storage of its own and usually has asynchronous ASCII communications built in, it can be used to combine local processing with "emulating" a terminal. For libraries, this has permitted the development of "front ends" that interact with remote systems over networks designed for terminals. Bibliographic utilities, commercial information services, and libraries all have developed software for personal computers that allows users to prepare transactions on the personal computer and connect to the remote computer only to perform the task. In addition to keeping communications costs down, this prevents the central computer system from being overloaded by trivial operations. In many cases, front-end software has been developed also to provide interfaces to information retrieval services that are more friendly and easier to use than the underlying retrieval system and allow the user to capture or download the information shown on the screen. Even with a network designed for terminals, personal computers used as workstations can provide powerful capabilities to the user, and, for several years to come, libraries can assume that this is the only type of access available to some of their users.

However, the new generation of computer networks provides much greater potential for the electronic library. These peer-to-peer networks are designed to support more general forms of communication than terminal-to-host networks can provide. The underlying model no longer assumes masters and slaves. Computers on the network, whether large mainframes or personal workstations, are attached to the network as equals, each identified by a unique address. Network traffic consists of individual messages from one computer to another, with communication between workstations as easy as communication from a workstation to a large time-sharing computer. Built on the low-level network capability of sending messages from one address to another, protocols of specified sequences of messages perform particular higher-level tasks. Among the services for which protocols exist are electronic mail, file transfer, and terminal emulation for logging on to time-sharing systems.

While offering all the capabilities of a terminal-to-host network, peer-to-peer networks also can be the basis for much more powerful services that integrate access to information resources more conveniently into the user's routine activities. Programs developed for a personal computer on this type of network can reach out and communicate with any number of other computers as particular services are needed. A common concept used when describing network services is that of client and server. A file server provides shared access to files stored on its disk; to a client workstation, these files are a seamless extension of its own file storage. A mail server may act as a post office, holding mail in electronic mailboxes until the recipient runs a client mail program on his or her personal computer, and picks up the mail. A recent development is that of a database server, which holds the basic "search engine" that manages the data stored in a database, and can search for and retrieve items according to specified criteria. The user interface software runs entirely on the client workstation, which sends out occasional messages to the server, requesting particular information to display or integrate with information stored locally. If necessary, the client can communicate with several servers simultaneously. All that is needed is an agreed protocol for sending database requests and responding to them. For business databases, SQL (Structured Query Language) has been ratified as a standard protocol by ANSI and is under consideration as an international standard. Many vendors are now adapting old products and developing new ones to support this standard and to allow database applications and servers from different vendors to operate together. Of more direct relevance for libraries is the development of an information retrieval protocol designed specifically for handling bibliographic information. This standard, known as Z39.50, was developed as part of the Linked Systems Project, a cooperative venture by the Library of Congress and some of the bibliographic utilities to facilitate exchange of information between their data bases. Both SQL and Z39.50 define the protocols for machine-to-machine communication. They do not preclude the option of a customized user interface that constructs the query for the user from a simplified set of options on a menu, a series of simple prompts, or entries typed into boxes on a form displayed on the screen. If adopted widely, Z39.50 could be the key to more powerful information services that will be able to link the user to resources across the country as easily as to those of his or her own library.

High-speed peer-to-peer networks are becoming standard on campuses, either replacing or in addition to terminal-to-host networks. They rely on families of layered protocols, with the lowest layer supplying the basic physical connection, and the highest layer (application protocols) supporting particular tasks, such as information retrieval or electronic mail. A number of different families of networking protocols exist. The most important are protocols developed by specific vendors (for example, IBM's System Network Architecture, Apple Computer's AppleTalk, or Digital Equipment Corporation's DECnet), TCP/IP (developed under the sponsorship of the Department of Defense), and the family of standards being developed by ISO. The ISO protocols are being developed within the framework of the Open Systems Interconnection (OSI) networking model, itself adopted in the late 1970s. The ISO/OSI protocols have been emerging only slowly, and the higher-level protocols are not yet in widespread use. Until this family of protocols matures and is more complete, it cannot serve as the basis for a general-purpose high-speed campus network. Most campus networks currently support TCP/IP for cooperation between computers from a number of vendors; many support one or more vendor-specific networking protocols as well. TCP/IP is also the basis for many regional networks and for the NSFNET, which provides nationwide access to the supercomputers sponsored by the National Science Foundation.

In the past, the library community and the academic computing community have used the word "network" to describe two rather different phenomena. To the computing community, a network is a general-purpose structure that links computers and supports a wide variety of activities. It is like a highway system, providing a basic facility, a means to get from one place to another. This facility can be used both by individuals and by organizations that build on its capabilities in order to offer higher-level services, such as long-distance haulage, express delivery, or nationwide bus service. Like a highway or telephone system, a computer network is an infrastructure. Library networks, on the other hand, are organizations that provide high-level services, such as shared cataloging or interlibrary loan; these services usually are based on a computer network of some sort, but the justification for a library network is the service it provides, not the communication facility itself.

The two communities have not yet developed a unified approach to networking on a national scale, but the differences are not as great as might be imagined from a superficial scanning of the literature. Both communities, for example, see the need for nationwide links; considerable confusion, however, derives from the differing interpretations of the term "national network." In the 1970s, the library literature was full of proposals for a national network—a master national library organization that would combine the roles of bibliographic utility, leader in the innovative application of technology, and setter of standards. The concept depended primarily on the principle that large computer systems provided economies of scale. No consensus emerged as to whether such a network should build on a bibliographic utility such as OCLC or on the Library of Congress, which is the closest U.S. equivalent to a national library, and neither organization seemed anxious to take on the role explicitly. Equally importantly, no federal funding materialized.

While discussion continued, libraries made decisions based on the changing technological context, and, over time, it became obvious that a single centralized system made less sense than a more loosely connected federation of libraries. A recent assessment on library automation in North America, prepared by Charles Hildreth for the Commission of the European Communities, includes the sentence, "A single physical national or continental bibliographic network will not come into existence in the foreseeable future."[11] Such a statement might surprise a computing specialist who is aware of the substantial efforts, including those by EDUCOM's Networking and Telecommunications Task Force, to create a national computer network. This network is extending NSFNET by linking to it many of the other computer networks that have grown up to provide basic connectivity within regions and for specialists in particular academic disciplines.

Libraries require networking links for two different aspects of their operation: they need links with other libraries and with bibliographic utilities to support their traditional processes and links with the academic community to carry out their primary mission of providing students and scholars with access to information. Until now, most libraries have concentrated on the former, since patrons usually would come to a library to use its services. Independent networks were needed since the emerging general-purpose computing networks reached only a small number of academic institutions. OCLC, RLG, and the other bibliographic utilities developed independent, dedicated networks to support access from libraries to their centralized services. More recently, network links have been established between participants in the Linked Systems Project. The first phase of this project has developed procedures and protocols for sharing authority records among the bibliographic utilities. This is an important foundation for the effective sharing of information resources nationwide, facilitating the uniform use of names and subject headings throughout the library community, not merely within individual collections.

Networking protocols for library applications are being developed based on the lower-level standard protocols established by ISO, initially on the X.25 standard that was designed to support medium-speed communication (56K bits/second) on regular copper telephone lines over long distances. This standard is particularly suited to supporting bidirectional communication sessions maintained for a sequence of messages somewhat like a conversation. Most X.25 networks, including commercial networks such as Telenet, primarily support terminal-to-host services. The ISO/OSI standards also include low-level protocols more suitable for the higher speeds and truly distributed processing needed on campuses to provide transparent access to printers, file servers, and other shared services. Such protocols include Ethernet and IBM's Token Ring. Unfortunately, the middle-level protocols crucial to providing the services needed on campuses have been emerging only slowly for the ISO/OSI family of standards, and products have not been available commercially.

Meanwhile, high-speed campuswide computing networks that can deliver electronic information to every desk are proliferating, and most are linked to the emerging national computing network based on TCP/IP. Known as the Internet, this network integrates the NSFNET, the ARPANET, and around fifteen regional networks. TCP/IP can use a wide variety of low-level protocols, including Ethernet and Token Ring, and support a broad range of high-level application protocols.

The Department of Defense has announced that suppliers will be expected to support the ISO/OSI standard protocols in future. The national computing network will move to conform to the international standards, but this process may take many years, as the ISO/OSI protocol family matures. For academic libraries to serve their communities now, it is essential for their information retrieval services to support access from networks based on TCP/IP. Many individual library systems now support such access, and OCLC is promoting the development of capabilities to support the Z39.50 protocol for information retrieval on TCP/IP networks and to provide gateways between the two types of network. Nevertheless, there has not yet been a concerted effort to move in this direction.

New Media for Storing Information
Some technological developments can be adopted with less coordination, less reorganization, and less financial outlay. This is demonstrated by the popularity of information services based on the compact disk technology first developed for high-quality audio reproduction. Personal computers with compact disk readers are now found in reference areas in many libraries. This alternative to print or online searching requires

training and adjustment but no major restaffing or reorganization. Reference librarians can show a user which databases are appropriate and guide a user through a search, just as they would with the print equivalent. New databases and information services on compact disk are appearing monthly, many of them derived from print publications or databases previously available online.

The technology, usually known as CD-ROM (for Compact Disk Read-Only-Memory) when used as a storage medium for computers, encodes digital information by creating minuscule pits and bumps on a metal-coated plastic disk. The digital coding is read by interpreting the reflections from the surface of a laser beam. A CD can hold about 600 megabytes of data, which is roughly equivalent to two hundred thousand printed pages, or four hundred large books. Copies can be pressed from a glass master disk for around $3 a disk. A reader to attach to a personal computer costs between $500 and $1,500. The basic cost of storage capacity on CD-ROM is incredibly low; magnetic tape to store the same data would cost twenty times as much, and floppy disks two hundred times as much. The cost of the physical process of creating master disks has dropped dramatically in the last few years and can be under $2,000. The real cost of a compact disk derives from collecting, organizing, and indexing the information for convenient access. Since the market for services based on CD-ROM is still small, prices are high; typically, an indexing or abstracting service on CD-ROM is priced 50 to 100 percent higher than the equivalent service in print. As the market continues to expand and particularly as more individuals invest in CD readers, prices will come down. For full-text products that might be part of a personal library, such as an encyclopedia, the complete works of Shakespeare, or a cumulative subscription to a professional journal, prices eventually should be comparable to those of audio CDs.

Although the cost of storing information on CD-ROM is very low, the technology has important limits and will not supersede the more conventional magnetic disk technology that is now the primary medium for data storage. Once the compact disk has been pressed, the information stored on it cannot be modified. Hence, it is not suitable for applications that require absolute currency or for information that changes very rapidly, although it is ideal for material that can be conveniently revised annually, quarterly, or even monthly. The other problem with the technology is its speed. It takes ten times as long to locate a particular area of CD-ROM as it does to find an area on today's fast hard disks, and it takes twice as long to read data. Reading a document file from CD-ROM into a word processor is more comparable in terms of time to reading from a floppy disk than from a hard disk. So, while CD-ROM may be ideal for a personal environment or a dedicated stand-alone system, it may not be appropriate for sharing a heavily used database. A printed index often runs over many volumes, and several users can use a single copy simultaneously; if the same index is on CD-ROM on a stand-alone system, it is only available to a single user. For this reason, librarians often are unwilling or unable to cancel a subscription to a print indexing service when they acquire the CD-ROM equivalent. Software to support shared access over a local area network is now available, but, so far, little experience has been accumulated to guide librarians in designing configurations. Shared access may be appropriate for full-text databases where users retrieve large contiguous segments of information after a simple search and peruse it on the screen, but it may prove unsuitable for a heavily used indexing service where a search is likely to involve substantial disk activity to locate many small items. Mounting the most popular databases on a mainframe or minicomputer with high-speed disks and campuswide network access may be more satisfactory and less expensive.

Standardization has played an important role in the development of the CD-ROM market. The underlying technology and the size of the disks were standardized by cooperation between Philips N.V. and the Sony Corporation in the early 1980s. But that was only a basic level of standardization, similar to the accepted standard for the physical composition of floppy disks. (Computers from Apple Computer and IBM both use the same floppy disks but cannot exchange data because they store it in incompatible formats.) As long as each CD-ROM product used a different format, potential customers were hesitant to invest in systems that might serve only a single purpose or quickly become obsolete. In 1985, a group of thirteen companies interested in establishing a market for CD-ROM met at the High Sierra Casino on Lake Tahoe in Nevada. The High Sierra Group developed a proposal for a file structure appropriate for CD-ROM and presented it to the National Information Standards Organization (NISO). Once the format had been proposed, products that conformed to it began appearing, and the market started to expand more rapidly. And, by late 1987, ISO had ratified the proposed format, almost unchanged, as a standard (ISO 9660). Such rapid progress from an initial design to official ratification is unusual.

Standardization at another level is desirable but less likely to be achieved quickly. Information retrieval services have two components: the database and the search system that allows the user to retrieve particular items. Currently, these are packaged together, and services that perform essentially the same task present the user with different procedures, conventions, and displays. One reason for this is that, for efficient retrieval, the indexes to be used have to be stored on CD-ROM with the database; if the items being stored are short, heavily indexed bibliographic records, the indexes may need more physical space than the data itself. Since every search system uses a different approach to indexing, each CD-ROM product can only be used with a particular search system; this problem is alleviated somewhat when several CD-ROM databases are acquired from a single publisher. However, if databases from several sources are mounted on a larger, shared computer, they all can be indexed for retrieval using the same search software. It is then straightforward to provide a common user interface with which users can become familiar. On the other hand, it certainly uses less manpower to exchange compact disks when the new issue arrives than to load and index a database from magnetic tape. Still, cost is only one of the factors that guide decisions on how to deliver information. The ability to provide it in the most effective fashion for the particular community may be even more important.

The economies of scale for mammoth centralized computing systems have disappeared. There is no doubt that the computing environment of the future will consist of workstations on individual desks, linked to a campus network that provides resources to meet most of the general computing and information needs of the scholar. The campus network also will be the gateway to more specialized resources around the country and even across the world. But, in today's changing technological context, no clear pattern has emerged indicating which resources will be on the desktop and which will be stored at the departmental, campus, or national levels. As the existing technologies develop and as new ones appear, librarians will continue to face tough decisions concerning how to harness the new potential in a way that will serve their clientele best. The contributors to this volume all have recognized the potential and forged ahead. Not all of them have made the same choices, but their example and experience will help to shape the future of the academic library.

References

1. Pratt, E. Carl. "International Business Machines' Use in Circulation Department, University of Florida." *Library Journal* 67 (April 1, 1942): 302–303.
2. Perlis, Alan J. "The Computer in the University." In *Management and the Computer of the Future,* ed. Martin Greenberger (Cam-

bridge, Mass.: MIT Press and John Wiley & Sons, 1962),
p. 181.

3. Goldhor, Herbert, ed. *Proceedings of the 1963 Clinic on Library Applications of Data Processing* (Urbana-Champaign, Ill.: Graduate School of Library Science, University of Illinois, 1964).

4. Rohrbach, Peter T. *FIND: Automation at the Library of Congress, the First Twenty-five Years and Beyond* (Washington D.C.: Library of Congress, 1985).

5. Davison, Wayne. "Minicomputers and Library Automation: The Stanford Experience." In *Proceedings of the 1974 Clinic on Library Applications of Data Processing,* ed. F. Wilfrid Lancaster (Urbana-Champaign, Ill.: Graduate School of Library Science, University of Illinois, 1974).

6. Salmon, Stephen R. "In-Depth: University of California MELVYL." *Information Technology and Libraries* 1:350–358.

7. Bush, Vannevar. "As We May Think." *Atlantic Monthly* 176, no. 1 (July 1945): 101–108.

8. Kemeny, John, G. "A Library for 2000 A.D." In *Management and the Computer of the Future,* ed. Martin Greenberger (Cambridge, Mass.: MIT Press and John Wiley & Sons, 1962).

9. Overhage, Carl F. J., and R. Joyce Harman, eds. *INTREX: Report of a Planning Conference on Information Transfer Experiments* (Cambridge, Mass.: MIT Press, 1965).

10. Arms, Caroline R., ed. *Campus Networking Strategies,* EDUCOM Strategies Series on Information Technology (Bedford, Mass: Digital Press, 1988).

11. Hildreth, Charles R. *Library Automation in North America: A Reassessment of the Impact of New Technologies on Networking* (München, West Germany: K. G. Saur, 1987).

Chapter 2

OCLC
Online Computer Library Center

Michael McGill
Drew Racine

Authors have been talking about "paperless information systems" and the "electronic library" for more than a decade.[1] Campus administrators have often wished for an electronic library so that they would no longer have to plan for the space needed to house the "paper" library. The idea is so commonplace that it was illustrated recently in a cartoon appearing in the *Chronicle of Higher Education* (see Figure 2.1). Yet the electronic library is not a reality, much less a paperless information system.

The campus library often is described as the university's heart, but those in charge of the university budget might be more likely to describe it as a "black hole" in the university's midst. The inflation rate for higher education is greater than that for the economy at large: in 1987, the Higher Education Price Index was 293.9, while the Consumer Price Index was 280.0. Within higher education, the inflation rate for books and periodicals is second only to that for fringe benefits, with the index for books and periodicals within the 1987 HEPI index at 580.6. In large measure because of heavy purchases of foreign materials, which are affected strongly by the falling value of the dollar abroad, libraries need ever-larger infusions of funds in order to remain the resource that campus researchers, faculty, and students need.

How the concept of the paperless information system and that of the library as black hole relate may not be immediately apparent. Quite simply, automation of library processes and electronic provision of information services have been counted on to reduce actual expenditures for libraries (partly by saving space) or at least to slow the rate of increase. Libraries have been automating processes since early circulation systems using punched cards appeared in the mid-1950s. Because libraries have been in the interlibrary lending business for many years, librarians also understand that cooperative efforts can deliver, through synergy, economic benefits that one library alone could never hope to achieve.

As an organization consisting of cooperative member libraries, the OCLC Online Computer Library Center achieves many of these benefits. It is a "bibliographic utility" for its members, maintaining an enormous database of information about books, periodicals, and other library materials. It operates an international telecommunications network. It helps scholars to obtain the information they need and libraries to operate more efficiently. It acts as a change agent to further the electronic revolution in the information industry. OCLC is a member of EDUCOM, the Corporation for Open Systems (COS), and many other organizations leading the way into the future.

Figure 2.1 *The Electronic Library.* **A cartoon by Jody Millard. Reprinted by permission of the artist from the** *Chronicle of Higher Education* **24, no. 46 (July 27, 1988): B4.**

Background

The origin of the OCLC Online Computer Library Center can be traced back to 1963, when the Ohio College Association engaged Wyman Parker to devise a cooperative library center in Ohio to help academic libraries and their parent institutions cope with the explosion of research that began in the 1950s.[2] Libraries could not keep up with the creation of information: they could not own everything their faculties and students needed, and even what they could acquire often was too much for their staffs to catalog in a timely manner. It was hoped that a cooperative center would be able to help libraries select appropriate materials and speed up the processing of acquisitions.

Parker's report recommending the establishment of a union catalog listing the holdings of all academic libraries in Ohio was used to solicit bids from several companies to implement such a catalog. Two men, now considered pioneers in library automation, were hired to analyze the bids and recommend which firm should be awarded the contract. Ralph H. Parker, then of the University of Missouri, and Frederick G. Kilgour, then at Yale University, rejected all of the bids, instead suggesting that the

Ohio College Association should create a "total information system by using computers and associated equipment [in which] individual processes become an integral part of the whole."[3] The association agreed and hired Kilgour to create the system. In 1967, Kilgour founded what has become the largest bibliographic computer system with the largest, broadest, and deepest bibliographic database in the world. The corporation, referred to here as OCLC, was originally the Ohio College Library Center. The name was later changed to OCLC, Inc., to reflect its new status with members outside Ohio. Its official name is now the OCLC Online Computer Library Center, Inc.

Kilgour and R. Parker, both from academia, understood the processes of research, publication, and scholarly communication; they were also familiar with acquiring and cataloging library materials and with interlibrary lending. Both were experienced at husbanding the scarce resources entrusted to them and their libraries. Their design, and the system Kilgour subsequently created, reflected their knowledge of the university community and a desire to contain rapidly increasing costs. The goals of OCLC were twofold: first, to support the objectives of member institutions, making it possible for academic libraries to cooperate in the educational and research activities of their individual users by supplying information to them when and where they need it; and, second, to make the resources of all member libraries available to the faculty and students at each institution by means of an online union catalog of library holdings.[4]

The Online Union Catalog

The online catalog of bibliographic records is the basis for shared cataloging and many of the other services offered by OCLC. OCLC went online with its shared cataloging system for colleges and universities in Ohio in 1971. The first library acquiring a book would catalog it, transmit the data from a terminal to OCLC over a multiparty synchronous transmission telephone line, and receive catalog cards by mail in a week or so. The next library acquiring the book could retrieve the existing record in the OCLC online union catalog database, add its holding symbol to show that it, too, held the title, and order its catalog cards. A third library then might decide that, since two libraries in its region already held the book, it would borrow the title rather than purchase it. A network of cooperating libraries could reallocate funds from processing or acquisitions budgets to other areas because full use of the OCLC online system provided savings. For the system to be effective, library members had to supply bibliographic records for titles that they held for which no record existed, and they had to add their special codes, or "holding symbols," to existing records when they used them for cataloging purposes. A cooperative such as OCLC can work only when all its members cooperate fully.

The online catalog has grown continuously and increasingly rapidly since 1971, as indicated in the chronology in Table 2.1. New options for access to the catalog have been added as technological developments such as commercial data networks and personal computers have emerged. In 1972, OCLC first provided online cataloging to libraries outside Ohio. It used Sigma computers from Xerox Data Systems; access was from Spiras LTE terminals. (OCLC still uses Sigma 9 computers for online operations and will continue to do so for the next two or three years.) In 1973, OCLC switched to Beehive International terminals, many of which are still in use and will be supported on the network until 1990. In 1984, OCLC introduced a new workstation based on an IBM PC, and, in 1986, a workstation was developed to support Chinese, Japanese, and Korean characters.

The private telecommunications network, which uses lines leased from the telephone company and protocols designed and developed by OCLC, was the standard method for accessing OCLC. In 1974, members were provided the option of accessing the database by dialing in through a public data network.

Bibliographic records are available, not only for books, but for audiovisual materials, serials, manuscripts, maps, music scores, and sound recordings. The database had one million bibliographic records in 1974; by 1981, it had eight million. Today, the online catalog has over nineteen million bibliographic records with over three hundred million holding library symbols attached. The catalog database is growing at the rate of about two million bibliographic records and twenty-three million holding symbols per year. OCLC's system currently runs on sixteen Xerox Sigma 9 computers, sixty Tandem computers, and one large IBM processor. More than ninety-five hundred terminals and workstations worldwide can access the system, and peak load averages over seventy transactions per second.

The online catalog of bibliographic records is the basis for shared cataloging and for many of the other services offered by OCLC. Over the years, online subsystems have been developed for related library tasks: acquisitions, control of individual issues of journals, and interlibrary loan. As hardware costs have fallen, OCLC has provided products and services appropriate for libraries with their own local computer systems. As the technological context has changed, OCLC has adapted its activities, always following the philosophy and vision of its founder and the board of trustees.

Table 2.1   OCLC Chronology

1967	OCLC is incorporated as a not-for-profit corporation.
1971	OCLC begins online operations in Ohio.
1972	OCLC begins to operate interstate, in Pennsylvania.
1973	OCLC Model 100 Beehive terminals are installed.
1974	Dial access to OCLC becomes available. The one-millionth record is added to the database in September.
1975	The first Xerox Sigma 9 mainframe goes online in February.
1976	The two-millionth record is added to the database. In October, the third Sigma 9 goes online.
1977	The three-millionth record and the fourth Sigma 9 are added.
1978	The database processor is activated, allowing hardware expansion and greater data security.
1979	The interlibrary loan subsystem becomes operational. OCLC goes international with operations in Canada.
1980	The serials union listing capability is enabled. In September, the one-millionth interlibrary loan transaction is made over OCLC.
1981	The eight-millionth record is added to the database; the two-millionth interlibrary loan is made; the sixth Sigma 9 is added. The OCLC European office is opened. The acquisitions subsystem is introduced.
1982	The University of Minnesota is the first nonmember library to add records to the database via batch tapeload.
1983	The first OCLC LS/2000 integrated local system is installed at Hampshire College.
1984	The first OCLC M300 workstation (IBM PC) is installed. Micro Enhancer software for cataloging and interlibrary loan is developed and delivered, making processing more efficient for large libraries.
1985	OCLC's microcomputer-based serials control system is introduced. The thirteenth and fourteenth Sigma 9s are added; the twelve-millionth record is added to the database; the nine-millionth interlibrary loan transaction is made. Records from the British Library enter the database.
1986	The ten-millionth interlibrary loan is made in May, the eleven-millionth in July, and the twelve-millionth in November. The database contains fifteen million bibliographic records with 240 million holding symbols attached to them. The OCLC CJK (Chinese-Japanese-Korean) vernacular workstation and software are tested. OCLC has fifteen Sigma 9s and eighty-eight mini-computers online. OCLC installs its eighty-sixth LS/2000 local system. The OCLC microcomputer-based acquisitions system is

Table 2.1   (continued)

	released. The first Asian library, Tamking University Library in Taiwan, joins OCLC in June. A prototype CD-ROM reference database is displayed in July at the American Library Association conference.
1987	The WYSEpc 286, Model 2112, becomes the OCLC M310 work-station. The seventeen-millionth record is added to the database. Kinki University Library in Osaka becomes the first Japanese OCLC user.
1988	The OCLC database contains over nineteen million bibliographic records with over three hundred million holding symbols attached. The seventeen-millionth interlibrary loan transaction is made just seventy-seven days after the sixteen-millionth. OCLC now serves over eight thousand libraries in twenty-six countries. There are over ninety-five hundred terminals and workstations in the field, all of which can access OCLC at once. Fifty-four libraries are using OCLC CJK systems. OCLC is linked with the Library of Congress for record exchange over the Linked System using OSI protocols. Indiana University is entering records into the Library of Congress database over the Linked System through OCLC in host-to-host operation.

Note: This chronology is based on an earlier version by Philip Schieber, OCLC Public Relations Manager.

Philosophy

OCLC can be defined by the Mission Statement in its corporate charter:

> The purpose or purposes for which this Corporation is formed are to establish, maintain and operate a computerized library network and to promote the evolution of library use, of libraries themselves, and of librarian-ship, and to provide processes and products for the benefit of library users and libraries, including such objectives as increasing availability of library resources to individual library patrons and reducing rate-of-rise of library per-unit costs, all for the fundamental public purpose of furthering ease of access to and use of the ever-expanding body of worldwide scientific, literary and educational knowledge and information.[5]

In 1987, the Mission Statement was extended by the Board of Trustees in its Vision Statement:

> Resolved, that the Board's vision for OCLC is to remain preeminent in providing an international bibliographic database, and services based on that database, in electronic form, and, during the next ten years to go beyond bibliographic records and services, in providing expanded information services to libraries and other information users.[6]

OCLC is a private, not-for-profit corporation with a pro bono educational purpose of providing information to libraries and users of information, be they academic researchers, government employees, or the general public. Today, there are over eight thousand OCLC member libraries of all types in twenty-six countries. To meet their needs, OCLC utilizes up-to-date methods of data delivery, operates a telecommunications network that reaches around the globe, maintains a database of over nineteen million records, and employs over nine hundred people. Annual revenues approach $100 million. OCLC also finances the largest operation in the country for applied research and development in library and information science. It seeks to meet the needs of the scholar, the researcher, the information seeker, and the library, itself driven by users' needs. To fulfill its mission, OCLC provides a range of products, services, and programs.

Services and Products

OCLC's diverse services are consistent with its charter and build toward its vision. The core services function for the technical processes of the library.

Technical Services

Cataloging
OCLC's first service to libraries was to support shared cataloging. The cataloging function depends on the richness and breadth of the database, as do most other core OCLC services. The more "hits" libraries make when checking titles against the OCLC database, the lower the cost of cataloging. The comprehensiveness of the database, the precision of the retrieval system, and the quality of the data are what keep the hit rate high. OCLC constantly encourages input to enlarge and enhance the database. Currently, OCLC either is loading or working on agreements to load bibliographic records from numerous national libraries, including the Library of Congress, the National Agriculture Library, the National Library of Medicine, the National Library of Canada, the British Library, the Bibliothèque Nationale in France, the Diet Library of Japan, and the national libraries of Australia, New Zealand, Spain, Italy, China, Taiwan, and elsewhere. OCLC also seeks to acquire records from major public and academic libraries around the world, particularly in countries that have no national library. To increase the resources of its database through direct input, OCLC provides credits to members that enter original records into the database and charges less for records derived

from retrospective conversion projects. OCLC also has worked out exchange agreements with the Research Libraries Group so that both databases can be enriched through an exchange of classes of records.

OCLC's cataloging system is effective. The typical research library can find existing bibliographic records in the OCLC database for between 60 and 95 percent of the titles it acquires, depending on the subject, the languages, or other characteristics of the collections. The great majority of titles does not, therefore, have to be cataloged originally, thus avoiding the most labor-intensive and costly process in the technical services of a research library. When an existing cataloging record is found on OCLC, a student or clerical worker can complete the cataloging task, rather than a librarian or paraprofessional staff member.

Along with its online capabilities, OCLC also has created offline products for libraries. Over two-and-a-half million catalog cards are shipped to libraries each week. By far the most important offline products are machine-readable records of a library's current cataloging activity. Records on magnetic tapes, written in the standard MARC (MAchine-Readable Cataloging) communications format, have become the foundation of many local online catalogs. Tapes are shipped from OCLC for input to systems at academic libraries. However, more and more libraries now have integrated online systems, and the tapes do not arrive fast enough for them; they need direct online downloading of cataloging records as they are created. An interim arrangement now permits a record displayed on the screen of an OCLC workstation to be copied to another system, although OCLC expects soon to provide a more formal facility for transmitting records in standard MARC format. In future, direct downloading will be the preferred method of record transmission.

OCLC also has several programs to assist libraries to convert the catalog records for their existing collections to a machine-readable form. These programs allow libraries to convert their records directly online, offline via microcomputer and diskette, offline by magnetic tapes (for substandard or nonstandard existing records), or offline by OCLC staff at OCLC. These records are delivered back to the libraries on magnetic tapes so that the libraries can enter them electronically into their online catalogs.

Some special programs are offered to assist libraries in cataloging their materials. For example, OCLC operates a Major Microform Set Project. Under this program, a library or cooperating group of libraries catalogs a complete set of materials issued on microform, perhaps the *Spanish Drama of the Golden Age* set. Then, the bibliographic records for the dramas in the set are merged into the database individually, but they also can be acquired as a set, so that, with one transaction, a library can catalog each item in the entire set of over four hundred titles.

Another special service OCLC has developed—primarily for academic libraries—is a non-Roman alphabet capability. OCLC's Chinese-Japanese-Korean (CJK) program involves a workstation with a special keyboard for inputting and searching in the vernacular CJK languages and the software and database structure to allow this searching, while, at the same time, displaying romanized data for those who cannot read the alphabets.

CAT CD450 is another of OCLC's specialized cataloging products. It incorporates cataloging software, which runs on a microcomputer, and a strategic section of the main database. This subset of the online catalog was chosen for greatest applicability and put on a CD-ROM disk. Primarily designed for the smaller library, the distributed cataloging system reduces costs for libraries that do not need the entire nineteen million bibliographic records to catalog their current acquisitions. Recognizing the need to continue to build up the holdings database, OCLC has built into CAT CD450 the ability to contact OCLC and upload the holdings information offline during nonprime hours of operation.

Serials Control

OCLC's second online subsystem, for automated recording of the receipt of individual issues of journals, was introduced in 1976. This service has been used less than other OCLC services, but it has been successful for those who have participated. For this function, a distributed capability based on local microcomputers is more compatible with local needs. A microcomputer-based serials control system (SC350) is now available, and the online service is being discontinued. The product includes support for checking in journal issues, for automatically generating claims for issues not received, for fund control, and for binding notification.

Acquisitions

In 1981, OCLC made available an online acquisitions subsystem that allowed libraries to enter bibliographic "short" records for items being ordered from cooperating publishers. As for serials control, this function now is carried out more conveniently at the library. OCLC provides distributed acquisitions services in a product (ACQ350) that can run in a library over a local area network. A powerful microcomputer using the Intel 80386 processor is the platform for the system.

Resource Sharing

The three processes just described are directed more toward containing costs. The resource-sharing services, however, are intended to make data available when and where users need them, although they also help libraries contain costs of borrowing materials from their peers.

Interlibrary lending is the most obvious example of sharing resources. Libraries can see from the online union catalog which institutions hold a particular title, since holding symbols are attached to the bibliographic record. But the third major OCLC subsystem, introduced in 1979, facilitates interlibrary loan further. It supports electronic requests to borrow an item and transmits electronic responses. The borrowing library specifies a list of libraries that own the needed title. The system sends borrowing requests to the libraries seriatim until one agrees to lend the material. At this point, the borrowing library is informed electronically which library will lend the title. The loaned material must be sent via the U.S. Postal Service or UPS. Over one million requests were made in the first year of operation. In 1988, the eighteen-millionth loan was processed.

Libraries frequently borrow issues of journals or individual articles. Clearly, borrowing will be more efficient when the borrowing library knows which library is likely to have a particular issue. "Union listing" for serials, another function of the OCLC online system, facilitates such interlibrary lending. A union list is a single grouping of titles held by a cooperating group of institutions. Libraries in the group record the issues of journals that they own and share this information with other participating libraries. Whereas a regular bibliographic record in the online catalog identifies which library holds a title, a union list goes one step farther and shows holdings for individual parts of a title. For example, if a library owns the title *Science,* this fact will be identified in a bibliographic record through the attached holdings symbol for the library. However, the more specific information that the library has volume 241, number 4689, of *Science* will be identified in the union list record. Offline printouts of union lists are also available.

OCLC offers other products that make it easier for libraries to form networks to operate more efficiently and more effectively. One such program is the Group Access Capability (GAC). Under the aegis of GAC, separate libraries agree to group together to access OCLC for many kinds of services. One library acts as the lead library, through which the others will generally use OCLC. Bibliographic records generated by the libraries are added to the OCLC database, usually by batch tapeload, and access to the resultant group database is available to all members of the GAC for resource sharing. Costs are shared among the group, so GAC libraries can avail themselves of OCLC services at a lower cost than would be the case if they were direct members.

Local System

OCLC offers an integrated local system—the culmination of a generation of products and services for automating traditional library processes. Introduced in 1983, LS/2000 provides libraries with modules for acquisitions, serials control, cataloging, and circulation; it also supplies management information in the form of reports and statistical summaries. It is a minicomputer-based system that runs on Data General hardware. The basic system was developed as the Integrated Library System (ILS) at the Lister Hill National Center for Biomedical Communications, which is part of the National Library of Medicine. The first ILS was put into operation at the Pentagon in 1980. ILS was licensed by two firms, Online Computer Systems, Inc., and Avatar Systems, Inc., both of which developed it further. OCLC purchased Avatar Systems and signed a joint development agreement with Online Computer Systems. OCLC then merged the two versions of ILS, retaining the best elements of each, and enhanced it further to create LS/2000. LS/2000 marked OCLC's entry into the arena of local systems for library automation, allowing OCLC to assist libraries, not only with their technical processes, but also with services directed toward their users.

Reference Services

OCLC probably is best known for its cataloging, interlibrary loan, and acquisition services. However, for a long time, it has been clear that OCLC's database and related resources provide a strong base for reference services.[7] To date, OCLC has not created true reference facilities; fortunately, things are changing.

Recent work in one OCLC department has focused on reference and enhanced information services. This department will provide the products and services necessary for efficient and effective access to the information contained in OCLC's online union catalog and in other appropriate reference databases. Access will be provided through state-of-the-art information retrieval capabilities, including full Boolean searching with many enhanced features. Services will move quickly beyond the simple retrieval of bibliographic records to handling full text and other materials. A single OCLC search engine, Newton, will be used in microcomputer-based products, as well as in products based on minicomputers and mainframes. This software will permit coordinated access to a range of databases.

The first product from this group is OCLC's Search CD450, a full retrieval package for information on optical compact disks (CD-ROM). This service lets the user search a large database—typically, two hundred thousand to five hundred thousand records—using a microcomputer. No telecommunications nor large-scale central computing facility is needed. At present, OCLC has published fourteen separate databases on CD-ROM, including databases from indexing and abstracting services such as NTIS, ERIC, AGRICOLA, and CRIS. The Search CD450 user interface, shown in Figure 2.2, gives the user constant access to the search statement, retrieval documents, and summary results.

The same interface will be used for the Online Reference Service (EPIC), a centralized information retrieval facility that OCLC is developing. This service will provide access by subject to OCLC's online union catalog of nineteen million unique records, identifying books, serials, machine-readable databases and software, sound recordings, and a variety of other valuable resources. The database will be accessible by any term or combination of terms from the fields of the database records, including the author's name, title of the work, dates, subject headings, geographic identifiers, language, publication type, Dewey Decimal Classification, corporate name, and many other identifiers. The database is international in its coverage and represents 370 languages. It has become a unique resource for scholars. Through the reference service, access will be available to a number of databases beyond OCLC's own online catalog.

By providing full access to the online union catalog and related reference databases, OCLC has begun to enhance its services beyond bibliographic data and to give its users far more effective access to information, including full text, graphics, and perhaps sound. The first service of this nature will be to make accessible approximately one hundred and fifty books of critical reviews of American literature, the Twayne Series. The full text of these books will be accessible by every word or combination of words in the text, indexes, or title, by the names of authors, or by the names of reviewers. To accomplish this, OCLC has joined forces with a publisher, G. K. Hall, to form OCLC Electronic Publishing, Inc., bringing together the best resources of the library and the publishing worlds to provide a service that both organizations recognize as new and exciting for scholars. This type of arrangement probably will become more common as OCLC's users expect increasingly sophisticated access to more information.

Database: CIJE 82–

RETRIEVED: 383
Record: 2

1 > kindergarten
2 >

F2 = Index   F3 = Fields   F4 = History   ↵ Enter Query

Accession Number: EJ302602

AUTHOR: Swartz, Janet P.
Walker, Deborah Klein

TITLE: The Relationship between Teacher Ratings of **Kindergarten** Classroom Skills and Second-Grade
Achievement Scores: An Analysis of Gender Differences.

SOURCE: Journal of School Psychology (v22 n2 p209–17 Sum 1984)

ABSTRACT:

Used the **Kindergarten** Performance Profile to analyze the relationship of classroom skills in the fall and spring of
kindergarten to second-grade achievement. Results indicated **kindergarten** work skills were significantly related

F5 = Previous   F6 = Next   F7 = Print   F9 = Format   Use ↑↓ PgUp PgDn to view text
Search CD450   v2.0   **F1 = Help   F10 = Quit**

Figure 2.2 Sample display from Search CD450 system.

Access to OCLC

OCLC operates a dedicated telecommunications network that uses over two hundred thousand miles of communication lines.[8] This synchronous, polled, multidrop network is designed to meet the specific needs of OCLC's cataloging services. It continues to be very effective and fully supports over eight thousand terminals that have dedicated access to OCLC. Access is also possible over the commercial CompuServe network. The network and computer system handle in excess of sixty-five transactions per second.

As good and reliable as this network is, it needs to be even better, allow for more types of access, and provide mechanisms to use emerging international standards.[9] Thus OCLC is committed to supplying a network that will support the Open Systems Interconnection (OSI) model for telecommunications, and the related ISO standard protocols. This is consistent with the direction taken by most of the library community. OCLC already is involved in an OSI networking project with the Library of Congress and the Research Libraries Group: the Linked Systems Project, which supports the direct exchange of records between databases.

Unfortunately, the ISO/OSI networking standards are not directly compatible with the current approach taken by many academic campuses in the United States. Most campus networks, as well as regional and national networks such as NSFNET, are based on the TCP/IP family of protocols. OCLC has recognized the need to work with the TCP/IP community to provide for access to OCLC reference services. With EDUCOM and NYSERNet, it has begun an experiment that will interconnect OCLC's current OSI network with NYSERNet's TCP/IP network. This project is based on the National Information Standards Organization (NISO) Information Retrieval Protocol for Library Applications (Z39.50), a newly adopted protocol specifically designed for the retrieval of bibliographic records, developed as part of the Linked Systems Project.[10] The structure of the proposed gateway is shown in Figure 2.3. If successful, this development could let scholars have direct access to OCLC's reference services from their workstations on a campus network. While this is only an experiment, it demonstrates the potential for such a capability in the near future.

In supporting reference capabilities OCLC is striving to provide access to information that is of benefit to users directly, not only through services to libraries. The services described above have identified some resources available through a large central facility and others stored at the workstation. Economics will determine for the user which databases and which approach are most appropriate. When a small database will

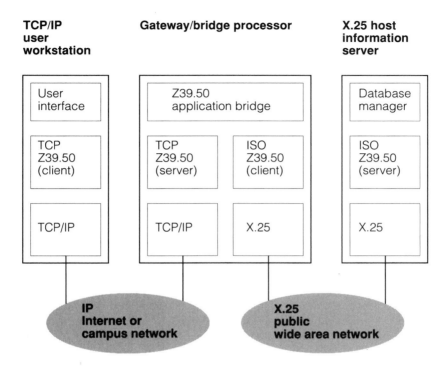

**TCP/IP
user
workstation**

Gateway/bridge processor

**X.25 host
information
server**

User interface	Z39.50 application bridge		Database manager
TCP Z39.50 (client)	TCP Z39.50 (server)	ISO Z39.50 (client)	ISO Z39.50 (server)
TCP/IP	TCP/IP	X.25	X.25

**IP
Internet or
campus network**

**X.25
public
wide area network**

Figure 2.3 Structure of proposed information retrieval gateway between ISO and TCP/IP networks.

be accessed frequently, it may be more economical for a user to purchase one on a compact disk for direct use at a workstation. When access to a particular database is infrequent, it probably is more sensible to gain access through a large centralized facility. In the latter case, the user obviously is faced with the additional cost and complexity of a telecommunications connection.

Some circumstances suggest a need for an intermediate level of service, based neither at the user's workstation nor at a national information facility like OCLC. It may make more economic sense to have an information service based at the user's campus if individual users cannot justify copies of a database directly at their workstations but the aggregate of their needs dictates that the information resource should be available on the campus. OCLC is considering an information retrieval product that will work in conjunction with local library automation systems. This campus-level system would complement the capabilities already accessible from a user's workstation on local CD-ROM disks through

Search CD450 and from the Online Reference Service at OCLC. Together, the three services would form a compatible information retrieval system with the same user interface, retrieval software, and indexing conventions. The user would have access to a continually increasing body of information with no need to shift mentally when moving among resources at the workstation, across the campus, or in the national information utility.

Research at OCLC

For years, OCLC has supported a research group working in the information science field. This group of research scientists and their support staff, with backgrounds in library, information, and computer science, seldom conducts "basic" research, although some basic studies have been and probably will continue to be performed. Several OCLC products and services have resulted from the group's efforts, including OCLC's full range of Micro Enhancer software, which has increased substantially the cataloger's productivity and simultaneously reduced library cataloging costs. Using a Micro Enhancer, a user can prepare a batch of transactions to be carried out by an unattended microcomputer interacting with OCLC. A more recent outgrowth of the research is the OCLC Collection Analysis System, a self-contained optical compact disk product that will make it possible for a library to compare its collection with collections of similar libraries to determine size, overlap, gaps, and so on. This statistical tool will allow administrators to plan acquisition policies much more thoroughly.

OCLC's research also has generated a number of prototypes. One example is Graph-Text, an early implementation of a complete electronic information facility.[11] Graph-Text combined a variety of tools and techniques into a single, unified information environment: typesetting tapes from publishers, scanned images, sophisticated display fonts, a significant knowledge of user displays and layout, techniques for browsing, and early hypertext experience. The system provided the full text and graphics of journal articles, reference works, and other complete documents. The prototype ran on a user's workstation, which can be an IBM PC/XT or equivalent or a powerful workstation from Sun or Apollo. The user could retrieve, browse, scan, "explode," and otherwise traverse the documents in the collection. What appeared on the screen was virtually identical to the printed page (see Figure 2.4). A user who found a useful document could request that it be printed (published). The printer of choice was a laser printer; however, the system worked very well with an inexpensive dot-matrix printer. Many of the capabilities of the Graph-Text

Figure 2.4 A page of the *Kirk-Othmer Encyclopedia of Chemical Technology*, displayed using Graph-Text.

prototype have been patented and incorporated into OCLC's reference services; they will continue to have an important role in future releases.

OCLC's Office of Research performs and sponsors many other projects that are relevant to the goal of providing expanded information services.[12] Studies of user interfaces focus on the identification and exploration of the more significant characteristics in a full-text environment, supplying appropriate keys to the user to allow access to large bodies of information, and enhancing feedback to users to help them carry out tasks effectively. The research group also is examining the utility of information resources in new contexts. "Authority" files contain records that establish authoritative forms for names, titles, and subject headings and list any known alternative forms. For instance, Aaron Copland is the authoritative spelling of the composer's name, but the record also will list Aaron Kopland, since that form appears on one record label. Authority files are an important means for catalogers to ensure consistent use of names and subject headings; they can be of value to users, too. In a manual catalog, an entry for Kopland would point the user to Copland; in online catalogs, authority files can form the basis for automatic cross-referencing. Authority files have been created by such organizations as the Library of Congress, the French National Library, and the National Library of Canada. Such authority files, particularly for subject headings, have the potential of providing significant knowledge structures to characterize the information contained in documents and may help provide for consistent retrieval of documents.

Nontextual information is also very much of interest to OCLC. An OCLC postdoctoral fellow began a study of authority control for music. It is very important that the title and related information about a musical score, performance, or other musical record of information be retained consistently and correctly within the database. This is accomplished best with a strong, consistent authority file. However, it was quickly discovered that it was possible to go well beyond the typical bibliographic information and store a copy of the score and the sound associated with the bibliographic record. Soon it was feasible to retrieve information about a performance or score, see the score directly on the screen, and hear the music. This system exists as a prototype from which OCLC is learning a great deal about the storage, retrieval, and use of nonbibliographic and nontextual information.

Conclusion

OCLC is committed by its charter to "furthering the ease of access to and use of the ever-expanding body of worldwide scientific, literary, and educational information."[13] This has been accomplished to date primarily by facilitating technical processing, thus ensuring that the materials within a library are accessible quickly and economically to its users. In the process, OCLC has promoted the sharing of resources and, with its members, built a collected body of bibliographic information in electronic form that has no peer. This body of bibliographic information has added increasing value, not only to the technical services of the library, but also to the reference needs of library patrons and the entire scholarly and research community.

OCLC is moving judiciously to meet research needs by furnishing a range of reference services, which will be available in a variety of system environments. Information will be available through remote, centralized reference facilities, from campus-based services, and directly at users' workstations. In addition to its own vast information resources, OCLC is providing access to a number of valuable related databases, such as

ERIC, NTIS, AGRICOLA, and so on. These services have the twofold purpose: easier and cost-effective access, and access to a much broader range of information.

Bibliographic information is, by itself, an incomplete resource—the user must take further action to obtain the item that ultimately will be used. The fulfillment of this complete information need goes beyond bibliography. OCLC is taking steps to fill part of this need and to explore the options in other areas. Products will be offered that permit access to enhanced bibliographic records and to full documents. Delivery of graphics and other types of information, such as sound, is being explored. The breadth and depth of information-related products, services, and research are growing continually. The problems and opportunities that this growth produces are the challenges to be met by OCLC and its academic partners.

References

1. Lancaster, F. W. *Toward Paperless Information Systems* (New York: Academic Press, 1978).

   ———. "The Paperless Society Revisited." *American Libraries* 16, no. 8 (September 1985): 553–555.

   Battin, Patricia. "The Electronic Library—Vision for the Future." *EDUCOM Bulletin* 19, no. 2 (Summer 1984): 12–17, 34.

2. Parker, W. Wyman. *The Possibility of Extensive Academic Library Cooperation in Ohio: A Survey* (Columbus, Ohio: Ohio College Association, 1963).

3. Parker, Ralph H., and Frederick G. Kilgour. "Report to the Committee of Librarians of the Ohio College Association." In *Collected Papers of Frederick G. Kilgour* (Dublin, Ohio: OCLC Online Computer Center, 1984), p.1.

4. Kilgour, Frederick G. "Objectives and Activities of the Ohio College Library Center." In *Indiana Seminar on Information Networks (ISIN),* ed. Donald P. Hammer and Gary C. Lelvis (West Lafayette, Ind.: Purdue University Libraries, 1972), p. 34.

5. OCLC Online Computer Library Center, Inc. "Amended Articles of Incorporation of OCLC, Inc." (Online Computer Library Center, Dublin, Ohio, January 29, 1981.)

6. OCLC Online Computer Library Center. Minutes, users council meeting (OCLC Online Computer Library Center, Dublin, Ohio, February 1988).

7. Online Computer Library Center. *A Guide to Special Collections in the OCLC Database* (Dublin, Ohio: Online Computer Library Center, 1988).

8. Online Computer Library Center. *OCLC Annual Report 1986–87* (Dublin, Ohio: Online Computer Library Center, 1987), p. 1.

9. Datapro. *Transmission Control Protocol/Internet Protocol TCP/IP: An Overview, Datapro Report on Data Communications* (Delran, N.J.: Datapro, November 1987).

10. National Information Standards Organization, *Proposed American National Standard for Information Sciences—Information Retrieval Service Definition and Protocol Specification for Library Applications, ANSI/NISO Z39.50/1988* (New Brunswick, N.J.: Transaction Publishers, 1989).

11. Hickey, Thomas B., and John C. Handley. "Interactive Display of Text and Graphics on an IBM PC." In *Impact of New Information Technology on International Cooperation: Essen Symposium (9th: 1986),* ed. Ahmed H. Helal and Joachim W. Weiss (Essen, Federal Republic of Germany: Gesamthochschulbibliothek Essen, 1987), pp. 137–39.

12. Online Computer Library Center. *Annual Review of OCLC Research, July 1986–June 1987* (Dublin, Ohio: Online Computer Library Center, 1987).

13. OCLC Online Computer Library Center, Inc. "Amended Articles of Incorporation of OCLC, Inc."

Chapter 3

The Research Libraries Group

David Richards

T

he Research Libraries Group (RLG) is a nonprofit corporation owned and governed by thirty-six of the nation's major universities and other research institutions. It is dedicated to improving the management of and access to the information resources necessary for the advancement of scholarship.

RLG was established in 1974 as a regional consortium comprising Harvard, Yale, and Columbia universities and the New York Public Library to enable their research libraries to address cooperatively the challenge of providing access to scholarly materials in the face of rapid increases in their rate of production and in the cost of acquiring and cataloging them. The early activities of the group led the members to conclude that the best way to achieve their goals would be to share a computer-based bibliographic processing system. In 1978, after evaluating available systems, RLG concluded an agreement with Stanford University to acquire BALLOTS, the library automation system developed in the late 1960s and early 1970s for the Stanford University libraries. Stanford joined RLG and became the host institution for RLG's staff and computer operations. These changes transformed RLG from a regional into a national organization, and a period of rapid membership growth followed.

Table 3.1 presents a complete list of RLG members as of late 1988. The thirty-six governing members jointly own RLG; each has a seat on RLG's board of governors. More than sixty nongoverning members also participate in RLG, with several memberships pending at the time this was written.

RLG's activities are organized into a set of programs, each of which addresses specific aspects of interinstitutional cooperation in the management and provision of information resources for scholarship. RLG staff coordinate these activities. However, much of the actual work is carried out by representatives of member institutions meeting in various program committees and task forces.

RLG operates an international computer network and a large mainframe computer system (Amdahl 5890-300E) to provide a technical infrastructure for its cooperative programs. Collectively, this infrastructure is called the Research Libraries Information Network (RLIN). Interactive applications support various aspects of library operations, such as acquisitions, cataloging, and interlibrary lending. These services are designed to meet the needs of large research libraries and incorporate special capabilities required by various RLG programs. RLIN services are provided directly by RLG to its members and are available to nonmember

Table 3.1   RLG Members (as of November 22, 1988)

Governing Members

American Antiquarian Society
Brigham Young University
Brown University
Colorado State University
Columbia University
Cornell University
Dartmouth College
Emory University
Florida State University
Johns Hopkins University
Louisiana State University
The New-York Historical Society
The New York Public Library
New York University
Northwestern University
Pennsylvania State University
Princeton University
Rutgers University
Stanford University
State University of New York at Albany
State University of New York at Binghamton
State University of New York at Buffalo
State University of New York at Stony Brook
Temple University
University of California at Berkeley
University of California at Davis
University of California at Santa Barbara
University of Florida, Gainesville
University of Iowa
University of Michigan
University of Minnesota
University of Oklahoma
University of Pennsylvania
University of Rochester
University of Southern California
Yale University

Associate Members

Harvard University Library
Syracuse University Libraries

Table 3.1 (continued)

University of Chicago Library
University of Illinois at Urbana-Champaign Library
University of Texas at Austin Law Library
University of Toronto Library
University of Wisconsin at Madison Library

Special Members

Alabama Department of Archives and History
American Philosophical Society
Arizona State University
The Art Institute of Chicago
Boston University Law Library
Brandeis University
The Brooklyn Museum
California State Archives
Canadian Centre for Architecture
The Cleveland Museum of Art
Commonwealth of Massachusetts Archives
District of Columbia Office of Public Records
Fashion Institute of Technology
The Folger Shakespeare Library
Freer Gallery of Art/Arthur M. Sackler Gallery Library
Georgia Department of Archives and History
Graduate Theological Union
Hagley Museum and Library
Historical Society of Pennsylvania
Henry E. Huntington Library and Art Gallery
Library Company of Philadelphia
Los Angeles County Law Library
Massachusetts State Archive
The Metropolitan Museum of Art
Minnesota Historical Society
The Museum of Fine Arts (Boston, Massachusetts)
The Museum of Fine Arts (Houston, Texas)
The Museum of Modern Art
National Archives and Records Administration
National Gallery of Art
The Nelson-Atkins Museum of Art
Nevada State Library and Archives, Division of Archives and Records
New York State Archives
New York State Library

Table 3.1   (continued)

Oregon Secretary of State, Archives Division

Pennsylvania Historical and Museum Commission's Division of Archives and Manuscripts

The Philadelphia Museum of Art

The Pierpont Morgan Library

Princeton Theological Seminary

Radcliffe College

Rhode Island School of Design

Rockefeller Archive Center (The Rockefeller University)

Rosenbach Museum and Library

The Saint Louis Art Museum

State Historical Society of Wisconsin

Sterling and Francine Clark Art Institute (Williams College)

University of Hawaii at Manoa Library

University of Tulsa Libraries

University of Utah Law Library

Division of Archives and Records Service for the State of Utah

Utah State Historical Society

Virginia State Library and Archives

Whitney Museum of American Art

Henry Francis du Pont Winterthur Museum

RLG Affiliates

Frick Art Reference Library

Getty Center for the History of Art and the Humanities

Kimbell Art Museum

institutions worldwide through a broker, the Cooperative Library Authority for Systems and Services (CLASS), based in San Jose, California.

The size and comprehensiveness of the RLIN databases, along with the system's powerful and flexible searching capabilities, make RLIN a significant scholarly resource. As a result, RLG's role as an information provider rapidly is becoming as important as its role as a provider of processing services and is likely to overshadow it in the long run. In fact, this evolution is reflected in the rate structure adopted by RLG's board for the 1988/89 fiscal year, which made searching the main activity for which charges are imposed. Until this year, charging was based on technical processing transactions, such as cataloging a book or sending an interlibrary loan request. By responding to its members' needs, RLG expects to play an important role in the strategies developed by its members for libraries and electronic information in the twenty-first century.

RLG Programs

RLG operates four principal programs and a number of subject area programs that, together, provide a framework for interinstitutional cooperation.

The principal programs focus on primary library activities.

- *Collection Management and Development.* The goal of this program is to achieve the broadest possible coverage across the membership of materials of interest to scholars while, at the same time, reducing duplicate purchasing.
- *Shared Resources.* This program is concerned with facilitating access by scholars at RLG member institutions to the collections of other members. A major focus is maximizing the ability to transfer information and materials among RLG member libraries freely, flexibly, and promptly.
- *Preservation.* The physical deterioration of library collections, primarily due to acid paper, is a problem that is now receiving public attention nationally. Preservation of these materials, usually via microfilming, is labor-intensive and expensive. Therefore, coordination of preservation activity and the elimination of duplicative effort is a major program activity of RLG.
- *Library Technical Systems and Bibliographic Control.* This program aims to provide immediate access at every member institution to all bibliographic records. Program activities are directed at RLIN system development, policies for effective, efficient record use, and means to achieve better bibliographic control over collections.

The subject area programs focus on particular aspects of each of the principal programs that present special problems or opportunities for a given discipline. A further goal of these programs is to identify and provide information resources and tools to support scholarship in the respective areas. Currently, there are programs in the following subject areas:

- Archives, manuscripts, and special collections
- Art and architecture
- East Asian studies
- Law

- Medical and health sciences
- Jewish and Middle East studies
- Music

A relatively new venture for RLG is the Program for Research Information Management (PRIMA). Its objective is to make new types of information easily accessible to scholars by developing management frameworks analogous to the familiar bibliographic control mechanisms for traditional library materials. A major activity of this program has been a comprehensive assessment of information needs across a wide range of scholarly disciplines. The results of a survey of the humanities disciplines already have been published.[1] Similar surveys of the social sciences and sciences are nearing completion. The information gained from these surveys will guide RLG in the design of future programs and services.

RLIN Databases

The RLIN databases are managed with the Stanford-developed database system, SPIRES, whose original design goals included support of the BALLOTS library automation application. As a result, SPIRES has the necessary facilities to support storage and retrieval of bibliographic and textual data. Key characteristics of such data are that fields are highly variable in length and that records must allow for multiple entries for a particular field.

RLG Union Catalog

RLG's largest and most heavily used database is a union catalog of the holdings and in-process acquisitions of RLG members and other contributing institutions. While this database will not be complete until the cataloging data of all members has been converted to machine-readable form and loaded, it already contains more than thirty-two million records, representing more than thirteen million unique bibliographic entities. Combined with the powerful searching capabilities of RLG's database software, this database is itself a significant scholarly resource.

The union catalog database is divided into eight files representing books, serials, visual materials, maps, sound recordings, musical scores, the archival and manuscripts control (AMC) format for manuscripts, collections of letters, memorabilia, and other archival materials, and the machine-readable data file (MDF) format for computer data files and software. In addition, the Library of Congress name and subject authority files—which define the approved forms of personal names and subject headings for use in catalog records—are available online for use in conjunction with the bibliographic files.

Records may contain Chinese, Japanese, Korean, Hebrew, or Cyrillic characters as well as Roman characters from the extended set recognized by the American Library Association (ALA). Such data can be input and displayed on an appropriately configured personal computer running RLG-developed multiscript terminal software. Terminals that cannot support the additional character sets will display data in Roman characters only.

Each institution cataloging an item has its own record for that item in the database. This supports variations in cataloging practice and allows institution-specific information to be stored in addition to the usual bibliographic information. Records may contain ordering or processing status, local subject headings or notes, preservation decisions, and item-level holdings; the AMC and visual materials files also contain additional information required to manage the processing of archival materials.

Table 3.2 shows the approximate current sizes of the files (number of records and number of unique titles) as of November 1988.

Approximately one hundred thousand records are added to the database every week via online cataloging by libraries. In addition, records are loaded regularly from a variety of other sources, including the Library of Congress, CONSER (the CONversion of SERials project), the National Library of Medicine, the Government Printing Office, the British Library, and RLG member libraries.

Special Databases

The RLIN special databases are not intended for general-purpose shared cataloging; instead, they are information resources, each covering a specific subject area, for scholars and librarians working in a particular discipline. As in the central bibliographic database, new records constantly are added and existing records updated, but a special database generally is maintained by a single library or small cooperative group. At present, there are four special databases; this number will increase as RLG identifies particular subject areas in which gaining access to scholarly information is particularly difficult or of special concern to the research community.

The On-line Avery Index to Architectural Periodicals

Avery is an online version of the Avery Index to Architectural Periodicals, which was published by Columbia University and G. K. Hall and Company from 1963 to 1979. The database is produced and maintained by an operating unit of the J. Paul Getty Art History Information Program at

Table 3.2   Holdings in the RLIN Union Catalog as of November 1988

	Records	Titles
Books	28,350,000	10,539,000
Serials	2,583,000	1,769,000
Visual materials	115,000	105,000
Maps	151,000	140,000
Sound recordings	223,000	156,000
Musical scores	486,000	323,000
Archives and manuscripts (AMC)	156,000	156,000
Machine-readable data files (MDF)	5,000	5,000
Total	32,069,000	13,193,000

Columbia University. It indexes articles published since 1979 in over one thousand journals in the fields of architecture, architectural design, history and practice of architecture, landscape architecture, city planning, historic preservation, and interior design and decoration. Presently, Avery includes over fifty-seven thousand records and is supplemented by a reference file of more than twenty-seven thousand subject headings used in the bibliographic records.

SCIPIO—The Art Sales Catalog Database
SCIPIO (Sales Catalog Index Project Input On-line), a listing of art sales catalogs, is produced and maintained jointly by the Art Institute of Chicago, the Cleveland Museum of Art, the Metropolitan Museum of Art, the Getty Center for the History of Art and the Humanities, the National Gallery of Art, the Clark Art Institute, the Nelson-Atkins Museum of Art, and the University of California, Santa Barbara. The database contains over eighty-eight thousand records of catalogs listing works of art and related materials sold at auction from the late sixteenth century to the present. These catalogs are valuable aids in tracing the provenance of works of art, establishing collecting patterns, and analyzing the contemporary art market.

The Eighteenth Century Short Title Catalogue (ESTC)
The ESTC database contains bibliographic records for eighteenth-century publications from Great Britain and its colonies, as well as for English-language materials printed anywhere in the world during the same period. The British Library created the initial database, and the

North American Center for ESTC (located at the University of California, Riverside) is adding North American holdings information to existing records and creating new bibliographic records for British imprints held by North American libraries. Records for American imprints are being compiled by the North American Imprints Project at the American Antiquarian Society and will be added in 1990.

ESTC now has over 209,000 records. The completed database is expected to contain 500,000 titles related to every aspect of eighteenth-century studies.

The RLG Conspectus On-line

Created in 1982, the RLG Conspectus On-line is a tool for comparing and analyzing existing RLG collection strengths and future collecting policies and for distributing primary collecting responsibilities among the membership. Assessing each member's collection in seven thousand fields, the conspectus is primarily a resource for librarians and collection-development planners, although it can be a useful aid to locating desired materials, because it identifies libraries with strong collections and/or active collecting policies in many fields.

RLIN Services

A large mainframe application program, known as the Integrated Technical Processing System (ITPS), provides a number of related RLIN services based on the union catalog database. ITPS integrates searching, cataloging, acquisitions, interlibrary loan, and archival control facilities, making it possible to move from one activity to another in a natural progression. This software replaced the original BALLOTS system in 1982.

Other RLIN services include special database searching, the generation of batch products such as catalog cards and tapes of member records, batch and online retrospective conversion, electronic mail and conferencing, and intersystem communication.

Searching

RLIN offers sophisticated, flexible access to bibliographic records through twenty-five "general" and fifteen "local" indexes, as well as eight character indexes to Chinese, Japanese, and Korean material. Commands and indexes use natural language. Indexes can be combined using the Boolean operators "and," "not," and "or." An "also" qualifier can be used to restrict results to those records satisfying specified criteria on the values of selected fields.

The general indexes are for bibliographic access points like author, title, series, and subject, as well as for alphanumeric codes like the Library of Congress control number, classification number, ISBN, Geographic Classification code, and Superintendent of Documents number.

In title and corporate author searches, the user can search for selected, distinctive words (for example, "imperial earthquake" for *Imperial Valley, California, Earthquake of October 15, 1979*) or type in an entire phrase. Records also can be retrieved by subject headings, either by searching for the entire phrase or for a subject subdivision such as "20th century" or "Addresses, essays, lectures." (Subject subdivision searching currently is not available in the books file.)

Depending on the amount of information available, a user can perform author searches with the personal name index (PN), which permits use of the surname alone or the surname and selected initials, or with the exact personal name index (PE), which requires the complete name. For example, a user could search for "Faulkner" or "Faulkner, W.," using PN or for "Faulkner, William," using PE. Like the phrase index, the exact personal name index is an efficient searching tool; it creates a very specific search request that eliminates many unwanted records from the result.

Some general indexes are unique to particular material types. For example, the publisher and number indexes retrieve records in the files for recordings and scores according to the publisher name or the issue/matrix/publisher number.

When several libraries own the same item (that is, the same edition of a given work), the multiple individual records are clustered together for retrieval purposes in all files except MDF and AMC. This streamlines the user interface for searching and minimizes retrieval time. One record that will satisfy a searcher's needs in most instances is chosen to represent the cluster as a whole. This Primary Cluster Member (PCM) is accessed first during a general index search, making it unnecessary to access any of the other cluster members, called Secondary Cluster Members (SCMs). If the searcher's library owns one of the SCMs, that SCM, rather than the PCM, is used for the display.

Each local index is specific to a single library, which uses it primarily for technical processing and, with one exception, only to retrieve its own records. The exception is the ID index, which retrieves specific records by the unique record identifiers that are assigned by the system as each record is added to the database. The other local indexes include a call number index for locally assigned call numbers and a queuing date index that makes it possible to retrieve records for materials that the library has decided to microfilm. Acquisitions and circulation numbers can be indexed in the local data number index. A library can retrieve easily all the records that it has added or updated on the current day and all of the records waiting for revision in "saved" status, either for the current day or for an earlier day or period.

Cataloging and Acquisitions
RLIN includes extensive facilities to support cataloging and acquisitions activities. In fact, the original purpose behind the creation of shared bibliographic utilities like RLIN was the dramatic reduction in cataloging costs that results from sharing bibliographic records.

Catalogers using RLIN are able to search the database for appropriate records from which to derive the new records that they wish to create. When records are found, their bibliographic information can be copied to the new records and modified as necessary to conform to the standards of the cataloger's library. Detailed local information also can be appended.

The RLIN acquisitions facilities allow a library to track the status and location of each item, beginning with the original order and proceeding through claiming, receipt, and cataloging. This in-process information supports the RLG cooperative collection development and shared resources programs.

Interlibrary Loan
Participants in RLG's shared resources program are supported by RLIN interlibrary loan facilities. Users of this system can create loan requests and send them to other program participants through RLIN. Bibliographic information can be copied from an existing record to expedite the creation of requests. Requesters can be notified that a request is being filled, and unfilled requests can be forwarded to another potential lender. The system allows users to inquire about the status of requests, renew loans, recall loaned materials, or send overdue notices. Users can examine online statistical reports of interlibrary loan activity for their libraries and for the network as a whole.

Archival and Manuscripts Control
RLIN includes special facilities to allow repositories to track all stages of the processing and management of archival materials. Manuscripts and archives of unpublished papers are complex to catalog; they also may need special physical preparation to be ready for access. A record in the

AMC file initially describes an unprocessed collection or item and is updated as the material passes through stages of processing. Related but independent bibliographic records (for example, one record describing the collection as a whole and other records describing the collection's individual series) can be linked by including common access points in the records. The system can produce various status reports and alerting lists derived from the database that can help the repository to control its holdings and manage its resources effectively.

Batch Products

An RLIN user can request that catalog cards be produced as part of a cataloging transaction. These are formatted to the library's specifications, printed on a Xerox laser printer at Stanford, and shipped to the library on a daily or weekly basis. Although the production of catalog cards is declining as more libraries switch to online systems and close card catalogs, RLG still prints over fifteen million cards per year.

Through an acquisitions transaction, order, claim, and cancellation forms can be printed either by RLG or on a printer at the requesting library.

A library also can request tapes of its records, usually in order to load them into an online catalog or the local library automation system. These can be either special "snapshot" tapes or regularly scheduled tapes containing records generated by online use of RLIN.

Management and statistical reports of database contents, tailored to a library's needs, can be produced on request by the RLIN Reports System. Examples are lists of new holdings, finding aids, action alert notices, and breakdowns by language or Library of Congress classification.

Retrospective Conversion

RLIN includes support for online retrospective conversion, basically a mode of operation of the cataloging facility intended to expedite the entry of existing manual cataloging records. RLG also provides a batch retrospective conversion system. Using a simple, offline, PC-based interface, users create search records containing minimal bibliographic information and detailed holdings information. These records then are uploaded to RLIN for comparison with the union catalog database. When records match, complete records, including the institution's holdings data, are added to the database, producing cards and/or tape records if they have been requested. For each batch of input records, the institution receives a report indicating which records were created successfully and which generated either no hit or multiple hits in the database. This information can be used to guide subsequent completion of the conversion online.

Electronic Communication

RLG members can exchange messages with each other and with RLG central staff using RLIN's electronic mail facilities. In addition, the RLIN system is a node on BITNET and on the national Internet, so mail may be exchanged with any institution with access to these networks.

RLG committees, working groups, and others who need to share information quickly can communicate with each other using RLIN's electronic bulletin board system. Users may select and process conference notices posted by other users and post notices themselves. Within a given "conference," posted notices can be categorized by several predefined "topics" for improved retrieval.

Intersystem Record Transfer and Information Retrieval

RLG has been a pioneer in the development and implementation of computer-to-computer linkage for the exchange of library information. This work, funded by the Council on Library Resources, began in 1980 as the Linked Systems Project (LSP). RLG, the Library of Congress (LC), and the Western Library Network were the original participants; current active players are LC, RLG, and OCLC. The ultimate goal of this work is to link the participating systems so that cataloging and interlibrary loan data can be shared among them, creating a virtual national bibliographic network.

Two facilities were developed by the Linked Systems Project. Intersystem record transfer enables queues of records created on one system to be transferred to a second system at its request. Intersystem information retrieval enables search requests to be sent from one system to another in a standard syntax and includes means to manage the transfer of retrieved records back to the system that originated the search. Normally, this is done by translating a user's search from the familiar language of his or her own system into the intersystem syntax; as a result, use of this facility does not require a user to learn the searching language of the target system.

Use of these facilities began in 1985, when the Library of Congress began distributing updates for its name authority file to RLG on a daily basis. Subsequently, RLG began contributing to LC on a daily basis the records created by member libraries participating in the Name Authorities

Cooperative (NACO) Project. LC staff use LSP intersystem searching to retrieve and examine NACO records created on RLIN as part of a review and approval process. The NACO project, whose goal is to allow many libraries to share the burden of maintaining the LC's name authority file, would not be practical without the real-time access to shared information made possible by computer networking technology.

The Library of Congress has initiated a National Coordinated Cataloging Project (NCCP), modeled after NACO. To support member libraries participating in NCCP, RLG is developing the necessary application-software enhancements to allow intersystem searching and record transfer to be used for bibliographic records.

As local library automation systems suitable for large libraries have become available commercially, many RLG members have begun to use them to carry out at least some of the acquisitions and cataloging work once done on RLG's system. To ensure the continued viability of RLG's cooperative programs, it is necessary to facilitate the contribution of data created on local systems to the union database and to make the union database accessible to local systems. Intersystem linkage between these systems and RLIN appears to be the most effective way to achieve this, and RLG staff are working with member institutions and several library-system vendors to implement this capability.

Access to RLIN Services

RLIN services currently can be accessed via RLG's private network, the GTE/Telenet public data network, or the national educational Internet.

Terminal Access

Two different types of terminals are used with RLIN. Special-purpose synchronous terminals are used for data entry (recent versions are based on personal computer hardware); these support the full-screen interface used by the library technical-processing applications. Asynchronous terminals can be used for search-only access to RLIN databases. Unlike the synchronous terminals, asynchronous terminals do not have an end-to-end, error-free link to the host; therefore, update of the databases is not permitted from these devices.

Originally, the approximately eleven hundred synchronous terminals in the RLIN network were connected to the host system via leased multipoint telephone lines and Paradyne synchronous modems. In 1988, the old leased-line network was replaced by a private packet-switching network using the X.25 communications protocols, which also are used by public packet-switching networks such as Telenet. The installed base of RLIN terminals now is supported by special PAD (packet assembler/disassembler) software that is run in the network nodes.

Figure 3.1 shows the configuration of the new network. The RLIN host system and network control center are located at Stanford University. Switching nodes are located at New York University, Johns Hopkins, Northwestern, Colorado State (not yet installed), the University of Southern California, and Stanford. These nodes and the lines connecting them make up the backbone network. Nodes at the other sites shown in the figure function as terminal servers for RLIN terminals and concentrators for X.25 traffic. The switching nodes provide terminal server functions for the institutions at which they are installed. The figure does not show the multipoint terminal lines outboard of the nodes.

At present, asynchronous terminals can be connected to RLIN in several ways. Eight dial-up ports are available for Northern California users, while more distant users access RLIN through GTE/Telenet, which is connected to the host system via an X.25 link. The new RLIN network makes possible a third alternative that is likely to replace much of the Telenet usage: asynchronous traffic can be routed through standard PADs connected to one of the network nodes. Such PADs are available from many vendors, and, even taking into account depreciation of the equipment, this service is significantly less expensive than Telenet for locations that are close enough to an RLIN network node.

The private RLIN network is necessary to support intensive production use of RLIN services with the requisite level of control over network operation and reliability. However, RLG recognizes the importance of making RLIN services available via the national educational Internet and is taking steps to make this possible. The first step, completed in early 1989, was to connect the RLIN host to the Internet and support the Telnet virtual terminal protocol, so that users of terminals or workstations with Internet access can log on to the RLIN system and search its databases.

Intersystem Access
Current RLIN support for intersystem access was developed in the context of the Linked Systems Project. The project participants decided to base their work on the seven-layer ISO Open Systems Interconnection (OSI) Model, rather than on any vendor-specific protocol suite, and, where possible, to utilize ISO standard or draft standard protocols for the various protocol layers. Thus, CCITT Recommendation X.25 was adopted

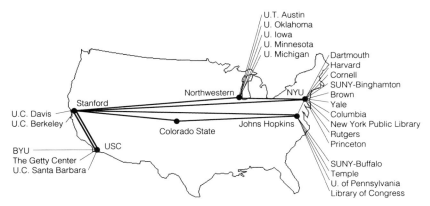

Figure 3.1 Configuration of the new RLIN network. Switching nodes are shown as dots, access nodes as names fanning out from the switching nodes.

for layers 1 through 3. The layer 4 and 5 protocols nearly conform to ISO Class 2 transport and ISO session protocols; the differences stem from minor changes that were made between the draft and final versions of the standards after LSP implementations had been started. Although support for the original LSP protocols will be continued as long as it is needed, RLG intends to migrate to the final versions of the ISO protocols. A null presentation protocol was used at layer 6, and application protocols for record transfer and information retrieval were developed by the project; the information retrieval protocol is now a national standard, adopted by the National Information Standards Organization (NISO) and known as Z39.50. These application protocols have been described by Ray Denenberg of the Library of Congress in a number of publications.[2]

The library community had begun work on intersystem linkage long before it became clear that the higher education community had chosen to use the TCP/IP protocol suite for extensive wide area networking. The Department of Defense intends to phase out the TCP/IP protocols in favor of ISO protocols as support for the latter becomes widely available from vendors; in the meantime, it seems important for information and service providers in the library community to support connection via TCP/IP networks in addition to the ISO transport protocol. RLG plans to provide such support for workstations that run the appropriate ISO session, presentation, and application protocols on top of the TCP transport protocol.

The Future of RLIN Services

Most RLIN computer services are implemented as host-based application programs accessed via terminals. Except for the screen-editing facilities of the data-entry terminals used in RLG's private network, all intelligence is provided by the RLIN host computer. Such terminal access is likely to remain important for some time to come. However, RLG believes that eventually most application software (that is, the software providing the interactive user interface and data-manipulation and -display facilities) should be run on the increasingly powerful workstations now being used by scholars and students. The RLIN system then would function primarily as a large-scale "database server" in a wide area network (or networks).

Much of RLG's current development effort is focused on repositioning RLIN for such a role. Work to establish new connectivity options has been discussed already. In addition, architectural changes are being planned that will repackage the database management software as a database server with a uniform message-based interface to applications, whether they are run on the RLIN host or on remote workstations and local library systems. In the process, this software is being enhanced to support very large databases and high transaction loads more efficiently and to provide substantially more hours of availability of the RLIN databases. The next generation of RLIN applications is being designed for the workstation environment.

Until now, RLIN has offered access to bibliographic databases, which describe the contents and location of published materials. As the Program for Research Information Management identifies additional needs of the scholarly community, the scope of RLIN databases will expand to encompass other categories of "metainformation" (i.e., information about information) and primary information (textual, numeric, image) of interest to scholars but not provided by commercial information suppliers. Some examples are already being developed:

- The Medieval and Early Modern Databank, a database of quantitative information (such as currency exchange and census records), compiled by scholars at Rutgers University, concerning this period in history;
- A database of research in progress, produced by the Modern Language Association, containing prepublication information concerning papers submitted to selected journals in the humanities;
- A geodata system to provide access to the vast and growing body of information referenced geographically (for instance, aerial photography, satellite remote-sensing data, and census data);

- Enhancements to RLIN to enable retrieval of image information from a terminal-controlled videodisk player in conjunction with the retrieval of related bibliographic records, being applied initially to the collection of architectural drawings held by the Avery Art and Architecture Library of Columbia University.

Obviously, these projects only scratch the surface of what is possible. What is clear is that providing access to an expanding variety of scholarly resources will be a major endeavor for RLG over the next decade.

References

1. Research Libraries Group. *Information Needs in the Humanities: An Assessment* (Stanford, Calif.: Research Libraries Group, 1988).
2. Denenberg, Ray. "Linked Systems Project, Part 2: Standard Network Interconnection." *Library Hi Tech* 10 (1985): 71.
   ———. "Network Interconnection Protocols." In *The Linked Systems Project: A Networking Tool for Libraries,* ed. Judith G. Fenly and Beacher Wiggins (Dublin, Ohio: OCLC, 1988), pp. 19–49.

Chapter 4

Northwestern University

John P. McGowan
Karen L. Horny
Betsy Baker

Northwestern University Library has been and continues to be a pioneer in library automation. The decision to assume this role dates from the early 1960s, when a planning committee was formed to identify the service features necessary for a new building for the main library. This committee included a number of highly influential faculty members who took an active interest in all aspects of the design process and commissioned a series of studies by respected leaders in the field of automation and data processing. The recommendations that came out of these studies set directions for library automation at the university.

The initial goal was a fully integrated online system tailored to local academic needs. To meet this goal, the library has developed automated support for ordering materials, receipt recording, fund accounting, cataloging, and controlling circulation, as well as for course reserve services and an online public access catalog. When the Northwestern Online Total Integrated System (NOTIS) was first implemented in January 1970, it supported circulation, including self-service check-out of items in the collections. Building upon that strong beginning, the library has pursued a steady process of development. Faculty, students, and staff all rely on computer-based services for their library needs.

Although the goal of developing and operating an integrated local system remains primary, it has been modified; NOTIS has evolved into a product, a software package now adopted by over a hundred other libraries. A combination of changing circumstances are responsible for this shift. Among these was the receipt of significant external funding to help automate the operations of the National Library of Venezuela; once the software had been released for use at one other library, it was hard to refuse purchase offers from others.

As anticipated, the decision to market NOTIS had significant ramifications, particularly in terms of the time expended to demonstrate the software, not only at Northwestern, but also at conferences and on visits to other institutions. Also expected was the growing pressure to address the interests of other libraries, regardless of Northwestern's priorities. The eventual hiring of additional programming staff specifically to meet external demands has alleviated this pressure significantly. In 1987, the marketing group was formed into a separate corporation owned by the university. This step acknowledges the important position of NOTIS in the market for library automation software.

At Northwestern, the library continues to develop new opportunities for access to machine-readable information. The support of teaching and research at the university is the library's first priority.

The Context

Northwestern is the only private university among the "Big Ten" Conference institutions. It is also the smallest, with some 7,400 undergraduates and 5,700 full-time and 3,150 part-time graduate, continuing education, and professional-school students. The university occupies two campuses: the main campus is at Evanston; the continuing education program and the schools of law, medicine, and dentistry are in Chicago.

The university offers a wide variety of academic programs. In addition to strong programs in technology and the liberal arts, Northwestern has important schools of journalism, music, and speech, emphasizing studies in theater, radio, TV, and film. The Transportation Center, one of the premier institutions for transportation research and education in the United States, offers special programs, including conferences and seminars, to executives in industry as well as academic researchers.

Northwestern's libraries' collections total over 3.3 million volumes, supporting the university's emphasis on both research and teaching. The central library system serves the 12,750 students and 850 faculty on the Evanston campus and in the continuing education and masters in management programs on the Chicago campus. The University Librarian, who holds the Charles Deering McCormick Distinguished Chair of Research Librarianship, reports to the provost. The head librarians of the separate medical, dental, and law libraries report to the deans of their respective schools.

Statistics reported to the Association of Research Libraries for 1987/88 covering all of Northwestern's libraries recorded 33,226 current serials subscriptions, 114 professional staff, 146 support staff, and 100 full-time-equivalent student assistants. Over $3.4 million are spent annually on library materials. Northwestern is an active member of the Research Libraries Group. Library operations in Evanston are highly centralized, with a main library complex, a separate science-engineering library a block away, and only two small branches, for mathematics and geology. Processing for the separate branches is performed centrally. The library has been a leader in the development of online operations in the academic community at Northwestern. When NOTIS was introduced in 1970, it was the first online, interactive operation providing a public service in the university. The central library's in-house computing center is accessible through campus networking services.

Until recently, network growth on campus has progressed on a number of independent tracks. Three different networks offer terminal-to-host communications. Terminals and personal computers in public clusters are linked to academic time-sharing computers and the library system through a data switch. From offices, these computers can be reached through the Northern Telecom telephone PBX using modems or data-interface units. A separate IBM SNA network supports administrative computing. Meanwhile, an Ethernet serves science and engineering departments in five buildings, providing peer-to-peer networking based on the TCP/IP family of protocols. This network also provides access to supercomputers and the NSFNET for the whole academic community, since terminals using the data switch or PBX can connect to a Digital VAX computer on the Ethernet. At present, a proposal for a more unified approach based on a high-speed campus backbone is under consideration. Plans to support network access from all offices and dormitories also are being discussed.

Library users currently have access to the online catalog from all public clusters of terminals and personal computers and from any telephone. The library also has a computer-to-computer link with Northwestern's University Management Systems, which allows the library's financial manager to access the university's accounting system records from the same terminals used for the library's NOTIS system. The connection currently does not allow direct passing of records, but this feature is a candidate for future development.

Strategies for Success

The process of introducing computer technology into library services has been time-consuming and continuous. For such a program to succeed, every sector of the university community must understand, accept, and be involved in the undertaking. Faculty, students, staff, and the university administration need to recognize that the library's operations will always be in transition. A steady state never will be reached; further improvements should always be expected. At Northwestern, involving the university community in NOTIS developments has yielded excellent cooperation as each new step has been taken. The University Library Committee, composed of faculty, students, and librarians, gave particularly effective support when the closing of the card catalog was proposed in 1981. Subsequently, the proposal was approved by the University Senate without a single dissenting vote.

Each stage in the evolution of NOTIS has required a new set of technical and administrative decisions. These have been shaped by the state of computer technology, by funding considerations, by the availability of experienced and qualified staff to design and program the systems, and by the cooperation of library staff, who have to be trained and retrained as each new NOTIS module is developed, tested, and moved into the library's operations.

Most of the principles and decisions of the sixties that determined the early direction of Northwestern's library automation program and its philosophy of operation are still valid today. A progress report prepared in December 1968 for the university administration described that philosophy and the subsequent direction of the program. One section of the report states:

> The results of the analysis indicated that Technical Services and Circulation control were the areas which could benefit most by the new techniques. A computer system, if it were to become an effective solution to the problems of these departments, would have to meet the following requirements:
>
> 1. The system must be based on a unified centralized computer file of records for books and serials. The file must contain order, catalog, and locational data, captured as soon as possible after the initiation of a request for an item.
> 2. The file must be able to reflect change in the status of an item without delay; the user wants to know where a book is now.
> 3. It must be possible to interrogate the file from a number of different physical locations, within and without the main library building. This requires multiple terminals and time-sharing capability.
> 4. The time necessary to order, receive, pay for, catalog, and physically process a book must be substantially reduced.
> 5. The system must include provision for financial accounting and inventory control. It must be able to supply management with information on which to base planning.
> 6. Computer files must be available for library use throughout the day and evening hours; hence multi-programming, to permit various non-library jobs to be processed during intervals between library transactions, is desirable for economical and effective computer utilization.
> 7. In addition to serving the needs of library operations, the files should be so constructed as to be useful for information retrieval.
> 8. The system must have provision for expansion and refinement, and must be reasonably compatible with systems presently being developed by the national library.
> 9. The library system must be compatible with the overall university information system.

While these requirements are accepted widely today, they were not so in the late sixties.

In the early days of library automation, it was common practice to seek large amounts of external funding to support individual projects. Northwestern was one of very few libraries that did not use external funds to support their automation programs. The decision to develop the NOTIS computer system with university funds has affected all subsequent activities. It also is at the root of Northwestern's philosophy of operation: the development of a tightly designed system that places the primary emphasis on economy at all stages—design, development, and operation.

Using university financial resources placed some constraints on the development of NOTIS, but these were far outweighed by the advantages, a fact that became increasingly apparent as Northwestern's program developed. Libraries that received significant federal funding for automation in the late sixties and seventies tended to launch large-scale, overly ambitious, and unwieldy projects that could never be supported locally. They also suffered from a paucity of experienced and qualified systems and programming personnel and from a batch-processing technology that was not designed to meet the requirements of large research libraries. As soon as it became apparent that batch processing was inadequate, a few libraries received funding to develop online systems. The obstacles were many—the technology was untried and vastly more complex, with inadequate software packages, expensive terminals, and storage devices of limited capabilities—and the outcome was predictable: as soon as funding agencies withdrew their support, many libraries were unable to continue the development and operation of their online systems.

Northwestern escaped this fate. Because the library entered the era of automation at the right time, when the online mode of operation was replacing the batch mode, and because its efforts were supported by local funds and directed at the practical objective of applying technology to a new building, its approach was well-defined, incremental, affordable (of necessity), and, ultimately, successful.

A second factor in the success of automation at Northwestern was the decision to adhere to standards as closely as possible. The library was fortunate to begin automating just as the Library of Congress was introducing the second version of the U.S. MARC format for bibliographic information. This standard furnished the basis for the major current library automation systems, including the networks operated by the Research Libraries Group and OCLC.

A key principle that has guided Northwestern's automation efforts from the start has been a commitment to involving all library staff in the design and development of NOTIS. The library's operations staff have been encouraged to interact with the systems design personnel. Suggestions and opinions are welcomed, and library committees are formed to review and analyze all design specifications, new features, and enhancements to NOTIS. These committees regularly address recommendations and criticisms from staff using NOTIS in their operations. Individuals from every division of the university's libraries on both campuses participate in these committees. This wealth of knowledge and practical experience enriches the design process and ensures that any new feature or enhancement will function effectively and to the satisfaction of the staff and the public.

NOTIS development also has been guided by the decision to test system enhancements in regular library operations as soon as possible so that design and programming flaws can be detected and corrected quickly. Changes suggested by library staff thus may be incorporated in the current version of NOTIS or may influence succeeding versions. This quality control at the design, development, and implementation phases of the project guarantees that each release of NOTIS is fully tested and reliable.

Two decisions most affected the system's operation and its ability to function efficiently and continuously for almost twenty years. When the choice of equipment was made, the library had the good fortune to predict—accurately—that IBM would provide a growth path in both hardware and software. The IBM equipment also offered a more suitable architecture for text processing than other options intended primarily for scientific computing. The choice eventually proved especially advantageous for other libraries, for whom IBM equipment, supported by the CICS communications subsystem, has been an attractive environment for running NOTIS.

The other critical choice was the decision to establish an in-house computing staff. Two members of that resident staff, James Aagaard, who is also a professor of computer science and electrical engineering, and Velma Veneziano, Systems Analyst and Design Coordinator, have worked together on every phase of the NOTIS project. In 1985, in recognition of their superb contributions to library automation, the Library and Information Technology Association granted them its highest honor: the LITA/Gaylord Award for Achievement in Library and Information Technology. Continuous service by these two individuals and their active and productive collaboration with library staff have been major factors contributing to Northwestern's success in library automation over the last two decades.

Evolution of Automated Services

Automation of traditional library services began with the circulation module, introduced simultaneously with the opening of the new main library building in January 1970. The following year, Northwestern implemented modules for technical processing, including acquisitions, cataloging, and serials control. Some of the important steps in the evolution of NOTIS at Northwestern are shown in the accompanying chronology.

At first, the library shared the university's computer for administrative data processing, but, in 1979, the library acquired its own dedicated computer, operated in-house. This computer has been upgraded periodically over the last decade. The database has now grown to over a million records, and the system is available over 99 percent of its scheduled 110 hours per week.

Beyond the self-service check-out feature, public access to NOTIS began in 1975 with the installation of a terminal from which library users could make direct inquiries about item circulation status. This service was received enthusiastically and proved to be a valuable precursor to the Library User Information Service (LUIS) online catalog that was made available to the public in 1980. LUIS can be accessed easily from a terminal or microcomputer at a remote location, either over the Academic Computing and Network Services terminal network or through a modem. A handout prepared by the Reference Department provides basic instructions to facilitate dial-up use.

NOTIS/LUIS has evolved through several versions, and development continues. LUIS currently provides author, title, and subject access to a database of over one million bibliographic records. A series of online introductory and help screens provides assistance. The simplicity of the design allows easy access to the library's holdings. Recent enhancements to LUIS include a full cross-reference structure (cross-references, such as pseudonyms, now are followed automatically), expanded index displays, and a search qualification methodology that enables a user to narrow the results of a search in several ways, such as by type of publication (books or serials), by record type (map, video, etc.), by date, by volume, or by place of publication. Another enhancement provides access by specialized subject headings, such as those devised by the university's Transportation Library.

The database, too, is changing to match university needs; catalog records for machine-readable data files, including those housed in the campus computing center, were added recently. Authority control for the database and inventory control to assist in collection management are among other features that have been implemented over the past two decades. The library's services now depend entirely on the automated NOTIS system. Few paper files are maintained, and card filing in the traditional catalog has ceased. For the million titles already represented in the online database, only a shelflist card remains in the card catalog.

Table 4.1   Chronology of NOTIS Development

1962–64	Planning Committee for new library building foresees development of an automated library support system and provides a room for a dedicated library computer in the plans.
1967	Velma Veneziano is appointed Library Systems Analyst. Dr. James Aagaard from the faculty of Computer Sciences and Electrical Engineering joins the project.
1968	Programming begins. Keypunching of nearly a million cards for book circulation starts.
1970	Circulation module is introduced successfully when new main library building opens. Self-service checkout terminals are provided. The library shares the university's computer for administrative data processing. Conversion of serials information to machine-readable records begins.
1971	Version 2 of the library system, with full support for technical services, is implemented. Acquisitions, serials control, and cataloging all rely on the automated system to provide their services. Typewriter terminals are used for input and display.
1974	Screen displays replace the typewriter terminals.
1975	A public terminal is installed to display circulation status information.
1976	The name NOTIS (Northwestern Online Total Integrated System) is adopted. The libraries of the Garrett Evangelical and Seabury Western theological seminaries, which adjoin the Northwestern campus, join the system.
1977	The National Endowment for the Humanities grants $275,445 to demonstrate the feasibility of distributed components in a national library network. Northwestern library operations are converted to the third version of NOTIS.
1978	Northwestern's Transportation Library begins to use NOTIS. Input of records for music scores and phonorecords begins.
1979	Input of authority records begins. NOTIS is installed at the National Library of Venezuela at the conclusion of a $1.3 million joint bibliographic project. The library now operates its own computer, an IBM 4331.
1980	The Medical School library at Northwestern begins using NOTIS. The online public access catalog, known as LUIS (Library User Information Service) and providing author/title access, is introduced. A team of EDUCOM consultants recommends that the university market NOTIS to other libraries. Sales begin. The Law Library at Northwestern begins using NOTIS. Filing of cards in the main author/title catalog ceases. The online catalog becomes the primary source for bibliographic information.

Table 4.1   (continued)

1981	The University of Florida becomes the first customer to install NOTIS. A cable to the university's academic computing center allows remote access to the online catalog. Access by subject is added to the online catalog. A grant from the Council on Library Resources funds development of computer-to-computer applications protocols. A special office within the library is established to market the NOTIS software.
1985	A new circulation system is implemented, using item records and bar-code labels in place of the punched cards. Circulation status information is now integrated into LUIS.
1986	The authority file of Library of Congress subject headings is loaded into NOTIS. A preliminary version of new indexes, including a full cross-reference structure, is made available to staff for testing. The Dental Library at Northwestern begins to use NOTIS.
1987	A grant from the Council on Library Resources funds implementation of Linked Systems protocols for the interconnection of computer systems. The marketing department is restructured as NOTIS Systems, Inc., a for-profit corporation owned by Northwestern University.
1988	The database at Northwestern contains over one million bibliographic records. The new indexes, with cross-referencing, are introduced into LUIS. NOTIS is in operation at more than one hundred other sites, some supporting several libraries.

NOTIS is a fully integrated system, which allows information from operations supported by the various modules to be used jointly. Among the most impressive features of an integrated system is its ability to provide information in the online public access catalog that was never available in the traditional card catalog. Circulation information for most items is displayed with the bibliographic record. For new items, the order status is displayed. A library user can determine immediately if an item is on order, received but in process, or already checked out. Up-to-the-moment information on which issues of a serial have been received also is visible in the online catalog.

Automation has provided opportunities to reevaluate old rules and methods—for example, creating a separate record when the title of a journal changes makes catalog cards easier to handle in a manual system but makes little sense in an automated system. Building on their positive experience with computer-based applications for library services, Northwestern's staff are always ready to review traditional methods of operation and seek out opportunities to use electronic information to add another dimension to the library's role.

NOTIS Beyond Northwestern

Up to 1976, the library's policy had been to keep its staff fairly small and to place primary emphasis on designing and developing an efficient computer-based support system to serve our own academic community. That year, representatives of the National Library of Venezuela asked the university about the possibility of establishing a project to identify and record in machine-readable form bibliographic information about Venezuelan works held in libraries in the United States. This led to a $1.3 million project that began in the fall of 1976. By the spring of 1979, the NOTIS computer software was installed in Venezuela, where it was used initially to maintain and enlarge the database created by the project. NOTIS, with displays translated into Spanish, now supports the technical and reference services of the National Library, the public libraries, and several university libraries within Venezuela. In addition, staff from Venezuela's National Library helped to install NOTIS at the National Library of Chile and the Banco de la Republica in Bogotá, Colombia.

At the completion of this ambitious bibliographic project, Northwestern's librarians and systems and programming staff had small interest in actively marketing the NOTIS software for use in other libraries. The Venezuela project had drained time and resources from the regular staff as well as the project personnel. Because of the significant impact on operations, the library administration determined that, unless there were basic changes in the organization, marketing the NOTIS software would interfere with the library's primary mission. The scores of librarians who visited the library to see the system in operation and to inquire about its availability were informed that the university could not market and support the NOTIS package with its current resources.

Continuing pressure from the external library community and careful evaluation and expansion of staffing resources eventually changed the library's view. The decision to market NOTIS was influenced greatly by the recommendations in a report by a team of consultants from EDUCOM that was submitted to the president of Northwestern University in August 1980. The team, consisting of Hugh F. Cline, Senior Research Sociologist, Educational Testing Service, John W. McCredie, then president of

EDUCOM, and Robert Scott, Director of Financial Systems, Harvard University, was invited to review the status of library computing activities and to recommend new directions and a course of action. In their report, the consultants noted that "the Northwestern computer-based library system is an outstanding information system. An excellent small staff has achieved what most other libraries are still only discussing." They recommended that the university make NOTIS available to the library community and predicted that "at the appropriate time NOTIS could produce substantial income for the Northwestern University Library." They also suggested "that it might be necessary to invest additional funds in the library to cover production and travel expenses as well as expand the staff to support installation and maintenance of NOTIS in other locations if large numbers of external sales were to become a university goal."

By September 1981, a special office within the library had been established to market the software. With substantial assistance from the University of Florida (the first NOTIS purchaser), a version running under IBM's MVS operating system had been developed to supplement the original VSE version, and sales of both were being made regularly. Gradually, additional staff were hired, and, in December 1983, Jane Burke was appointed director of the NOTIS office. As more libraries purchased the software, the staff expanded rapidly, and, by 1987, it was clear that the library could no longer provide the space and administrative resources to accommodate the operations necessary to support the burgeoning clientele. The library's software marketing division was restructured as a for-profit corporation owned by the university, and Jane Burke became president and chief operating officer of the newly formed NOTIS Systems, Inc. (NSI).

The library continues to develop the system, in close cooperation with the corporate group. Within the library, the development team, still led by James Aagaard and Velma Veneziano, has four other staff members for systems analysis and programming. This team provides enhancements to NOTIS under contract with NSI but concentrates on the developments deemed most important locally, working closely with the Northwestern librarians, as in the past. At NSI, another team focuses on extensions requested by customer libraries. For instance, a module supporting keyword searching has been provided by modifying software licensed from BRS Information Technologies.

By mid-1988, more than one hundred systems had been installed at other institutions. Three-quarters of the customers are academic libraries; among the others are public, corporate, state, and special libraries.

Choosing a Local Library Automation System

Expanding Northwestern's focus both on the library's own direct development activities and on the marketing of NOTIS identified some general issues that all libraries examining automated systems should consider. These fall into four categories: hardware selection, software selection, the ability to upgrade and expand, and the local and institutional context.

- *Hardware selection.* Hardware considerations are extremely important, and many library administrators are guided by the advice and counsel of computing center directors and university administrators, who generally recommend the adoption of software packages that run on a computer already in service or on standard equipment. Of significant concern is the long-term viability of a vendor; resources and capital must be available to develop new configurations and generations of hardware and to offer software that can be supported and maintained in the field. Another consideration is the desirability of versatile and standardized terminals and personal computers. These should be widely available to the academic community, compatible with other university hardware and software, and able to interact with the library system from many locations. At Northwestern, these considerations led to the choice of IBM equipment.

- *Software selection.* The selection of a software package is a key element affecting the outcome of library automation. The inclusion of source code in a standard programming language as part of the purchase is often a very important consideration, particularly if the hardware is acquired separately. The availability of the source code enables an organization to modify and customize a system and maintain it locally. It is also very important that the software run with a standard operating system from a well-established company if a local library automation system is to be maintained and upgraded.

  Understandably, some vendors are reluctant to provide the source code and may write their programs in nonstandard programming languages in order to protect their products. This practice is understandable and defensible, but not always beneficial to the customer. Some such vendors supply hardware and software as a single product; this can be a real service since it relieves an institution of the responsibility for separate maintenance. Each type of vendor has its place: some NOTIS customers choose to modify the software to suit their own interests and others do not. As long as many vendors offer different types of local library automation systems the community will be well served, benefiting from a market shaped by competition.

- *Ability to upgrade and expand.* An integrated system will undergo many changes and refinements and must be able to accommodate upgrades and expansion without requiring major reinvestments in hardware and software. At Northwestern, it became clear early on that each introduction of a new automation feature prompts both staff and users to demand yet more capabilities.

- *Local and institutional context.* The local area networks that are emerging at universities will facilitate transmission of data across and among campuses. One very important class of data is held by the library, and, to use it over local or wide area networks, the library automation system must use standard transmission protocols. Adherence to standards will be important for the exchange of bibliographic data through the many tiers of an organization and between different organizations. Without this capacity, a local library automation system inevitably will be isolated.

Teaching Information Retrieval: The Online Catalog and Beyond

The introduction of new information technologies into libraries has created special challenges for those most directly concerned with the education of library users. The online catalog was only the first in a series of innovations in service affecting both librarians and their public. Many of the new educational challenges stem from the growing number and variety of information systems that users now encounter as they seek information, both within and, increasingly, outside the library. New technologies that have provided electronic tools for managing information have also facilitated growth in published literature. This proliferation of information often has complicated the task of retrieving the particular information needed. The rapid pace of change and the diversity of access methodologies compound the confusion.

While technology commonly is viewed in physical and technical terms, a broader perspective envisions technology, not just as machines, but as the interaction between machines and people. As more automated systems are introduced into libraries and elsewhere, the importance of this interaction increases. Until educators are able to understand and identify the various elements of the human-machine relationship, designing flexible library instruction to accommodate many possible approaches to research will be difficult.[1] Northwestern librarians continually explore new instructional methods, including printed brochures, workshops, and sessions integrated into other courses. The strategy is to offer instruction of several different kinds and levels and to attempt to identify the forms of instruction best suited to specific user groups.

Technology can be a powerful ally both for librarians and for library users interested in efficiency. Electronic information storage and retrieval technologies are not simply different versions of manual tools; they offer substantially different capabilities and efficiencies when applied to the goals and priorities of library users. The power of well-conceived and well-applied retrieval technology lies, not in the automation of manual tools, but in the elimination of many of their limitations. Using interactive, flexible retrieval strategies, including sophisticated logic and searching for words within text, it becomes possible to investigate complex relationships and conceptual subtleties that were inaccessible through the card catalog and printed indexes. Most important, because the technology can be distributed, library tools can be integrated conveniently into the information-seeking patterns of clientele working outside the library. Technology has the power to improve the intellectual lifestyle of the academic community, not just to reincarnate the old tools that historically embodied the interests and needs of libraries.

Early instructional efforts concentrated on the online catalog. During recent years, Northwestern has been involved with various studies of online public access catalog usage, some funded by grants, others pursued as individual research projects. In particular, transaction logs have been used to study user behavior with the automated system.[2] These studies have led library instruction planners to believe that future efforts should be more general: instruction should focus on building skills that can be used to access a variety of information services. There are clear indications that instruction in generalized concepts of information retrieval, linked to the academic curriculum, is more appropriate and also increases student motivation.

New components of library instruction programs are being developed to teach the technological skills and conceptual issues that are becoming increasingly important to a society in which educational and research processes rely more and more on computers. New teaching efforts have been directed toward particular academic areas where the availability of large bibliographic databases can be especially significant. To give only a few examples of areas where special user instruction has proven useful, the language departments find access to the Modern Language Association Bibliography especially helpful, the School of Education is a heavy user of ERIC, and Psychological Abstracts has proven valuable to several departments in the social sciences. Library staff conduct lectures on automated information retrieval systems as part of the Microcomputer Literacy Course offered by the College of Arts and Sciences, and computerized literature search seminars have been developed for the graduate school's Teaching Assistant Workshop series, as well as for specific departments.

Other Projects

Northwestern's libraries have developed a number of specific strategies to integrate electronic information into the work of the academic community. One of the most popular developments, called BIBLIO, is a simple, PC-based utility program that permits users to edit bibliographic information downloaded from the online catalog for use in research papers. This program is available at no charge from the library's Reference Department.

Two of the university's microcomputer laboratories are now housed in library facilities. One is in the main library, in a study area near the reserved book room. The other is located in the Schaffner Library, which serves the continuing education and masters in management programs on the Chicago Campus. In addition, the medical library provides access to microcomputers and assists users in producing computer graphics.

The Schaffner Library also functions as an "electronic library laboratory." Because of its separation from the rest of the main library system, this branch depends primarily on electronic sources for delivery of information; innovation and experimentation with microcomputers are natural consequences of this dependence. Projects undertaken at Schaffner include the first introduction in the university of search facilities (such as WILSEARCH or CD-ROM systems) for end users, training users in online searching, and the development of a variety of microcomputer applications for the management of library operations. Library science students from local professional schools serve as microcomputer consultants, gaining valuable experience in user instruction, online searching, and microcomputer operations. The systems and techniques explored in this small, controlled setting, if effective, can be shared with other Northwestern libraries.

The library at Northwestern participates in beta testing of various CD-ROM services, including a project to introduce graduate business students to DIALOG's Business Connection and an investigation of potential uses of the Library of Congress Authority Files on CD-ROM. The Reference Department is using Apple Computer's HyperCard to develop a "tour" of the main library building, to be available on Macintoshes in all campus microcomputer laboratories.

One area in which the interests of libraries, computing centers, and researchers have converged is the acquisition and accessibility of machine-readable data. The Research Libraries Group is coordinating a group of related studies in this area, which are being conducted at Northwestern, Cornell, Dartmouth, the University of Florida, New York University, and the University of Pennsylvania. Northwestern's contribution focuses on universitywide policy development regarding the acquisition of machine-readable data, whether by a research library or an academic computing center. The project, on the Evanston campus, is exploring several related issues, among them, the relationship of research grant support to computing data resource management, the questions surrounding bibliographic access to data files that are not under the physical control of the library, and the allocation of responsibility for dataset purchase among computing center, library, and school and departmental stakeholders.

Northwestern is taking an active research approach to the project, with surveys and interviews of faculty, discussions with research administrators and other senior managers, and negotiation between computing center and library staff all part of the process. Publication of results can be expected by mid-1989, and it is hoped that the Northwestern model will help other institutions establish processes for policy development in this difficult and potentially contentious area.[3]

Currently, the library also is involved in a universitywide study of academic, administrative, and library computing that should result in increased cooperative development at Northwestern for the future.

Northwestern has been involved for many years with projects to explore and develop capabilities for sharing bibliographic information across networks. Beginning in 1977, Northwestern and the Library of Congress cooperated in a test to demonstrate that a system of decentralized centers for cataloging and bibliographic control could be used to build a national bibliographic database that would be of consistent, high quality. Funded by the National Endowment for the Humanities with partial matching from the Carnegie Corporation, this test was conducted using materials from Northwestern's preeminent collection of Africana materials. A central finding of the study was "that successful creation of a consistent national bibliographic database depends heavily on the successful and efficient sharing of authority data" to ensure consistent usage of names and, particularly, subject headings.[4]

In 1981, the Council on Library Resources funded the development of computer-to-computer applications protocols for library and information science applications. Another grant from the Council on Library Resources in 1987 supports the implementation within NOTIS of the protocols developed in the Linked Systems Project. The initial phase of the Linked Systems Project has involved searching and distributing authority records among the Library of Congress, the Research Libraries Group's RLIN system, and OCLC. The protocols developed for information exchange have wider application, however, and can support interchange between library automation systems and bibliographic utilities such as OCLC and RLG and between automated systems at different libraries. They will be the basis for access to remote bibliographic databases over networks.

Evaluation and Plans for the Future

As a result of automation, library operations have become more efficient, and staff levels have been reduced.[5] Developments in the NOTIS system continue to utilize advances in technology. The library's systems staff are involved actively in the Linked Systems Project. As well as implementing the particular applications protocols for exchanging information between library systems, this involves incorporating into NOTIS the standard ISO communications protocols that are the basis for this project. Northwestern also is considering providing support for terminal access across TCP/IP networks, since many campus, regional, and national networks will continue to be based on TCP/IP protocols until products based on ISO protocols are more widely available. Providing "gateways" from NOTIS to external databases, both online and on CD-ROM, is high on the library's priority list; with such gateways, the end user would no longer need to be aware of the varying characteristics of systems consulted.

Staff enthusiasm has led to highly productive use of both the locally developed NOTIS and automation-based products from external sources. While Northwestern's librarians constantly pursue a wide variety of computer-based options, the principles established early in the development of automation for the library have served and will continue to serve the university well. Looking back at the requirements for NOTIS that were identified in 1968, it is possible to say that each was met and did indeed contribute to successful services for Northwestern University and beyond. The system is unified, online, and interactive; it can be interrogated from dispersed locations; the time to acquire and catalog library materials has been reduced significantly; the system is reliably available, and information in the database is readily retrievable; expansion and refinement have been continuous; standards are maintained consistently, and the system is compatible with both national and local developments. Northwestern University takes justifiable pride in the library's strategies for electronic information services.

References

1. King, David, and Betsy Baker. "Human Aspects of Library Technology: Implications for Academic Library User Education." In *Bibliographic Instruction: The Second Generation,* ed. Connie Mellon (Littleton, Colo.: Libraries Unlimited, 1987), pp. 85–103.

2. Baker, Betsy. "A New Direction for Online Catalog Instruction." *Information Technology and Libraries* 5, no. 1 (March 1986): 35–41.

   Nielsen, Brian. "What They Say They Do and What They Do: Assessing Online Catalog Use Instruction Through Transaction Monitoring." *Information Technology and Libraries* 5, no. 1 (March 1986): 28–34.

3. Nielsen, Brian. "Fees and Service Quality: Old Problem, New Dilemmas for Academic Libraries" (Paper presented at I. T. Littleton Seminar on Academic Library Issues, North Carolina State University, Raleigh, N.C., May 20, 1988).

4. Hill, Janet Swan. "The Northwestern Africana Project: An Experiment in Decentralized Bibliographic and Authority Control." *College and Research Libraries* 42, no. 4 (July 1981): 326–332.

5. Horny, Karen L. "Fifteen Years of Automation: Evolution of Technical Services Staffing." *Library Resources & Technical Services* 31, no. 1 (January/March 1987): 69–76.

Chapter 5

Clemson University

George D. Alexander
Richard W. Meyer

Clemson University, founded in 1889 by Thomas Green Clemson, is a state land grant institution. Located on the former plantation of statesman John C. Calhoun, the campus occupies 1,800 acres in the Blue Ridge foothills of northwestern South Carolina. Surrounding the campus are an additional 20,860 acres of university farms and woodlands devoted to research in forestry, agriculture, and agricultural engineering. Another 10,447 acres throughout the state are used to support the research conducted at the five agricultural experiment stations.

Clemson's programs are oriented toward science and technology. The university offers degrees in sixty-four undergraduate and ninety-seven graduate programs in the Colleges of Agricultural Sciences, Architecture, Commerce and Industry, Education, Engineering, Forest and Recreation Resources, Liberal Arts, Nursing, and Sciences. Present enrollment is about 14,700 students, of whom 3,000 are graduate students. The university maintains the state's primary programs for instruction and research in agriculture, city and regional planning, building construction and management, textiles, forestry, ceramic engineering, and environmental engineering.

Introduction to the Library

The Robert Muldrow Cooper Library serves the community in an innovative manner, encouraging the patronage, not only of Clemson students and faculty, but also of all citizens of South Carolina. Its current holdings of 1,470,750 volumes consist of 668,861 books and bound periodicals, 656,130 documents and reports, and 145,759 microforms. The library has 6,900 serial subscriptions and 71,000 slides.

In 1983, the library installed the Northwestern Online Totally Integrated System (NOTIS) from Northwestern University to automate most of its technical processes. The online catalog portion of NOTIS, called Library User Information Service (LUIS), provides access to the catalog from over two thousand terminals on campus, as well as from about three hundred terminals on a statewide network. Dial-up access is also available. The card catalog was closed officially in May 1985.

In 1987, Clemson acquired the software product BRS/Search from BRS Information Technologies and began making information databases produced or acquired by Clemson available on the computing network. This service, called the Document Online Retrieval Information System (DORIS), provides access to the full text of databases and allows the user to search for specific terms of interest and display the relevant portions of text. Databases in DORIS include commercial indexes such as the Magazine Index, national bibliographies such as AGRICOLA, and such local documents as procedure manuals, organization minutes, and the Clemson campus directory.

Today, providing electronic information access services has become a vital part of the library's mission. The development of these services involves close cooperation with Clemson's computing organization. As shown in Figure 5.1, both the library and the Division of Computing and Information Technology report to the provost. Library automation projects are pursued jointly by these organizations.

Computing at Clemson

Because of Clemson's technical orientation, computing has played a fundamental role at the university since the early 1960s. At that time, like many institutions of higher education, Clemson established a computer center, which was the focal point of all computing activities. Today, computing power is dispersed widely in the many academic programs. However, a computer network that provides access to large mainframe and midrange processors is the foundation of academic and administrative computing.

Clemson's computing facilities are operated by the Division of Computing and Information Technology (DCIT), whose administrative offices are located at the new Information Technology Center. DCIT is composed of three departments: the Computer Center, the Department of Administrative Programming Services (DAPS), and Information Systems Development. The last group develops information systems under contract to other state agencies. DAPS develops administrative systems for the university and provides all software support for library automation. The Computer Center operates the computing network used for all major applications, including library automation. It also runs the central time-sharing computers and provides support to academic users through the Consulting and Technical Services Office.

DCIT operates a statewide computing network incorporating processors from several vendors. Because of Clemson's mission as a land grant institution, the computing network provides support to extension agents and agricultural experiment stations throughout South Carolina. It also provides service to various state offices. As shown in Figure 5.2, the network has an SNA component and a VAX/Ethernet component; these are connected by an SNA gateway device. All administrative computing,

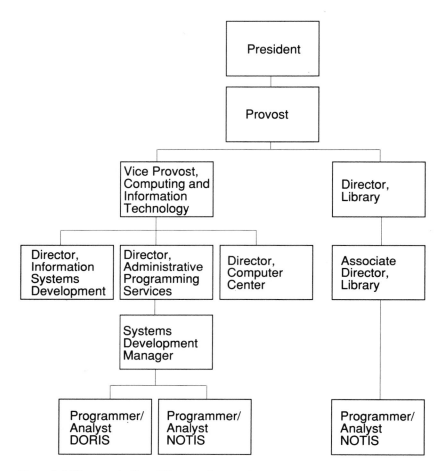

Figure 5.1 The organization of library and computing services at Clemson University.

including library automation, runs on the SNA side of the network, although databases can be accessed from the Ethernet side as well.

A major resource is a large IBM-compatible NAS AS/XL mainframe computer running the MVS/XA operating system. The library services run on this computer, using IBM's CICS transaction-processing communications subsystem. The network also provides access to several VAX computers, ranging in size from the MicroVAX II to the VAX 8820. Three VAXes sharing disks and tapes form a VAXcluster, which runs the VAX/VMS operating system. Another VAX runs ULTRIX, Digital Equipment

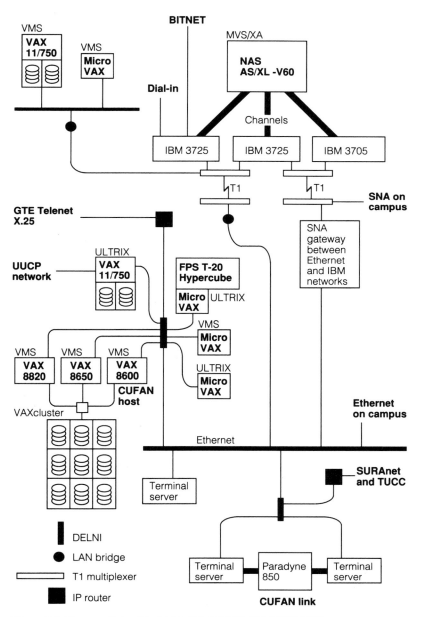

Figure 5.2 Clemson University computing network, November 1988.

Corporation's version of the UNIX operating system. Parallel computing for massive calculations is provided by a Floating Point Systems Hypercube array processor.

The Computer Center attempts to provide free access to as many students, faculty, and staff as it can. Those with research grants and contracts, however, are expected to pay for central computing services consumed. To augment funds provided directly by the university, the Computer Center contracts to perform services for other South Carolina state agencies. While this approach has fueled some lively debates, it is clear that the services provided to faculty, students, and staff would be much less without these outside contracts.

The Clemson administration has refrained from requiring students to bring their own computers to campus, although it is estimated that about 10 percent of the student population owns a computer. Currently, there are almost four hundred microcomputers and three hundred networked terminals in unrestricted areas available to all students. Additionally, over seventeen hundred networked terminals, personal computers, and advanced workstations in laboratories, faculty offices, and administrative areas provide access to Clemson's facilities and to computing resources off campus.

Library Automation Strategy

Administrative Environment

The Clemson administration encourages each division to pursue its own goals as it sees fit within the overall university mission and within general guidelines. An entrepreneurial spirit supports new initiatives and approaches. Often, it is not certain whether resources will be available for the duration of projects. This certainly was true for the library automation initiative. Nine years into the project, however, the systems continue to grow and address additional needs.

The library and the computing organizations realized early on that it would be necessary to redirect resources to accomplish objectives. A substantial infusion of funds to support automation efforts was neither anticipated nor received. The allocations of $10,000 in 1980 for a library automation consultant, $26,000 in 1983 for the purchase of NOTIS, and $33,000 in 1987 for additional terminals were the only instances where "new" funds were directed toward the project. Of course, additional funds were needed, but they were obtained by rechanneling the existing resources of the library and computing organizations. No new positions have been allocated to the library, the Computer Center, or Administrative Programming Services specifically to support library automation.

The entrepreneurial environment at Clemson has both positive and negative aspects. The positive aspect is demonstrated when a major state-of-the-art accomplishment emerges, as with the library automation project. The negative aspect is revealed when separate units take duplicative or conflicting approaches to solve similar problems. While the project has produced dramatic positive results, at least one interesting problem with campuswide coordination has surfaced. Because development of the systems for library circulation and dining services was separate and uncoordinated, many students need two identification cards. A project is now under way to design a standard identification card that will be used for all access-control systems on campus.

Such problems can be expected when university units act independently and aggressively to initiate services. Almost always, there is ultimately a reconciliation among related services, yielding a more coordinated and integrated solution. In fact, the portion of the computing network providing service to the agricultural extension agents and experiment stations was originally a project of the College of Agricultural Sciences, funded by a grant for that purpose. This innovative service, called Clemson University Forestry and Agricultural Network (CUFAN), is still under the auspices and direction of Agricultural Sciences, but now it is managed as a node of the computing network by the Division of Computing and Information Technology. Such innovation and cooperation are central to the manner in which Clemson staff meet the needs of the campus and state constituencies.

Access to Library Services
The strategic aim of library automation at Clemson is to provide access to information with as few barriers for the users as possible. This parallels the computing philosophy of the past ten years—like the computing organization, the Clemson library actively has promoted access to its facilities for many years. Thus, in 1979, when the library staff first began discussing an integrated library automation system allowing access to the catalog, the Computer Center and Administrative Programming Services were very supportive. The emerging computing network appeared to be an ideal avenue by which to provide such access. Although the decision as to which specific computer would run the software was deferred, there was from the beginning a shared objective to distribute library resources across the entire network.

The Integrated Library Automation System

Goals of Library Automation

The major goals of library automation at Clemson are interrelated: increased productivity, reduced costs, and improved service. The effect of automation on productivity is easily discernible. The same number of staff are able to maintain better control of bibliographic data and records of holdings and produce a catalog and other bibliographic files that are accessible from hundreds of locations within and outside the library. Patrons now can search online catalogs and indexes with much less time and effort than was needed for manual searches.

An online catalog that can be accessed both locally and remotely also results in considerable cost savings for users. The need to walk to the library and root through card catalog drawers is a substantial impediment to research. Online bibliographic access through a computing network makes the literature search that must accompany research less painful and, therefore, more likely to be accomplished thoroughly. The ease of searching for information in an automated system allows students to locate more and better citations; this results in higher-quality papers. Decreasing the time required for faculty to identify citations important to their research yields a higher return on their efforts. All these considerations profoundly affected the planning for library automation at Clemson.

The combination of effects described here produces an overall improvement of service. Patrons in offices as distant as two hundred miles from the library can avail themselves of the same online information access as those who are in offices on campus.

Planning: Phase 1

In November 1979, the library organized a study team to develop an automation plan. Until then, the only automated systems used in the library were a circulation system developed in the early 1970s and the OCLC bibliographic utility. The circulation system employed a thoroughly outdated technology that recorded all transactions using cards punched with Hollerith coding. Cards were stored with each item, and faculty, staff, and students had similar cards for identification. The technology to produce and read these cards was outdated and expensive to maintain. OCLC access, made available through a consortium called the Southeastern Library Network (SOLINET), was through high-speed leased lines. OCLC services were purchased for the production of catalog cards and for the development of a computer file of bibliographic records.

The library staff felt that it was important to automate all the processes within the library—both those normally seen only by staff members and those that directly supported patrons. From the start, the objective was an integrated and comprehensive automation system, because this would allow all units of the library and all patrons to benefit simultaneously from updates to central databases. For example, additions or modifications made to the central bibliographic file by acquisitions staff would be immediately available to staff in cataloging and users throughout the network.

Administrative philosophy played a strategic role. At the outset, it was decided that planning would be systematic, that a maximum return on Clemson resources in the long term would be sought, and that key political relationships with state and university officials would be established to minimize the difficulties frequently experienced by libraries with bid-oriented purchasing approaches.

Purchasing library software by means of a bid process frequently leads to a dissatisfied customer. The bid process requires that detailed and complete specifications be developed before products are examined. Once the bid is released, little further opportunity is afforded the library to refine the results. Clemson opted instead for a strategy that allowed informally solicited descriptions of available systems to be compared to draft specifications. This allowed for a stepwise refinement of the specifications, with additional information being obtained from vendors as software inadequacies and desirable features were discovered. This systematic strategy allowed Clemson to locate the system best suited to the environment. Although the evaluation identified a system that required a larger initial investment, long-term costs were projected to be lower than for alternatives.

The methodology used for the initial study was the Application Transfer Team (ATT) study technique designed and refined by IBM.[1] This approach, which is based on structured interviews, works particularly well in developing applications that solve operational problems. It was used to determine the information needed by all units of the library as well as the interrelationships of the units. Interviews were conducted with members of the library staff, library patrons, and university staff routinely involved in business interactions with the library. The information gathered pertained to interfaces between units, problems, volumes and cycles of activity, and possible improvements and benefits. The study team consisted of the associate director of the library, the head of the circulation unit, the serials cataloger, a reference librarian, the director of Administrative Programming Services, and an IBM representative. Sponsorship of the ATT study by an associate vice-president contributed to establishing fruitful political relationships with upper-level university administrators and the state purchasing office.

The ATT methodology was used to fulfill four needs. First, it was necessary to develop a librarywide automation plan to present to the library and university administration. Second, objectives and implementation estimates were required to provide a basis for the development of system specifications and evaluations. Third, the planning process had to provide a forum for meaningful participation by library staff and users. Fourth, the planning process needed to be completed rather quickly.

The study team decided that the new system should address the needs of the serials unit first. This unit is involved primarily with the acquisition and receipt of magazines, journals, and other periodical literature. The function requires repeated transactions over time for thousands of subscriptions. Workflow relating to acquisitions and bibliographic control in this unit was clogged with clerical detail. Receipt of each serial issue was recorded in a manual check-in file. After check-in, first issues of a new journal were taken to the cataloging unit for further processing. The serials unit maintained a second, nearly redundant, manual file, which provided limited information on serials holdings to users. As an example of the workload, the entire claiming process for issues not received required over five thousand hours of clerical time each year. It was felt that much of this effort could be redirected toward providing more productive information for users if an automated system was installed.

While the automation of procedures was important, the primary goal of the proposed system was to make information more accessible. Ideally, library patrons all over the state should be able to access the catalog in several ways: by subject, author, title, and keywords, as well as by truncated portions of these. Furthermore, the system should give the circulation status of all items. Complete serials holdings information must be accurate. In 1979, the library maintained five card catalogs, and patrons usually had to visit one of the libraries on campus to determine if material was available. Since much of the library user community was off campus, increased accessibility to bibliographic information was crucial.

The seventy-three-page study report was submitted to the university administration in March 1980.[2] It contained a description of the existing library environment, the objectives of the proposed system, components and data needed in the system, cost and benefit considerations, and implementation recomendations. After considering the report, the library administration decided to review available systems to find the one most suitable for replication at Clemson.

Planning: Phase 2

A fundamental strategic decision was made during the development of design specifications in the ATT study. The estimates for designing and programming an integrated library automation package indicated that five years and approximately $320,000 in development expenditures would be required to complete the task. These estimates did not include hardware or allow for contingencies. Knowledge of the efforts at other institutions led librarians to suggest that these estimates were optimistic. In addition, it was unlikely that library staff would benefit from any automation during the development period. On the other hand, by 1980, many turnkey systems were being marketed nationally and appeared close to meeting the full ATT specifications. Also, other universities had developed packages that might be replicated at Clemson. The library administration decided to evaluate existing systems before venturing into a costly development project. If an appropriate system could be identified, not only would substantial cost and effort be bypassed, but the benefits of automation could be realized sooner.

It was important to the library to utilize a systematic methodology to review available systems. With the help of an outside consultant, the associate director designed a procedure to identify and rank systems. The steps followed were:

1. Compile a list of general system requirements.
2. Identify desired features, questions, and hardware/software considerations (about two hundred items based on the original ATT design requirements).
3. Draw up a list of candidate systems.
4. Screen out unsuitable candidates using the general requirements.
5. Evaluate the remaining systems using the detailed list of features, questions, and considerations.
6. List the local modifications that would be necessary to operate each system at Clemson.
7. Calculate the implementation costs for each system, including all hardware, software, and other costs identified in the evaluation.

Twenty-nine candidate systems were identified for analysis. All but nine were screened out by the general requirements as unsuitable to Clemson's hardware environment, difficult or impossible to replicate, or lacking key functional elements. Secondary screening based on contacts with the software developers left only three systems that were totally suitable for thorough analysis. These were evaluated carefully against the detailed features, questions, and considerations. In May 1981, about nine months after the study had begun, the final report on library automation was submitted to the university administration.[3] It concluded that Clemson should purchase NOTIS from Northwestern University.

Implementation

After the decision to purchase NOTIS, library staff began to nurture contacts through the university purchasing channels with the state purchasing office. Because of the thorough planning and evaluation that had been done, state officials allowed the university to bypass the ordinary purchasing procedure of soliciting proposals—the analysis was considered to have accomplished the essential purpose of the normal procurement procedures. This allowed the library and DAPS to begin implementation plans immediately. However, budget difficulties and contract negotiations delayed the acquisition of the software until January 1983. Tapes containing the software were delivered in March.

During the period between the decision to purchase NOTIS and the delivery of the actual tapes, two important projects were initiated. First, library staff began the vital task of creating the database of bibliographic records representing the library's catalogs. Many catalog entries were available on magnetic tape through OCLC, which maintains an archival collection of machine-readable records as a by-product of regular catalog card production. The Clemson Library had begun to use this online system for cataloging in July 1975; therefore, machine-readable records describing every book and journal added to the collections between 1975 and the beginning of NOTIS implementation already were available. In 1982, the cataloging staff began conversion through OCLC of catalog card records for items acquired before 1975.

Second, steps were taken to allocate staff to the NOTIS implementation project. Given the estimates made during the planning phase, it was decided that two programmer/analysts would be needed for implementation and continued maintenance. Since no new positions were available, two positions had to be reallocated to the project. When a high-level clerical position became vacant, consolidation of tasks and simplification of some manual procedures allowed the library to reclassify the position to programmer/analyst and assign it to the NOTIS project. A programmer/analyst was hired by the library in late February 1983. Similarly, DAPS was able to assign to the project the programmer/analyst who had maintained the old circulation system as well as other systems. These two positions still share the responsibility for supporting and maintaining NOTIS. With assistance of staff from various units of the library, the associate director and the two programmer/analysts began to devise the implementation plan in early March 1983.

Clemson's library, like most academic libraries, is organized according to function into units. The acquisitions unit handles the business-oriented aspects of purchasing, receiving, and paying for books. Another unit performs similar duties for serials and also records systematically the multiple receipts of individual issues of periodicals. A third unit, for cataloging, concerns itself with the bibliographic description of books and journals and the creation of cataloging records. Finally, the circulation unit is responsible for inventory control and charging books and journals to users.

This breakdown into acquisitions, serials control, cataloging, and circulation closely parallels the major modules of NOTIS. Each module can be implemented separately, but the acquisitions, serials, and circulation modules depend on the presence and continued maintenance of a central bibliographic file, that is, a catalog file. It was recognized quickly that implementation had to begin with the creation of this file and the start-up of the cataloging module. Once the bibliographic file was in place, it would be possible to begin implementing the remaining modules. (The initial release of NOTIS to Clemson did not contain the circulation module, since it was still in the design phase. This consideration lent further support to the decision to implement the cataloging function first.)

The first implementation step, in the spring of 1983, was to specify the format for a tape of Clemson's catalog records to be loaded from OCLC archives. Arrangements had been made with SOLINET to compile the tape from the OCLC tapes. By this time, records developed through OCLC to this point covered nearly 80 percent of the collection. Records for the balance of the collection were generated over the next two years. While the tape was being created, preparation for NOTIS continued. The CICS teleprocessing monitor required for NOTIS was installed on the IBM mainframe by May 1983, and, during the first three months of the project, the library programmer/analyst and the associate director outlined an implementation schedule. This was a simple diagram summarizing project tasks in a logical sequence. Based on that summary, the NOTIS implementation proceeded as shown in Table 5.1.

This schedule warrants several comments. First, terminals were installed as little in advance as possible. Experience at other universities indicated that, if terminals sit idle in production units for too long, staff start to think that they aren't useful. That attitude is likely to have substantial negative impact on the already difficult transition from manual to automated procedures.

Table 5.1   Implementation Schedule for NOTIS at Clemson

May 1983	NOTIS package installed on IBM mainframe
June 2, 1983	First online query of NOTIS conducted at Clemson
July 1983	Terminals installed in cataloging
August 1983	Staff training begun in cataloging
November 1983	Archive tape of bibliographic records loaded
January 1984	Interface program linking OCLC terminals with in-house terminals installed and debugged
April 29, 1984	Corrections to archive tape of bibliographic records loaded
April 30, 1984	Routine production begun in cataloging
June 1984	Final tape of archive records for the transition period of August 1983 through April 29, 1984 loaded
January 1985	LUIS made public in the library and throughout the network
January 1985	Training of acquisitions and serials staff begun
February 1985	Routine production begun in acquisitions and serials
May 1985	Planning begun by circulation implementation task force
May 1985	Card catalog closed
May 1986	Collections bar-coded for circulation
June 1986	Staff training begun in circulation
July 1986	Routine production begun in circulation; NOTIS implementation completed
November 1987	IBM system replaced by NAS mainframe

Second, interfaces between the OCLC terminals and in-house terminals were installed to optimize record loading. For each OCLC terminal, a null modem cable was installed to link the serial printer port on the OCLC terminal to a serial input port on a specially ordered terminal used for NOTIS. This terminal was compatible with an IBM 3270 terminal but had an input port designed to accept a data stream from either a bar-code reader or another input device. With a slight modification of the cable, it serves equally well for input from the OCLC terminal. This approach was not common when Clemson installed it but has been used extensively by subsequent users of NOTIS.

When Clemson orders items, the OCLC system is checked for matching bibliographic records already produced by the Library of Congress and other libraries. Matching records are transferred directly into NOTIS through the special link between the two terminals. Typically, records are found in the OCLC database for 90 percent of the items acquired by Clemson; the savings derived from avoiding redundant keying are sub- stantial. The transfer technique also greatly speeds up the process of cataloging. The new catalog record is instantly available, a major improvement over manual processes or transfer from archive tapes.

Third, users acquired online access to the library catalog throughout campus slightly over five years after initial planning for automation. Had delays caused by budget difficulties and administrative changes in the university not occurred, this could easily have been cut to three-and-a- half years. Even five years is short compared to the time and effort expended at Northwestern to design and develop the system internally.

Following our planning and implementation strategies, nearly every functional process in the library is now automated. We have had substan- tial success in meeting our three major goals of cost reduction, increased productivity, and improved service, with an optimal balance against resources. No additional staff were required. Funding to support the entire project was made available almost wholly from routine sources. The availability of information on library holdings has been enhanced dramati- cally and expanded throughout the user community.

Library Automation Extended

The one remaining function typically falling within the domain of libraries, but not mentioned in the previous section, is reference service. The automation of library procedures that support users by providing easy access to more complete and timely information about holdings has had the further effect of improving reference operations. Online access by reference librarians expedited the processes of interpreting resources, answering telephone inquiries in a timely manner, and handling routine chores associated with collection development, such as bibliographic verification of purchase requests. However, forces at work outside the library also have had an impact on reference service.

In the past few years, there has been a burgeoning market in alterna- tives to the printed index and reference book. Indexes and reference aids on compact disk (CD-ROM) and videodisk are widely available. Some indexes are even marketed in more than one version by competing companies. In addition, online access to DIALOG and other commercial database services has become more widespread and simpler to use. All of this has caused reference departments to consider extending their traditional book and index collections to accommodate a large assortment of products based on CD-ROM and do-it-yourself versions of online databases. This phenomenon is complicated by the variety of formats, record structures, and approaches to the design of search software. Few, if any, standards exist for this fast-growing market that would help reference librarians maintain consistent control of access to electronically stored information. In effect, reference departments could soon become information video arcades. Realizing this possibility, Clemson library administrators sought a way to bypass this confusion by using local automation to offer online access to indexes through one consolidated searching system.

During this same period, Administrative Programming Services began to receive requests for an online system to support access to full-text databases produced locally. For example, the university's personnel division wanted to provide campus access to the complete set of personnel policy documents without having to distribute bulky, frequently outdated printed versions. Better access to the minutes of campus organizations, to the catalog of campus office supplies, and to other full-text files had become increasingly desirable over the past few years. To fulfill the demands of the library reference department and those of the campus administrative operations, DAPS and library staff undertook a second joint project in 1987. This one sought to augment and expand the earlier integrated library automation system in order to provide access to bibliographic and textual information beyond the library's catalog.

Implementation of DORIS

Developing software capable of retrieving information from a combination of full-text files and citation files would have presented DAPS and the library with another long and expensive task. Because software developed elsewhere had filled Clemson's earlier needs so successfully, project leaders immediately looked for existing software. This time, the project moved quickly.

Several criteria affected the decision. First, it was desirable to install software that would run under CICS so that it could complement NOTIS readily. Second, the new software would be required to operate efficiently as an information retrieval system yet need not be effective as a text processor. The full-text files to be loaded into the system were generated on other systems. Many were produced on microcomputers with word-processing software and others from mainframe-based systems from which the files are precursors to printed output. Furthermore, the intention was to purchase large files of bibliographic citations; it was not to provide users with an integrated information management and word-processing environment. Third, year-end Computer Center revenue available in June 1987 provided the means to acquire a package if the appropriate software could be identified.

DAPS and the library discovered that several available commercial software systems could handle the tasks at hand. Among these, the BRS/Search package had proven itself over a number of years. As required, the package's strengths lay in its powerful information retrieval capabilities, not in text management. Library staff already were familiar with BRS/Search as a normal part of reference activity. It was available at a reasonable price and ran in the same environment as NOTIS—in fact, the search engine for the keyword module in NOTIS is a version of BRS/Search. These factors combined to convince project leaders that the BRS/Search package would be the best investment.

In June 1987, the package was purchased, and a vacant position in DAPS was filled by a programmer/analyst with CICS experience. As with the first automation project, resources were reallocated to initiate the extension project. The new programmer/analyst was assigned to it half-time. The associate director of the library assumed the task of soliciting and loading full-text files, including minutes of organization meetings and procedure manuals. The library administration and reference staff se-lected citation databases to load and negotiated with vendors for the information files. Resources previously used to purchase indexes on CD-ROM were diverted to cover the cost of some computer files. Addi-tional resources were made available by users through a grant secured from outside the campus. Decisions as to which databases to acquire first were based on experience with online searching in the library through DIALOG and other information brokers.

LUIS Meets DORIS

By November 1987, the BRS/Search package was running on the NAS mainframe as the Document Online Retrieval Information System (DORIS), loaded with a variety of full-text information files developed locally and the AGRICOLA citation database. To create a sense of anticipation among the patrons and to promote the availability of the new service, rumors were planted that LUIS possibly had a new companion named DORIS. Librarians discreetly denied such rumors while confes-sing that DORIS would indeed serve as a worthwhile complement to LUIS. More concretely, several campuswide demonstrations of DORIS were held in March 1988.

In November 1988, DORIS contained the databases listed on the menu screen in Figure 5.3. Each database is searched using terms entered on an input screen tailored to that particular database with Mentor, a

```
                        DORIS Database Selection

The following databases are available.
Type the number that corresponds to the database you wish to search and press
ENTER. If you need a more detailed description of the databases, type h
and press ENTER

     1.  CU Organization Minutes            (MINS)
     2.  AGRICOLA (1/83 thru Current Month) (CAIN)
     3.  AGRICOLA (Current Month Only)      (CNCM)
     4.  CU Campus Directory                (CUCD)
     5.  University Stores Catalog          (CSCT)
     6.  Magazine Index                     (MAGS)
     7.  National Newspaper Index           (NOOS)
     8.  Management Contents                (MNGT)
     9.  Trade and Industry Index           (TRAD)
    10.  Computer Index                     (COMP)




Type a selection number and press Enter  or
Type  q  to Quit or  h  for Help and press Enter --->
```

Figure 5.3   Database selection screen for searching in DORIS.

BRS/Search module. Mentor allows search results to be presented in a unique format for each database. A patron is not required to be familiar with the BRS/Search package to use DORIS. Rather than require users to memorize the commands and syntax of BRS/Search, the interface presents them with the appropriate commands at each stage in a search. It is not readily apparent to the user that searches are being processed by BRS/Search. However, the full capabilities of BRS/Search are available to the experienced user.

The screen displays used for the local database that provides an online campus directory are shown in Figures 5.4 and 5.5. The user can enter search terms next to any of the "paragraphs" listed on the input screen. These terms are combined using a Boolean "and" and presented to the BRS/Search software in the appropriate format. Entries in the directory meeting the criteria are retrieved and presented to the user in the output format designed for the directory.

Initial reaction to DORIS has been extremely favorable. For example, prior to installation of the AGRICOLA database (the largest nationally available bibliography of agriculture) in DORIS, library staff assisted faculty researchers with roughly two hundred searches a year of this file through DIALOG, at an annual cost of $5,000. Current activity on the local version of this file amounts to nearly three hundred searches per week by students, faculty, and staff.

```
                        Search Screen for the
                 Clemson University Campus Directory
                            (CUCD) Database

Name     --> peggy
Major    -->
Depart.  --> library
Building -->
General  -->
========================= Suggested Search Methods =========================
1) To search for someone's phone number, type the name of the person in
   the Name field in the following manner john and smith and press
   ENTER.
2) To search for a person in Computer Science whose name is Nancy, type
   nancy in the Name field and 820 in the Major field and press
   ENTER.
3) To find the phone number for Gary in Sikes, fill in only the name and
   building fields with the appropriate information and press ENTER.
4) Use the General field to find information not in the other fields -
   such as computer userids, telephone numbers, and so forth.
============================================================================
In any field, type c to Change databases,
or h for Help, or q to Quit, then press ENTER
```

Figure 5.4   Input screen for the Clemson Campus Directory.

```
Type Doc # or press ENTER -->
Enter q to Quit      h for Help      s to Search

   Record  1   of 2                    OFFICE PHONE : 656-5171.
   NAME : BLACK PEGGY    C.             HOME PHONE : 654-2576.
   TITLE : LIB TECH ASST III.           USER ID : PCBLACK.
   DEPARTMENT : COOPER LIBRARY.
   OFFICE : RM COOPER LIB CAT.

   Record  2   of 2                    OFFICE PHONE : 656-5173.
   NAME : COVER PEGGY    H.             HOME PHONE : 654-3639.
   TITLE : HD REF/ASSOC LIBN.           USER ID : CUREF.
   DEPARTMENT : COOPER LIBRARY.
   OFFICE : RM COOPER LIB REFER.
```

Figure 5.5   Output screen for the Clemson Campus Directory.

Although the implementation of DORIS seems much less systematic than that of the library automation project, discussions between the library and the Division of Computing and Information Technology regarding the concept began in 1985. These discussions served to focus the strategy, and the development of the DORIS service benefited from the teamwork and creativity that were essential throughout the library automation project.

Future Directions

The basic strategy of providing widespread access across the entire computing network, with LUIS and DORIS as comprehensive information access tools, will continue as long as it proves successful. Clemson staff will go on seeking new ways to meet emerging needs for information without acquiring substantial new resources. Academic institutions are subject to change; as older objectives decline in importance, resources can be reallocated to new objectives. Putting those resources to work in an effective fashion will continue to be important, because additional funding will not be easy to generate. Therefore, DAPS and the library will be cooperating on more joint ventures. Several projects already are under way or in the early stages of discussion.

The success of DORIS has motivated the library to direct additional resources to the project. A vacant position in the circulation unit, made available through clerical savings stemming from the use of NOTIS, has been redefined as librarian for Electronic Information Services. The position is assigned responsibility for soliciting and loading additional databases and information for DORIS and for researching techniques for gateway access to other systems. Also, information describing data files available at Clemson, such as the U.S. census data, will be added to DORIS to increase patron awareness of the availability of these databases.

One major immediate goal is to link NOTIS and DORIS. Users who search DORIS for citations in the report and journal literature often generate long lists of relevant items. They can print copies of these lists but must then search LUIS separately to determine whether the items are available in the local collection. Obviously, it would be a major enhancement if citations retrieved in DORIS were sought in LUIS automatically. Furthermore, it should be possible for users, not only to search both systems and locate needed items as part of the same operation, but to transmit their requirements to library staff electronically. Users then could avail themselves of all library services without leaving their offices or homes. As soon as the implementation of DORIS is complete, staff will initiate activities to design these enhancements.

The next step will be to enhance both NOTIS and DORIS directly by linking them to other systems offered by vendors and other academic institutions. For instance, serials staff use the database of one major vendor every day through a dedicated online terminal. Nearly all periodical subscriptions are ordered through this vendor, who then consolidates Clemson's orders with other libraries' and transmits them to publishers. Linking staff terminals to this vendor through a gateway would allow staff to seek direct information about price and availability of titles in NOTIS. Since a multisession terminal capability is available at Clemson and the necessary gateway software exists, this enhancement will be added as soon as budgets allow. Similarly, means are being sought to link users through a similar gateway to the databases of at least one major information vendor as soon as possible. A gateway through Clemson's BRS/Search system to remote BRS databases is being considered. Negotiation for access to nine important databases is under way.

Links to Clemson from other libraries around the state also are developing. Currently, the State Library can access the Clemson VAX cluster through the CUFAN network established to support agricultural extension agents. This network allows all Clemson extension agents access to LUIS and DORIS. Additional nodes on this network soon will make it possible for a large number of state agencies, schools, colleges, and public libraries to access the Clemson library systems. Likewise, Clemson can use this network to gain access to the catalog of the State Library now and to others as they develop systems of their own. These systems and links are coalescing quickly into an information system that will make the resources of the entire state available to users statewide. Although access to commercial databases mounted at Clemson currently is restricted to faculty, staff, and students, other libraries in the state are being encouraged to obtain licenses that will permit statewide access to these files.

Conclusion

The entrepreneurial environment and a willingness to venture into new areas with reallocated resources have allowed the library to provide users with an effective and innovative library automation system. Bypassing the currently popular CD-ROM technology with its inherent limitations on access, the library has made information widely accessible over a comprehensive computing network. Use of citation databases and the library catalog is two orders of magnitude greater than that of manual predecessors. The catalog is available over a terminal network extending into every county of South Carolina. Library automation has improved dramatically the information available to the statewide constituency. All users retrieve substantially more information now, for the same investment of effort, than they ever did before.

The success of these efforts has yet to be measured fully. However, unsolicited comments thus far indicate strong approval and appreciation of the new services. Strong motivation exists to continue to find additional ways to improve service to patrons. First LUIS, then DORIS—who knows what will happen next?

References

1. International Business Machines Corp. *Application Transfer Teams: Application Description* (White Plains, N.Y.: International Business Machines Corp., 1977).

    ——— . *Application Transfer Teams: Realizing Your Computing Systems' Potential* (White Plains, N.Y.: International Business Machines Corp., 1977).

2. Meyer, Richard, George Alexander, Frances Colburn, Francisco Diaz, and Beth Reuland. *Total Integrated Library Information System: A Report on the General Design Phase,* ED 191,446 (Syracuse, N.Y.: ERIC Clearinghouse on Information Resources, 1980).

3. Meyer, Richard, George Alexander, and Ringgold Management Systems. *Total Integrated Library Information System: A Report on the Specific Design Phase: Identification and Evaluation,* ED 207,533 (Syracuse, N.Y.: ERIC Clearinghouse on Information Resources, 1981).

Chapter 6

University of Illinois
at Urbana-Champaign

William H. Mischo
Beth Sandore
Sharon E. Clark
Michael Gorman

With over 35,000 students and 11,500 faculty and staff, the University of Illinois at Urbana-Champaign (UIUC) is the largest institution of higher education in the state of Illinois and one of the ten largest in the United States. While the student body is drawn from all fifty states and over a hundred foreign countries, the majority of undergraduates, as would be expected in a state university, come from within the state. Education at UIUC is provided through the university's twenty-one colleges and schools. As a comprehensive graduate and research institution, the UIUC has many top-ranked educational programs, including accounting, education, engineering, music, and psychology.

The UIUC Library is one of the largest state university libraries in the United States. The size of its collection ranks third among all U.S. academic libraries. The collection consists of more than seven million volumes and eleven million items, with subscriptions to over ninety-four thousand serial titles. It is housed in the main library bookstacks and in more than thirty-five departmental libraries, area studies centers, and special collections. The total library budget for 1986/1987 surpassed $15.3 million, and the staff numbered 547.

Philosophy and Strategy for Information Services

Automation of the UIUC Library began in the early 1970s and has evolved in ways that reflect the library's unique nature while supporting the multifaceted needs of both public and academic libraries throughout the state. This philosophy of cooperation, which continues to guide the development of electronic information delivery in the library, has been a factor in the key role played by the UIUC Library in the development of the statewide ILLINET Online catalog. This online union catalog, growing out of initiatives at UIUC, is emerging as the culmination of interlibrary resource-sharing efforts throughout the state. From its early beginnings in 1978 as a shared circulation system among a handful of academic libraries in Illinois, this system has grown into a database of over eight million records representing materials at over eight hundred libraries of all types across the state, with enhanced access through an expanded command language with powerful retrieval capabilities.

The aim of integrating automation into the information-seeking patterns of a statewide user community has been expanded within recent years on this campus to include the crucial link between mainframe and microcomputer capabilities. Currently, the UIUC Library is designing and

developing distributed microcomputer workstations with interface software intended to optimize user access to the statewide resources and
other supporting information resources, including remote bibliographic
databases.

These efforts have led to the development of a strong statewide
electronic network for resource sharing. The network fulfills two important
goals at once: an institution's internal objective of providing efficient,
enhanced access to information while alleviating the burden of manual
circulation and technical processes and the aim of a broader educational
community to share research materials. This sharing of resources
strengthens the collections and services that each library can provide to
its user group and provides a link among these user groups.

Throughout the years, initiatives in Illinois have received dedicated
support from several key agencies—the Illinois State Library (through
funding from Library Services and Construction Acts), the Illinois Board
of Higher Education, and, more recently, contributions by individual
academic library member institutions.

Although the UIUC Library undertaking is ambitious, its practical aim
of facilitating large-scale resource sharing and access to materials is at
the core of all library service. Simply put, effective library service involves
librarians linking users to the desired information sources. Neither users
nor collections need to be tied physically to only one institution. The role
of electronic technology in this effort has been threefold: (1) to provide
faster, more efficient access to information than previously was provided
manually; (2) to increase access to information not available through a
manual system; (3) to explore and set in place innovative means of
access to disparate forms and sources of information.

Early Initiatives that Shaped Automation in Illinois

The first plan for large-scale interlibrary electronic resource sharing in
Illinois dates back to actions taken well over a decade ago. The impetus
for this plan can be traced to two initiatives. The original call for electronic
resource sharing within the state emanated from the Library Committee
of the Illinois Board of Higher Education in 1969. It specified that the
establishment of a statewide automated network to support interlibrary
activity be investigated. With this directive in mind, in the mid-1970s, the
late Hugh C. Atkinson, then University Librarian at the UIUC Library,
proposed the implementation of the Library Computer System (LCS)
circulation system. This system, developed by IBM in the late 1960s, was

already in place at Ohio State University, where Atkinson had previously pioneered its installation. Combined with his unique qualities of leadership, this experience equipped him well to address the Illinois challenge. His vision inspired a pervasive enthusiasm and engendered the support that has enabled this network to move in unprecedented directions.

The First Phase: Developing a Multicampus Circulation System

Atkinson's vision began as a local plan—the ambitious effort to automate the management of and access to the collections of the UIUC Library. In the mid-1970s, the UIUC Library was struggling with the myriad problems characteristic of large research libraries. Magnified by the sheer size of the UIUC Library, these problems made the prospect of an automated circulation system seem attractive.

The first comprehensive step was the installation of the short-record system known as LCS. Illinois's use of the LCS system differed from the Ohio State installation in two important respects. First, the software was almost entirely rewritten, partly for technical reasons. More importantly, LCS was used at Illinois as the basis for the statewide resource-sharing network. Initially installed at the UIUC Library in 1978, it was extended in 1980, with Illinois Board of Higher Education funding, to the library of the University of Illinois in Chicago and then to other college and academic libraries in the state.

Prior to the implementation of LCS, Illinois borrowers were, of necessity, limited to OCLC and the microform catalogs of some of the larger collections in the state when they needed materials not held by their local libraries. LCS furnished many improvements, including currency of information and increasingly broader coverage as new academic institutions joined the network. Further, a feature crucial to successful resource sharing—shuttle document delivery—was provided through the establishment of the Intersystems Library Delivery System.

LCS proved immensely popular among librarians in the state, but the impact was even more dramatic at UIUC, affecting all areas of library operations and services, as well as staff and users. Internally, LCS functioned efficiently and successfully as the library's master shelflist, the on-order file, and the only record of current location. The important seeds of public acceptance of automated access to this vast collection were sown early on. LCS terminals were available to patrons in public areas throughout the library and large campus, and users soon grew to appreciate the easily remembered commands, the excellent response time, and the degree of control the system offered over immediate information needs. The simplicity of the command structure in LCS was no mistake: LCS was a resounding success.

On the UIUC campus, users now enjoy a number of options for information delivery through LCS. Books can be checked out directly by a user at any of the one hundred public terminals in the library or from home or office using dial-up access. Patrons can pick books up at the library or opt to have them delivered to an office. This capability extends to materials throughout the entire LCS network. A user on the UIUC campus can charge directly a book from, for example, Southern Illinois University at Carbondale. Books checked out in this manner usually are delivered within five working days through the statewide shuttle system. In most cases, users can renew books themselves at a terminal or through the UIUC Library's Telephone Center, a unit set up to search the database and renew items for patrons by telephone.

To date, among the twenty-nine libraries in the network, the UIUC Library alone allows users such a high degree of control over their access to the collections via LCS. Some predicted that remote charging and renewal of materials would weaken the library's control over timely returns and renewals; this problem simply has never materialized. Rather, the emphasis on the role of the library has shifted: once a vast, passive storehouse of volumes, it has become a dynamic, easily accessible collection of information resources for the user community. This increased accessibility encourages an average yearly circulation of a least one million items on the UIUC campus alone.

Today, with over eight hundred terminals online, processing an average of fifteen thousand transactions an hour, LCS is the largest circulation system in the country. Completing its eighth full year as a statewide system, the LCS network represents the most extensive automated resource-sharing enterprise in the United States. Its membership now encompasses fourteen privately supported colleges and universities, thirteen state-supported universities, and two publicly supported community colleges. The materials represented in this database now exceed ten million titles and seventeen-and-a-half million volumes. In fiscal year 1987/88, intercampus borrowing among LCS institutions totaled over 240,000 transactions.

LCS, despite its smashing success, is limited in its potential. The limitations do not arise from LCS's original design as a single-library circulation control system. Rather, they are the result of a short record for entries, the lack of authority control to ensure consistent use of names and terms, and the inability to support sophisticated information retrieval operations. LCS does not support searches by subject, keyword, or series title, nor does it support Boolean combinations of search criteria.

The Second Phase: Enhancing the System with an Online Catalog

Clearly, LCS could not be viewed as a replacement for the card catalog, despite its many virtues and capabilities that go well beyond those of manual files. The problem was simple to pose but difficult to answer: How could the virtues of LCS be preserved while its capabilities were expanded or supplemented? The very question ruled out certain answers. A separate catalog system was not acceptable, nor was a simple expansion of LCS itself. Ohio State University library has expanded its single-campus LCS system successfully to create an online public-access catalog. However, both the major modification of the Illinois LCS software and its installation as a statewide network militated against choosing the same direction. The statewide dimension of LCS could not be compromised in seeking an alternative to the card catalog.

An early decision was that the supplementary system, which, with LCS, eventually would form an online catalog, should be sought among existing systems and off-the-shelf software rather than developed locally. This decision was made on economic grounds (such internal development is inordinately expensive), on grounds of human resources (few if any libraries possess a cadre of individuals with the necessary expertise to develop an acceptable major automated system), and on philosophical grounds, relating to the potential for cooperative development and other forms of cooperation that come with the purchase of existing systems. The last requirement was that the purchased system should complement LCS, not replace it. Given this decision, a link between LCS and the new system was imperative. This link became the single most important and difficult technical problem of this phase of development.

Specific attributes of the desired system were:

- it should be based on MARC, with full bibliographic records derived from use of OCLC, with all standard access points, especially subject headings;
- it should allow full authority control, including a hierarchical subject structure;
- it should be capable of being linked to the existing multicampus LCS circulation system in such a way that the user would perceive the two as a single comprehensive system;

- and, most important, it should have the potential to form the basis for a statewide union catalog.

The job of identifying suitable software for this Full Bibliographic Record (FBR) system was undertaken by staff from the UIUC Library and from UIUC's computer services agency—the Administrative Information Systems and Services (AISS) organization. After a thorough examination of several systems, they determined that the software that came the closest to meeting all the requirements was that used by the Western Library Network (WLN), formerly Washington Library Network. Key arguments in favor of this software were that WLN had been conceived and created within a network environment and that, within that environment, it was a fully functioning and fully developed system.

Once the choice was made, a package of grant and local funding was assembled late in 1979. Funds were approved by the Illinois State Library for the purchase of the WLN software and its attendant database management system, ADABAS, from Software AG. Additional funding from university and other local resources was secured for the mounting of the software on university computers, the generation of the database, the construction of the link between LCS and FBR, and the purchase of additional hardware and telecommunications equipment. The essential condition of the grant from the state library was that the money be used to research and to demonstrate the feasibility of a statewide union catalog. To this end, the UIUC Library sought and won the collaboration of the River Bend (Illinois) Library System. This association provided an opportunity to show the practicality of cooperative bibliographic control between libraries of different kinds that also are separated geographically. The River Bend staff were also invaluable in helping to arrive at design specifications suited to the special needs of public libraries and in evaluating the project from that perspective.

The next three years brought several challenges in the implementation of the FBR system and the construction of the initial shared bibliographic database of the UIUC Library and the River Bend Library System records. The next formidable phase was to create the link between the full bibliographic records and the circulation records. The idea was that a catalog search should yield, not only bibliographic information, but also an indication of the availability of the sought item and the means to gain access to it. This was the important distinction between the online catalog and all of its predecessors. Technically, it was important that both systems be accessible from the same terminal and, while maintaining their separate software identity, appear to the user simply as different aspects of a unified system.

The online catalog has been completely operational on the UIUC campus since 1984. Many aspects of the catalog and its implementation were described in detail in *Information Technology and Libraries* in 1985.[1]

Involvement of Users and Staff in Planning and Implementation

A crucial factor in the success of the enhanced system was the involvement of users and library staff at all stages. From the beginning, the online catalog project was planned to reflect all views of all components of the UIUC Library and the River Bend Library System. To this end, a large committee of representatives from all "public" and "technical" service units of the library was established. This Policy and Implementation Committee met monthly with colleagues at River Bend, using a conference telephone. The committee also was divided into a number of subcommittees to deal with such topics as terminals, priorities, content of databases, and screen displays. A complementary committee on technical matters composed of library faculty and computer center staff also was established. The whole process was monitored by a steering committee consisting of senior library staff (including the University Librarian) and senior computing center staff. Once the project became a reality, a considerable contribution was made by the User Education Committee, which devised and conducted training sessions for staff and wrote and disseminated printed materials, ranging from fliers to a detailed reference manual.

In the four years since the online catalog was installed on campus, the committee structure within the library has undergone several changes aimed at integrating this function firmly into the overall administrative and committee structure of the library. The ad hoc Policy and Implementation and User Education committees have been disbanded, while the steering committee has been retained. In place of the initial structure used during the catalog's implementation, two coordinating positions have been established—Online Catalog Coordinator for User Services and Online Catalog Coordinator for Operations and Development. In addition, two standing committees have been established to assist in ongoing user, technical, and policy development issues both within the library and in the UIUC campus community—the Library Online Catalog Advisory Committee and the Online Catalog Technical Committee.

The evolution in committee structure reflects the transition from the early planning and development stages, where substantial involvement was necessary, to a more stable operational environment, where online catalog activities are now integrated into ongoing policy and operations.

The Third Phase: Expanding to a Statewide Online Catalog

In 1985, a project was begun to expand the catalog database for the UIUC Library and the River Bend Library System to create a statewide union catalog to include the holdings of every OCLC ILLINET (Illinois Library and Information Network) library in the state. The ILLINET organization has brokered OCLC services for libraries in the state since the mid-1970s. This statewide online catalog, named ILLINET Online, is now fully operational, with records for new titles being loaded weekly. The retrospective loading of records from OCLC continues, with completion scheduled in March 1989. It is expected that the database then will represent over thirteen million holdings associated with over four million unique titles from over eight hundred libraries of all types—academic, special, public, research, school, and regional library systems.

The project has involved several major efforts:

- developing procedures for the ongoing database processing of all the OCLC cataloging records for the OCLC ILLINET libraries;
- loading retrospective OCLC archive tapes from the ILLINET libraries;
- enhancement of "scoping"—a WLN software feature that enables searching by selected libraries or geographic groups of libraries across the state;
- expanding and upgrading the telecommunications and terminal network that supports access to the database;
- expanding LCS's existing governance and financial structure to include ongoing support for the FBR system.

By late August 1988, with the statewide database load over halfway completed, ILLINET Online contained over 3.4 million bibliographic records, of which 2 million could be linked with circulation information, and an online Library of Congress–based authority file of over 5.7 million headings. The catalog can be scoped over fifty different ways; for instance, records can be retrieved from (1) an individual LCS institution (2) LCS institutions as a group, (3) each of the eighteen ILLINET regional library systems, (4) the Illinois Research and Reference Centers, (5) the Center for Research Libraries, or (6) the entire state. In particular, the system's ability to perform keyword searching over title and corporate author fields provides access capabilities not present in OCLC. For public-service and interlibrary loan staff, the sophisticated retrieval features of ILLINET Online play an important role in citation verification and location of materials.

The UIUC Library then had a fully operational online catalog with three components: LCS (short bibliographic records for complete inventory control and circulation functions), FBR (full MARC records and Library of Congress authority file plus powerful searching capabilities), and links between each full bibliographic record and its associated LCS record. Access by the public is through a user-friendly interface developed locally. In essence, the success of this pilot project for the UIUC Library meant that each library in the LCS network could adopt this model of online catalog. The pilot project's success for the River Bend Library system—a public library system not using LCS for circulation—meant that the FBR component, based on WLN software, could be adopted in a public library for use as a union catalog. Since the online public access catalog promised by OCLC had not yet come to fruition, the libraries in the state that were using OCLC for cataloging were especially happy to take advantage of the ILLINET Online union catalog, with its access points that offered the much-needed option of searching by subject.

Role of Committees for Statewide Expansion

In each stage of automation at the UIUC Library, committees were created to handle issues of policy, finance, and implementation and to facilitate communication internally between library units, as well as externally between the library and the University of Illinois computing staff and the campuses of the University of Illinois. This committee structure has undergone dramatic changes as ILLINET Online has evolved from a single-campus circulation system into a statewide online catalog.

To ensure that diverse user needs were met during the development of ILLINET Online, the Illinois State Library appointed a statewide Online Catalog Advisory Committee. This twelve-member committee, representing all types of libraries, reviewed and approved technical specifications and addressed a myriad of issues from quality control to funding. In addition, members of online catalog committees at the UIUC Library assisted throughout the process in various capacities, compiling reports and writing programming specifications with members of the AISS organization.

Experience with the two systems that each were implemented first at the University of Illinois and then extended statewide revealed several prerequisites to success.

- The planning and development stages and the later operational form require different organizational structures.

- Substantive input on the statewide planning committees from members of the campus library committees that already have experience with the implementation and use of the system is essential.
- Involvement and education of library staff and users are vital and should be planned for in the same way as technical implementation.

The implementation of the ILLINET Online project is described in detail in the forthcoming proceedings of the Twenty-fourth Annual Clinic on Library Applications of Data Processing.[2]

The Budget and Financial Planning Process

For almost a decade, from 1978 through 1987, funding to support this massive project through its various phases has been provided in the form of grants and nonrecurring monies from a number of agencies: the Illinois State Library, the Illinois Board of Higher Education (IBHE), and the University of Illinois. Details are given in a recent article describing the history of ILLINET Online.[3] In 1987, a budget and funding package was proposed that began to address the question of future network development and sought to involve the LCS member libraries in the financial support of the network. Table 6.1 shows the proposed plan for funding ILLINET Online for the next five years. It is anticipated that LCS membership may increase from twenty-nine to as many as forty-five libraries during this period. It is hoped that the combination of more members and slightly increased member assessments will stabilize member contributions and support for the network.

Although the actual funding support from the Illinois Board of Higher Education and the Illinois State Library did not reach its anticipated goal for fiscal 1988, commitments for fiscal 1989, totaling nearly $1.8 million, are firmly in place. As ILLINET Online moves closer to being an operational statewide resource-sharing network, its benefits for the entire user community are clearly evident, strong arguments in favor of firm continuing support from these agencies.

Network Support for a Statewide Database

This ambitious project has been supported by a telecommunications network, which itself has undergone considerable restructuring recently. Since equipment and software are integral components in the operation of any network, a brief overview of the structure of the ILLINET Online network in the campus and the larger statewide environment may be helpful.

Table 6.1   Budget Plan for Sources of Funding for ILLINET Online (in thousands of dollars)

Funding Source	Fiscal Year						
	1988	1989	1990	1991	1992	1993	1994 and after
IBHE	$150	$800	$1,100	$1,200	$1,000	$800	$700
State Library	300	431	431	431	431	431	431
User libraries	383	569	669	769	819	819	869
Total	$833	$1,800	$2,200	$2,400	$2,250	$2,050	$2,000

Computing resources for administrative data within the University of Illinois are provided by AISS through the Administrative Computer Network (ACN), which is shared by the Urbana and Chicago campuses. This network is generally accessible to staff and faculty of the university. The administrative network supports a number of online systems, such as administrative database applications and the ILLINET Online catalog. Other services include file-transfer facilities and electronic mail. The mail service uses IBM's PROFS office automation system and provides access to BITNET.

ILLINET Online is supported by an IBM 3081 GX mainframe computer located on the University of Illinois at Chicago campus. The telecommunications network that supports communication between the mainframe and terminals across the state includes central nodes (front-end processors) in Chicago and Urbana. A diagram of the ILLINET Online telecommunications network is shown in Figure 6.1. The network structure implemented by AISS is based on the IBM Corporation's System Network Architecture (SNA) using the Synchronous Data Link Communications (SDLC) protocol. The SNA/SDLC architecture enables all types of administrative users to obtain direct access to a number of applications and databases, regardless of their location or specific access methods. The two most widely used terminal protocols supported on this network are for IBM 3270 terminals and asynchronous ASCII terminals.

The SNA/SDLC network was implemented by AISS during 1988. Primary internal considerations in the decision to adopt this architecture were that SNA/SDLC enabled centralized management and control of the existing IBM-based network, assured consistently speedy response time, and facilitated administrative analysis and evaluation of network performance. This architecture also allows access to multiple computing facilities

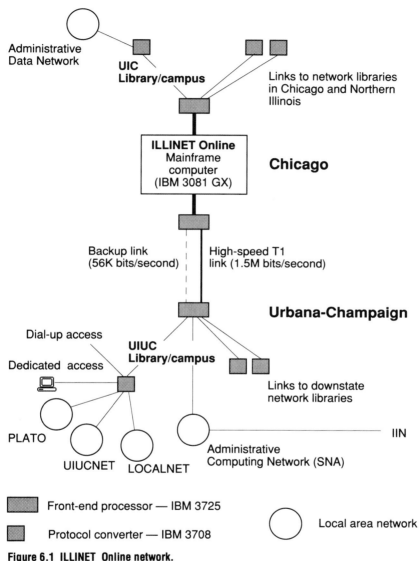

Figure 6.1 ILLINET Online network.

within the network, as well as connections to other SNA networks of special interest to the ILLINET Online community. During the first half of 1989, the network will be testing the feasibility of using ILLINET Online as a gateway to other services through the IBM Information Network (IIN), particularly to subscription services for serials, such as Faxon Linx and

Baker & Taylor, and to commercial bibliographic databases, such as those available through BRS and DIALOG.

Elsewhere on the University of Illinois campus, ILLINET Online is available through dial-up access, LOCALNET (a campus academic computing network), ADN (the University of Illinois at Chicago Administrative Data Network), and from PLATO terminals used primarily for computer-assisted instruction. Users of UIUCNET (a campus fiber-optics network that utilizes the TCP/IP protocol) also have access to the online catalog through asynchronous links between the two networks. AISS also is moving toward connections with networks at other LCS institutions.

Linking the ILLINET Online network to non-SNA networks is an important issue for future development. Of primary interest to libraries is the Open Systems Interconnection (OSI) network architecture, the standard family of protocols used in the Linked Systems Project endeavor for libraries.

User Interfaces and the Role of Microcomputers

Microcomputer workstations play a major role in the UIUC Library's online systems. They are used to facilitate user access to the central systems, to distribute the processing load away from central functions, to provide a gateway function to external, complementary databases, and to furnish access to bibliographic, referral, and directory information stored in microcomputer hard disk and optical-disk files. The effective utilization of microcomputers is made easier in the Illinois setting because ILLINET Online employs microcomputers as public-access terminals.

The User Interface for ILLINET Online

How the catalog information would be presented to the user was a critical area in the development of ILLINET Online. LCS and WLN use different command languages. Forcing users to learn both could have caused confusion and frustration. Instead, the library commissioned an integrated user interface for an inexpensive microcomputer. Written by C. C. Cheng, a professor of linguistics at UIUC, the interface builds search queries in the command-mode language of the two systems by prompting the user for input in clear, natural English. This menu-driven system presents the user with a range of options that allow basic searching of both systems using author, title, subject, author/title combinations, and call-number search capabilities—these being the most commonly used commands. The interface program runs on IBM PCs at a majority of public

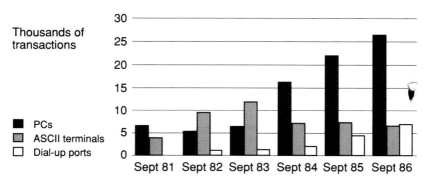

Figure 6.2 Monthly catalog transactions per terminal by type of public access terminal.

service locations throughout the library system. The interface employs some expert system techniques that mimic the actions of a reference librarian—particularly in the subject searching process—to navigate users through search sessions. If a search results in too many matches, the user is prompted for additional terms to narrow the results. Searches for subject headings that do not find a match can be expanded to search titles for the same terms; alternate subject headings identified in this way then can be extracted and used as the basis for further searches. The interface maneuvers the user between the catalog and circulation and provides access first to local holdings and then, if desired, to the statewide database. The interface program distributes the processing by refining the search request at the microcomputer level, thereby limiting the number of transactions with the mainframe computer as the interface formulates the search arguments.

This user interface to the catalog has proven its popularity and has been adapted for use by all of the LCS institutions and each of the ILLINET Regional Library System headquarters offices. About three times as many transactions occur per terminal on terminals on which the interface runs (IBM PCs) as on ASCII or "dumb" terminals, which require knowledge of commands in order to search both systems. Figure 6.2 shows per terminal transaction volumes from 1981 to 1986 at both ASCII terminals and public PCs in the library's "Public Information Desk" area. Users are "voting with their feet;" the results of that vote are very clear. It is not uncommon for students and faculty to queue up to use interface terminals, while an adjacent command-language ASCII terminal remains unused.

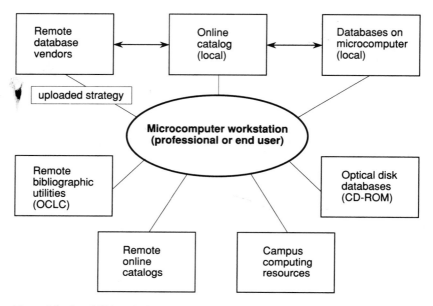

Figure 6.3   Capabilities of microcomputer interface software.

Microcomputers Used as Public-Service Workstations

Different interfaces are appropriate for different classes of use. The UIUC Library has developed customized interface and retrieval software to maximize retrieval capabilities for public-service staff and to facilitate user access to periodical information databases. Desktop personal computers with faster processors and larger, faster disks have made complex library database applications much easier to implement. Figure 6.3 illustrates the possibilities for enhanced access offered by microcomputer interface software.

The library utilizes microcomputers at public service points to expedite reference work and provide expanded access to information resources for library staff. These workstations employ intelligent gateway software to provide access to multiple, discrete information sources, both remote and local. Figure 6.4 shows the opening menu for ILLINOIS SEARCH AID, a software package used primarily by public-service staff at patron contact points. This menu details the various weapons in the reference librarian's arsenal. SEARCH AID is used to access ILLINET Online, remote database vendors, remote bibliographic utilities, local databases stored on the microcomputer's hard disk (via the Reference Information

```
ILLINOIS SEARCH AID
Database Vendors or Networks:
     0.  Online Catalog -- Direct Connect
     1.  BRS -- Telenet
     2.  BRS -- Tymnet
     3.  Dialog -- Telenet
     4.  Dialog -- Tymnet
     5.  OCLC -- Compuserve
     6.  OCLC -- Telenet
     7.  RLIN -- Tymnet
     8.  SDC - Telenet
     9.  SDC -- Tymnet
    10.  BITNET
    11.  Continue search
    12.  Print previously downloaded data
    13.  ENX/PHX Serials Listing
    14.  Logon by searcher
    15.  Online Catalog -- Dial-up
    16.  Reference Information
    17.  Knowledge Index -- Telenet
    18.  Knowledge Index -- Tymnet
    19.  BRS After Dark -- Telenet
    20.  BRS After Dark -- Tymnet
          CHOOSE ONE OF THE NUMBERS
```

Figure 6.4 Search options for public-service staff.

module), and the campus computing center for BITNET and electronic mail.

SEARCH AID offers a number of features to facilitate the searching process and provide enhanced access to information.

- Search strategies can be prepared, edited, and stored offline. Some checking for errors in command strings is performed.
- Strategies entered offline can be uploaded and executed.
- Logging on to remote systems is done automatically, and passwords are masked for security.
- Function keys control selective downloading and printing of search results.
- Search results can be saved for later printing.

The software allows the user to type ahead and contains several features to facilitate searching of the online catalog by combining and/or executing several command strings sequentially. SEARCH AID can search and display files created on word processors and allows simultaneous connections to a database vendor and the online catalog.

Figure 6.5 shows the menu of local data files stored on the microcomputer's hard disk and accessible under the Reference Information

```
REFERENCE INFORMATION SYSTEM

   0.  Exit
   1.  Faculty Interest File
   2.  Table of Contents
   3.  New Books File
   4.  Reference Collection Database
   5.  Continuations File
   6.  Staff Message Board
   7.  Artificial Intelligence Holdings
   8.  Databooks
   9.  NASA Holdings
  10.  IEEE Collection
  11.  ENX/PHX Periodicals
  12.  Problem Citations

Choose a number
```

Figure 6.5 Search options within the Reference Information module of SEARCH AID.

module in the opening SEARCH AID menu. These files, in this example from the Engineering Library, are generated locally. They are searched through locally developed database management software that features keyword searching and browsing capabilities. These databases comple- ment or expand on information available in the online catalog. For ex- ample, the records in the Institute of Electrical and Electronic Engineers (IEEE) Collection file have been downloaded from ILLINET Online to allow more detailed searching than is possible in the online catalog.

Software to extend and distribute these enhanced information retrieval functions to library users via campus electronic networks is being devel- oped. The UIUC Beckman Institute Library, which opened in January 1989, is centered around a networked approach to library service, featur- ing accessibility to the type of customized local data files described above, facilitated end-user access to remote bibliographic databases, and a communications and bulletin board function. Figure 6.6 shows the library function menu for networked Beckman Institute researchers. In this environment, a journal table of contents service and new title listings can be customized to the individual researcher and delivered to his or her networked terminal.

```
UNIVERSITY OF ILLINOIS BECKMAN INSTITUTE LIBRARY SEARCH OPTIONS:

  1. SEARCH ONLINE CATALOG FOR ITEMS IN THE LIBRARY SYSTEM:
     Look for books, journals, theses etc., by author, title,
     author/title, subject, call number.

  2. SEARCH FOR CURRENT ARTICLES IN JOURNALS AND MAGAZINES:
     Self-service database search of an index (e.g. Physics Abstracts)
     to retrieve references to articles on a topic.

  3. Search Engineering Library New Books List.

  4. Search Selective List of COMPUTER SCIENCE/COGNITION/INTELLIGENCE
     journals, incl ENGINEERING LIBRARY JOURNALS, PHYSICS LIBRARY JOURNALS.

  5. Search database of Library's Artificial Intelligence Holdings.

  6. View personal TABLE OF CONTENTS and NEW TITLES list sent from Library.

  7. REQUEST AN ITEM FOR DELIVERY TO OFFICE.

  8. INTERLIBRARY LOAN REQUEST.

CHOOSE A NUMBER:
```

Figure 6.6   Search options for networked library service for the Beckman Institute.

Enhanced Access to Periodical Literature

Users of online catalogs exhibit overwhelming enthusiasm for the technology and general satisfaction with search results. However, transaction log analyses show that even satisfied catalog users are not necessarily performing effective and successful searches. Formal user studies of online catalogs have revealed that users experience serious difficulty with subject searching and that they expect online systems to provide enhanced access to a broader range of library materials, particularly periodicals. Access to information about individual articles in periodicals has been identified as an important focus of development in academic library automation efforts. The technology currently permits several approaches to providing end-user or direct patron access to periodical information. Computer-searchable periodical indexes are being made available as a component of online catalogs, on optical disks, in local stand-alone retrieval systems, and through services that allow end users to search remote databases. The UIUC Library is committed to exploring various techniques for providing enhanced access to periodical literature.

Optical-Disk Systems

CD-ROM technology offers access to bibliographic databases from microcomputer workstations without connect-time costs, telecommunication fees, and printing charges. The UIUC Library has used part of a computing fee levied on students to purchase a wide range of CD-ROM products. This fixed-cost searching technology has caused a great deal of excitement and interest, but there are concerns about the aggregate cost of subscriptions and the lack of standardization among what are presently single-workstation systems. Furthermore, because of existing limitations in database size and retrieval software, the large scientific databases do not lend themselves to this solution. For these reasons, libraries are investigating complementary means of providing networked end-user access to periodical databases. This can be done through gateway software linking users to remote "information supermarkets" (such as DIALOG or BRS) or by loading periodical databases into online catalogs or into separate, parallel local retrieval systems.

Search Software for End Users

The UIUC Library has developed an extension to the ILLINET Online interface that allows simplified end-user searching of remote periodical-information databases residing on commercial vendor systems. While libraries have provided online access to periodical databases since the late 1960s, until recently direct interaction with these systems usually has been the exclusive province of trained librarians functioning as intermediaries. The role of the end user has been to supply information for formulating and modifying the search strategy and to interact with the intermediary searcher. In the past several years, however, the number of libraries offering direct patron searching of bibliographic databases has grown dramatically. To a large extent, this change has been driven by the technology. Libraries and information centers have instituted formal training programs for patrons and established walk-in search services to support end users, often using the less expensive after-hours services.

Studies of the direct end-user searching of online catalogs, remote bibliographic databases, and optical-disk retrieval systems show that

- users are enthusiastic about performing searches on easy-to-use, quickly learned, inexpensive search systems;
- the searches that they perform themselves often are not as effective as those performed through intermediaries;
- search strategy formulation is the most troublesome problem for end users;

- end users have considerable difficulty with Boolean logic;
- end-user search services demand a significant investment of library staff time in training and assistance; and
- end users resist formal training sessions and the use of printed instructions, preferring computer-aided instruction and direct one-on-one instructions from library staff or peers.

Understandably, one of the most active areas of development in end-user information technology has been in search-assistance software, or front-end interfaces, intended to help end users access bibliographic databases. Numerous laboratory systems and commercial products have been reported.[4]

Because of inadequacies in the search engines of the commercial packages and a desire to link local and remote information resources within a single user interface, the UIUC Library undertook the project of developing customized microcomputer interface software for end-user searching of remote databases. This effort has produced an enhanced microcomputer interface that permits searches of periodical databases to be performed as a search option within the local online catalog. From a public terminal linked to the online catalog, users may search for periodical information and then link search results with local holdings and availability information. This "one-stop-shopping" approach provides library users with an online catalog that supports access to multiple information resources from a single terminal and includes information on individual articles within periodicals.

The interface software features include:

- conversational guided assistance and suggestive prompts in search strategy formulation;
- offline preparation and storage of search strategies;
- term selection from customized thesaurus term displays;
- software formulation of Boolean statements;
- automatic truncation of terms and stopword removal;
- replacement of user-entered terms with terms from a predefined substitution table;
- uploading of strategy and ranking of resultant search set combinations;
- software modification of a search strategy, including limiting results to titles and controlled descriptors and using sophisticated search proximity operations, to optimize results;

```
YOU WILL NOW BE ASKED TO ENTER THE CONCEPT TERMS FOR YOUR SEARCH.

    The terms making up the separate concept groups will be
    used to find references to journal articles and reports.

** To help identify your concept terms, please begin by typing
   a one-sentence title of an imaginary (or real) article that
   would best meet your information needs.

This title will not be directly searched.  Rather, it should help
    focus on a specific topic and help to identify concept terms.

    (TYPE ARTICLE TITLE BELOW, FOLLOWED BY ENTER KEY)

PLEASE TYPE A RELEVANT ARTICLE TITLE BELOW.



Interface software for end-user searching
```

Figure 6.7 Screen from a sample end-user search: starting from a sample title.

- dynamic modification of a search strategy based on user feedback; and
- selective downloading and printing of citations and search history.

This expert system software approach incorporates search techniques employed by trained searchers and seeks to expedite the search process for end users. The user is guided through the search process by a series of menus, suggestive prompts, and software manipulations that construct and modify the search strategy. Figures 6.7 and 6.8 show screens from a sample search as it is being constructed. Based on the "concept terms" entered here by the user, the software will generate a sequence of searches on the remote database. For instance, if the ERIC database is being searched on DIALOG, the central concept is used first as a search term by itself; if less than forty references are found, the most recent twenty-five are downloaded for the user. If more references are found, the search is refined; subsidiary concepts are combined successively with the key concept (using a Boolean "and"), and the combination producing the largest set of references is chosen. If further refinement is needed to reduce the number of references to fifty or fewer, the software will try

```
Your search title:

Interface software for end-user searching

You will be asked to enter the words in this title as separate search concepts.

You will be able to enter up to three concept groups.

Type below a term (word or phrase) describing concept 1 of your search request.

Type the word or phrase followed by the ENTER key.

Concept 1 should be the central or most important topic of your search.
   For a search title like 'Microcomputers used in CAD/CAM', concept 1
   would be entered as: CAD/CAM.

If you need to use chemical formulas, check with a site attendant.
Is this concept: Supercomputing, AI; Cognition; Computational Geometry? (y/n) n

Concept 1 (word or phrase):   end-users
```

Figure 6.8   Screen from a sample end-user search: establishing the central concept.

limiting the search to certain fields, such as the title or description of an article, and then try constraining the concept phrases to be found in close proximity to each other. The interface software controls the search process, minimizing connect time and limiting the number of references printed to twenty-five per search session, although many users perform multiple searches. This essentially fixes or places a ceiling on the cost of the search service. (The issue of search costs and the provision of fixed-cost access to bibliographic databases remains a serious concern in academic libraries.)

The enhanced interface is being used at several departmental libraries; over sixteen hundred end-user searches were performed in 1988. User questionnaires and transaction log analysis reveal that the system is regarded very favorably by users; it is rated as easy and effective to use.

The development and testing of the interface have provided some insights into interface design issues and needs.[5] Clearly, the interface plays a particularly critical role in effective end-user searching of bibliographic databases. This has ramifications for online catalogs, bibliographic services, and optical-disk systems.

Summary and Future Focus

The goal of providing improved access to library materials has been the cornerstone of the development of all electronic information systems at the University of Illinois at Urbana-Champaign. With the installation of LCS, the library's online circulation system, the user immediately benefited through improved access to library resources. Creating the statewide online catalog improved access to materials for library patrons throughout the state. Within the LCS colleges and universities, a quarter of a million volumes per year are shared through intercampus borrowing.

Providing effective access to library materials and complementary bibliographic databases is of paramount concern to academic libraries. Studies of end-user searches emphasize the importance of the user interface in effective information retrieval from databases. The development of a microcomputer-based interface that facilitates user access to ILLINET Online and an extension of this interface that provides access to periodical databases residing with remote commercial vendors are just a start. At the University of Illinois at Urbana-Champaign Library, improving access to periodical information—in particular, the role of microcomputer interface software in providing this enhanced access—will continue as a primary focus.

References

1. "Special Section: In Depth—The Online Catalogue at the University of Illinois at Urbana-Champaign." *Information Technology and Libraries* 4, no. 4 (December 1985): 306–351.

   Gorman, Michael. "The Online Catalogue at the University of Illinois at Urbana-Champaign: A History and Overview."

   Potter, William Gray. "Linking LCS and FBR: The Library's Perspective."

   Salika, Catherine. "Linking LCS and FBR: Technical Perspective."

   Romero, Nancy, and Arnold Wajenberg. "Authority Records and Authority Work in the Online Catalogue."

   Clark, Sharon E., and Winnie Chan. "Maintenance of an Online Catalogue."

   Woodard, Beth, and Gary A. Golden. "The Effect of the Online Catalogue on Reference: Uses, Services, and Personnel."

   Cheng, Chin-Chuan. "Microcomputer-Based User Interface."

2. Clark, Sharon E. "The Online Catalog: Beyond a Local Reference Tool." In *Twenty-Fourth Annual Clinic on Library Applications of*

Data Processing, Questions and Answers: Strategies for Using the Electronic Reference Collection, ed. Linda Smith (Urbana-Champaign, Ill.: University of Illinois at Urbana-Champaign Graduate School of Library and Information Science, in press).

3. Sloan, Bernard G., and J. David Stewart. "ILLINET Online: Enhancing and Expanding Access to Library Resources in Illinois." *Library Hi Tech* 6, no. 3 (1988): 95–101.

4. Mischo, William H., and Jounghyoun Lee. "End-User Searching of Bibliographic Databases." *Annual Review of Information Science and Technology* 22 (1987): 227–263.

5. Mischo, William H., and Melvin E. DeSart. "A Microcomputer Interface for End-User Searching." In *Twenty-Fourth Annual Clinic on Library Applications of Data Processing, Questions and Answers: Strategies for Using the Electronic Reference Collection,* ed. Linda Smith (Urbana-Champaign, Ill.: University of Illinois at Urbana-Champaign Graduate School of Library and Information Science, in press).

Chapter 7

Brigham Young University
Law Library

David A. Thomas

Sponsored by the Church of Jesus Christ of Latter-day Saints (familiar to many as "Mormons"), Brigham Young University is located in Provo, Utah, a community with a population of about eighty thousand, approximately forty-five miles south of Salt Lake City. With twenty-seven thousand under-graduates and about two thousand graduate and profes-sional students, it is the nation's largest church-related university. In addition to very good law and business schools, the university's most popular or prominent programs are in languages, edu-cation, engineering, communications, and fine arts. The meticulously maintained campus, nestled at the foot of the Wasatch Mountains, is regarded as one of the most attractive in the country. In recent years, the Provo area's economy has gained a respectable sector in technology development and manufacturing.

Although in operation since only 1973, Brigham Young University's J. Reuben Clark Law School and Law Library have assumed national leadership in applying automation to legal education and law library processes. This achievement has been driven more by necessity than by a quest for prominence: except for the nearby University of Utah College of Law, the nearest law school is over five hundred miles away and the nearest law library of comparable size is seven hundred miles away. This geographic isolation both stimulates the need for communication and resource sharing and fosters a spirit of independence in forming technol-ogy strategies. Other factors, too, have contributed to the unusual strength of technology application at BYU's law school: several BYU law professors possess both the skill and the interest to help develop com-puter-assisted law practice systems and classroom projects; the law school is located in an area that has become a hotbed of software development—WordPerfect and Novell headquarters are only minutes away; the law school student body has exceptionally high academic credentials and strong computer backgrounds; and the staff of the law library has been able to achieve significant economies and service upgrades through automation.

BYU law school is served by its own local, integrated computing facilities, which are linked to other campus facilities as shown in Figure 7.1. All faculty, librarians, and other full-time staff have terminals or personal computers in their offices. They all have access to the school's Digital VAX 11/750; many also are linked to a local area network. Through the local area networks, users have access to file servers, shared printing, and other university local area networks through the campus broadband. Data switches in the law school and elsewhere on campus also provide asynchronous terminal access to campus computing facilities, such as

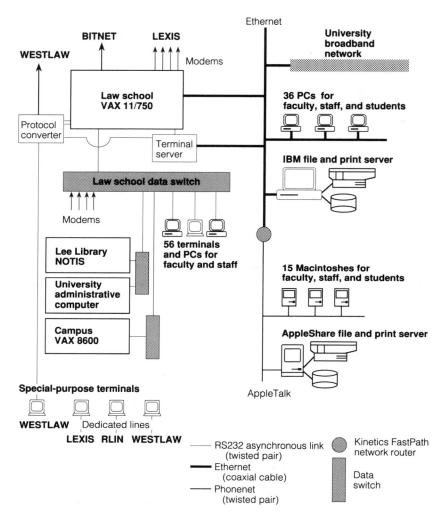

Figure 7.1 Linked computer networks at the J. Reuben Clark Law School.

the online catalog in the main campus library, the VAX 8600 in the engineering building that supports statistical packages and other software for science and engineering applications, and the university's administrative computer system.

About three dozen IBM or IBM-compatible personal computers in the law library are used heavily by the 450 law students during the school year. These computers are linked in a local area network for access to shared printers, software, and databases. A network of Macintosh computers was added recently, providing sophisticated publishing and graphics capability for students, faculty, and staff. All of these personal computers can connect to the university's facilities over the campus broadband network and to the VAX 11/750, the focus of the law school's computing services.

The law library has fully automated and integrated its cataloging, acquisitions, serials management, public catalog, circulation, fiscal control, inventory control, security, photocopy and printer accounting, and most reference and interlibrary loan functions. The library also provides distributed and remote access to huge local and national databases. Retrospective conversion of the substantial collection, which now numbers 315,000 volumes, was completed in 1982 without the aid of special funding or staffing.

As a direct benefit from these capabilities, the law library has effectively eliminated backlogs in cataloging, acquisitions, and serials management, despite an increase in the rate of acquisitions. Since 1976, when library automation began in earnest, the library has voluntarily reduced its full-time staff from twenty to thirteen. Some of this reduction resulted directly from automation, and all of it was made more manageable by automation. For library users, automation has meant that new books are on the shelf faster, new journal issues and bindery items are tracked more efficiently, the collection bibliographics can be searched faster and with greater accuracy, and interlibrary loan is much more responsive. With the efficiencies of word processing readily available, law students can spend more time in substantive studying, writing, and editing. Their intensive training in legal-research databases has made them more attractive to prospective employers.

Philosophical Commitments as Bases for Strategies

While the automation of the BYU law library has been evolutionary and many plans have been revised along the way, certain philosophical commitments have remained constant. These have been the bases for long-term strategies, which are still intact even after heady breakthroughs in computer capabilities and the rise of new technologies directly relevant to libraries.

The philosophies that animate an academic library are perhaps so obvious or self-understood that they are seldom, if ever, articulated. But they are the foundation of technology strategies and therefore must be dusted off and examined. One basic philosophical commitment of the BYU law library is to gain access to or actually obtain as many information resources as possible that pertain to the mission of the law school. Another commitment is to provide access to these resources as broadly and easily as possible, at least for the specific constituencies of the law school. These constituencies are very diverse and extend well beyond the university community itself; for example, the law library serves, not only students and faculty in the law school and elsewhere at BYU, but also law school alumni, lawyers who are members of the sponsoring church, and, indeed, the public generally. A more inward-looking philosophical commitment, relating to the way a library is administered, is to reduce as much as possible the tedium and error incidence of labor-intensive library work in order to improve the quality of both workers' lives and library operations. An obvious corollary of all of these is to accomplish them at the lowest possible cost.

Deriving strategies for electronic information from these philosophies follows more or less naturally, but not without some serious tests of the philosophies along the way. For instance, if we really are committed to obtaining all the pertinent information resources, are we ready to accept them in some form other than print? Librarians and users alike have occasionally rejected an information technology such as microforms, even when it was the only available format for certain resources. Similar inconveniences are attached to electronic information. For example, a number of law librarians have refused to subscribe to a periodicals index on CD-ROM, with its swift and comprehensive searching, because its cost is several times that of its print counterpart. For the most part, however, forming strategies for introducing electronic information into a campus library is characterized by eagerness rather than restraint. Electronic information promises direct and dramatic progress toward the philosophical objectives: more resources, better access, and efficient management. Cost is often a sobering consideration, but, in many automation applications, it is possible actually to reduce normal expenditures and, in others, to improve the value obtained.

Academic libraries, and perhaps law school libraries more than most, typically divide their electronic information strategies into two distinct efforts: one directed toward obtaining access to electronic information resources available commercially or from outside the institution, perhaps through library networks; the other toward developing local or internal capability to access and distribute those resources. The development of internal capabilities is also important for performing a multitude of library management tasks, all of which ultimately affect user services. In candor, however, it must be conceded that progress in these efforts depends less on pursuing strategies of preconceived stages and schedules than on opportunistic funding, serendipitous technology developments, and pragmatic compromise.

Automation at the BYU Law Library

This pragmatic approach is amply illustrated in this brief history of automation at the BYU law library. If a single motive has guided the efforts to bring electronic information sources into the law library and then to develop the internal capability to manage and distribute those resources, it has been the desire to reduce complexity—to provide access for the user to all the library's electronic information through a single terminal, with facile transition between databases and systems, and to support this access with reliable, swift, convenient communications and printing capability. The goal has not yet been achieved, but it is now well within sight.

Bringing in the Outside Electronic Information

The principal electronic information resources sought by any law school library are the huge, full-text, interactive databases consisting of judicial opinions, state and federal statutes, administrative materials, and scholarly literature. Only two vendors offer this resource. In a very general sense, there is much parity in their data and their search modes, but the competition between them is brisk, and most law school libraries subscribe to both.

The first of these was LEXIS, which was introduced commercially in 1973 by its owner, Mead Data Central, initially among large New York law firms. It quickly became apparent to both the vendor and the law schools that the dramatic changes in legal research portended by this facility needed attention in legal education curricula.[1] The BYU law library was an early adherent to this view and subscribed to LEXIS in 1976. Access to the database was from a dedicated terminal through a direct-line dial-up connection. Soon minimal competency in computer-assisted legal research on LEXIS was required of all BYU law students.

Getting a later start, the rival West Publishing Co., America's largest publisher of printed legal materials, committed itself to a similar system in 1973, introducing a somewhat incomplete database and system in 1975. An extensively and successfully redesigned service was offered in 1980. That same year, the BYU law library subscribed to WESTLAW, becoming one of the first law school libraries to provide both databases. BYU law students were required to be trained on both systems. Now over

90 percent of the 175 American law school libraries subscribe to both systems, and mandatory training for law students on both systems is clearly the trend.[2]

The annual charges are about $25,000 each for the comprehensive LEXIS and WESTLAW law school subscriptions, permitting unlimited usage of the services. Despite the expense, the services have become an indispensable resource for law libraries and legal education: both LEXIS and WESTLAW do more than train law students to function comfortably in private law practice; they are crucial supports for law faculty and student scholarly research. Moreover, numerous related or derivative databases are available through these subscriptions, including NEXIS and DIALOG, either as part of the subscriptions or on a fee-for-use basis, and these, too, enrich the law library's holdings of electronic information.

At first, the BYU law library provided these services exclusively through dedicated terminals in communication with the remote databases. It became apparent early that, while a single terminal located near a reference librarian who taught computer-assisted legal research to large numbers of law students served an educational function, it did not foster an ambience conducive to scholarly research. As a consequence, the law library sought ways to distribute LEXIS and WESTLAW directly to terminals in faculty offices without incurring the expense of buying more subscriptions and more dedicated terminals. The vendors, however, who based subscription rates for law schools on flat fees with little or no profit, worried that distributed access would vastly increase faculty use and slow response time for commercial customers. They were also reluctant to expose newer users to noncustomized keyboards.

A breakthrough occurred in 1982, when BYU's law school equipped itself with the VAX 11/750 and installed terminals in all faculty offices. Using the asynchronous Develcon data switch attached to the VAX and a program developed at the law school and taking advantage of the willingness of West Publishing Co. to participate in the experiment, the library made WESTLAW accessible in every law faculty office. The number of simultaneous users that the system could accommodate was still limited; the program selected communication links on a single, multiplexed line, assigned available passwords, and signaled when all passwords were being used. Both vendors since have extended similar arrangements for access through nondedicated terminals to all their users. LEXIS has been available at BYU law school on a distributed basis since the spring of 1989.

Now fully committed to the proposition that student training is the key to commercial acceptance, both vendors offer substantial training assistance at law schools. Most impressive are the so-called TLCs—temporary learning centers. One or more times during the school year, at the convenience of the law school, each vendor delivers several additional terminals and connects them to the home database. Training is conducted with groups of law students clustered at these terminals, either by the standard law librarian trainers, student trainers, or company trainers or by combinations of all three. TLCs, which were in place in the BYU law library for six months of the eight-month 1987/88 school year, are provided by the vendors at no charge. TLCs are now evolving into PLCs (permanent learning centers), which require some investment by the law schools.[3]

Lurking beneath the grand strategy of bringing full-text databases into the law library are troublesome tactical considerations relating to the virtues of full text as a research medium. The theoretical advantage of searching full-text data with Boolean techniques (the ability to sharpen searches through combinations of search instructions) is the possibility of swiftly sweeping through the entire universe of that data, from every rational perspective, to extract all relevant information. In practice, however, the variable skills and knowledge of searchers and the inevitable inconsistency of terminology in the databases have led to search results falling far short of the theoretical possibilities. In the common task of searching for judicial opinions, electronic full-text searches often yield no more relevant cases than do manual searches, and the lists of particular cases retrieved by the two methods are often disturbingly different. Lawyers, who already tend to be paranoid in their competitive professional environment, constantly confront the specter of more and better undiscovered authorities awaiting only the command of a more perceptive researcher. Law students, of course, are instantly tuned in to that culture.[4]

Despite the unresolved intellectual challenges of full-text searching, full-text databases do offer some important mechanical advantages. For libraries always seeking new economies, such databases make it possible to eliminate some print holdings and subscriptions, at least of titles not in heavy demand. Retrieval and display are often more efficient. Downloading of data to local systems, for further searching, manipulation, or cut-and-paste publication or class preparation projects, is a popular capability, especially with so much legal data already in the public domain.

In addition to LEXIS and WESTLAW, other publishers of legal materials occasionally have attempted to offer full-text databases. The necessity or appeal of these offerings is considerably less in the law schools than it is in private law firms, corporate law libraries, or government agency legal offices, and some of these services have not survived in the legal education market.

The greatest interest currently centers on possible uses for CD-ROM (compact disk) and videodisk in law libraries. Vendors are busy determining what information resources can be offered advantageously in these media at prices attractive to law school and other law libraries. Several training programs for lawyers and law students have been produced. Two vendors of legal periodicals indexes offer CD-ROM as a companion to their print publications, supplying monthly updated replacements for the disks and using dedicated hardware. The searching and printing capabilities of these installations are so powerfully attractive to users that some law librarians feel compelled to subscribe despite their reservations about the extraordinary cost. The BYU law library subscribed to the first such service, then quickly switched to a competitor who introduced a much less expensive service a year later.

Several considerations surround the strategic objective of expanding library resources electronically. Providers may price new databases exorbitantly in order to recover their development costs quickly. Because prices tend to come down as customer lists grow or competitors appear on the scene, the impulse to be the "first on the block" with a new database should be tempered. Also, some new electronic services require investment in hardware but simply will not survive; again, restraint is counseled. On the other hand, if a new offering genuinely will enhance the law library resources and has good backing, earlier acquisition is better than later. And if the new service can be provided through hardware already on hand, so much the better.

A persistent issue is whether a print resource duplicated by an electronic service should be discontinued (most are in serial form). The answer often depends on how many users can be accommodated by the electronic service compared to the printed volumes or, at least, on whether adequate access is available electronically. The issue is further complicated by the facts that books never "go down" and that, once purchased and delivered, the availability of books is never subject to the commercial success and survival of their publishers, whereas electronic media are at the mercy of their vendors' fortunes. Virtually no cancellations of print subscriptions have occurred at the BYU law library; high use usually has required the broader availability of the print versions.

A special category of electronic information resources is the bibliographic information about collections at other institutions now widely available through utilities such as RLIN and OCLC. Compared to LEXIS and WESTLAW, this information is of limited usefulness because it is not the primary information needed for research; instead, it mostly is used to discover and seek access to the conventional primary sources. BYU is a charter member of the Research Libraries Group, the nonprofit owner of RLIN; the BYU law library has been an RLIN participant from the beginning, and RLIN searching is available to both users and staff. If this utility were useful only for sharing resources through interlibrary loan, its return on cost might be questioned, but, of course, it has performed other important functions for member libraries, such as providing support for cataloging and acquisitions. Indeed, at the BYU law library, RLIN fees represent an instance where automation actually has reduced costs, compared to the old manual procedures.

Strategies for Internal Automation

Although the goal for law library automation at BYU is to achieve full integration of all functions, in fact, the various library functions have been automated individually, sometimes on disparate systems. Partly, this is because automation began a few years too soon; packages with a high degree of integration are now available that were not ready for market just five or ten years ago. However, the BYU law library has proceeded from the viewpoint that, if the automation of an individual process can be justified, it is better to go forward and reap the benefits, rather than waiting indefinitely until an acceptably integrated package is announced. Moreover, transitions from individual systems to an integrated system have seldom been difficult or expensive.

Internal Automation with the Main Library

The first library function to be automated at BYU was serials management in 1976. For this function, as well as for others to follow, it clearly was better for the main campus library and the law school library to join forces, both to strengthen proposals for funding and to refine the processes once they were installed. Computer communications and staff working relationships were firmly and positively established while developing this excellent in-house system. The small costs for terminals and computing time were justified fully by the conversion of check-in, routing, accounting, claims, and bindery control to full automation. Law library input in software refinement was meaningful because of the high proportion and variety of serials typical of a law school library collection. This serials management program originally ran on an IBM mainframe housed in the university computer building, with terminals in both the main library and the law library. Recently, it has been merged into the integrated library system, described below.

Soon thereafter came the introduction of RLIN in 1978 and the blessed concept of shared cataloging. This function, too, was adopted by both main and law libraries acting in concert, and it resulted in immediate savings over old manual methods. Later, acquisitions functions also were conducted on RLIN, with benefits similar to those of cataloging. For these two functions, no additional computer was required, but more dedicated terminals were used, creating yet another separate system.

Feeling secure in the sophistication and high quality of the RLIN database, the BYU law library staff decided early to conduct a full retrospective conversion of the law collection catalog to machine-readable form. With some temporary additional clerical staff, the project was completed in about eighteen months, helped by high "hit rates," since many titles owned by BYU had already been cataloged by other RLG members. This early conversion was to prove of immense benefit for the next stage of automation.

That next stage was the selection of an "integrated system" to perform all library management functions from a single bibliographic database. Again, the main library and law library joined in the proposal and selection processes and have remained joined ever since in the implementation of Northwestern's NOTIS system, which eventually was chosen and installed.[5] This system requires yet another mainframe computer, this one devoted to library functions and located in the main library; the law library communicates fully through the law school data switch, as well as by direct lines. The system, called BYLINE at BYU, principally provides an excellent online public catalog (now the only law library catalog), cataloging, acquisitions, and some accounting functions. BYLINE was first made available to the public in 1986. The transitions from using RLIN for cataloging and acquisitions are taking place; RLG sees this as a proper and normal evolutionary development. The serials management program developed in-house has been modified recently and mounted as part of the integrated system.

In summary, the BYU law library enjoys automated public catalog functions and support for cataloging, acquisitions, serials management, and circulation on the BYLINE/NOTIS system; cataloging, interlibrary loan, and some reference searching on RLIN; and full-text research databases provided separately by vendors. The seeming fragmentation of this arrangement largely is overcome by the accessibility of most of the data needed by patrons on virtually any individual terminal or personal computer in the library or law school.

Internal Automation at the Law School

The BYU law library's ability to share in automation developments at the main campus library is aided immensely by the presence of the law school computer system, built around a Digital VAX 11/750, installed in 1982. The ability of this system to distribute data throughout the law school and law library, coupled with its power to communicate with systems outside the law school through its data switches, opened new dimensions of library automation. A compelling impetus for the VAX acquisition was development of the law school's computer-assisted practice systems (CAPS), involving several faculty and many students. CAPS programs were designed to provide highly interactive checklists, interview prompts, and forms-creation routines for such areas as estate planning, real estate transactions, adoptions, and litigation support. In addition, typical office automation capabilities would be available through the VAX, and their benefits would extend to the law library as well as to the law school faculty and staff.

Of these office automation capabilities, word processing alone, with associated facilities for communications and file transfer, would have justified the cost of the system. The productivity of some law faculty members increased fourfold. Library staff members experienced similarly increased efficiency in many of their tasks, such as compiling bibliographies and performing research, writing, and editing. Extra benefits arose because all users were connected directly to the same computer, rather than working on separate, unconnected personal computers. At the same time, most of the original workstations were DECmate IIs that also could function offline, thus relieving the VAX of some burdens at peak times.

The other major attraction of the system was that it would provide word processing to law students, which, it was hoped, would improve both their ability to meet the heavy writing demands of law school and the quality of their work, as well as freeing more time for study. About three dozen student workstations were installed on three of the four floors in the law library. They functioned offline as independent workstations but were monitored by and scheduled through the VAX. In the years since this initial installation, the equipment has been replaced by personal computers joined in a local area network (called the JRC network). A file server on the network is loaded with numerous useful databases and software.

The hope for greater student efficiency has been realized, and so the law school has introduced more substantial writing requirements.

The law library has benefited from the integrated VAX network in numerous, unanticipated ways. It has installed electronic door locks on floors other than the main entrance floor and introduced a system of coded plastic cards for student ingress and egress, especially outside regular operating hours. The computer network can monitor the time and identity of each individual card use, and this helps control unauthorized entry. The same cards are programmed and coded for fee-based student use of computers, printers, and photocopiers. The law library maintains high-speed photocopiers that produce about three million copies annually; accounting and maintenance of individual copy accounts are handled by special programs developed locally.

Dissatisfaction with delays in the university accounting system has prompted development of the law library's own automated bookkeeping, which yields daily balances on each account in the law library's budget. This is particularly valuable for acquisitions and personnel. Systems for inventory control, for compiling statistics (both institutional and for the American Association of Law Libraries), and for tracking gifts have been developed at the law library to run on the law school computer. Staff members have been encouraged to suggest computer applications for their own areas of responsibility and to help in developing useful programs.

Issues

One crucial element in the creation of the law library's automation facilities has been the ability to conduct successful joint ventures with the main campus library and with the law school administration. In the main library partnership, the law library obtains access to the entire NOTIS system and its ongoing developments and also is able to play a substantive role in RLG matters. Differing viewpoints on bibliographic issues have been resolved amicably and with respectful restraint by the larger library, which could dominate the joint committees because of its greater representation. The relationship between the law school and the law library is more symbiotic. The law school provides financial support for system development, maintenance, and supplies; in return, the law library, in cooperation with the VAX system manager, actually supervises use and training for the entire law school computing system.

All partnerships are vulnerable to breakdowns in human relationships and communications. At BYU, the partners strive to strengthen those links however possible. Especially helpful are full participation in regular, frequent committee meetings, widespread distribution of minutes, much advance deliberation before reaching important decisions, and an attitude that acknowledges the impermanence even of wrong decisions in this fast-changing milieu.

Automation has also brought increased requirements for technical skills in workers, and some clerical positions have been upgraded. The cycle, however, is not yet complete. Soon, virtually all clerical workers will need some of these technical skills, and then even the technically trained will resume their former positions at the low end of the organizational hierarchy. Library directors should try to preserve the upgrades. They also should continue development of computer applications that remove the tedious and mundane elements from jobs. Some issues of health and safety remain unresolved and should be watched closely. Some mature professionals cannot or will not adapt to new ways. After a few years, all these concerns will have been laid to rest; in the meantime, library administrators must reduce costs in human emotions. At the BYU law library, the screen and keyboard tasks are intermixed with traditional tasks to minimize tedium and possible health hazards.

Money continues as an issue. Obsolescence, repair, maintenance, and enhancements exact high expenditures even after initial investments. Whether and what fees should be paid by users is a continuing concern, as is the expensive appeal of new technologies. The only user fee charged at the BYU law school is one dollar per hour for student use of word processors. LEXIS and WESTLAW are free for educational use by students and faculty.

Finally, even in the academic setting, security remains troublesome. Invasions of examination files or student records are rare, but even a few incidents threaten the integrity of an entire system.

Perhaps more urgently in the academic setting than elsewhere, the institution must not become so preoccupied with automation that traditional educational values are ignored, curricula distorted, or library collection development compromised. Similarly, even though it is fun to be first, automation innovators often incur greater costs and longer start-up times than their fellows who wait long enough to learn from others' experience. On the other hand, the sooner an institution begins the automation journey, the sooner begins the time of actual experience that is always necessary to get the most from the innovations.

At BYU's law school, students have a unique opportunity to become "computer literate" in ways that are especially valuable for their professional careers. Even though some equipment and some software have had a short useful life at the law school, all the installations have served useful purposes and constituted improvements over former facilities. Fortunately, the law library never has installed a system that reached dead-end obsolescence; it always has been possible to "trade up" to newer or better equipment. The improvements in professional life for the librarians and scholarly life for students, staff, and faculty have been and will continue to be profound.

References

1. Harrington, William G. "A Brief History of Computer-Assisted Legal Research." *Law Library Journal* 77 (1985): 543–556.

2. Thomas, David A. "1986–87 Statistical Survey of Law School Libraries and Librarians." *Law Library Journal* 80 (1988): 485–537.

3. Thomas, David A. "Training American Law Students in Computer-Assisted Legal Research." *Law Librarian* 19 (1988): 59–61.

4. Dabney, Daniel A. "The Curse of Thamus: An Analysis of Full-Text Legal Document Retrieval." *Law Library Journal* 78 (1986): 5–40.

   McDermott, Jo. "Another Analysis of Full-Text Legal Document Retrieval." *Law Library Journal* 78 (1986): 337–343.

   Runde, Craig E., and William H. Lindberg. "The Curse of Thamus: A Response." *Law Library Journal* 78 (1986): 345–347.

   Dabney, Daniel A. "A Reply to West Publishing Company and Mead Data Central on 'The Curse of Thamus.'" *Law Library Journal* 78 (1986): 349–350.

   Burson, Scott F. "A Reconstruction of Thamus: Comments on the Evaluation of Legal Information Retrieval Systems." *Law Library Journal* 79 (1987): 133–143.

   Bing, Jon. "Performance of Legal Text Retrieval Systems: The Curse of Boole." *Law Library Journal* 79 (1987): 187–202.

   Warnken, Kelly. "A Study in LEXIS and WESTLAW Errors." *Legal Economics* 13 (July/August 1987): 39, 58.

   Coco, Al. "Full-Text v. Full-Text Plus Editorial Additions: Comparative Retrieval Effectiveness of the LEXIS and WESTLAW Systems." *Legal Reference Services Quarterly* 4 (1984): 27–37.

5. Thomas, David A. "Peaceful Partnerships: Suggestions for Law School Libraries Sharing Local Computer Systems." *Law Library Journal* 77 (1985): 26–35.

Chapter 8

Georgia Institute of Technology

Miriam A. Drake

The Georgia Institute of Technology, a unit of the University System of Georgia, is located on the northern edge of downtown Atlanta. The institute's charter states, "The purpose of the Georgia Institute of Technology is to contribute to the fulfillment of the scientific and technical needs of the state of Georgia through education, research and service."[1] In addition to its educational and research missions, the institute's charge includes promotion of "a partnership between public and private sectors for the transfer of technology into the economic base of the state of Georgia."

With 65 percent of its undergraduates and 60 percent of its graduate students enrolled in engineering programs, Georgia Tech is the most engineering-intensive university in the nation. Enrollment in fall 1987 was 9,105 undergraduates and 2,666 graduates. The institute grants degrees in engineering, science, architecture, management, and psychology. The average SAT score of the 1987 freshman was 1,206, approximately two hundred points above the national average. The student body of Georgia Tech ranks first among publicly funded universities in terms of National Achievement scholars and second in terms of National Merit Scholars.

In 1988, Georgia Tech received $120 million in grants for sponsored research. The institute also houses the Advanced Technology Development Center, established by the governor of Georgia. The ATDC serves as a business incubator to provide support to new companies and works to attract the research and development operations of large national and international companies. Seventy-six companies have participated as members of ATDC since 1980.

The Library

There are two libraries at Georgia Tech, the main library and a branch serving the College of Architecture. Eighty percent of the libraries' collections are in science and technology. In addition to holding an outstanding collection of books and journals, the library is a depository of U.S. government documents, patents, standards, specifications, and technical reports from a variety of public and private agencies. We like to think of ourselves as the largest specialized library in the United States. Georgia Tech has a reciprocal agreement with Georgia State University, located in downtown Atlanta, for library loans to students and faculty. Georgia State University Library concentrates its collections in the humanities, social sciences, education, and business.

The Georgia Tech library is a client-oriented service organization that focuses on the information, research, and instructional needs of faculty, students, and local business. Emphasis is on services rather than the collection. High-quality services have been a tradition for over sixty years.

The library has a history of experimentation and innovation. In the 1950s, it was a test site for MARC I, the first version of the standard for exchanging machine-readable catalog records. In 1975, the card catalog was replaced by a microfiche catalog, which was distributed to all buildings on campus and to local businesses. This distribution facilitated operation of the LENDS service, a document delivery service available to faculty and staff. The LENDS truck delivers books, documents, and other items to campus buildings twice a day. More recently, the library has been using fax (facsimile transmission) to deliver documents to research faculty and staff at off-campus sites and to corporate clients around the world. Since 1985, the catalog has been available online as part of the Online Information System, which also offers other bibliographic and full-text databases. Many faculty are heavy library users but have not entered the library building for years.

Computing and the Campus Network

Georgia Tech is a computer-intensive campus. Almost every faculty member has a terminal or personal computer in the office. Access to personal computers is available to the entire academic community in the several public clusters on campus. Many faculty and students own personal computers that they use at home or in the dormitories. For several years, the Georgia Tech Foundation has partially subsidized the purchase of personal computers by faculty.

The library houses three public clusters. One, with twelve terminals and six printers, provides dedicated access to the library's Online Information System. A second holds approximately forty IBM PCs and PS/2s, two printers, and several terminals. This equipment may be used independently or for access to campus computers. Recently, a third installation, of forty Macintosh computers, has been installed.

The campus network, GTNET, has been in place since 1979. A five-mile fiber-optic, broadband backbone connects 128 buildings and supports approximately twenty-five hundred ports. Network access is available from many faculty offices, from the public clusters of terminals and personal computers, and from dormitories. GTNET functions as a three-level hierarchical network with group, department/building, and campus levels. It has gateways to national networks, such as SURAnet (Southeastern Universities Research Association Network) and the statewide PEACHNET. The protocol of choice is TCP/IP. Local area networks in buildings or departments may be token rings or Ethernets and are linked to the Ethernet backbone through bridges or routers. The network permits access to more than twenty campus mainframes and minicomputers in the Office of Computing Services and satellite locations. Almost all devices on campus can access the library's Online Information System, which runs on an IBM mainframe in the computer center.

Library 2000

In 1984, the president of Georgia Tech indicated that he wanted the institute to have the most technologically advanced library in the nation. The library staff participated in a planning process that addressed the following questions:

- What are the attributes of the present and future campus and technological environments?
- Why should the library exist?
- What role should the library play in supporting instruction and research?
- How should services be provided so that people will succeed because of the library, not in spite of it?
- What technologies should the library use?
- How could these technologies be implemented?

The staff concluded that the campus and the current environment are characterized by rapid technological change, lack of information awareness, costly scientific and technological literature, increasing interdisciplinary research, a networked campus, bright students, star faculty, and high expectations of the library. During the planning sessions, the staff developed goals for a special project to shape the future of the library as an information-service organization. The project is named Library 2000.

Goals
The goals of Library 2000 are to:

- increase the amount of information available through the campus network;
- deliver all forms of information (textual, graphic, bibliographic, and numeric) to the workstation or personal computer;

- increase faculty productivity;
- increase information-resource productivity;
- create personalized information systems;
- study the human/information-system interaction;
- create a rich learning environment for students; and
- ensure that Tech graduates will be information literate.

During the planning sessions, it became clear that the library was an underutilized campus resource. While faculty and staff could use a phone call or electronic mail message to seek information, they often did not think of doing so. Students used the library for study and class assignments but generally were unaware of the volume of information available and of the importance of information in their lives. While the campus had been focusing on computer literacy, little attention had been paid to information literacy. Forest Horton has pointed out,

> Information literacy...as opposed to computer literacy, means raising the level of awareness of individuals and enterprises to the knowledge explosion, and how machine-aided handling systems can help identify, access and obtain data, documents and literature needed for problem-solving and decision-making....[2]

In order to reach the goals of Library 2000—to achieve information awareness and increase productivity—data and information would have to be delivered to library clients in their offices, homes, and dormitories.

Online Information System

The first phase of Library 2000 was the installation and implementation of the Online Information System, to provide online access to the library catalog and other bibliographic databases. The Library Systems Department, the Office of Computing Services, and the Information Systems Applications Department collaborated on the project. Each group brought specialized knowledge and talents that contributed to the rapid success of the project: the Information Systems Applications Department provided software support and testing; the Office of Computing Services was (and is) responsible for computer operations, systems programming, and network access; and the Library Administration was responsible for coordination of the project.

The library selected the BRS/Search software from BRS Information Technologies because it allows the full text of records to be searched for a word or phrase and supports full Boolean logic for combining search criteria. The software also includes modules to format data, provide customized searches, and handle messages between users and library staff. In 1985, the software was installed on the campus IBM 4381, and the library catalog database was mounted. Each student, faculty member, and staff member was issued a user number, a password, and a user guide. The user numbers and passwords are for remote access; public-service terminals in the library do not require a user number. The message component of BRS/Search also was used to enhance the document delivery service for faculty. The new service was more convenient for both faculty and library staff.

Since 1985, five commercial databases have been added to the system. Magazine Index, Computer Index, Management Contents, and Trade and Industry were leased from Information Access Company. INSPEC, published by the Institute of Electrical Engineers in Great Britain, was added in December 1987. (INSPEC was chosen for its coverage of electrical engineering, physics, and telecommunications.) In February 1988, the Georgia State University Library catalog database was added—a significant enhancement, since Georgia Tech faculty and students borrow materials from the Georgia State library. Likewise, Georgia State has installed the Georgia Tech catalog database locally. The library recently has added Applied Science and Technology Index and the full text of the Commerce Business Daily. Test databases for use by library staff also are installed from time to time.

The Online Information System operates in command mode and is relatively easy to use. It has only one menu—a list of databases and the periods that they cover. The rest of the system is not menu driven and uses the BRS command structure. Since most students and faculty at Georgia Tech are computer literate and have a basic knowledge of mathematics, access at the command level is appropriate. The library staff were distressed initially by the decision to forgo a menu-driven system. However, they quickly realized that the command structure brought greater flexibility to the user, as well as the ability to define a search more precisely. For example, someone searching for recent articles on fiber optics could enter

Fiber adj optics and 1988
Books by Saul Bellow could be found by entering
Bellow.AU.
whereas books about Saul Bellow could be found with
Bellow.SU.

Someone wanting to know if the library had a subscription to *Management Solutions* could enter:

Management Solutions.TI. and Current

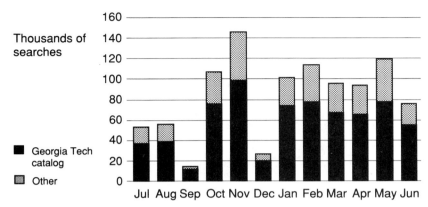

Figure 8.1   Searches on the Georgia Tech Online Information System in 1987/88 (by month).

People using the system in the library can consult staff at a help desk in the library's terminal cluster. People using the system in their offices can consult staff from the Library Systems Department by telephone. Starting in the spring of 1989, the library will give formal classes both for beginners and for advanced users. The classes will cover searching skills and other aspects of information finding.

The Online Information System's seventeen thousand users performed over a million searches in 1987/88. Figure 8.1 illustrates the distribution of searches through the year. The fall and winter quarters generally have higher enrollment than the spring and summer quarters, and the institute is closed for ten days in December; this accounts for the differences in numbers of searches from month to month. Figure 8.2 shows searches by database. The Georgia Tech database accounted for 70 percent of the searches; Magazine Index is the next most heavily used database, accounting for 14 percent of searches. It should be noted, however, that, since INSPEC had been available only since December, the usage shown in the figure is misleadingly low.

The Online Information System represents the first module of Library 2000 and brings bibliographic and full-text information to users' workstations. Future modules will include numeric, graphic, and video information.

Services on CD-ROM

The Tech library makes only limited use of CD-ROM. While abstracting, indexing, and other services are available on CD-ROM, the medium is not particularly effective for service to large populations over a campus

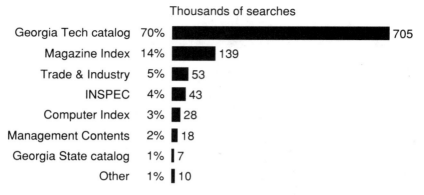

Thousands of searches

Georgia Tech catalog	70%	705
Magazine Index	14%	139
Trade & Industry	5%	53
INSPEC	4%	43
Computer Index	3%	28
Management Contents	2%	18
Georgia State catalog	1%	7
Other	1%	10

Figure 8.2 Searches on the Georgia Tech Online Information System in 1987/88 (by database).

network. Most current information services based on CD-ROM are designed as single-user systems, largely because the technology is not fast enough to support simultaneous interactive searching. If the library were to acquire abstracting and indexing services on CD-ROM, it would need about fifty workstations and multiple copies of the disks. Another disadvantage is that CD-ROM forces people to come to the library for information rather than delivering it to them. The library offers one heavily used service on CD-ROM because it is available only in that form. DATEXT provides financial and other information about publicly and privately held corporations in the United States and abroad. Faculty have requested that the service be made available on the campus network so that they can access it remotely and download data to their personal computers. The library has been working on getting permission to extract data from CD-ROM disks and make it accessible within the Online Information System. It is not clear, at this time, which vendors will supply data on corporations for access over the campus network.

The library has been a test site for CD-ROM products for the U.S. Bureau of the Census and the U.S. Patent Office. The census project provided access to demographic data by zip code. The software was limited in application and was not flexible enough to handle the myriad requests for population data. The U.S. Patent Office issued its CASSIS classification system on CD-ROM for testing. The test program, intended to support searching for patent information, was designed to reduce the use of the Patent Office's online system. This program has been moderately successful. Both tests used single-user personal computers with CD-ROM players.

Digital Software Library

One CD-ROM service offered over the campus network is Digital Equipment Corporation's Education Software Library. Departments with one or more Digital workstations subscribe to the Software Library on an annual basis. This entitles them to access and use any or all of the thirty programs offered. When they access the system, they identify themselves and download the software they need to their hard disks from a VAX file server with a CD-ROM reader. Users have downloaded an average of five packages per computer. Prior to the installation of this system, library staff members would carry tape cassettes across campus and install the software on the user's computer. CD-ROM access, though slow, is faster than waiting for a library staff member, and software can be downloaded on demand.

The Education Software Library has made it easy for subscribers to use software legally and to evaluate various software packages without purchasing them individually. The service has been implemented by other universities, but Georgia Tech is the only location where it is operated by the library instead of the computing center.

Other Library Systems

The Tech library has focused on delivering information to the user; therefore, it has chosen not to implement an integrated library automation system. Market offerings do not satisfy our requirements for full-text searching or efficient housekeeping and accounting; the systems appear to mechanize manual functions without enhancing library operations. Their limited capabilities make them a poor choice for the future.

Many librarians argue that users should have access to circulation and order records so that they can determine if a needed document is on order or checked out. Such a service is hardly necessary at Georgia Tech. Here, faculty and staff do not have to come to the library in order to use its services; documents and other materials are delivered to them directly. The Tech library staff are responsible for obtaining documents or information and will find them locally or through another library or document delivery service. When copies of articles are supplied, faculty do not care whether they come from the Tech library or elsewhere.

Circulation

In 1988, the library's circulation system, SIRSI, had been running on a Texas Instruments 990 for eight years. That fall, the system was upgraded and is now running on a MicroVAX. The SIRSI circulation system now will serve as an inventory control system and a backup to the Online Information System. During the three years that the online system has been operating, downtime on the IBM has been minimal. However, should the network or the IBM mainframe go down, staff can search the catalog on SIRSI.

Purchasing and Receiving

Library acquisitions are controlled manually. While several acceptable library purchasing systems are on the market, they are bundled into integrated systems that the Tech library does not want.

Serials control—keeping track of individual issues of periodicals—currently is done through a vendor in Boston. That system, based on a remote mainframe, will be transferred to a local system on a personal computer by 1990.

Communicating with Users

Technology has enabled new services that enhance productivity and staff communication. For example, all staff at the library, from the shipping room clerk to the director, have access to electronic mail and an electronic library bulletin board. Using electronic mail, staff members can communicate with the institute's faculty, students, and staff, as well as with each other. The internal bulletin board allows communication with the staff as a whole and reduces the need for phone calls and paper memos.

The library also maintains two news systems on campus mainframes for faculty, staff, and students. A library bulletin board operates on a Cyber 990 computer used by students and faculty. News, such as the acquisition of new databases or journal subscriptions, is announced on the bulletin board, which also functions as a forum where users can air problems, ask questions, and make suggestions. The library staff responds to questions and other items daily. A news service also is maintained for the IBM mainframe users on the PROFS office automation system.

We also have taken steps to prepare students for the increasingly complex, information-oriented world into which they will graduate. In 1985, the W. M. Keck Foundation gave a grant to the library, based on the premise that the success of a learning society in the information age will be determined by the ability of people to find, obtain, and integrate information and knowledge to enrich their personal and professional lives. The specific goals of the grant are to develop innovative, discipline-oriented information courses in management, electrical engineering, and chemistry and to develop student skills in information and data retrieval, storage, use, and analysis using online information systems and personal computers.

As part of this program, the existing course in chemical literature was enhanced to provide greater access to online sources of chemical information. New courses were developed for the College of Management and the School of Electrical Engineering. Initially, enrollment was limited to graduate students and seniors. Now the courses are open to all upper-level undergraduates. They involve lectures, demonstrations, and labs where students gain hands-on experience with a variety of databases. The management course stresses information for management and practical experience with internal and external bibliographic, full-text, and numeric databases. The course in electrical engineering includes modules on patents, specifications, standards, manufacturers' catalogs, legal resources, and other sources. Both courses include discussions of copyright and access to information for personal use, such as airline fares and schedules, movie reviews, or advice on how to buy a car. Students have been enthusiastic in their praise of the new courses and their instructors.

Learning in the classroom and the self-motivated learning that takes place in the library are different experiences. The benefits of self-motivated learning are intangible. The Online Information System and the information courses, both those being taught now and those under development, are intended to help students to learn how to learn. The grant has supported progress toward the goals of Library 2000: creating a rich learning environment for students, and ensuring that every Tech graduate will be information literate.

Issues Facing Today's Librarians

The context in which today's librarians must make decisions is changing rapidly. Externally, they must deal with a publishing industry that is wrestling with rising costs and the problems of pricing new types of products. Internally, delivering information to users' desks, instead of requiring them to come to the library, raises new operational issues and requires new expertise. As Georgia Tech has been developing its Online Information System, some particular issues have emerged as important.

External Issues
While electronic information will be applied in many areas and become increasingly essential, print will not disappear. The publication of books and paper journals and magazines will continue and increase. Dreams of the reforestation of the United States are not likely to become reality.

Books intended to be read from cover to cover will survive. People are not likely to read poetry, drama, fiction, history, or philosophy from a screen. Books can be taken anywhere. Paper magazines can be carried in a briefcase or backpack. Although some scholarly journals will become totally electronic, many probably will survive on paper. People like to skim and browse through new issues, and this is much easier to do in print than on a screen.

Libraries will continue to buy paper products for many years to come. However, they may not store paper copies of journals and magazines, since media such as optical disks offer great advantages and binding, maintaining, and housing paper volumes are becoming increasingly expensive. Economics and technology will favor electronic storage in the library of the future.

Books and journals will escalate in price whether they are published electronically or on paper. The major cost associated with publication is editorial, intellectual, "people" cost. This cost is unlikely to decline in the future. Journal issues are larger than they were ten years ago and contain more information. Costs increase with the number of pages. In science and technology, the price problem has been exacerbated by the declining dollar: most foreign science and technology journals have almost doubled in price in the past three years. Since libraries are the primary customers for journals, pooling subscriptions does not reduce cost; instead, it simply causes publishers to raise prices on the smaller number of subscriptions so that they can recoup costs and realize a reasonable return on investment.

Traditional publishers of serials derive the major portion of their revenues from the sale of print subscriptions. Many scholarly publishers rely exclusively on libraries for their revenues. During the last few years, this revenue base has been eroded by cancellations and the use of online services. Publishers are still experimenting with pricing products on tape and CD-ROM. Many publishers have yet to formulate rational pricing schemes for electronic products; they continue to follow the pricing practices developed for print. In the long run, publishers of abstracting and indexing services, statistical compendia, directories, and other items containing information that must be kept current must adjust to a new environment in which print is not the medium of choice. Both libraries and publishers must adapt to the new conditions.

Internal Issues

Delivering information to users rather than forcing them to go to a library poses new challenges that were not critical to the operation of a paper-based, collection-driven library. A major issue is the cost of an online information system; another is the organizational responsibility for such a system. Perhaps less obvious are issues arising from the changing expectations of users and the penalties of success.

Costs of Information Delivery

The installation of an online information system does not reduce cost. Online information systems require additional staff, computing support, networking, and database licenses. While the library may be able to cancel subscriptions to abstracting and indexing services, it cannot cancel core journal subscriptions or curtail the purchase of books.

At Georgia Tech, we have canceled print versions of indexing and abstracting services now available on our own online system. We also have canceled subscriptions to little-used services or those that are accessed more efficiently online. From 1986 to 1988, we canceled approximately $45,000 worth of subscriptions.

The cost of operating Georgia Tech Library's Online Information System was approximately $1 million in 1987/88. Seventy percent of searches were performed on the Georgia Tech and Georgia State catalog databases, but there were also 280,860 searches of commercial databases leased from publishers. If these searches had been done using remote commercial services, the cost, at an estimated $25 per search, would have been $7,021,500.

While the cost per search on a local computer is substantially lower than the commercial equivalent, leasing databases is significantly more expensive than buying the corresponding services in paper. A key question is how these services should be financed. If users are charged for the service, use will decline. However, since the value of information is intangible, it is not possible to determine the value lost. At Georgia Tech, the funding for the Online Information System has come from the institutional budget and from grants. Expansion of the system will require additional funds or the imposition of user fees.

Collaboration with Computing Services

While computers and networks are making it easier for people to acquire data, the data-processing operation alone cannot convert that raw data into useful information or knowledge. The computer cannot think, intuit, invent, or innovate. Despite the tendency to confuse means with ends in information operations, the fact remains that books, journals, databases, networks, and software are all tools, the means by which people acquire information to answer questions, solve problems, make decisions, and achieve a desired result. Each information seeker or computer user brings a unique mind-set to problem solving and responds differently to systems designed for general use. The problem is not new: tailoring information systems to users' needs has been a challenge since 300 B.C., when the first library to manage information and make it available for individual use was established in Alexandria.

Data-processing staff bring knowledge of systems, hardware, and software to the organization. Their main preoccupation is to make the hardware and software work. Their systems process raw material—data—into a useful product—information. However, they rarely deal with the behavioral or cognitive aspect of information. Librarians, on the other hand, have been dealing with the personalities and cognitive styles of individuals for over two thousand years. They are trained to ask the information consumer the right questions about needs, context, and forms of information. They add value to the raw material. Both sets of talents are needed to produce a successful online information system.

Both the computing center and the library use significant portions of institutional funds to perform their functions. Merging their operations is not likely to result in cost savings. Coordination and collaboration at Georgia Tech has been achieved by each organization recognizing its unique talents and contributing those talents to a common project.

Changing Consumer Expectations

Consumers of both computing and library services increasingly demand more service and value. The shift in consumer expectations has changed the way computing centers and libraries do business and will continue to stimulate more changes. It is also moving the costs of doing business away from the consumer and placing a greater burden on the institution. In the old days, when faculty or students wanted information, they traveled to the library, searched a card catalog, found books on shelves, and hoped that they had found the information or data they needed. The major cost associated with this activity was the value of the user's time. Under the new system, an information-finding problem that once might have consumed an hour of time takes five to ten minutes and can be completed without the user leaving the office or home. Cost and inconvenience have been reduced for the user, but the cost to the institution has increased.

The success of the online system has created another new problem: it has raised expectations that cannot be fulfilled in the near future. Faculty routinely request that the full text of particular journals be made available online at no cost to them. They fail to realize that, even if the publisher were willing to provide the tape, the price of the journal and cost of disk storage would be unaffordable. At Georgia Tech, we are working with publishers to come up with solutions acceptable to all parties concerned.

Off-Campus Use

Another serious issue has been raised by success. Georgia Tech receives several requests each month from people and businesses off campus wanting to access the online system. These requests have been refused, because contracts with database producers prohibit the resale of the service to anyone and limit usage to Georgia Tech faculty, staff, and students. However, by the end of 1989, the Georgia Tech catalog will be made available to off-campus users through a commercial database vendor.

Staff

The new library environment has caused some discomfort and uncertainty among some members of the staff, who are not sure what their new role is or how to make the changes necessary to integrate the technology into their daily activities. Some would like to return to the familiar paper library, but others have been excited and enthusiastic and want to move faster to bring on new services.

In order to overcome insecurities and anxieties, staff have attended workshops and training sessions to improve their searching skills, learn new techniques, and find out about new databases. In meetings with staff and faculty, the library administration stresses service to people rather than the collection. In recruiting new staff, potential employees are told that the Georgia Tech Library is not a traditional academic library and that the emphasis is on solving problems for people, not on providing books.

Toward the Goals of Library 2000

The goals of Library 2000 are gradually being realized. Information available over the campus network now includes bibliographic and full-text databases. Students, previously denied access to commercial databases like INSPEC, now have free access. Searches that used to require many paper volumes and many hours now can be done in fifteen minutes from an office, dormitory, or campus cluster.

Productivity

Productivity of faculty and students is difficult to measure, but anecdotal accounts indicate that it has increased. Faculty and students have reported that database searches have allowed them to save time, acquire new information, and avoid costs. For example, several people have said that using the Computer Index has led them to make better decisions when buying computer hardware and software. There also have been some unexpected testimonials. For example, a member of the English Department, who teaches technical writing, reported that the INSPEC database, which covers physics and electrical engineering, is the best service the library has provided.

Information-resource productivity has increased dramatically. During the year prior to the local installation of INSPEC, library staff performed fewer than five hundred searches of that database through commercial services, at a cost of $45,000. During the first six months of local INSPEC service, more than forty-three hundred searches were done by faculty and students. More library materials are being used by more people. This increased usage is reflected in higher photocopying volume, an increased number of requests from faculty for delivery of documents, and greater in-house use.

Information Delivery
The library has not yet succeeded in delivering all forms of information to the user's personal computer or workstation; however, it has made a solid start. The bibliographic databases and the full text of the Commerce Business Daily are the beginning. The next stage will move beyond bibliography and include more full-text databases, numeric data, and graphics. Numeric data from several U.S. government agencies soon will be available on a file server. Software for statistical analysis will be available on the server, and users will also be able to download files across the campus network in standard formats for use with spreadsheets or other personal computer software.

The library has been working very closely with two U.S. government agencies on graphics and mapping projects. By 1991, these projects should be ready for campus use. Implementation will depend on the availability of funds to purchase equipment and of systems staff time to devote to the projects.

Learning Environment
Students have a richer learning environment than they had three years ago. For both course work and personal needs, they have access to a larger store of information that is easier to use. Graphics, full text, numeric data and audiovisual facilities will add further enrichment.

The goal of ensuring that every Tech graduate is information literate is gradually being realized. The expansion of course offerings and training sessions will contribute to its fulfillment. The W. M. Keck Foundation grant has made it possible to acquire databases and provide facilities and funds for the development and implementation of discipline-oriented information courses.

Personalized Systems

Personalized information systems are still in the pilot stage. The Online Information System was created for general use and has no facility to accommodate individual styles. While BRS/Search provides great flexibility, individuals may want a front-end or user interface tailored to a particular problem set or style. Both users and library staff have much to learn about how people articulate their needs and how these specific needs can be satisfied on an ongoing basis.

During the pilot stage, library staff and faculty will test customized search profiles—sets of searches, specified by the user, that will be performed automatically as new records are added to the databases. The faculty members will receive search results by electronic mail. After three to six months, they will be interviewed about the overall effectiveness of their profiles and the usefulness of the citations or data received. Profiles will be adjusted and tested until they satisfy user needs. This program was implemented in the spring of 1989.

Challenges

The Library 2000 program is achieving progress toward its stated goals. However, some areas still need attention and improvement. The study of human/information interaction has not begun nor even been scheduled. Ideally, this study will be an interdisciplinary effort that will lead to the more effective design of information systems and user interfaces. This is just one of the important challenges ahead for librarians.

John Sculley, writing about information technology, said,

> This is a new vision that looks at information technology as a transport for the mind, a way of expanding our personal boundary of knowledge, our creativity, and our ability to be more productive, and it will help us learn to communicate, to work, and to entertain ourselves in ways we never before imagined....This poses a formidable challenge to educators—teach the rest of us how to cope with the acceleration of knowledge and especially teach the young people (who are going to spend the majority of their lives on the twenty-first century) the process of learning.[3]

While most students entering college or university today are comfortable with computers, they often lack learning skills, general knowledge about the world, and the motivation for learning on their own. Many students are technically competent but socially and culturally ignorant.

Successful living in the twenty-first century will depend on lifelong learning and the ability to integrate and synthesize information to create new knowledge. Sculley's challenge is formidable.

In the old days, the librarian served as the keeper of books, journals, and catalogs and also as an advisor, teaching the reader how to find and use the information in the collection. These basic purposes have not been subsumed or supplanted by technology as the library has taken on new roles and functions.

As Vartan Gregorian recently observed,

> The libraries carry our nation's heritage, the heritage of humanity, the record of its triumphs and failures, the record of man's intellectual, scientific and artistic achievements....They are windows to the future. They are sources of hope, self renewal, self determination, autonomy, and—to use a new word—empowerment.[4]

Librarians have an obligation and responsibility to preserve the records of humanity's achievements, failures, history, and culture. In the Georgia Tech Library collection is the history of science and technology. Our students can see, touch, and read the original works of Newton, Pascal, Einstein, Bernoulli, and others. We have an obligation to preserve this history for future generations.

Our role also includes the functions of information specialist and information manager. The value of information in any form depends on the ability of a person to use it. By itself, the information has no value. Libraries can be critical links between people and information they need to use.

We also have an obligation to prepare young people for life in the twenty-first century. We no longer can be merely custodians of the books. As well as preserving the history of the institution and the history of science and technology, our role at the Georgia Tech library is to provide the environment, motivation, tools, and guidance for lifelong learning.

References

1. "Georgia Tech Fact Book 1987–88" (Georgia Institute of Technology, Atlanta, Georgia, 1988.)
2. Horton, Forest Woody, Jr. "Information Literacy vs. Computer Literacy: Raising the Level of Awareness to the Knowledge Explosion." *ASIS Bulletin* 9 (April 1983): 16.

3. Sculley, John. Foreword to *Information Technology: The Trillion Dollar Opportunity,* by Harvey L. Poppel and Bernard Goldstein (New York: McGraw-Hill, 1987), p. xiii.
4. Gregorian, Vartan. *Research Libraries Group News* 15 (January 1988): 11.

Chapter 9

University of Southern California

Margaret L. Johnson
Peter Lyman
Philip Tompkins

T

he history of the University of Southern California parallels that of the city of Los Angeles itself, and USC's academic programs reflect the dynamic economic and social life of the city. From its schools has come the leadership of the city: business and law; aerospace and engineering; communication and the arts, including cinema, music, and drama; medicine and medical research, dentistry, and pharmacy; education; the sciences; and the social sciences.

USC is a private university, with the traditions and culture that that suggests, but its size is that of a public institution, and its academic programs provide the educational foundation for much of the region's culture and economy. USC offers degrees in 183 fields of study and supports twenty professional schools in addition to the central College of Letters, Arts and Sciences. Nearly two thousand full-time faculty members serve 30,500 full- and part-time students. In 1988/89, USC also employed approximately fifteen hundred part-time faculty on the University Park campus.

On the same site since USC's founding in 1880, the University Park campus now comprises one hundred major buildings spread over approximately 150 acres about five miles south of downtown Los Angeles. Seven miles away, the Health Sciences campus has eighteen buildings on approximately fifteen acres adjacent to the Los Angeles County–USC Medical Center. Since 1960, the university has been a member of the Association of American Universities, the body that unites the fifty-six most prominent research universities in the United States.

Recent years have been a time of change and growth both in computing services and in the library at USC. In its 1986 reaccreditation self-study, the university identified the development of the library system and a new-generation computing environment for the campus as two high priorities necessary to support the academic community. Close cooperation between the University Librarian and the Vice Provost for Academic Computing led to joint initiatives for developing new information technologies and resources. A convergence of interests is reflected in the creation of a jointly sponsored Center for Scholarly Technology that is to coordinate activities between the two divisions and provide leadership in developing new information technologies for a Teaching Library, a new facility that will use information technologies to foster teaching and learning at every level of the curriculum.

This chapter focuses on the priorities, goals, and decisions that have guided development and innovation in the library during this decade, most especially since June 1984, when Charles Ritcheson assumed leadership of the university libraries.

The Library and Its Strategy

The Central Library System encompasses the Doheny Memorial Library (which houses the general collection and the undergraduate College Library), twelve specialized subject libraries that support the major academic programs on campus, and six satellite libraries. The system is administered by the University Librarian, who also has the rank of Dean and Vice Provost. The two affiliated special libraries—for Law and Health Sciences—function separately.

The central library system now holds two-and-a-half million volumes and over two million microforms, receives eighteen thousand serials, expends $3.8 million annually for library materials, and employs 94 professionals and 140 support staff. Its total budget is $12 million.

Physical access to information sources is through the library's fourteen campus collections, document delivery services, and interlibrary borrowing from research libraries throughout the United States. Library collections are augmented by cooperative collecting arrangements with other major research libraries in the region, facilitating access to needed materials regardless of location.

Technical processing operations are automated to provide access to the most current information about the acquisition, organization, and location of the library's collections. Public-service units provide specialized collections and user-oriented services according to the characteristics and needs of the disciplines. Instructional programs teach the university community how to use new kinds of library resources.

Electronic access to bibliographic records is available through the online catalog, known as HOMER, and through USCinfo, USC's electronic library of bibliographic databases, which runs on an IBM mainframe housed in the University Computer Center and may be accessed over the campus networks. In addition to the USC community, USCinfo's users include members of the Electronic Library Consortium, five private liberal arts colleges in the Los Angeles basin. USC also is linked to a number of national online networks. Its membership in the Research Libraries Group (RLG) is pivotal because it provides electronic access to some forty of the premier research collections on the North American continent and in Great Britain.

The University Library also supports the development of software for accessing and manipulating information and provides hardware and training through "satellite libraries," storefront libraries located in student activity areas. These satellites contain microcomputers that can access USCinfo over a campuswide network and are staffed by librarians ready to train students in the use of information resources. Currently, there are six such satellites; in 1989, another four will be opened.

To quote from a self-study done by the library four years ago, "the basic goal of the USC Library system is to support instruction and research at the University by collecting, preserving, and disseminating recorded knowledge through both automated and conventional services." Following this general statement, the library further defined its role in the area of academic information services: "Leadership in innovative campus information services is exemplified by coordination of automated academic information; through monitoring the development of and interaction among information technologies, collections, and users; and through instruction and assistance in the application of information technology to scholarship, research, and teaching. Services and programs developed by local experts are actively publicized and marketed."

The role of the librarian has been reexamined, particularly in relation to teaching and the dissemination of information. Even though there is great potential for storing and transmitting information electronically, the printed book will remain a primary format for storing and disseminating information for years to come. The library maintains the responsibility for printed materials and their relationship to the instructional and research activities of the institution but also seeks to identify how access to information can be increased through the use of computer technology. Planning for the future must include strategies for providing economical access to information regardless of format and, ideally, for supplying library patrons with the materials they need in the format of their choice.

The Teaching Library

A primary instrument for executing this transition is the Teaching Library, planned to open in the fall of 1993, which will contain materials that support the instructional activities of the faculty, while the Doheny library and the thirteen specialized subject libraries will contain research materials. The working assumption is that, for the next five to ten years, most of the information in electronic form will be of a bibliographic nature (such as indexing and abstracting services) but that the full text of some material will be available.

The Teaching Library will be built around the new roles that technology should play in teaching and learning. It will integrate new technologies with traditional information sources, interweaving research materials and technology in attractive, flexible space conducive to basic research and study. Here, students will find a place to read, interpret, discuss, and synthesize information developed from books, journals, optical disks, computer-assisted instruction, microforms, and other audiovisual materials. There will be workstations, study spaces, individual carrels, group discussion rooms, and rooms for working with the various audiovisual materials. Faculty and students will come to the Teaching Library to learn about the resources and to locate information, no matter what the format. The intention is to provide an environment where students can learn to master any technology or information resource they may encounter in a world in which the pace of technical change and the volume of information available continue to increase.

The Center for Scholarly Technology was established recently as a joint project of the University Library and Academic Computing to coordinate planning between the two organizations and to foster the close cooperation that their common goals and projects obviously require. In the next year, it will be the mechanism for developing new kinds of library environments to encourage faculty to use information technologies for teaching and research. The center will play a major role in planning for the Teaching Library.

The Campus Computing and Networking Environment

Reflecting the reality of a computing culture in which faculty typically prefer desktop computing, USC's strategy for academic computing is based on campus networking services. Within Academic Computing, the University Computing Services (UCS) operate two IBM mainframes (an IBM 3090 and an IBM 3081), three Digital VAX/VMS time-sharing systems, an Alliant FX/8, and numerous networked workstations. Since computing power is increasingly moving from the computer center to the users' offices or homes, mainframes and workstations are being defined conceptually as nodes on a network. Two main campus networks exist. The first, based on asynchronous data switches from MICOM, provides terminal access over five thousand lines to three thousand ports on a variety of time-sharing hosts. The second is a high-speed campus backbone, USCnet, which is a fiber-optic network based on Ethernet. Each network provides access to regional, national, and international networks for research (SDSCnet to the San Diego Supercomputer Center, ARPANET, NSFNET, and CERFNET) and education (BITNET).

The networking orientation has two great advantages. First, it encourages rational planning because it enables faculty and students to share scarce and expensive resources, while giving them immediate control over dedicated local resources—the greatest (and most interesting) challenge to Academic Computing is making a complex and heterogeneous network of computing resources appear seamless to the network users. And, second, with its networking orientation, Academic Computing seeks partnerships with USC's academic programs. USCinfo, the bibliographic information system, is an example of a joint project: the library's IBM mainframe is viewed as a network database server; Academic Computing provides programming and maintenance support, while the library defines the information needs of the campus, designs the interfaces, and provides training.

The networking orientation requires close cooperation with the library, since every network node should have access to the electronic resources of the library. This principle was established on campus by the library itself, through the creation of the satellite libraries in 1985, and has since become part of the university's academic computing policy.

The Convergence of Library and Computing Services

In 1986, the library participated vigorously in discussions within the university administration about the organization of computing. These discussions were occasioned by the departure of the senior administrative officer responsible for administrative and academic computing. An organizational convergence of the library and academic computing services, like that at Columbia, was considered, but the final decision was to create the new position of Vice Provost for Academic Computing. This vice provost and the University Librarian are both senior members of the staff of the provost, the chief academic officer of the university. Although organizationally separate, there is a functional interdependence between the two organizations, focused on USCinfo and the design of the Teaching Library.

The two organizations are separate except for the Center for Scholarly Technology. The director of the new center reports to both the University Librarian and the Vice Provost for Academic Computing. The center's interests naturally overlap those of library services. As curriculum software is developed, it should be made available as a library service. In some instances, the curriculum software should incorporate library resources (such as access to general bibliographic information or to special databases created by librarians of citations or full-text material related to the curriculum). Specialized software for areas such as music, cinema, and art are under development through cooperative projects involving teaching faculty, librarians, and technologists. The center also provides microcomputer training and consulting for instructional and information software applications. It includes a Software Development Group, which designs software for personal computers and workstations, with special focus on developing applications for the Teaching Library. The applications will be both for instruction and for accessing and manipulating information. Some of these applications will also be used in research libraries across the campus. The library satellites have become prototypes and test sites for new technologies. Through them, the center conducts experiments with hardware and software that may be incorporated into the new Teaching Library when it opens its doors in 1993.

Electronic Information at USC Today

During this decade, the library at USC has automated existing library processes and taken important steps toward establishing an electronic library.

Automation of Traditional Library Processes

The library began the automation of traditional library processes in 1980. Committees were formed to review state-of-the-art systems. The projected cost of developing and maintaining an in-house system suggested that a complete system supplied by a vendor would be more feasible. The original request for proposals identified all requirements for an integrated library system. After reviewing existing systems, the library selected the GEAC system. GEAC's response indicated that a circulation module was already available and that others (for acquisitions, cataloging, and an online catalog) were under development.

With the arrival of the hardware and software for the circulation system in February 1981, the arduous task of determining circulation parameters and loading the database began. Existing circulation policies were reviewed and translated into "computer tables" or changed to take full advantage of the automated system.

While the library was looking for a library automation system, it had begun retrospective conversion of the catalog to machine-readable form. Two separate studies were done to determine what records to convert. The first compared circulation statistics and call numbers for the collection as a whole. Based on the results of this comparison, the most frequently circulated parts of the collection were selected for conversion. As the library got closer to implementing the circulation system, the second study was done, to check whether the library had met its goal of having 60 percent of each specialized subject area converted before starting to use the circulation system. Like the first study, it compared the part of the collection circulating to the overall size of the collection; however, comparisons were made by subject area, rather than for the collection as a whole. It revealed different circulation patterns in certain subject areas, particularly philosophy, music, art, and architecture. Additional catalog records were converted as necessary to reflect these patterns so that the library could meet its overall goal.

Staff also reviewed the full bibliographic record that eventually would be used for an online catalog to determine what elements should be included in the circulation record. A task force studied the capabilities of the GEAC circulation system and decided to load complete bibliographic records to take advantage of the public access mode. This feature permitted the library to use the circulation system as an interim catalog and so gain experience with a public online catalog from the start.

The first terminals were put in the College Library when the circulation system/interim online catalog became operational in January 1983. It had taken two years from the arrival of the hardware and software to convert catalog records and implement the system. Over the next five years, additional terminals were added, the card catalog in the main library was closed, and access to the catalog was provided through the University Computing Network.

In late 1983, the vendor made the acquisitions module available; it was reviewed, approved, and purchased. This system was much more difficult to implement, because of the accounting and invoicing functions. Setting up and handling accounts required a basic understanding of accounting principles, placing new demands on the acquisitions staff. In a manual system, if mistakes are made when an order is placed, it is not too difficult to correct them later; an automated system, however, takes the original ordering information and automatically applies it to the receiving, invoicing, and accounting functions. The staff had to learn how the software programs interacted. Thus, although acquisitions software was used in fiscal year 1986/87, it was not until fiscal year 1988/89 that the system was implemented fully.

In mid-1984, a committee reviewed available online catalogs from a number of vendors. None offered any special advantages, and, given the ease of integrating software from the same vendor, the library decided to acquire GEAC's online catalog module. The process of planning for the online catalog and reviewing hardware and staffing needs then began.

Up to this point, a staff of two had operated the circulation system and implemented the acquisitions system. Additional staff were necessary if the library was to have a completely integrated, dependable system from which management information could be gathered. Two additional staff members were requested in the budgetary process: a professional librarian to head the unit and a computer operator for night operations. The unit head position was posted in January 1986 and filled the following April; the computer operator position was authorized in July.

Parameter requirements for the online catalog were defined, and the processes involved in reloading the database were identified. The entire bibliographic database, containing records created as early as 1976, was sent to UTLAS, a vendor of library bibliographic services, to be processed through their authority control service. This was to ensure that all name and subject headings in the catalog would be consistent and conform to current standards. After UTLAS returned the database tapes, the information was reloaded into the GEAC catalog system. Catalog records were linked to the circulation database, so that records displayed on the online catalog also would show the circulation status of items. The implementation of the online catalog was completed by August 1988.

USC does not have an automated serials control system, although it does have an automated union list of serials with issue holdings. This system was developed in-house and runs on the IBM mainframe. Titles are input manually after cataloging. This software originally was written in the late 1970s and redone in 1980. In the future, the library plans to provide access to the union list of serials through USCinfo. Existing systems for serials control are being evaluated, with the aim of integrating detailed information on serials holdings into the online catalog. At this point, about 80 percent of the titles currently received are in the online catalog.

Steps toward an Electronic Library

Once activities were under way to implement an integrated system for automating traditional processes, the library administration began to look toward the future. Since 1984, the library at USC has taken experimental, but practical, steps to to develop new kinds of library services and to provide new kinds of access to information. The first step was taken in July 1985 with the creation of a Division for Academic Information Services (AIS) within the library. AIS manages all automated library services, including the integrated library system (which was already well under way). AIS is also responsible for developing new projects related to electronic access to information, such as the establishment of the satellite libraries and the USCinfo system.

Satellite Libraries

The first activity of this division was to develop a proposal for a $2 million grant intended to fund the purchase of hardware and software and the support of staff to create new library programs using microcomputer technologies. The primary goal was to provide indexing and abstracting services in electronic form, with access in-house and from remote locations, including dormitories and homes. Integral to the proposal was the development of library satellite operations. Each satellite was to be located in a student activity area. Microcomputers linked to the university's MICOM computer network would provide students with access to word processing, bibliographic databases, reference works, and other campus computing resources.

The project was fully funded by the Ahmanson Foundation for a three-year period, supporting a staff of three and the cost of equipment and database leases. At the time of the grant request, academic and administrative computing services on campus were being reorganized. The library had been the prime mover in implementing its integrated library system and obtaining a grant for further development of electronic services; Academic Computing did not play a significant role until after major decisions had been made on hardware and software. From a management viewpoint, the project was treated as separate from the other day-to-day activities of the library. This enabled the division director to proceed quickly and in innovative directions.

Once the project was funded and a project librarian hired, detailed plans for the operation of the satellite libraries were developed. Two initial satellites were set up, one in a dormitory and the other in a student activity center. Students were hired to help maintain the operation. At the time, the IBM PC was the most logical choice as microcomputer, and the 3Com local area network that the library already had installed internally became the network of choice in the satellites. The initial activities included word processing, access to the online catalog, and an encyclopedia on CD-ROM. The CD-ROM software was on the file server, and a menu on the microcomputer directed students to the specific computers with CD-ROM capability.

At a minimum, all workstations now provide access to the online catalog and USCinfo, the ability to download and print bibliographic citations, and word-processing software for taking notes and preparing research papers. The satellite libraries also act as a research laboratory for developing new approaches to accessing information and incorporating access to library resources into the curriculum. Teaching and instruction in the use of the library's information services is an integral part of the mission of the satellite libraries. They are where students go to learn about the services and to receive hands-on instruction in accessing information for research and term papers.

USCinfo

While the satellite libraries were readied for operation, work progressed on the selection of hardware and software for loading and maintaining USCinfo, a major information database of indexing and abstracting services, aimed at the undergraduate students.

The choice of software was addressed first. The BRS/Search software was the most logical candidate: it already was being used for this purpose by a major database vendor and at other universities, could be used to develop local databases, would be easy for librarians to use, and could have a customized front end developed for end users. In the future, a gateway to the larger world of databases maintained by BRS could be added without additional training or support. Once the software was selected, the choice of hardware was easy—BRS/Search primarily runs on IBM mainframes. Advised by a part-time consultant, the library defined the hardware configuration and, in 1986, purchased an IBM 4381 with 20 gigabytes of storage.

Academic Computing agreed to maintain the library's IBM mainframe and to provide applications programming support to tailor the BRS front end to local needs, in exchange for being able to use the mainframe's surplus capacity as a time-sharing host for users of other software running in IBM's VM operating system. In 1988, the mainframe was upgraded to an IBM 3081D; it is now the major VM server on the campus network. The library is responsible for defining the user interface, determining the appropriate software for information needs, and defining and managing projects.

The library had been a pioneer in the use of microcomputers, databases, and networks and, as a result, considered itself a partner of Academic Computing in the development of campus computing resources. It became dependent on the resources of Academic Computing at about the time that Academic Computing began to redefine its philosophy away from the provision of computer cycles for expert users and toward a philosophy based on networking and reaching out to new computer users. In principle, the roles of the library and the computing organization as they relate to the provision of access to information are understood clearly; in fact, the library must compete with other projects for the time of an applications programmer. The arrangement undergoes constant discussion and adjustment; the library must depend on programmers from the computer center but, thus far, has no direct organizational control over them. Most recently, the liaison work has been led by the Director of the Center for Scholarly Technology, who is appointed to both departments.

As software and hardware were being selected for USCinfo, the library staff began corresponding with a large number of database vendors to determine their interest in leasing databases to individual educational institutions. Initial responses were not encouraging. Vendors either did not understand the project or required payment based on the number of searches or the amount of searching time. Since the project was using limited grant funds and usage could not be determined in advance, there was concern about making a financial commitment that could not be maintained. This is not an uncommon problem in the development of campus computing and information services and policies; vendors often are unprepared to deal with academic environments and needs, and a patient dialogue is required to inform each side of the other's needs. Over the last three years, the situation has improved significantly, and most vendors now are willing to lease database tapes for an annual subscription fee.

Aside from finding willing vendors, the project team had to identify potential databases to start the electronic library. A review of USC's search histories for remote DIALOG and BRS services identified the most heavily used databases. Keeping in mind the needs of undergraduates, the staff chose five indexes of general interest, all available from Information Access Company—Magazine Index, Trade and Industry, Computer Database, Management Contents, and the National Newspaper Index. These indexes were installed during 1987/88. Funds are available to maintain them and to add an additional nine bibliographic databases during the 1988/89 fiscal year. The additions planned are MEDLINE, PAIS, PsycINFO, and six indexes from the H. W. Wilson Company: Applied Science and Technology Index, Art Index, Humanities Index, Library Literature, General Science Index, and Social Sciences Index.

USCinfo first became available in a test mode in November 1987. A straightforward menu system was designed by librarians in the Academic Information Services Division. The menu system allows students to type in a string of words for searching purposes; the system assumes the Boolean operator "and" and searches for items containing all the specified words. Through the help system, training classes, and written documentation, students can learn more sophisticated search techniques. Early usage indicated that students found the database easy to use and were enthusiastic about its potential. Between March and October 1988, usage increased sevenfold, and statistics indicate that it continued to increase during the fall semester of 1988. The success of the service led to the decision to add the new databases. With more training and publicity, usage should be even heavier.

The USCinfo service is intended to introduce students to searching for references through online indexing and abstracting services (and, in principle, to extend their computer literacy to include database searching using Boolean operators). For the immediate future, reference librarians will continue to act as intermediaries for remote access to the more sophisticated databases, such as the citation indexes provided by the Institute for Scientific Information. USCinfo is available in the main library and the specialized subject units, in the five satellite libraries, from any computer hooked to the university's computing network, and from home. In time, it is expected to be the primary central information resource on campus and the anchor of the campus information networks.

The Electronic Library Consortium

As a major research library, we have accepted a community responsibility to assist smaller academic institutions through access to our collections. To this end, we developed the USC Electronic Library Consortium. One of the primary goals of the consortium is to give the faculty of small liberal arts colleges in the Los Angeles area access to research materials.

Five colleges belong to the consortium (there is a nominal annual fee for membership). They have electronic access to the online catalog and to some of the USCinfo databases. (Access to the databases is subject to negotiations with specific vendors.) The consortium members also have electronic access to the USC Doheny Express to request delivery of materials that they have located through the online catalog. A user services librarian at USC is responsible for training librarians at the member institutions, providing them with microcomputer disks for access to the service, and generally managing the services.

Project Jefferson

With the advent of Macintosh computers and, in particular, the development of the Mac SE and Mac II, the library, in partnership with faculty from the Department of Industrial Engineering and the Freshman Writing Program, began to develop curriculum software that would help students prepare research papers and use library resources. This cooperative effort, known as Project Jefferson, is being pursued under the auspices of the Center for Scholarly Technology. Apple Computer provided machines for the development of the software and for a microcomputer laboratory where the software could be used.

The software originally developed for this project made use of the new hypertext capability of Apple's HyperCard. It allowed students in the Freshman Writing Program to receive an assignment, search a limited database on the constitution that resided on the Macintosh computers in the laboratory, and prepare their research papers. The next version of the software will also enable students to search mainframe databases and download the results.

Management and Organizational Issues

In any organization, change raises issues for management. Organizational structure, funding, and commitment from the institution are particularly important for supporting the growth in automated library services and the new roles assumed by the library.

Organizational Structure

In the USC library, the organization of Academic Information Services points beyond the traditional role of library automation. AIS is responsible for the selection, design, installation, and maintenance of the library's automated integrated library system (circulation, acquisitions, online catalog, and serials). AIS also supports the automation of the library's administrative services, which are served through a local area microcomputer network with an internal electronic mail system and shared software on a file server. This support includes the operation of the local area network in the libraries and the satellites, the selection of appropriate hardware and software for personal computers, and the training of library faculty and staff.

AIS is responsible for electronic access to scholarly information and, in general, for the Central Library System's management and development of information technologies. It coordinates the technical aspects of the operations for USCinfo with the Director of the Center for Scholarly Technology. These technical aspects include equipment requirements and descriptions of machine-readable elements for the databases. AIS also monitors the installation, electrical wiring, and cabling of data-communication lines within the Central Library System.

Funding

Since 1984, costs for new projects have been supported by increased university operating funds and successful fund-raising by the library from private sources. The campus administration has supported the leadership role of the library since the receipt of the $2 million grant from the

Ahmanson Foundation in 1984. In 1989, the Center for Scholarly Technology will administer and develop instructional and information software and facilities across campus; these activities represent a new phase in the development of the original library satellites. They mark a transition to intensive program planning for the new electronic Teaching Library planned for 1993.

The Teaching Library will require major infusions of operating funds in the budgets of the University Library and Academic Computing, which already support USCinfo. Projections of requirements for new staff, hardware and software development, and user training currently are being developed. Much of the capital funding for the Teaching Library is secure, and an architect was selected in early 1989. The operating budget will be built incrementally over a three-year period beginning with the 1989/90 fiscal year; it will represent new funds allocated by the university administration to both the library and Academic Computing.

Institutional Commitment

Institutional commitment to academic computing, including the library's particular mission to support instruction and research in new creative ways, remains high. The commitment of the university's president to the design of a state-of-the-art electronic library—the Teaching Library—further confirms the allocation of resources necessary. The collaboration of librarians and faculty through the Center for Scholarly Technology in the Teaching Library will prove to be the single most revolutionary activity in integrating access to instructional and informational software at the University of Southern California. The Teaching Library will serve as a catalyst for change in the classroom, the culture of learning, and the role of libraries.

Evaluation and Future Plans

Lessons Learned

USC is committed to exploring the new library roles made possible by information technologies. Up to now, it has concentrated on networks, databases, microcomputers, and software development; in the future, it will build on new technologies for the delivery and storage of information, such as multimedia workstations and optical media. This has been a period of experimentation, in which the library has been the focus of development for microcomputer hardware and software, claiming a central role in using information technology to support the research and teaching missions of the university. This leadership is now redefining the relationship between the University Library and Academic Computing, on the one hand, and between the staff of "the electronic library" and the traditional library on the other.

The relationship with Academic Computing was uneasy when the library was dependent on computer center support but had no organizational leverage to give its projects priority. With the creation of the Center for Scholarly Technology, it is hoped that an organizational "umbrella" now exists that will be able to coordinate the activities of the two departments. The functional convergence and interdependence brought about by new technologies has led, by design, to a joint venture rather than an organizational merger.

The relationship between Academic Information Services and other library services is also evolving. Library automation projects have been integrated into the traditional library, but this has not been so easy for the new teaching missions implied by software development and the satellite libraries. In part, integration has been consciously avoided so that new directions could be explored fully without seeking a consensus. Since the support provided by the Ahmanson Foundation grant has ended and many of the experiments have proved successful, it is now necessary to define strategies for mainstreaming information technologies and new formats into the library units. Yet it is also important to continue to experiment.

What Next?

The introduction of technology into the library has given birth to new kinds of information cultures and to a second generation of projects that seek to resolve the thought-provoking contradictions that technology has brought into every research library. At USC, the Teaching Library program is the focus of this process of inquiry and experimentation aimed at discovering the library of the future in the contradictions

- between the traditional print library with its emphasis on the conservation of knowledge and the potential electronic library with its emphasis on the distribution of knowledge;
- between the need to create a library that will be an enduring and permanent part of scholarly life at USC and the need for a library that can keep pace with changes in technology and learning; and
- between a humanistic library of the spirit and the library of high technology.

We believe these contradictions are creative, not destructive; nevertheless, they do imply a fundamentally new direction in the library's vocation.

The Teaching Library must provide a humanistic setting for technology. This means, first of all, the humanistic use of computers to teach, to create a culture of learning among students, and as a medium for communication and for creativity. Until now, two voices have conducted the conversation of knowledge—those of human beings in dialogue, whether students, student and teacher, or librarian and student or teacher. The computer is to be the third voice in that conversation, raising or changing the level and type of information available and providing tools for analysis, tutorial advice and training necessary to use new technologies, and a medium for communication and expression.

But the challenges implicit in the contradictions are not limited to the Teaching Library—they affect every aspect of the library. The library is moving beyond the automation of paper processes to the creation of new kinds of information-intensive services in every dimension. We must ask some hard questions in this era of intensive change but limited budgets. How can technology-intensive services be integrated into the traditional print library? How can technology-intensive services based on different hardware and software—like GEAC, USCinfo, and different microcomputer operating systems—be integrated into coherent systems so that libraries and patrons do not have to learn new techniques for each new kind of information service? How can the academic computing organization and the library learn to be interdependent and perhaps build cooperative cultures, given their quite different histories and traditions?

At one point, critics imagined a future in which the library would become like the university museum, once a center of research, but now an anachronism. At USC, the goal is to create a library that will lead the information revolution in humanistic directions.

Chapter 10

Columbia University

Paula T. Kaufman

The administrators at Columbia responsible for providing traditional library and computing services recognized early in the decade that emerging computing and communications technologies would have an impact on the way that scholars do their work, necessitating a reexamination and rethinking of the organization, scope, and type of operations for which they were responsible. The Scholarly Information Center was created in response to such a reconceptualization and redefinition of the information infrastructure necessary to support the work of the institution's faculty and students.

The Scholarly Information Center (SIC) is designed to provide a total array of information services to the university community, typically envisioned as a user working at a desk or workstation and seeking information for the intellectual task at hand, regardless of format or computing capacity. The new organizational integration of library and academic computing activities has enabled the university to bring together a broad range of talents—disciplinary, technical, and managerial—with knowledge of and access to scholarly materials in a broad range of formats—from manuscripts and incunabula to electronic texts—in order to meet the needs of students and scholars whose academic requirements encompass all the human mind can imagine.

Library collections today are more than just the books held in the stacks of an individual institution. As scholarly output rises, as materials budgets fail to keep pace with inflation in publishing, and as the economies of scale in managing large research collections diminish, the "collection" must be considered to be whatever provides access to and delivers as much of what is needed as possible. Several factors are key to the success of this collection concept: the identification of collection strengths and individual items; the commitment and means to share resources among institutions; delivery mechanisms to speed the transmission and receipt of scholarly information and documents; reliable national and international telecommunications networks; and trained scholarly information specialists to help users identify, access, acquire, and use the raw materials of their work.

No university can develop these capabilities on its own. As well as working closely together within an institution, library and computing organizations must participate in national and regional cooperative efforts. Columbia, and the SIC in particular, is committed to collaboration and to sharing resources, expertise, and experience.

Just as the new national library will hold a virtual collection, the SIC is a conceptual organization—one without walls. It has brought together its impressive arsenal of resources without making physical changes or relocating staff. Like all dynamic organizations, the SIC is evolving. Created in January 1986 from the Columbia University Libraries and the Academic Computing division of the Columbia University Center for Computing Activities (CUCCA), the SIC's original configuration has changed only slightly since then. Figure 10.1 shows the organization chart in September 1988. Additional modifications undoubtedly will come as needs change and as the information landscape becomes ever more complex and costly.

Columbia University

Columbia University, a private, nonsectarian institution of higher education, ranks among the nation's top universities. Its two major campuses— Morningside Heights and Health Sciences—are in New York City; other campuses—most notably the Lamont-Doherty Geological Observatory— are in nearby New York counties. The university's 1,760 full-time faculty members teach in sixteen faculties and seventy-three departments of instruction, through which the university's academic activity is primarily conducted. Various other educational institutions, hospitals, and medical research institutes also are affiliated with the university.

The total enrollment at Columbia is approximately 18,500 students: two-thirds of whom are graduate, professional, and special students, and one-third of whom are undergraduates. The distribution of enrollments, joined to the university's traditional strengths in the arts and sciences, the institution's emphasis on research, and its location in New York City, places different demands on library and computing services than those found at many other major universities in the United States. Research library materials, for example, are used much more heavily at Columbia than they are at the libraries of many colleague institutions.

Columbia University Libraries

The Columbia University Libraries (CUL) date to the beginnings of King's College in 1754 and now contain one of the most notable research collections in the country. Library resources on campus are centralized (all libraries except the Law Library are part of the CUL system), and CUL is organized in twenty-six units designed to provide materials, services, and support to disparate parts of the university community. Columbia's statutes prohibit the establishment of formal libraries outside the CUL system.

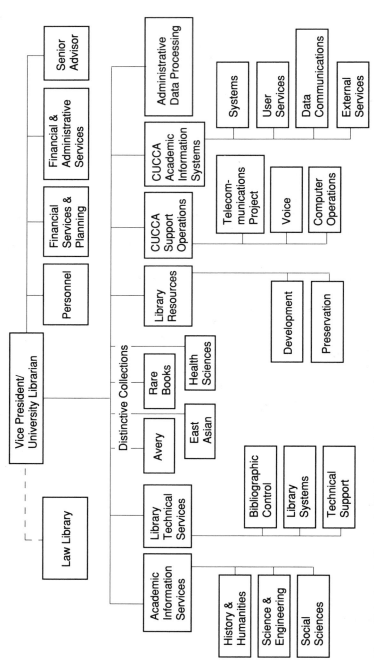

Figure 10.1 Organization chart of the Scholarly Information Center.

The CUL collection, which is the seventh-largest academic library collection in the United States, holds more than five-and-a-half million volumes, with more than one hundred thousand added annually. Additionally, the collection contains more than three-and-a-half million microform pieces, more than twenty-four million manuscript items, and a sizable number of CD-ROMs and other resources in electronic format. There are also important collections of maps, audio materials, scores, and pamphlets. As important to the university community, however, is the access CUL provides to resources held elsewhere. Columbia is a member of (and often helped to found) many local, regional, national, and international consortia and other organizations through which virtually the entire world of published scholarly information can be reached.

Of the twenty-six library units on three campuses (Health Sciences, Lamont-Doherty, and Morningside), twenty-two are grouped in three divisions within the Academic Information Services Group: Humanities and History, Science and Engineering, and Social Sciences. The other four libraries are designated as "distinctive" collections, so called because their collections are of unique depth and national significance: the Augustus C. Long Health Sciences Library; the Avery Architectural and Fine Arts Library; the Rare Book and Manuscript Library; and the C. V. Starr East Asian Library. The current organizational structure has evolved from that created after a 1970/71 study by Booz, Allen & Hamilton, Inc.[1] This study, carried out with support from the Council on Library Resources and the involvement of the Association of Research Libraries, has served as a model for some major research libraries. The organizational structure that it produced at Columbia permitted a fairly easy transition to the SIC.

Nearly fifteen thousand individuals use the libraries each weekday during the academic year, and about one million items are circulated annually. The collections are developed, organized, and processed by a staff of 156 librarians, 317 supporting, technical, and supervisory personnel, and a student work force equivalent to some 151 full-time employees. The University Librarian's position has been at the vice-presidential level for more than fifteen years.

Columbia University Center for Computing Activities (CUCCA)

In marked contrast to library services, academic computing at Columbia is highly decentralized. CUCCA comprises two divisions: Administrative Data Processing (ADP), with which we will not be concerned in this chapter, and Academic Computing, composed of Academic Information Systems and support groups for communications and computer operations, which merged with CUL in 1986 to form the Scholarly Information Center.

CUCCA Academic Computing (CUCCA for the remainder of this chapter) operates time-sharing services, a small number of microcomputer facilities for some instructional and research activities, and consulting and microcomputer prepurchase advisory services. It also manages a set of networks on campus and provides connections to local, regional, national, and international networks as well as direct connections to the John von Neumann supercomputer center in Princeton. CUCCA's staff of 125 maintains the backbone network (which uses the TCP/IP family of communications protocols), operates the central voice/data networks on the Morningside campus, maintains communications links to Columbia's other campuses, oversees the machine room and most of its equipment and systems, and provides consulting assistance for faculty and students. However, an ever-increasing proportion of academic computing done at the university, not unexpectedly, is under the aegis of individual schools and departments.

University Reporting Structure

In the early 1980s, Columbia abandoned a triprovostial structure in favor of a single provost who is responsible for developing, implementing, and periodically evaluating the university's academic programs and activities. At the same time, library and computing services were moved from the provost's office to that of the Executive Vice President for Academic Affairs, whose portfolio included athletics, the registrar and bursar, affirmative action programs, and the office of investments. After the creation of the SIC, the Vice President for Information Services and University Librarian, who is directly responsible for SIC operations, continued to report to this office. The newly created position of Assistant Vice President for ADP also reported directly to the executive vice president.

Problems and Changes
Predictable difficulties arose from this reporting relationship: academic matters were under the provost's aegis; the academic information infrastructure necessary to carry out academic activities was not. The exclusion of the SIC from participation in the institution's academic strategic planning processes and in its routine tactical planning activities caused a widening disjuncture between the SIC and the provost and faculty. Difficulties in coordinating, planning, and setting institutional priorities also spread. Some operational problems produced by the split

of academic and administrative computing also arose. As a result, and with the arrival of a new vice president in the summer of 1988, the university changed the SIC's organizational structure and reporting relationships. CUCCA, ADP, telecommunications, and the libraries now all report to the Vice President for Information Services and University Librarian, who reports to the provost.

Advisory Committees

Several university committees provide formal advice and support to the SIC. Of longest standing (since 1969/70) is the Senate Committee on Libraries, Computing Activities, and the Bookstore. Its responsibility is to review and recommend university policies to advance the role of the libraries in effecting the university's educational purposes. The more recently established Information Processing Advisory Committee (1986/87) is charged with providing advice to the vice president about policies for the SIC's academic computing operations. The newly appointed Committee on Scientific and Supercomputing provides strategic advice to the Assistant Vice President for Academic Computing. A Telecommunications Policy Committee advises the vice president about issues relating to the installation of a new digital voice-and-data system. Finally, a newly appointed (in 1987/88) Budget Advisory Committee helps provide academic input during the preparation and submission of the CUL annual budget. There are also a number of small advisory committees, which work with librarians responsible for the operations of department libraries.

Philosophy and Strategy for Library and Information Services

Purpose

The purpose of the SIC is to meet the scholarly information needs of the students and academic staff of the university by providing recorded information in the pertinent subject fields and by forming and maintaining a robust information infrastructure for the institution. Further, because many of its collections are of national and international importance, the University Libraries recognize an obligation to serve, not only the Columbia community, but also certain scholars and students from outside the university who require access to unique materials or specific distinctive collections. Similarly, CUCCA recognizes an obligation to help develop, participate in, and support regional, national, and international networking activities. CUCCA's role is not to be a "leading edge" organization but rather to support the needs of its users as solidly as possible.

Role

The SIC strives to fulfill its purpose by

- identifying and acquiring, or otherwise making available, materials in all formats necessary for instruction and research within the university or required to maintain the quality of distinctive collections;
- developing reference, consultation, bibliographic, instructional, and other specialized services that effectively and imaginatively reinforce academic objectives;
- making resources accessible through the support services and facilities of central and specialized library units, computer center offices, labs, terminal rooms, and scholars' workstations; and
- assuring the security, preservation, and condition of the collections, the networks, and centrally owned computing and communications equipment.

To meet these objectives, the SIC must offer its resources and services effectively and efficiently; it must also maintain close working relationships with university officials, faculty, and students. In addition, the SIC must work with other research libraries, academic computing organizations, associations, and cooperative organizations to enhance access to other resources and to develop mutually advantageous solutions to collective problems.

Decision and Planning Processes

Historic Evolution

During the last fifteen years, CUL's leadership has recognized the need for a formal body to provide the organization's planning structures and processes. In the mid-1970s, the Library Operations Committee consisted of the three group directors, the Assistant University Librarians for Planning and Personnel, and the heads of the distinctive collections.

The Library Operations Committee felt that it would be more effective if the assistant directors, who were closer to daily operations, were included. It experimented with a variety of committee structures for library planning and operations. At one time, a separate operations committee of the assistant directors met monthly, but it seemed to serve merely as a substitute for informal corridor discussions and was an impediment to implementation. When the SIC was formed, the structure described below was established; it has operated fairly successfully for the last two years.

Planning Council

The Planning Council is chaired by the vice president and is composed of the SIC's group directors, its Director of Personnel, the Directors of Budget and Planning for CUCCA and CUL, and the librarians of the four distinctive collections. The Assistant Vice President for ADP is also a standing member and attends when appropriate. The Planning Council's activities include the development of a strategic planning process and the consideration of a broad range of planning and policy issues of critical importance to the university. The group meets biweekly and, as part of its charge, identifies policy issues to refer for discussion/input to the Operation and Planning Council.

Operation and Planning Council

This council is purely a library organization. Its members are responsible for addressing and resolving issues of emerging concern and for informing the membership of important and impending changes in operational issues. The group meets monthly and is convened by the vice president.

CUCCA Managers

With the establishment of the SIC in 1986, the vice president formed a working group, known as CUCCA Managers. Members were managers from both sides of the merged organization: from CUL, the four group directors (all except the Resources group) and the head of the systems department; from CUCCA, four group managers and the manager of Financial and Administrative Services; from both groups, the directors of personnel. The group, which was chaired by the vice president, met monthly to deal with operational and policy issues. As the SIC matured, however, it became apparent that these issues could be handled more expeditiously through the SIC organizational structure and that a number of immediate and far-reaching issues, particularly those relating to telecommunications, networking, and the implications of the decline in external income, were more urgent.

Thus, a new, as-yet-unnamed group now meets weekly. It consists of the vice president, the Assistant Vice Presidents for Systems and ADP, the Director of Telecommunications, and the CUCCA Budget Manager. The former Director of CUCCA, who currently works part-time as the Senior Advisor for Information Strategy, completes the group.

Current Priorities

Through the planning structures and processes described above, the SIC has identified a number of areas that it considers to be most important for both the short and long run:

- improving access to and control of the libraries' collections by implementing an integrated functional computer-based system;
- improving services provided directly to end users, including access services, reference and consultation, and access to materials and equipment;
- developing and managing the collections to meet the curricular and research needs of the university community;
- providing inexpensive connectivity, including electronic mail and access to Columbia Libraries Information Online (CLIO), to everyone in the university community;
- continuing to upgrade the quality of the campus backbone network and the ability to maintain it;
- continuing to recruit and retain the best possible staff; and
- improving and maintaining physical facilities.

Under other circumstances, separate computing and library organizations would include most of these items on their individual lists of priorities. However, because they were developed and will be pursued by the combined SIC, we believe that the user will benefit from a more effective environment for accessing and utilizing information. The decision to amalgamate was based on the knowledge that electronic information services will be increasingly important to both research and instruction and that advances in technology will affect almost all library services.

Information Services

Automation of Traditional Library Processes
CUL began its automation activities more than two decades ago, when it developed and implemented batch systems to support acquisitions, reserves, and circulation. A shortage of resources limited the impact of this computerization, and the second two systems were neither implemented in any but the very largest of library units nor upgraded in any meaningful way. They are still operative today, on their proverbial last legs. No other stand-alone systems have ever been used.

Columbia was a charter member of the Research Libraries Group (RLG), which was founded by research universities and independent research libraries in 1974 to manage the transition from locally self-sufficient and independently comprehensive collections to a nationwide system of interdependencies in order to preserve and enhance the national capacity for research in all fields of knowledge and to improve the ability to locate and retrieve relevant information. In 1977, CUL started to catalog its books and serials through the Research Libraries Information Network (RLIN), which is RLG's automated information system; it began to use RLIN for acquisitions operations in the early 1980s. CUL now also makes extensive use of the RLIN interlibrary loan facilities and its archives and manuscripts control functions. The RLIN database integrates eight bibliographic files representing archival materials and manuscripts, books, machine-readable data files, maps, sound recordings, musical scores, serials, and visual materials from more than thirty-five institutions; this database is used extensively by reference librarians and scholars.

Online Catalog

Columbia Libraries Information Online (CLIO) is an information system of which the online public access catalog is a major component. The online catalog consists of two databases: materials cataloged after 1977 and materials on order or in process. CLIO also contains a two-year subset of citations from MEDLINE and a database of information about the libraries—schedules, locations, and the like.

CLIO currently runs on software (BLIS) originally leased through a contract with Bibliotechniques, Inc. The BLIS system runs WLN searching software in an ADABAS environment. CLIO is installed on an IBM 3083 acquired through an IBM Advanced Education Project grant and located in CUCCA's machine room. The system is maintained by staff from CUCCA and CUL. Cataloging and acquisitions still are done on RLIN, with records added to CLIO weekly from tapes.

When Bibliotechniques, Inc., declared bankruptcy in June 1986, a consortium of five institutions, led by Indiana University, arranged license agreements with WLN and Software AG. After an intensive comparative analysis of all viable systems, the SIC concluded that it would be better not to run the current system over the long term, primarily because development of the other components needed to create a fully functional integrated system—circulation, serials control, cataloging, and acquisitions—was uncertain. NOTIS was determined to be the software that best met Columbia's needs. It was installed in June 1988, and the SIC expects to make the information on CLIO available under NOTIS in the fall of 1989. Until then, it will continue to maintain and keep updated the current CLIO system.

Document Delivery

CUL does not offer document delivery services in the traditional sense of the term. A market research study conducted in 1984 uncovered little enthusiasm for direct delivery of documents and even less willingness to pay for the service. CUL staff think that this attitude will change as access to CLIO becomes more widespread. A follow-up survey will be done soon.

In the late 1970s, when financial pressures caused the cancellation of most subscriptions duplicated on the Morningside and Health Sciences campuses, CUL began, and still operates, a service to deliver upon request copies of articles or tables of contents to the nearest library. Users pick up the materials themselves. A 1984 experiment to substitute facsimile delivery for hard-copy delivery was not successful. Costs were high, and the quality of reproduction was unacceptable. Recent improvements in fax technology have prompted another exploration of this option. Some table of contents services have operated for years in the libraries serving science and social science disciplines. Headline services, derived from online database services, also are provided to area institutions; CUL staff post daily headlines from an international newspaper database.

Interlibrary Loan

Materials not available at Columbia may be requested and obtained at no cost to the user through CUL's interlibrary loan services at the Health Sciences and Morningside campuses. Staff use formal interlibrary loan services over networks, such as RLIN, OCLC, NLM's Regional Medical Library Program, and New York State's NYSILL; informal electronic mail channels, such as BITNET and NYSERNet; and the U.S. mails. The Law Library uses facsimile technology to send and receive documents, and planning is under way to introduce this service elsewhere on campus.

Reference Service

Reference service is one of CUL's traditional strengths. CUL had one of the first academic reference departments in the country, and reference services offered to the research community always have been state of the art. The ten editions of the American Library Association's *Guide to Reference Books* were edited by the three Heads of Reference in Butler Library from 1912 to 1987. The *Avery Index to Architectural Periodicals* also is produced at Columbia, at the Avery Architectural and Fine Arts Library, and is published both in print format and electronically on RLIN.

Reference service is very different today from what it was even five years ago. No longer do professional librarians spend long hours at reference desks, waiting for questions to be asked. At Columbia, librarians work with user services consultants to help individual scholars or academic departments identify, acquire or access, and use information resources and tools.

Over the last few years, SIC staff have provided many new services, often designed to help scholars in particular disciplines locate, use, and manage scholarly information. Here are just a few examples:

- Access to the online version of Chemical Abstracts Service is provided through the Chemistry Library, which manages the university's account with the American Chemical Society and provides training, documentation, and support. Users do their own searching from their workstations.

- The SIC reference and consultation staff provide training and support for scholars' use of ARTFL (a remotely located online database of more than fifteen hundred French language texts).

- Staff in the Science Division and Health Sciences Library present seminars for faculty and students on managing reprint collections, focused on using software for commonly used microcomputers.

- SIC staff evaluated more than a dozen bibliographic database management packages and disseminated the information to all faculty and many graduate students. Demonstration software and help are available in libraries and computer consulting areas.

- Support for projects awarded equipment from Columbia's IBM Advanced Education Project is provided by SIC staff. This includes assistance in determining needs, configuring hardware, identifying and acquiring software and data, and using remote networks.

Staff supporting users of the Mathematics/Science Library have been particularly concerned about the lack of sufficient resources to provide adequate reference services much of the time. As part of the solution, they are developing a "reference desk librarian," a simple expert system that will provide assistance with very basic requests (e.g., locations, simple reference tool use, citation interpretation) and direct users to staff located elsewhere. If successful, the technique might be extended to other small locations. As yet, there are no plans to offer the system over the campus network, because of software and resource limitations.

Access to Databases/Information Services

As scholars and students become more sophisticated information users, they increasingly use data in electronic media directly, rather than using librarians as intermediaries. The SIC staff spends considerable time helping users identify, locate, acquire or access, and learn how to use online databases themselves. Access to many of these sources can be gained by:

- individuals contracting with database vendors individually;
- the SIC arranging group licenses for individual direct access;
- the SIC making remote online databases available for individual users on publicly accessible equipment at no charge;
- CUL contracting with database vendors for large-use contracts and performing searches for individuals on a cost-recovery basis;
- CUL purchasing and making databases on CD-ROM available to users at no cost.

Thanks to a grant from the Pew Charitable Trust, Columbia has been able to make more than two dozen CD-ROM databases available at the university; it is studying the impact of this storage and delivery mechanism on instructional and research activities. Various types of databases are offered in this format: bibliographic, full text, statistical, and graphic. Most of the CD-ROM systems were placed in library units; however, some have been sited in academic departments, including MEDLINE in the School of Nursing and Thesaurus Linguae Grecae in the Classics Department. Comparisons among print, remote online services, locally mounted files, and CD-ROM versions are being studied. Through the grant, the SIC also has sponsored some of the Lamont-Doherty Geological Observatory's development of an optical storage system for geological information with a map-based interface.

During 1987/88, SIC staff serving the social sciences worked with a professor of political science to convert a book that was required reading for two courses to machine-readable form. After overcoming some unexpected difficulties in the scanning process, the text was made available over the campus network at no cost to students in a large undergraduate course and a small graduate seminar. Students in both courses are required to submit their papers, and comments on their classmates' papers, electronically. There are more than two hundred terminals available on campus for them to use. Although the results of the year-long project still are being analyzed, it appears that, for the most part, students preferred to read and study the printed, codex format. The greatest weakness of the electronic version seemed to be that the software did not permit precise searching for trends and ideas. SIC staff are now examining alternative software and, despite the results of this experiment, plan to continue similar projects.

The SIC is also in the process of establishing a Scholarly Resources Center to support the use of full-text materials in electronic format. The center will be located in Butler Library, which houses the humanities book, microform, and manuscript collections, and will contain a wide variety of texts and the software designed to analyze and manage them. Staff will be available for consultation on an individual or group basis.

Like most of its colleague institutions, Columbia supports the purchase of resources in electronic formats, as well as access to information stored remotely, from its materials budgets. These expenditures cover all but the most intricate and individualized database searches. At present, both types of purchases absorb less than two percent of the CUL materials budget but are expected to grow as scholarly information becomes increasingly available in nonprint formats.

In 1985, a committee appointed by the Executive Vice President for Academic Affairs developed a set of university policies for databases, stating that: information for research and scholarly purposes, regardless of format, should be available to all members of the university community; the university should provide access to the widest scope of databases possible; there should be bibliographic control and access to as many databases as possible in the university; while respecting the private or confidential nature of some databases, database owners should normally make them available to all members of the university community; access to some databases may need to be on a cost-recovery basis; and the SIC should provide users with several tiers of services to assist them in the selection of information sources and the selection and use of databases accessible at the university. Although funding has not been available to implement many of these policies, they have served as guidelines to the SIC as it has developed its current profile of reference and consultation services and resources.

User Education and Information Instruction

The Scholarly Information Center is dedicated to providing a vital information infrastructure to support the university's research and instructional activities. It offers a variety of services to teach users how to help themselves and how to determine when it is more appropriate to ask for the individual expert assistance that the SIC also offers.

To help inform the scholarly community of available resources and current trends in information technology, the SIC issues a quarterly publication. *The SIC Journal* is distributed free of charge at the university and mailed directly to all faculty. In addition, the SIC sponsors seminars on topics of general interest—word processing for humanists, database availability and searching, scholarly communication, and the like. These meetings, held at lunchtime, are very popular with faculty, graduate students, and staff.

Instructional services range from one-on-one consultations to large group instruction. Traditional classes and instruction sessions (often called "bibliographic instruction" or "computer literacy courses") are offered routinely on subjects of general interest or tailored specifically for a course. SIC staff also have applied new technologies in an effort to make instruction more effective—and more cost-efficient.

As a supplement to its introductory sessions in freshman composition (a required course for all freshmen), SIC staff produced a computer-aided instruction (CAI) program. Anyone at the university can use this library instruction program free of charge from any of the terminals on campus. The CAI format has proven to be a useful way to make basic library information available to a much wider audience, and it will, in time, be marketed to more and more of the Columbia community.

In this institution with so many graduate students in the humanities and history, it has become increasingly apparent that these students must learn to operate successfully in the emerging information milieu of their disciplines, just as their mentors had to learn to cope with the admittedly less complex book/microform environment of the recent past. SIC staff developed and offered, first on an experimental basis, "Research in the Humanities: A Practicum on Resources and Methods." Now a regularly listed credit course in the Graduate School of Arts and Sciences, the course covers an introduction to library and archival research, reference tools and services (the class is divided into groups by discipline), computerized databases for bibliographic research (also discipline-specific), techniques for organizing scholarly information; computer-assisted textual analysis and critical editing, and scholarly communication and publishing. The Dean of the Graduate School of Arts and Sciences has asked that the course be required for all humanities students; unfortunately, the SIC does not have enough staff to support this at present. Perhaps some CAI-based applications will help. Another mark of the course's success was a request by the Religion Department for a modified version for its faculty. The department chair called the sessions "informative, challenging, and genuinely helpful to us all. I assure you that what we learned will have a significant impact on the way we go about our research in the future." This reaction prompted a significant reallocation of effort to exploring further programs such as these.

Integrated Academic Information Management System (IAIMS)
The Scholarly Information Center is working toward its vision of an integrated information environment accessible from the scholar's workplace. Searching for information should involve the same procedures whether the information is on a remote commercial database, in a univer-

sity-owned file, or part of one's own correspondence. It should be easy to collate information from different sources and to copy references and quotations into personal electronic notebooks. Many problems must be solved before this vision can be realized, but Columbia has been able to take advantage of active support from the National Library of Medicine for planning and implementing projects that move toward it. The project concentrates on providing facilities for the Health Sciences Division and the Presbyterian Hospital, which together form the Columbia-Presbyterian Medical Center (CPMC). However, SIC staff are involved closely with its planning and implementation, and facilities and services will be capable of extension or replication throughout the university.

Acting on the belief that effective management of the exploding knowledge base is one of the greatest challenges academic medical centers face today, the Health Sciences Division (HSD) applied for and, in September 1983, received from the National Library of Medicine (NLM) a contract to plan an integrated academic information management system (IAIMS). It subsequently received an implementation grant and has applied for additional NLM funds to provide partial support for further implementation of an institutionwide IAIMS. NLM's IAIMS initiative was designed

> to offer a planning framework, support, and encouragement to institutions that were ready to undertake a system-wide plan for the development of integrated information systems. Inherent in such a challenge is acknowledgement that wise management and problems of university-wide intellectual interaction loom as large as the technical and scientific obstacles to achieving an optimal system.[2]

There are several compelling reasons to develop an information management system at Columbia. First, the recent advances in biomedical research have generated new ways for preventing, diagnosing, understanding, and treating disease and maintaining health. The ability to produce new knowledge far outstrips the ability to learn and appropriately apply it; Columbia thinks IAIMS will play a central role in helping to deal with this challenge.

Second, Columbia is committed to practicing and teaching state-of-the-art medicine. Medicine of the future will depend on health practitioners having access to computers and being able to exploit the technology.

Third, in Columbia's view, computers are not a change to be contemplated for the future but a force to be managed and planned for now.

Finally, the medical center envisioned for the future is both larger and less centralized than today's center. Workers at remotely located primary care centers, a new tertiary care facility, and a research park, all of which are currently being planned or built, will need remote access to library resources, hospital records, and human resources. CPMC's building program depends on an information infrastructure that will link people and resources in a deinstitutionalized, decentralized setting.

Early Achievements
The IAIMS project at Columbia is marked by several notable achievements.

- Columbia has created an information management structure that encompasses the libraries, the Presbyterian Hospital, and the Health Sciences Division (see Figure 10.2).
- Important changes in culture and attitude have been achieved. A new and unprecedented unity between the hospital and the university has emerged.
- An institutionwide network was planned, and substantial portions have been installed.
- Electronic links have been established between CLIO and the Health Sciences Library, which also opened and operates a microcomputer lab and classroom, created an online catalog of institutional data files, and made a two-year subset of MEDLINE available through CLIO.
- Four prototypes of clinical information systems have been developed: Intensive Care Unit; Medical Records Project for Ward Patients; Pathology Reports Free Text Database; and Outpatient General Medicine Practice.

Concurrent with the IAIMS project, the hospital has implemented a network and systems for admission, discharge, and transfer; medical records; and order entry and results reporting for tests. Installation of a radiology system was completed in the fall of 1988. In addition, HSD's Department of Medicine has contracted with BRS Information Technologies to author an electronic textbook of medicine. This service should be available within the next two years, but final distribution plans are not yet complete.

Scholarly Information System
In its proposal for the next phase of its IAIMS grant, Columbia has set a number of ambitious goals. The first is a paradigm of the Scholarly Information Center: to develop and implement an integrated information management system that allows users throughout the institution to access clinical information, scholarly information, administrative information,

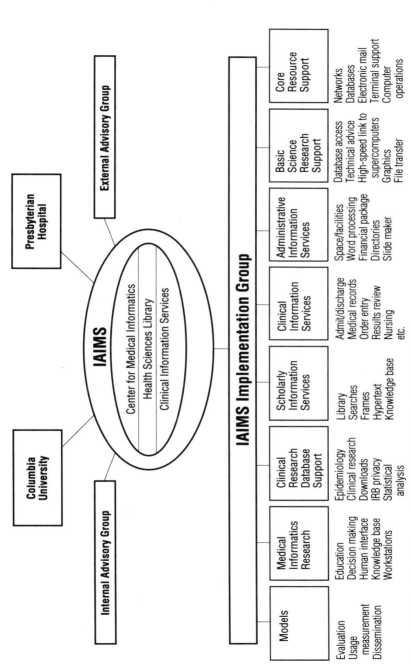

Figure 10.2 Overview of the organization for the IAIMS project at Columbia.

computing resources for basic research, and a comprehensive clinical database for clinical research. SIC staff will be involved particularly and specifically in the development of the Scholarly Information System (SIS). The SIS will provide seamless access to MEDLINE, CLIO, other locally mounted bibliographic and textual databases, such as the catalog of local data files, and other files that users identify as valuable. The SIS also will provide tools for managing a knowledge base, including activities such as acquisition, maintenance, and bibliographic control of new information resources, most particularly knowledge frames. Now under development in the medical community, knowledge frames will deliver expert-generated descriptions of new concepts, techniques, and other critical new knowledge. When the SIS is available, a medical practitioner, working at a patient's bedside, will be able to call up the patient's records, search bibliographic and textual databases for information about a specific illness or set of symptoms, review anonymous records of patients in the same hospital to ascertain local trends, communicate interactively with specialists, write orders, and get nearly any other type of information he or she thinks would be helpful to the case.

The goal of IAIMS, as of the SIC, is to permit the user to do as much of his or her work as possible in a preferred workplace, integrating information requirements into the system. Information sources may be local or remote, large or small, produced by others or by the individual; they may be bibliographic, textual, statistical, or graphic—or anything else the user defines. Final delivery is pictured as seamless, provided through a set of standardized interfaces, and linked to human experts who will furnish all of the information resources still in nonelectronic format. The goals and visions of IAIMS and SIC are very ambitious yet, ultimately, attainable.

Management and Organizational Issues

To work effectively toward the vision for the Scholarly Information Center, its management has identified important management issues that must be addressed.

Staff Training and Development

The continuing development of staff capabilities is vital to the SIC's future success. Effective staff development depends on training and recruiting programs to attract and retain qualified people and to foster individual growth and development. In addition to offering programs for training and general development, the SIC supports attendance at courses, workshops, seminars, conferences, and so forth, held at Columbia and elsewhere. This support, although significant, is not enough. Professional staff, with help from their supervisors, are expected to identify development needs and ways to meet them. The SIC supports these efforts with financial assistance and paid leave.

Promotional Opportunities

Managerial Positions/Development

As job requirements grow, it becomes increasingly more difficult to find and hire staff with the necessary technical, subject, and managerial skills. All professional positions in the SIC are advertised nationally; extensive recruiting efforts are made in each case. Very often, it takes many months to fill managerial positions. Whenever possible, a current employee, usually with little, if any, previous managerial experience, is given an opportunity to fill the position on a temporary, "acting" basis. This provides staff with a chance to learn firsthand what these jobs entail and management with the opportunity to observe and help job performance. About 50 percent of the people who have assumed acting positions conclude that they prefer nonmanagerial jobs.

Locating and recruiting senior-level managers is exceedingly difficult. Again, to provide opportunities for internal development, CUL sponsors one "internal management intern" per year. Chosen through a competitive application process, the intern spends six months working with a senior manager, participating in planning and operational meetings, and exploring areas of special interest.

CUL Staff

The CUL professional staff organization includes two long-standing parallel elements: a system of position categories and a system of professional ranks. Each professional staff member holds a position that is classified into one of five categories on the basis of the degree of administrative or policy-making responsibility involved. In addition, each staff member holds a title denoting professional rank, which reflects the level of professional achievement of the individual. Promotion of professionals is based on a peer-review system that evaluates performance, contributions to the university, and contributions to the profession. Although this is not a tenure review, it does bear some resemblance to the system by which teaching faculty are evaluated. Librarians at Columbia hold appointments as Officers of the Libraries that are equivalent to those of Officers of Instruction. Computing professionals at Columbia hold appointments as Officers of Administration.

Communications

The introduction and widespread use of electronic mail by SIC staff not only has improved internal communication by making it more accurate, timely, and efficient but has enabled staff to see quickly the potential of related applications of computing and communications technologies. The single largest barrier to effective communications between the SIC staff and the university's faculty and students is the lack of universal access to electronic mail by the latter group. With the assistance of the Information Processing Advisory Committee, SIC management is trying to achieve the objective of free availability of electronic mail to the community that was set in the 1984 report of a Task Force on Information Processing. The current effort is focused on designing a structure that SIC can support financially. As a start, small electronic mail accounts will be made available to all faculty. Recent support for faculty acquisition of microcomputing equipment by many schools and departments by the IBM Advanced Education Project has placed a large number of personal computers in faculty offices. The installation of an IBM-ROLM digital voice-and-data telecommunications system in late fall 1988 provided the means for universal connectivity to CUCCA's network and mainframe services, including and especially CLIO, at a modest cost ($15 per month for a connection). All classrooms, offices, dormitories, and other university facilities are covered by this project. Universal access to electronic mail, then, is almost a reality.

To exploit the possibility of widespread faculty access to electronic mail and the expected increase in access to CLIO (user identification is not necessary for on-campus access) after the new telecommunications system has been installed, the SIC has established online consultation facilities. Users now are encouraged to send their questions or suggestions about CLIO or other computing services electronically, with responses guaranteed within twenty-four hours. At this point, CLIO users must leave that system and log onto another to ask questions; as a result, they seldom bother to send their questions electronically. Changing this awkward arrangement is a high priority but not achievable until NOTIS CLIO is operational.

Requests for help with mainframe computing problems are received electronically more frequently. The Health Sciences Library, as part of IAIMS and together with CUCCA and CUL staff, will be the first site to test newly developing electronic reference services in the coming months.

Financing Information Services

Issues such as those discussed above epitomize a major paradox of the SIC. CUL always has operated on the principle of free and open access to all qualified users, with the understanding that enrollment or employment at the university entitles one to use nearly all the libraries' services at no additional charge. The unequal cost of various CUL services is characteristic of a university and not the subject of concern. There are a few exceptions to this entitlement principle (for instance, complex searching on commercial databases to meet individual needs is charged on an out-of-pocket basis), but they are, in the main, rare.

CUCCA's services, on the other hand, because they are newer, because, traditionally, they could be monitored, and because, until recently, they have been used by a relatively small portion of the university community, generally have been offered on a partial cost-recovery basis. Low fees were possible because much of the total cost was offset by selling excess capacity at a sizable markup to external users; however, that source of CUCCA's income has nearly disappeared. Additionally, much of the university community has now acquired its own equipment and demands access to a much richer infrastructure—an infrastructure whose use is hard to measure and whose importance equals that of the more traditional library. Users now want access to wide area networks, they want their LANs to connect to the university's networks, they want help in planning, installing, and managing their own LANs, and they want help in finding and using information and information management tools. They want all of this to be easy, cheap, and convenient. But, because CUCCA must recover some of its costs, it charges for some of its services, basing its fee structure on those developed at other institutions, most notably, Cornell.

Assessment of Current Structure

The creation of the SIC was a revolutionary step. The experience of the past two-and-a-half years has demonstrated the soundness of the concept for Columbia.

But all organizations are evolutionary. With the arrival of a new vice president in the summer of 1988, two important changes took place. First, Administrative Data Processing became an official part of the SIC. Work between ADP and CUCCA has been well coordinated, primarily because of the people involved. Nonetheless, issues concerning data communications, common machine-room space, and redundancy of services loom large, evidence that the organization will work more effectively after this change. Second, the vice president will report to the provost; this goal long has been sought to make the SIC an integral part of the academic operations at Columbia.

Since the creation of the SIC, information support services to the humanities have been affected most positively. CUCCA consultants, prior

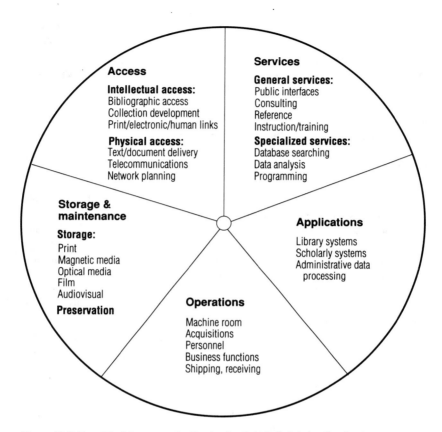

Figure 10.3 Possible future organization for the Scholarly Information Center.

to the merger, had no entrée to the humanities and history community. Together with their colleagues from the libraries, they have made a tremendous difference in the life of the average humanities scholar at Columbia. Cooperatively created databases, collaborative writing via network in a project spanning three continents, and CAI language teaching are representative of routine applications of new technologies in these disciplines. The implementation of the IAIMS program also exemplifies the success of the SIC. Still, in other areas, changes are less dramatic and sometimes not evident. The reasons are many, including the decentralized nature of the institution and the abandonment felt by some CUCCA staff at suddenly becoming "part of the library."

At the start of the SIC, CUCCA User Services was made a division of the libraries' public-services operations. During the transition from one vice president to another, the group was returned to CUCCA. Neither structure is ideal, but the experience of reference librarians and consultants working together has changed many attitudes for the better and continues to be a routine modus operandi, rather than an extraordinary measure. The smooth implementation of the BLIS CLIO system locally and the relatively easy shift to NOTIS CLIO are due to the close, positive relationship shared by librarians, computer consultants, and technicians.

The Future

There is no doubt that the SIC will thrive conceptually. There is also no doubt that the shape of the organizational structure will continue to change. Issues of span of control, logical arrangement, and depth of hierarchical structures will be addressed in the next few years. In the long term, the organizational structure of the SIC may be functional, perhaps as shown in Figure 10.3. Structures are merely means to an end, and the end remains a vital information infrastructure to support the scholarly life of the faculty and students of Columbia University.

References

1. Booz, Allen & Hamilton, Inc. *Organization and Staffing of the Libraries of Columbia University* (Westport, Conn.: Redgrave Information Resources Corp., 1973).
2. Lindberg, Donald A. B. "The IAIMS Initiatives of NLM: Institutional Planning for Advanced Information Services." *Journal of the American Society for Information Science* 39, no. 2 (1988): 105–106.

Chapter 11

Cornell University, Mann Library

Jan Kennedy Olsen

The Ithaca campus of Cornell University occupies approximately one square mile in the beautiful Finger Lakes region of the state of New York—"landscape which for variety and picturesqueness is unsurpassed by the site of any other university in the world."[1] It has been described by Eleanor Roosevelt as "magnificently centrally isolated," being a short flight from New York City, Philadelphia, Boston, Washington, D.C., Pittsburgh, and Toronto. The university also has a medical college in Manhattan and an agricultural experiment station in Geneva, New York.

Cornell has the unique distinction of being both the land grant university of the state of New York and an Ivy League institution. This was the vision of two men "whose names are indissolubly connected with Cornell University—from one of whom it took its name and its material prosperity and from the other its educational spirit and purpose—Ezra Cornell and Andrew Dickson White."[2]

The university was opened formally on Wednesday, October 7, 1868. The spirit and purpose of the new university were embodied in Mr. Cornell's words at the inauguration:

> I hope we have laid the foundation of an institution which shall combine practical with liberal education, which shall fit the youth of our country for the professions, the farms, the mines, the manufactories, for the investigations of science, and for mastering the practical questions of life with success and honor.[3]

Cornell has lived up to its founders' dream. Today, it is a university with thirteen colleges and schools. Four of these are supported partially by the state: the College of Agriculture and Life Sciences, the College of Human Ecology, the College of Veterinary Medicine, and the School of Industrial and Labor Relations. Nine are privately endowed: the College of Arts and Sciences, the College of Engineering, the College of Architecture, Art and Planning, the School of Hotel Administration, the Law School, the Johnson Graduate School of Management, the Medical College, the Graduate School, and the Graduate School of Medical Sciences. The university's annual budget is about $800 million, with research expenditures of about $250 million. Cornell enrolls 12,900 undergraduate students and 5,500 graduate students; faculty members number 2,555, and staff, 6,390.

In support of Cornell's Colleges and Schools, there are sixteen libraries. The second largest of these is the Albert R. Mann Library. The mission of Mann Library is tied closely to the land grant responsibility of the university:

Without excluding other scientific and classical studies, and including military tactics, to teach such branches of learning as are related to agriculture and the mechanic arts...in order to promote the liberal and practical education of the industrial classes in the several pursuits and professions in life.[4]

Mann Library traces its beginnings back to the late 1800s, when it was established as a rudimentary library to support the College of Agriculture. Today, Mann Library serves the 5,000 students, 692 faculty, and numerous extension staff of the College of Agriculture and Life Sciences, the College of Human Ecology, the Division of Biological Sciences, and the Division of Nutritional Sciences, as well as the agricultural experiment station through a separate library there. The collection now comprises six hundred thousand volumes and is considered to be the premier collection of the agricultural, life, and related social sciences of any academic institution in the United States.

Mann Library, together with the other libraries on the Cornell campus, belongs to the Research Libraries Group RLIN network. The libraries also jointly support a single online catalog (NOTIS). In addition, because it receives funding from the state, Mann is one of the libraries of the State University of New York (SUNY). The library's staff numbers 60, with 113 student assistants. Its influence has spread beyond the Cornell campus, throughout the United States—and, indeed, throughout the world. Scholars come from around the country and abroad to use the magnificent collection. Further, the library provides a training ground for librarians from developing countries; today, its professional staff has developed an excellent reputation for handling electronic information.

Mann Library is a research library. Its mission over the years has been to collect the definitive scholarly record within the disciplines it serves and to preserve this for posterity. In this spirit, it believes that scholarly information in electronic format must be incorporated seamlessly into the research library's collection.

Philosophy

It generally is agreed that we are now changing from an industrial society to a postindustrial—or "information"—society. The cultural, political, and economic consequences of this transition are so deep and so dramatic that we are considered a society in revolution.

At the heart of each revolution that has resulted in the shift of one society to another can be found a trigger technology. For the revolution that caused the shift from an agricultural society, the trigger technology was the steam engine. It spawned new machines, which produced new goods. It made possible mass production. It powered the rotary printing press, which produced the daily newspaper and stimulated mass literacy. It provoked new cultural, political, and economic structures. The revolution shifted the agricultural society to an industrial society in which the key resources were machines, manufacturing, and manpower.

The trigger technology of the information revolution is the computer, supported by telecommunications. The computer can generate types of information previously unthinkable, store information in small spaces, retrieve and manipulate it with dazzling speed, and transmit it to distant locations in seconds. It is creating a society in which the key resources are ideas, information, and the power of information technology.

As the traditional custodians of society's information and knowledge, librarians, and the nature of libraries, are under siege. Thomas Kuhn's conceptual framework of paradigms would suggest that the profession is in transition via revolution from one paradigm to another.[5] Long-held professional theories and practices, based in the tradition of print, are breaking down. The nature of the problems to be addressed is changing. The solutions to puzzles no longer fit. An anomaly is proving deep and persistent: access to knowledge is no longer only through print and its conceptual and instrumental tools of access. Information also is being generated in electronic form. It is dispersed widely and not subjected to the careful organization and classification given to print by librarians and publishers. The scholar does not need to come to the library; access to electronic information is through an inexpensive personal computer over telecommunications networks.

The paradigm, the model of theories, practices, and standards used to organize and provide access to this world's scholarly information is blurring. A new paradigm is needed, but its components will evolve only over a long period of time.

It is with this in mind that Mann Library is experimenting with the "library of the future." As is the case with any experimentation, certain assumptions underlie our activities:

- The fundamental purpose of the campus library remains unique and continues to be its responsibility to connect the scholar with the records of scholarship.
- Libraries will continue to share resources even in electronic form.
- The records of scholarship not only include electronic formats but increasingly will be stored electronically rather than in print.
- Scholars' microcomputers (workstations) will become more and more central to their professional work, including providing access to sources of scholarly information.

- Libraries have a critical stake in the nature of scholars' workstations, as well as the campus, national, and international telecommunications systems that link these machines.
- There is a fundamental innovation in the cognitive style with which scholars approach and interact with electronic information (especially full text) as opposed to print, which has serious implications for the design of interface capabilities.
- Scholars' access to information is not limited by their ability to pay nor by varying degrees of "rights" to access.

The Scholarly Information System

The vision that has driven the activities described in this chapter is simple and clear. The scenario for which the library is responsible is that of scholars at workstations (where "workstation" is each scholar's micro-computer), accessing data and the full text of literature regardless of their location and downloading, manipulating, and integrating pertinent segments into personal databases. The locus for scholars' access to scholarly information will be outside the four walls of the library: in faculty offices, laboratories, and homes. The library also must ensure that a wide variety of information resources is accessible, that this availability is publicized to scholars in an intelligible way, that the data resources are usable, that the scholar's workstation can perform certain functions well, and that the supporting telecommunications systems have sufficient bandwidth to support the sharing of information resources among institutions across the nation and the world.

The vision of this holistic scholarly information system, or electronic library, may be clear and simple; its realization is not. The practicalities of design and implementation are enormously complex. Mann Library's strategy has been to devise these through systematic research and development, rather than by choosing, for example, to put in place specific electronic resources as full operating services from the outset.

With this focus and the assumptions stated earlier, Mann Library entered into a partnership with Cornell Computer Services in early 1987 to create a prototype "scholarly information system," running on a central Cornell Computer Services computer attached to the Cornell communications network. This system makes substantial electronic information resources available to scholars in their offices and laboratories.

In this large-scale experiment, Mann Library is testing a number of questions:

1. Does a scholarly information system, accessible through the campus network, encourage and enhance use of scholarly information in electronic form?
2. Will scholars actually work with full text in electronic form?
3. If so, which materials are the most appropriate?
4. Where does optical storage fit in?
5. What is required for a scholar's workstation that will provide electronic information access, retrieval, and management in a networked campus computing environment?
6. What skills do scholars need in order to access electronic information efficiently?
7. How can the design of electronic full text of scholarly literature be made most effective?
8. What staffing patterns and skills must a library provide to support the scholar's access to electronic information?
9. How can the electronic resources of a library be shared with other libraries?
10. Given that knowledge should be freely available to the scholar, how are its acquisition, storage, and use funded?
11. How can information and knowledge in electronic form be reviewed systematically?
12. What evaluation criteria are suitable for electronic information resources?
13. What should be the relationship between the library and computer services?

The project is made possible through contributions from the National Agricultural Library, Apple Computer, the SONY Corporation of America, BRS Information Technologies, BIOSIS, Pergamon Press, RLG, and the U.S. Office of Education. Cornell Computer Services has contributed $50,000 for the purchase of magnetic and optical storage devices, as well as making computer time available to the project. The project has four tracks, each exploring a different aspect of the overall vision of a scholarly information system.

Track I
In the first stage of the project, Mann Library and Cornell Computer Services have created a computer system based on the DEC VAX, licensed and loaded the BRS/Search search-and-retrieval software pack-

age from BRS Information Technologies, and mounted four large bibliographic files on the system. Through our cooperative arrangement with
the National Agricultural Library, we have the entirety of the post-1980
portion of the AGRICOLA database. This preeminent database, compiled
by the National Agriculture Library, provides over a million references to
the worldwide literature of the agricultural sciences. With the permission
of the Biosciences Information Service (BIOSIS), Mann Library also has
mounted subsets of the BIOSIS database in the subject areas of genetics,
entomology, and nutrition. BIOSIS Previews, the parent database, is the
major English-language database for the biological sciences. Its coverage is international; over nine thousand primary journal and monograph
titles are indexed, and their contents abstracted. For researchers in
agriculture, the life sciences, and nutrition, the addition of these BIOSIS
subsets will enhance substantially the value of the bibliographic portion
of the scholarly information system.

Although experimental, this service is accessible from anywhere on
campus. At Cornell, two generations of campus network currently coexist.
A Sytek broadband network, installed in 1982, provides terminal-to-host
access from several thousand devices in offices all over campus to
central and departmental host computers. More recently, a high-speed
backbone network using TCP/IP protocols has been installed. Many
departments now have Ethernets, either connected directly to the backbone or bridged to an Ethernet in the Computer Center. Access to
centrally operated host computers is possible over either the Sytek or the
high-speed network. Since not all the schools served by Mann Library
have Ethernets installed, primary access to the scholarly information
system is initially over the Sytek network. As high-speed, peer-to-peer
networking facilities become more uniformly available on campus, the
library will take advantage of their more powerful features for linking
scholars' workstations to information services.

With a significant bibliographic resource in place, staff members at
Mann Library are analyzing and evaluating the response of a test group
of Cornell researchers to the system. In particular, they are analyzing how
these researchers consider a local scholarly information system, accessible through the campus network, compares with mediated searches of
commercial online systems such as BRS and Dialog. A two-year experiment is planned, to avoid the danger of interpreting the first flush of
enthusiasm as a long-term preference.

Track II

In a second stage of the project, Mann Library and Cornell Computer
Services will mount a full-text file of scientific journal literature "behind"

the citation files that already have been made available. With this substantial full-text resource, it will begin to be possible for researchers to secure, not only a list of references to the scientific literature through the scholarly information system, but an electronic copy of the document that they require. Key questions for the next generation of library information systems are how scholars will interact with full text in electronic form, and what sorts of materials they will prefer to use electronically. The intent is to begin this evaluation with the full text of scholarly journals.

The delivery of full text to the offices and laboratories of researchers will require sophisticated workstation hardware, equipped with high-resolution displays. Mann Library staff believe that current-generation Apple microcomputers begin to address this requirement, although much remains to be learned about how the software running on the local microcomputer must behave in order to function effectively as a true window of access to scholarly information systems on and off campus. Apple Computer has provided high-end microcomputers for the scholars who use the prototype system. Mann staff seek to determine what types of workstation hardware and software facilitate the interaction of the researcher with an information system of the sort being developed. In the future, the ability of a workstation to work smoothly with sources of scholarly information in electronic form will be a crucial element of the academic marketplace. Since journal literature is so vital to the scholar, it is important that the interaction with articles in electronic form be at least as productive as the interaction with the same material in print form. Beyond understanding the desirable specifications of the scholar's workstation is the necessity to understand the desirable characteristics and capabilities of the user interface to the full text. Aspects of this question are being addressed at Mann Library with funding from OCLC.

Optical-disk technology is being explored as a storage medium for large amounts of full text. The SONY Corporation has made available a "jukebox" that will store twenty optical disks. Each disk has 3 gigabytes of storage, which will hold roughly one-and-a-half million pages of text.

Track III

The third track of the system adds machine-readable, nonbibliographic, published data to the bibliographic and full-text resources. Preparation for this component has been under way since 1984.

A major grant from the Research Libraries Group and the Pew Foundation has allowed Mann Library to create a Computer Files Group within its Public Services Division. This unit consists of a computer files librarian, a programmer, and a statistician. The group is charged with assisting researchers to access and analyze nonbibliographic, published data in electronic form and with making these sources of scholarly information in electronic form easier for the scholar to use. The purpose of the research is to establish models and guidelines for the provision of services for nonbibliographic resources in an academic library. The project has focused on identifying staffing needs and service configurations, developing a user-friendly interface to data resources, identifying how acquisition, access, and servicing of machine-readable data files fit into the academic library, and examining the characteristics of novice users.

In the last two years, the group has initiated the development of a collection of electronic data resources in the subject areas of the library. These data resources, mostly stored on magnetic tape in a data archive, can be mounted on and accessed through the central mainframe computers of Cornell Computer Services. These now will be brought in under the umbrella of the scholarly information system.

The Computer Files Group has assisted researchers in creating subsets of data and in running computer analyses on the subsets. The programmer and statistical consultant have spent part of their time reformatting heavily used files into user-friendly systems. For example, with reference librarians, they have designed and implemented a front-end program that allows patrons to choose variables and perform data extractions from a file called the City and County Data Book. This file, from the Census Bureau, is a standard source of demographic data at the county level. Written in the C language, the program runs on a local area network of microcomputers within the library. The group also has conducted workshops for Cornell researchers in the use of published electronic data sets, helped coordinate access to genetic-sequencing software running on a departmental computer, and created a "metadatabase" that describes and indexes the data files that the Computer Files Group can help researchers to use.

Track IV

The fourth track of the scholarly information system is to provide access to Cornell's electronic data files for libraries and their scholars across the country . This phase is an extension of the age-old commitment of libraries to the sharing of resources.

Electronic information systems are expensive to develop and expensive to maintain. Reductions in the cost of computer hardware, while they encourage the development of new generations of information systems, do not counterbalance the costs of software, data resources, and personnel. Until recently, the central issue in networking for library resource sharing was how libraries could construct telecommunications networks to permit it. This remains relevant, of course, but the emergence of regional and national networks for education and research and the appearance of the microcomputer-based scholar's workstation in offices and laboratories now make it possible for libraries to share access to major information systems, not only with other libraries, but with the broader scholarly community as well.

The information system in place at Cornell's Mann Library is useful to scholars elsewhere. Cornell's telecommunications network has gateways to a regional New York State network (NYSERNet) and to the national NSFNET. Mann Library proposes to make its data files available, through these networks, to libraries and scholars at other institutions. This is made possible by collaboration with Cornell Computer Services and the libraries of those institutions.

This track, like the others, will be implemented in a research and development mode. Mann Library recently has received a large grant from the U.S. Office of Education to begin work.

The areas of investigation in this track give rise to such questions as:

- Which sorts of files are appropriate for interactive access?
- Which researchers use the interactive files system, and why?
- What library staff competencies and organizational arrangement are necessary to the development and implementation of an information system?
- What features and capabilities of data retrieval and manipulation are essential to the researcher when using an interactive data file system? Which system features must function on a central computer? Which features are best implemented on the workstation?
- What kind of support must libraries provide scholars who wish to use data files at another institution through the national network?
- What are the general operational and technological logistics of sharing electronic information resources among libraries across the national network?

Management and Organizational Issues

Mann Library's operating premise—that scholarly information in electronic format must be incorporated seamlessly into the research library's collection—has serious implications for the theories, policies, and practices of the organization. These are being identified through research, and, while there are still many questions to be studied, Mann Library already has faced a number of management and organizational issues. These issues will confront any library that decides to provide electronic information to scholars, whether it chooses to offer controlled experimental access or a full service.

Service Issues

Support of Nonbibliographic Data Files

Libraries are experienced in supporting mediated access to external information systems, such as bibliographic databases, usually through tightly controlled environments located within the library. In the last few years, librarians also have gained considerable expertise in teaching patrons to search these external, commercial systems independently (end-user searching). Now, one must question whether the models of support services that have developed are appropriate to the expanded scholarly information system or whether they must be modified to meet new requirements. One obvious difference between the scholarly information system under way at Mann and the electronic databases traditionally available is the presence of nonbibliographic files.

Providing quality service for a collection of nonbibliographic computer files depends heavily on the availability of adequate staff. While some libraries may be interested in acquiring and cataloging computer files, they often draw the line at providing service, which frequently is left to the computer services organization. No other library resource is treated in this manner, and, philosophically, there is no reason for the library to discriminate against computer files. The fact is, however, that few individuals currently working in libraries have the programming and statistical skills necessary to provide full service on nonbibliographic computer files. These skills, which include the "traditional" reference skills and a host of new ones, can be classified into four areas:

- *Hardware/technical skills*—This type of skill is needed to keep both microcomputers and mainframe running, to maintain tapes on a day-to-day basis, to move data around in the system, and to use mainframe housekeeping tools to keep track of the collection.
- *Software/programming skills*—The ability to reformat tapes into a usable format and to extract subsets of the data is essential. Also important is familiarity with many different types of software: communications programs and protocols, mainframe batch and interactive operating systems, database construction programs, and statistical programs.
- *Data issues*—The experience to discern how the data in a file was collected is needed, as is the ability to identify the best format for a particular set of data and to check for errors.

- *Reference skills*—Reference librarians need to know where to find data and how to judge when electronic form is more suitable than print. They need to be able to conduct a "reference interview" to establish the patron's requirements exactly and to describe the data files clearly.

At Mann Library, the new skills are provided primarily from two groups. The Information Technology Section (ITS) is composed of four full-time employees and several student programmers, an unusually large systems group for a library with approximately sixty staff members. The Public Services Division has a computer files librarian, a programmer, and a statistician—a level of technical computer expertise within the public services group of a library that is, to our knowledge, unique among the research libraries of North America.

Many of the hardware/technical requirements are handled by the ITS, which is responsible for testing, installing, and troubleshooting machines and networks. The Public Services programmer serves as backup and is responsible for all aspects of tape maintenance. Eventually, all the computer files staff will be familiar with the tape routines. The Public Services programmer also provides the software/programming skills, with the statistician serving as backup (having at least two people involved at the programming level is helpful for trading ideas when solving problems). The data issues are handled by the computer files librarian and the statistician—the combination of library and statistical skills is quite effective for evaluating the significance and validity of data sets.

There are several ways to build a staff with new skills. Personnel with the experience needed can be hired. Existing staff can be trained task by task. Or systematic training can be conducted through workshops, courses, and course sequences. For the computer files program, Mann hired some skills and trained for others. The statistician had a statistics minor and had worked with programs on the microcomputer and the mainframe. Both programmer and statistician learned about tape transactions, data manipulation, and other data issues on the job. The librarian learned data archive skills while in the position. (Evidently, quite a high percentage of data archivists learn their skills on the job.)

The next phase of staffing to service nonbibliographic computer files is to give the traditional reference staff the background they need to handle computer files as part of the library's resources. Through a series of demonstrations, anecdotal descriptions of transactions, and microcomputer-based finding aids, the staff of the computer files program will assist the reference staff to integrate the use of data files into daily reference service.

Most of the acquisition and processing of computer files has been absorbed into the normal library procedures. The selectors/bibliographers are learning enough about data collection and evaluation to judge whether a data set should be purchased. The acquisitions department is familiar with the different routines for acquiring tapes and other machine-readable files. Catalogers are able to create records for computer files.

User Information Literacy

A major service issue when providing users with electronic information is their ability to use it effectively.

A Nation at Risk recognizes that our society requires each person to be able to manage complex information in electronic and digital form.[6] Consequently, the report places great importance on computer literacy. This, however, is not enough—computer literacy is not information literacy. In its 1985 report, *Global Competition: The New Reality,* the President's Commission on Industrial Competitiveness concludes that success in international trade strongly depends on science, technology, and the control of information.[7] In *The Technology War: A Case for Competitiveness,* David Brandin and Michael Harrison take it a step further:

> ...the Technology War is about the worldwide race to capture the lead in the strategic technology information technology. Those that prevail in this war will control the resources of the world; they will control their Lebensraum; they will be the next global powers.[8]

If the United States is to remain internationally competitive in the "information age," not only must libraries take responsibility for applying modern information technologies to the retrieval and management of information, but they must also concern themselves with developing in the user an appropriate information literacy.

Mann Library proposes that, for a user to be properly sophisticated in the use of information, he or she must learn:

- the role, power, and uses of information in an advanced society;
- the variety of contents and formats of information;
- standard systems for the organization of information;
- methods for retrieving information from a variety of systems and formats; and
- ways to organize and manipulate information to achieve various ends.

Table 11.1   Skills Taught in the Curriculum in Information Literacy

- Searching bibliographic, full-text, numeric, and directory files
- Using information services on CD-ROM as well as on university mainframe computers
- Using telecommunications software and systems
- Searching computerized databases on remote systems
- Downloading information to floppy disk, and organizing, manipulating, and analyzing this information on a microcomputer
- Using citation-management, spreadsheet, and word-processing software
- Using online current awareness services
- Accessing library holdings records using the online catalog

Mann Library has conducted a large instructional program in the application of computer and telecommunications technologies to information retrieval and management for the past five years. The program has three tracks.

1. The *Workshop series in the Uses of the Microcomputer* is designed for both faculty and students. It is taught by information specialists from Mann Library, together with staff from Cornell Computer Services. The workshops, offered throughout the year, examine the computer's role, capabilities, and possibilities. Examples of specific classes taught are Bibliographic File Management with a Microcomputer, Spreadsheets, and Word Processing for Scholarly Information Management. The series is extremely popular: in the last four years, approximately eleven thousand faculty and students have attended the classes.

2. The *Curriculum in Information Literacy* is a fully rounded curriculum that is integrated into normal undergraduate coursework, woven into those courses that most naturally accommodate information technology concepts. There is a sequence to the material, which runs from the sophomore to the senior year, with each class building upon the content of the previous class. Table 11.1 lists some of the information literacy skills taught. Mann Library has two information literacy specialists on staff, and they teach the curriculum collaboratively with faculty. The prototype of the curriculum was initiated with the Department of Agricultural Economics. Since then, it has reached over one thousand students and has been woven into courses as

Table 11.2   Concepts Introduced in the End-User Searching Instruction Program

- What a database is
- What a bibliographic record, its fields, and its access points are
- How to divide a topic into component parts for development of a search strategy
- How to use controlled vocabulary and free terms effectively
- How to use Boolean operators or connectors to link terms or search components

diverse as Introductory Statistics, Managerial Accounting, Business Policy, and Marketing Management. For example, in the statistics class, instruction was given on data gathering and sources for statistical information. The assignment involved a search of the City and County Data Book, mounted as a data file on the file server of the local area network in the library's public computing facility. In the accounting class, students learned about a number of print resources concerning publicly held corporations and then completed a lengthy exercise using the Compact Disclosure database, a file on CD-ROM containing SEC information on approximately ten thousand United States corporations. Students compared the financial strength of companies within an industry, learning along the way how to download data to a spreadsheet for analysis.

3. The *End-User Searching Instruction Program* has been in existence since 1983. Mann Library information specialists teach the program, both in collaboration with faculty in particular classes and through open workshops. Its purpose is to train students and faculty in the concepts and technologies of searching computerized bibliographic databases. For a sophisticated understanding of any electronic bibliographic system, users need to develop understanding in certain conceptual areas (shown in Table 11.2). The range of concepts and skills presented is narrower than that covered in the information literacy curriculum, but represents an important component of information. Over four years, this program has reached four thousand learners and has been described several times in the professional literature, for example, in *Public Access Microcomputers in Academic Libraries: The Mann Library Model at Cornell University,* edited by Howard Curtis.[9]

Facilities for Access to Electronic Information

A third major service issue is the availability to users of appropriate equipment for access to electronic information. Cornell University is known for its lavish and sophisticated computing facilities. Cornell Computer Services supports two supercomputers, several other large IBM mainframes, five Digital machines, and one Hewlett-Packard minicomputer. In addition, many colleges, academic departments, and even individual laboratories have large-scale hardware.

Interestingly, Mann Library built the first microcomputer center on campus, which, in time, was followed by many others. Mann's was intended from the outset both to educate faculty and students in using the microcomputer to handle information and to provide access to local and remote information resources. Its success has been dramatic, and it enjoys the best reputation on campus in terms of the range of its software and hardware and the quality of its instructional staff and programs. In the impending renovation and expansion of Mann Library, this facility will triple in size.

A recent study at Cornell revealed that 90 percent of the faculty use microcomputers. Although most faculty are in the first phase of the computer learning curve (where one simply does better what one has to do anyway), the fact remains that there are enough computers to support more advanced uses. Added to the thousands of microcomputers owned by faculty, students and administrators are UNIX workstations manufactured by Sun, IBM, Digital, Hewlett-Packard, and AT&T.

Accessing online scholarly information requires a telecommunications infrastructure, or, in common parlance, a "wired campus." This infrastructure certainly must include a campus network, but that network alone is insufficient. If the scholar's workstation is to access the world of electronic scholarly information, it must be linked to national and world networks. In the words of Dr. Kenneth King, formerly Cornell's Vice Provost for Computer Services and now the president of EDUCOM:

> Networking is the glue that binds everything together....In the long term, the goal of networking efforts is to create a world university network connecting every scholar to every other scholar and to important sources of information, experimental apparatus, and computing resources. A major service of this network should be a knowledge-management system that permits scholars to access information on any subject in a uniform way.[10]

In pursuit of this, Cornell views its networking effort within the state, national, and world context. Cornell, a National Supercomputer Center, is attached to a regional network, NYSERNet (New York State Education and Research Network); to the NSFNET backbone; to ARPANET; to other regional networks attached to the NSFNET, such as SURAnet; and to CSNET. It is also one of the BITNET hubs and the gateway to NetNorth, BITNET's Canadian counterpart.

Cornell's long-range effort is motivated by the following vision, as described by Dr. King in *Campus Networking Strategies:*

- A universal communications network connected to national and international networks enables electronic communication among scholars anywhere in the world, as well as access to worldwide information sources, special experimental instruments, and computing resources. The network has sufficient bandwidth for scholarly resources to appear to be attached to a world local area network.
- Computing power is arranged hierarchically from desktop workstations to departmental and campus minicomputers, mainframes, mini-supers, and supercomputers on this world university network.
- The user interface is intuitive, consistent, and standard and makes effective use of dynamic high-resolution graphics and sound.
- All the computations and data appear to be in the workstation, with the actual origin of cycles and files transparent.
- A global knowledge-management system permits scholars to access information on the network in a uniform manner, using the library as a window to retrieve information in multimedia formats.
- The user has the illusion of total control.
- The response time is always fantastic.
- There are no user charges for basic network access and use.[11]

Today, planning at most universities for the new generation of networks involves administrators, faculty, and librarians. This is certainly true at Cornell, where Mann Library has served as an advocate for the faculty and students who will have to use the campus network in the future to work with scholarly information in electronic form. As universities begin to support large files of full text, the networking capabilities needed to deliver the text to the scholar's workstation will increase. Mann has established a library role in network developments that will ensure that the future needs of the electronic library are accommodated in the campus network structure.

Nature of the Operating Interface

A fourth significant service issue is the nature of the interface operating between the human and the computer. Ideally, this should be intuitive, offering branching capabilities to assist the user in the selection of an appropriate information resource, as well as common or uniform searching capabilities. What is needed is an entranceway to the system that combines an excellent screen design with a revelation of the system's functionality.

The area of human/computer interface design is burgeoning but still requires a great deal of research. The inherent questions have to do, not only with how to usethe power of the hardware and software to enhance the user's abilities to manipulate information, but, equally, with how the user's interaction with information is affected by retrieving and working with it in electronic rather than traditional print form. This is described by Donald Norman as the "discrepancy between the person's psychologically expressed goals and the physical controls and variables of the task."[12]

Mann Library has evaluated a great deal of software and analyzed a variety of user interfaces in information retrieval systems over the last several years. Some of this work has been published in the literature.[13] In addition, the staff has built individual front ends to several large computer files. However, the ideal remains to have an intuitive, uniform approach to searching all files in the scholarly information system. This ideal has not yet been realized; in pursuit of it, two things are clear: user-centered design is difficult, and there is no one way to approach it.

Mann has developed recently a first cut at a front-end interface to the NOTIS online catalog in the HyperCard "scripting" language, which runs on an Apple Macintosh computer. The front end is intended to simplify the use and increase the usefulness of a significant source of scholarly information in electronic form. This microcomputer-based "window of access" to the online catalog will then be expanded to enable access to a variety of information systems and resources through a single point of entry. The goal is to support access to the local online catalog, the local scholarly information system, and external academic and commercial information systems through an interface that is intuitive, helpful, and consistent. The interface also should assist the researcher in making the proper logical connections among the diverse information sources that he or she employs. Since the fundamental challenge is how best to organize information resources for identification and access by a user, it is well met by catalogers applying their principles of classifying, organizing, and providing access to information. For this reason, catalogers are involved with the programmers and public services librarians in the creation of this front-end interface. Mann Library certainly does not profess to expertise in the development of user interfaces but is convinced that, in the final analysis, the usability of information in electronic form will be highly dependent on the design and implementation of the interface with the user.

Creating Increased Expectations in the Scholar

A fifth service issue is that once scholars have access to electronic information, their expectations of the technology begin to increase. One typical expectation is a scholar's desire to manage his or her own electronic database of citations to important literature. When scholars have learned to search bibliographic databases and download search results, they then want to develop computerized control over their personal bibliographic files and import the results of an online search into them.

Bibliographic file managers are either specifically designed for, or capable of controlling, bibliographic records. Combining database management and text-editing functions, these programs allow long blocks of text to be entered and modified yet handle fields like a database manager. Since mid-1984, Mann Library staff members have collected and evaluated bibliographic management programs, distributed the evaluations within the university, and written software reviews for them. In addition, the staff teaches workshops on the use of bibliographic file managers for controlling personal literature files. To prepare for the workshops, the staff had to select and learn to use the software packages they would be teaching. This took a good deal of time, although, after learning one system thoroughly, subsequent ones were mastered more quickly.

The intent behind these classes is twofold: to offer users formal instruction in the evaluation and use of the bibliographic file managers and to establish the library as the campus consulting resource for these programs. Mann views its activities in consulting on, teaching, and evaluating bibliographic file management software as long-term commitments. Clearly, these services parallel to some degree the offerings of Computer Services. There is no duplication, however, since there is an understanding with Computer Services that Mann Library will cover the area of bibliographic management packages: the technical vehicle is the computer, but the users are being instructed in the organization and control of information, the library's long-time province. Users come to realize that the librarian's expertise extends to handling information in any format, not just print.

The next logical phase in the use of this type of software is integration with library online catalogs. After a scholar downloads the results of a database search into a local bibliographic database, the next step is to secure the actual documents. The scholar wants to be able to run the results of the search as a batch query of the online catalog from the workstation, with the details of the operation hidden. In fact, the scholar soon will be demanding that the full text of the literature appear on the screen of the workstation. This has been substantiated in a systematic series of interviews with scholars in various disciplines.

Administrative Issues

Perhaps the administrative issue most heavily debated in the professional literature today concerns the relative roles of the library and the computer center in managing scholarly information on the campus.[14] The debate hinges on the apparent convergence of the two organizations' evolving functions, as they both strive to support the academic community's use of personal workstations to access and handle information. The new similarity of functions provokes the question of whether the library and computer center should be merged or, at the very least, be governed by the same office—an Information Office.

Mann Library has a strong relationship with Cornell Computer Services. Mann has worked with CCS in establishing the library's innovative microcomputer center, in structuring a cooperative program of workshops in microcomputing for Cornell faculty, and in developing improved means of organizing and providing access to the software holdings of the two organizations. The two have joined forces to negotiate grants and contracts with outside agencies and conducted joint research in information technology. They have collaborated on the screening and interviewing of new personnel to be involved in some way, in either unit, with electronic information and worked together to create the Scholarly Information System described in this chapter and to formulate working arrangements for the maintenance and operation of Mann's Digital computer and internal network. Despite this degree of collaboration, there never has been any doubt or confusion about the role of each organization.

Doubt arises when the library or computer services wavers in its understanding of its mission in the university and falters in its grasp on the fundamental practices of its profession. The growing importance of research information in electronic formats has provoked a debate in libraries: should they handle this type of information? Beginning in the 1960s, social scientists confronted an increasing number of large numeric data sets. In most cases, research libraries were unwilling—partly because of their lack of expertise in coping with electronic information—to take on the responsibility of owning and servicing those files. As a result, many institutions created "data archives" to handle computerized information in the social sciences—in effect, removing computer files from the mainstream of scholarly information resources.

Yet, the application of computer and telecommunications technology to research information only changes the way that research data is stored and retrieved; it does not change its fundamental characteristics. Nor does it change the mission of the research library: to select, store, organize, provide access to, and train patrons in the use of the information that is critical to research.

And it does not change the mission of computer services on campus. At Cornell, that mission is to provide the computing and networking infrastructure to support all aspects of academic life. That support relates equally to the requirements of library activities, to instructional program needs, to research project demands, and to the requirements of the administrative processes. There is no more logic to the computer services organization taking over or merging with the library than there is to it taking over the administration of the research programs for which it also provides support.

There is no denying that, as institutions expand their in-house electronic information resources, questions will arise that must be answered. For example, who is responsible for negotiating with vendors of search-and-retrieval software; for installing software and scheduling upgrades and system changes; for database design and loading; for planning access to the information system through the institution's communications network; for the design and creation of front-end software; for consulting with and training users?

A second administrative issue is the impact on the library's organizational structure of the collection and servicing of electronic information resources. Mann Library has actively been handling the selection, acquisition, cataloging, storage, and servicing of electronic information resources in various formats for five years. The principle has been to absorb electronic formats into the traditional selection, technical processing, and access of information resources in the library. Mann has combined electronic format resources and traditional resources into one operational sequence and one integrated collection.

The impact, then, has not been on the basic pattern of organization, but on the procedures used in each division of the library and, particularly, on the skills and knowledge of the personnel involved. It is safe to say that everyone has been touched to some degree by the policy of admitting electronic formats seamlessly into the library's collection. In addition, several positions have been added, and some positions have reoriented their responsibilities to focus on the processing or servicing of electronic information (an interesting illustration of this is presented in "Mainstreaming CD-ROM into Library Operations," by Bill Coons and Linda Stewart).[15]

Eleven professional staff members (fifty percent of the professional staff) at Mann Library have responsibilities predominantly related to electronic information. A brief description of some key positions follows.

1. *Head, Information Technology Section*—This position has existed for four years. During that time, the individual in this position has built the entire Information Technology Section (ITS), a support unit to create and maintain the computing and telecommunications environment of Mann Library. ITS has three other full-time staff members, all new positions in the last four years—programmer/systems analyst, computer technician, and a coordinator for the Microcomputer Center in Mann Library. In addition, there are fifty student assistants, also new positions.

   The head of the ITS also designed and directed the building of the Microcomputer Center (which houses a software collection), provides workstations for information access and management, and conducts a workshop series in using microcomputers to access and manage information. This person also was charged with developing a high level of computer literacy in the staff of Mann Library. This was done over a period of two years in preparation for the installation of individual computers for every staff member. The installation is now complete.

2. *Computer Files Librarian*—This position, too, was created four years ago. To our knowledge, this is the only librarian in the United States whose full-time responsibility is the selection of and services on computerized, nonbibliographic data files in the agricultural and biological sciences. The computer files librarian has had the responsibility of creating Mann Library's program of services to incorporate computerized information (numeric, text, and reference) into normal library operations.

3. *Coordinator of Online Services*—This position has existed since 1983 but has expanded dramatically over the past five years. This person now coordinates the end-user education program. As described earlier, a major purpose of this program is to develop the skills to search computerized bibliographic databases. Having observed, at first hand, thousands of users interacting with computerized information systems, the coordinator of online services has focused on the key issue in these interactions—how effectively the user interface facilitates efficient and productive information access and retrieval. She has taken on the evaluation of many software interface and retrieval systems and conducted research projects to identify the most essential elements from the user's point of view. She is the resident expert in assisting the programmer with the development of user-centered interfaces.

4. *Information Literacy Specialist*—Two positions have been created by reorienting the responsibilities of existing positions. These librarians devise and teach a curriculum in information literacy at the undergraduate level.

5. *Computing Statistician*—This is a new position created in 1987. Its primary responsibility is to provide consulting on data-tape access in relation to statistical packages and on the production of data sets.

6. *Programmer, Public Services*—This new position has the primary responsibility of developing standard and custom products for accessing the computer files available through Mann Library. This includes designing and programming the products on mainframe, minicomputer, and microcomputer systems.

7. *Cataloger, Machine-Readable Data Files*—This position was created by reorienting the responsibilities of an existing position. It carries the responsibility for cataloging of computer-related materials, including microcomputer software, manuals, compact disks, and data files.

The Future

Taking a view from the bridge onto the full scope of the electronic library reveals serious implications for libraries in many areas: staff skills, development of end-user skills, the creation of adequate human/computer interfaces, storage of the data, its maintenance, pathways of access to it by the users, the sharing of resources with other libraries, and, eventually, the transformation of the physical plant that today houses predominantly print collections into one that will house predominantly electronic resources. One of the most significant concerns is to find a costing and payment structure that will uphold the ethics so vital to the development of knowledge in this country—free access to information and the protection of copyright.

Above all, two things appear to be true:

• Information and knowledge increasingly will be created using computers, organized and stored electronically, retrieved and disseminated by the power of computers and telecommunications.

• The skills that constitute literacy will be dramatically different in an electronic information world.

If the United States is to continue as a leading power, librarians will have to embrace a new paradigm for connecting the scholars of this country to the world's knowledge. Thomas Kuhn's analysis of the way that professions move from one paradigm to another reveals that an old paradigm is not abandoned until a new one can replace its components.[16] Mann Library is pursuing the research and development described in this chapter in an effort to identify the components of our new paradigm—a new model of theories, practices, and policies for connecting scholars to knowledge in a world of electronic information.

Acknowledgments

I wish to acknowledge the enthusiasm and superb capabilities of the staff of Mann Library, without whom the vision would remain only that. Special acknowledgment is due to Howard Curtis and Katherine Chiang for their tirelessness in working with and writing and speaking about the issues of electronic information in the library.

References

1. Sherwood, Sidney. *The University of the State of New York: History of Higher Education in the State of New York,* U.S. Bureau of Education Circular Information, no. 3 (Washington, D.C.: U.S. Government Printing Office. 1900), p. 321.
2. Ibid., p. 323.
3. Cornell University, "Proceedings at the Inauguration (October 7, 1868)" (Cornell University, Ithaca, N.Y., 1868), p. 4.
4. Public Laws of the United States, 1862, Chapter 130.
5. Kuhn, Thomas. *The Structure of Scientific Revolutions* (Chicago, Ill.: University of Chicago Press, 1970).
6. The National Commission on Excellence in Education. *A Nation at Risk: The Imperative for Educational Reform* (Washington, D.C.: U.S. Government Printing Office, 1983), p. 13.
7. President's Commission on Industrial Competitiveness. *Global Competition: The New Reality* (Washington, D.C.: U.S. Government Printing Office, 1985), vol. 1, p. 18.
8. Brandin, David H., and Michael R. Harrison. *The Technology War: A Case for Competitiveness* (New York: John Wiley and Sons, 1987), p. v.
9. Curtis, Howard, ed. *Public Access Microcomputers in Academic Libraries: The Mann Library Model at Cornell University* (Chicago, Ill.: American Library Association, 1987), chs. 9, 10.

10. King, Kenneth M. "Cornell University." In *Campus Networking Strategies,* ed. Caroline Arms, EDUCOM Strategies Series on Information Technology (Bedford, Mass.: Digital Press. 1988), pp. 164, 174.

11. Ibid., p. 164.

12. Norman, David A., and Stephen W. Draper, eds. *User Centered System Design* (Hillsdale, N.J.: Lawrence Erlbaum Associates, 1986), p. 33.

13. Stewart, Linda. "Picking CD-ROM's for Public Use." *American Libraries* 18, no. 9 (October 1987): 738.

    Chiang, Katherine S., Howard Curtis, and Linda Guyotte Stewart. "Creating Bibliographies for Business Use." *PC Magazine* 4, no. 23 (November 12, 1985): 249.

14. Molholt, Pat. "On Converging Paths: The Computing Center and the Library." *Journal of Academic Librarianship* 11, no. 5 (November 1985): 284–288.

    Neff, Raymond K. "Merging Libraries and Computer Centers: Manifest Destiny or Manifestly Deranged?" *EDUCOM Bulletin* 20, no. 4 (Winter 1985): 8–12.

    Woodsworth, Anne. "Libraries and the Chief Information Officer: Implications and Trends." *Library Hi Tech* 6, no. 1 (1988): 37–44.

15. Coons, Bill, and Linda Stewart. "Mainstreaming CD-ROM into Library Operations." *Laserdisk Professional* 1, no. 3 (September 1988): 29.

16. Kuhn. *The Structure of Scientific Revolutions.*

Chapter 12

Carnegie Mellon University

William Y. Arms
Thomas J. Michalak

Carnegie Mellon is a private research university in Pittsburgh, Pennsylvania. Total enrollment is 6,700, including more than 2,400 graduate students. About half the annual budget of $228 million comes from sponsored research. The university is particularly strong in engineering and computer science. At the end of 1988, the computer science department merged with several large research centers to form a school of computer science. Carnegie Mellon also has one of the finest drama departments in the country.

The university's strength in electronic information services is based on an exciting partnership involving computer science, campus computing, and the libraries. Strength in computer science has led to very advanced computing on campus; strong campus computing has become a basis for computing in the libraries.

Until the early 1980s, the libraries at Carnegie Mellon were sadly neglected. In this decade, however, their budgets have enjoyed rapid growth. This growth, in conjunction with strong campus computing, created a fertile environment for innovations in electronic library information. In 1986, the libraries proposed to the university that the best way to develop services for faculty and students was to combine campus computing and the libraries into a single unit. This proposal was based on the belief that the two big service units had many interests in common and that the area where they overlapped was likely to be the locus of future developments. The merger took place in July 1986; the new unit is known as the Academic Services Division. (Figure 12.1 shows the current organizational structure of the division.) The merger has been a success, and the division is rapidly reaching the point where the two groups would be difficult to separate; every year, they work together more closely. This cooperation extends to areas as mundane as recruiting student assistants or as strategic as building an electronic research library.

University Libraries

Carnegie Mellon maintains three principal libraries. Hunt Library serves the College of Humanities and Social Sciences, the College of Fine Arts, the Graduate School of Industrial Administration, and the School of Urban and Public Affairs. The Engineering and Science Library serves the Carnegie Institute of Technology (the engineering school), the Mellon College of Science, and the new School of Computer Science. The Mellon Institute Library, located half a mile from campus, serves the Departments of Biology and Chemistry, and the Mellon Institute for Research. Instruc-

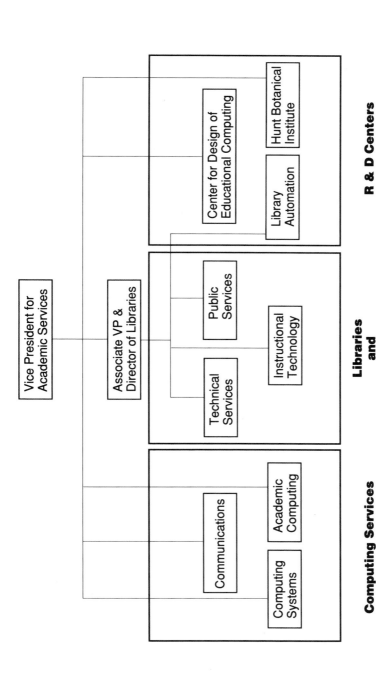

Figure 12.1 Organizational structure of the Academic Services Division.

tional Technology, providing audiovisual services, and University Archives are also part of the University Libraries.

Library materials are processed centrally, and cataloging is done through the Online Computer Library Center (OCLC). The library staff consists of 30 librarians and professional staff, 35 support staff, and 220 student assistants. The operating budget for 1988/89 was $3.6 million.

Overview of Library Computing

In 1981, the university undertook a major planning effort that had profound effects on both computing and libraries. As a result, the university and IBM embarked on the Andrew project in the following year; the aim was to provide an integrated network of personal computers for the whole university.[1] The story of library computing during the 1980s is the story of how, as the various parts of this campuswide network have been completed, the libraries have been able to use it to develop and deliver information services.

Library Automation

The first phase was the automation of traditional library operations. The most important achievement was the development of the online catalog; the card catalog was closed in 1984.

During this phase, the central computing service was on DECSYSTEM-20 time-shared computers, which were perpetually overloaded. Since computing equipment was a scarce resource, the library automation system was built on a minicomputer with a limited number of dedicated terminals. The main software used was the integrated library system now called LS/2000 and supported by OCLC.

The Library Information System I

By the middle of the 1980s, computing equipment was much more readily available. The libraries had access to large amounts of computer time on an IBM mainframe. This was used to mount a library information system, containing the library catalog and other databases, which was available to every terminal and personal computer on campus via the campus communications network. The system was fully operational by 1986.

The Library Information System II

By the end of 1988, almost all campus computing has moved away from traditional time-sharing services. Distributed computing is the principal form of computing on campus. Work on a second generation of the library information system is under way. Whereas the first library information system was designed to work with terminals over a low-speed network, this phase uses the power of personal computers and the high speed of the campus network.

The Mercury Electronic Library

Both generations of the library information system emphasize secondary information, providing indexes and abstracts that guide the user to the title and location of the items sought. The system also furnishes the full text of some reference material, such as an encyclopedia. The Andrew project, however, has brought sufficient computing power to the campus that it is now possible to store and deliver to the reader's computer the image of entire documents, complete with a full range of fonts, graphics, mathematics, and illustrations. Work on the Mercury Electronic Library was just beginning in late 1988.

Library Automation

Planning

Carnegie Mellon was not always enthusiastic about computing in the libraries. In 1968, the Long Range Library Planning Committee of the University Libraries recommended that the libraries follow the development of automation in large research programs and that the library staff become familiar with automation concepts but also recommended that the libraries not attempt a full-scale library automation program. This characterized the Carnegie Mellon approach to automating the libraries for many years, but, during the 1970s, computing began to creep in.

In 1975, the libraries received a grant from the State Library of Pennsylvania for the installation of equipment to use OCLC cataloging services. A policy decision was made that the libraries would receive machine-readable records of OCLC cataloging activities. At the time, there were no plans for using those records, but, in an institution with one of the leading departments of computer science, the day would surely come when they could be used. In that same year, the service of searching remote databases was instituted.

The first major collaboration between the libraries and the computing center was in 1978. Through the leadership of John W. McCredie, Vice Provost for Information Services, and Ruth Corrigan, Director of Libraries, the university received a grant of $210,000 from the Andrew W. Mellon Foundation. The grant supported a project to study the automation needs of middle-sized academic libraries, investigate available systems, develop recommendations for automating the libraries where appropriate, and begin the process of automation. As part of this grant, card catalog records were converted into machine-readable form, and items in the collection were bar-coded in preparation for machine-scanning.

In the fall of 1980, a new director of libraries, reporting directly to the provost, was appointed. The provost, Richard Van Horn, set the objective of accelerating the automation of the libraries and, specifically, installing an online catalog. As part of the universitywide planning and with the Mellon study as background, the University Libraries developed a strategic plan in spring 1981. The plan included an outline of what could be achieved through library automation and identified specific goals for library automation, including the development of a machine-readable file of journal holdings, an online catalog of information resources accessible through the campus computing network, a computerized system for handling materials on reserve for particular courses, and a database of machine-readable statistical files. The plan also itemized the capital requirements for automation. The following December, the university's Capital Allocation Board authorized $333,000 for library automation.

With the capital for hardware in hand, the libraries went back to the Mellon Foundation in 1982 with a request for a follow-up grant to develop a model electronic information system. This proposal addressed three areas: the automation of internal library operations, the development of an interactive information system through the online catalog, and the expansion of access to machine-readable databases on the campus.

Automating Technical Processes

Two classes of library operations have been automated: technical processes, such as cataloging, serials control, and acquisitions; and administrative and office tasks. (Table 12.1 lists developments in the automation of technical processes.) Based on the study sponsored by the first Mellon grant, the libraries had concluded that an integrated database management system would be the most cost-effective solution for small- to medium-sized academic libraries. Since such an integrated library database management system did not exist at the time, the decision was made to prepare systematically for automation and, where possible, to make use of existing campus software and hardware systems to automate some functions. The computing center provided time-sharing services on six Digital Equipment Corporation DECSYSTEM-20 computers, running the TOPS operating system. These computers were thought to be inexpensive and stable.

The first step was to begin an in-house retrospective conversion of catalog records, using OCLC. The second step was to use existing programs on the campus time-shared computers to develop an acquisi-

Table 12.1   Automation of Technical Library Processes

1975	Connection to OCLC is established for shared cataloging.
1979	Conversion of catalog records to machine-readable form begins. Bar-coding of the collection is instituted. Mellon Foundation funds a review of available automated library systems.
1980	Work begins on the design and testing of system for acquisitions.
1981	Local acquisitions system is completed and running on TOPS time-shared system.
Spring 1982	Agreement is made with Avatar Systems for purchase of ILS (Integrated Library System) software.
Summer 1982	Library minicomputer from Data General is installed in the university's computing center for ILS.
Winter 1983	Serials holding list is completed using TOPS system.
Fall 1983	Reserves system, using TOPS, is introduced.
Spring 1984	ILS (now known as LS/2000) online catalog is implemented.
Summer 1984	Library card catalog is closed. Dial-up and limited campus access to the online catalog is provided.
Spring 1985	Functions for electronic mail and online information on schedules and policies are integrated into LS/2000.
Summer 1985	Bib-Base/Acq replaces locally developed system for acquisitions.
Fall 1986	LS/2000 module for circulation is introduced.
Fall 1988	LS/2000 module for reserves is introduced, replacing locally developed system.
Spring 1989	SC350, a microcomputer-based system for serials control, is introduced.

tions information and fiscal control system. In this way, progress could be made toward automation. Since the libraries received substantial increases in the book budget beginning in 1981, this second effort proved to be critical.

The Integrated Library System

In 1980, the National Library of Medicine announced that it had developed a system called the Integrated Library System (ILS), which would be made available to the public. ILS seemed likely to meet the libraries' needs, and staff visited the National Library of Medicine to review the system. Its online catalog was both menu- and command-driven and appeared to be the most user-friendly system available. While it had a circulation system designed for the Army Library at the Pentagon, no other software was yet operational.

Developments at the National Library of Medicine were monitored closely throughout 1981. In the fall, several of the principals involved with ILS development formed their own company, Avatar Systems, Inc. Avatar Systems' goal was to provide turnkey installation of ILS, modify it to reflect the needs of academic libraries, and develop additional modules for functions such as cataloging, serials, and acquisitions. Avatar Systems approached Carnegie Mellon as one of its first prospective clients.

Negotiations with Avatar Systems took place throughout the late fall and winter, and, in April 1982, a contract was signed for the installation of Avatar's version of ILS. In 1983, the contract was modified to include additional software from Avatar, along with specific software modules that Carnegie Mellon library staff would develop. The contract was considered to be a collaborative development contract, in which each party would be responsible for specific software development. Carnegie Mellon developed an interlibrary loan module and integrated the National Technical Information Service release of ILS electronic mail. In 1984, OCLC purchased Avatar Systems and renamed ILS as LS/2000.

Hardware Installation

The computer chosen to run ILS was a Data General Eclipse, which was installed in the university computing center in May 1982. It was placed in the computing center for operator control and general maintenance and to ensure that the library system would be connected to the other campus computing facilities. Library staff, as well as other users, would be able to access ILS from the same terminals that they used for word processing and electronic mail.

To save money, the computing equipment was assembled from a variety of sources. The central processor came from Data General, but other hardware was supplied by System Industries, Control Data Corporation, and Mostek. Mixed-vendor systems are common at Carnegie Mellon, but this one was a sad mistake. Two days after installation, a disk-head crash occurred. From June to December 1982, as the tapes of the library's machine-readable records were loaded and indexed, one disaster after another occurred, largely in the form of disk and memory errors. Hardware staff pointed the finger at software. Software staff blamed hardware. Vendors of various hardware components blamed each other. All of this was particularly vexing because diagnostics showed no problem, yet disk errors continued to occur with annoying frequency. In October, an outside consultant was called in and, after a series of equipment replacements, the system began to run reliably at the end of January 1983. Maintenance contracts and warranties covered all the expenses, but the loss of staff time and morale was considerable. The system has been running reliably since 1983.

The year 1983 was spent completing conversion, loading and indexing records, profiling, designing menu screens and user support systems, and training library staff. Internal wiring of the libraries and connections to the computing center's terminal network were completed. The online catalog was made available in the Engineering and Science Library in March 1984 and in the other libraries at the end of the spring term. Because everybody was wary of the hardware, the system was introduced without fanfare. Students found the system easy to use, and the hardware was running reliably, so the decision was made to close the card catalog on June 30, 1984. Over the summer, facilities for dial-up and access through the campus terminal network were implemented.

The LS/2000 system is still in use, and new functions have been added over the years. In 1985, an electronic mail service was provided for staff, as was information about the libraries: hours, policies, services, announcements, and library publications.[2] A grant from the State Library of Pennsylvania provided funds to design an interlibrary loan service in the online catalog and to extend access to external sites. The interlibrary loan function combines the LS/2000 electronic mail with catalog searching and an interlibrary loan workform. A user at a remote location can search the catalog, fill out a request form online, and transmit the request in one terminal session. In September 1986, the LS/2000 circulation system was implemented, followed by the LS/2000 reserves system in September 1988.

Acquisitions System

The acquisitions system designed to run on the TOPS time-shared computers proved successful and was used from 1981 until July 1985. Eventually, however, maintenance grew complicated. The computing center began to make significant changes to support up-to-date versions of the operating-system software, not always with due consideration for all the applications running on the system. In 1984, changes in the operating system required the libraries to rewrite substantial parts of the acquisitions code. What originally had been simple and inexpensive to maintain became complicated and costly in terms of both systems and programming time. When the announcement came that time-shared systems would be phased out in favor of the new personal computer network, it became clear that the libraries would be well advised to identify an acquisitions system that ran on a personal computer.

In the spring of 1985, the Acquisitions Department selected and tested Bib-Base/Acq as a replacement for the system developed locally. It proved satisfactory, and the switch was made at the end of the fiscal year. In spring 1989, a microcomputer-based product from OCLC for serials control (SC350) was introduced. The libraries also expect to introduce OCLC's microcomputer product for acquisitions (ACQ350). These products are designed to interact closely with the LS/2000 integrated system.

Automating Office Operations

One of the most important contributions to increased efficiency in the libraries during the 1980s has been the use of word processing, electronic mail, and other central computer services in clerical support work. Initially, central computing facilities were used, but personal computers linked to the campus network are now standard. All staff have access to one or more of the thirty-five personal computers in the library, and eight of the professional staff have computers owned by the library in their homes.

The Use of Central Computing Resources

In 1981, university policy promoted the use of central computing facilities. The provost specifically encouraged the libraries to use these resources. At that time, the libraries had ten communication lines for terminals to the computing center: seven in Hunt Library, two in Engineering and Science, and one in the Mellon Institute Library. Data switches in the computing center allowed any terminal to be connected to any one of the TOPS computers.

The computer science department's research interests in electronic information had generated excellent facilities for editing and formatting text and for electronic mail on the TOPS computers. A text-formatting program called Scribe, originally developed within the department, is now a commercial product available for many types of computers. It provides useful features for academic documents, such as bibliographies and tables of contents. It emphasizes the structure of documents, rather than just typographic form, and is a precursor of languages used by publishers today to mark up documents for printing. The computer science department also had one of the earliest laser printers, and the computing center soon bought one for general use. Scribe supported both well, so the whole campus gained early experience in preparing documents with high-quality output and a choice of fonts.

The libraries began to take full advantage of the TOPS systems for electronic mail and document preparation. The diffusion process worked from the top down. Department heads were the first to learn and use the systems. Because of the limitations on communication lines available within the libraries, department heads were given terminals and modems for home use. This became a symbol of prestige and accelerated the learning process because the professional staff could learn in the privacy of their homes, without the potential for embarrassment. Gradually, more and more librarians identified a need to learn the systems.

The staff's vigorous use of central computing facilities provided a number of benefits and opportunities for the libraries.[3] Training in word processing and other computing systems helped to prepare staff for the introduction of the online catalog and other applications specific to the library. Morale improved as the staff began to feel a part of the intense computing environment of the university. The introduction of computing improved communications among the three libraries and smoothed the way for rapid change within the organization.

The Arrival of the Macintosh

The TOPS computers had one great disadvantage: everybody wanted to use them, and they became woefully overloaded. At the same time that the libraries wanted more computing power, so did the rest of the campus, and contention for access became severe. In response to this demand, the libraries acquired nine IBM PCs in late 1983 and early 1984. The PCs, however, required more training than the TOPS systems, and this was difficult to provide at the same time that LS/2000 was being introduced. Another problem was that, by the spring of 1983, 86 percent of the professional staff used computers daily for general office tasks, as compared to 15 percent of the support staff. The challenge facing the libraries was how to increase the number of support staff using computers for productivity.

In early 1984, the libraries received several Lisa personal computers as part of a general grant from Apple Computer to the university. The Lisa was much easier to use than the IBM PC, and with it came the promise of the Macintosh. Experience with the Lisa led to a freeze in the acquisition of additional IBM PCs and terminals for general use; instead, twelve Macintoshes were ordered in the spring of 1984. The university announcement that the TOPS systems would be phased out accelerated the need for stand-alone personal computers. By the end of 1987, the Macintosh was used for most word processing, although library publications continued to be produced on the time-shared system until the phase-out was completed in June 1988.

By late 1988, the Macintosh was established as the standard personal computer within the libraries. Thirty-five Macintosh computers and five

LaserWriter printers support word processing and other general computing applications. In the spring of 1988, the campus communications network introduced campuswide AppleTalk service, which allows the Macintosh computers to form a network within the libraries and also to be part of the full campus network. The transition from time-sharing is complete.

The Library Information System I

Providing Access to Bibliographic Databases
In May 1984, the libraries reviewed their accomplishments and presented a strategic plan to the deans and academic department heads. Building on the progress that had been made in automation, this plan proposed expanding the role of the libraries to provide a wide range of information services to the campus. In January 1985, the university published a statement of its goals and plans, in which the libraries' intention of providing more information in electronic form was tied to the goals set for campus computing:

> Carnegie Mellon intends to maintain its leadership in the area of research and academic computing. This will require the successful completion of the planned integrated personal computer environment and network, as well as continued research into and development of educational software. The library will be transformed into an advanced electronic information service.

This very explicit statement within an overall university plan was an important ingredient in the success of the libraries' efforts. The libraries' plans now were linked securely to the university's agenda. This approach has been used on many occasions to present the libraries' case for funds. While it is too often true that plans are not supported with dollars, linking the libraries' goals closely with those of the university has proved successful.

Because the Carnegie Mellon University libraries' collections had been weak, the library staff had always worked extra hard at providing service. The staff had a reputation for getting the material that users needed, regardless of its location. The concept of access to information, not necessarily ownership of it, was a strong tradition. As information became more readily available in electronic form, the libraries moved to provide access to these databases at as low a cost as possible to the user.

Bibliographic searching of remote databases began in 1975, using DIALOG; its use has grown every year since. Usually, a librarian carries out the search on behalf of a student or faculty member. The university is charged for each search, and these charges are usually passed on to users. In recent years, the libraries have experimented with several alternative approaches, such as installing databases on local computers, purchasing them on CD-ROMs, and searching remote databases through gateways that help the end user to conduct a search directly. One of the great advantages of a local database is that students and faculty are not inhibited from using it by the incremental costs of a remote service.

In its 1982 proposal to the Andrew W. Mellon Foundation, the libraries outlined their strategy to provide more databases once the catalog was online:

These new services, whereby the full text of journals and information resources are provided on-line, are the portent of the future for the electronic delivery of information and will have a significant impact on the nature of academic libraries. We anticipate that the amount of information retrievable on-line will increase. How libraries will provide this information on-line or substitute on-line availability for traditional print sources, pay for these services, and train library staff, students and faculty to make effective utilization of these new tools are all important questions facing academic libraries.

The proposal outlined an expansion of machine-readable databases on the campus, along with mechanisms to provide library clientele with direct access to remote databases. The strategy was to encourage students to search information systems directly. In this way, they would become accustomed to using the library workstations as a fundamental tool for seeking information. It was felt that students would set an example for the faculty.

Early Services for End-User Bibliographic Searching
The first machine-readable database to be made available on campus was Search Helper, which was installed in Hunt Library in April 1984. Search Helper, from the Information Access Company (IAC), used a free-standing personal computer and allowed users to do their own searching; user response to it was unreservedly favorable.[4] InfoTrac, another IAC product, arrived in December 1984. While reference librarians had reservations about its simplicity and inability to combine terms, users did not care about such sophistication and loved it because it saved so much time. Use was so heavy that the libraries felt it necessary to back up the system with IAC's Magazine Collection of article reprints on microfilm so that users had easy access to the items identified through InfoTrac. This practice of backing up electronic databases, particularly the most popular ones, with document delivery has continued.

So that library users could perform their own searches for a wider range of information, Easynet, a gateway product that provides remote access to six hundred bibliographic and numeric databases, was introduced in the fall of 1985. At first, students and faculty were provided unlimited access. This proved to be too expensive because some departments that had been frequent users of library-mediated searching simply shifted their searching to Easynet's unlimited access. Searches now are limited to two per semester for students, without charge, and faculty are required to pay a fee. The usage has dropped off considerably. WILSEARCH, a gateway to the H. W. Wilson Company databases, was added in 1986. There is no charge for WILSEARCH.

The Mainframe System

Despite the success of these commercial products within the library, little progress in providing information across the campus could be made without a larger computer system. In 1984, IBM gave an IBM 3083 mainframe computer to the university. The libraries proposed that some of the mainframe capacity be used to act as a database server for the campus. The goal was to provide an information system that was both easy to access and easy to use.

The new information system was to be open to every terminal and personal computer on the campus network. Because LS/2000 runs on a minicomputer, simultaneous access to it is restricted to a small number of terminals. IBM staff worked to permit access to the mainframe without the usual accounts and passwords. The Carnegie Mellon network staff provided a system by which typing a single word, such as "library" or "cat," would open a connection across the network and into the library information system.

Library staff were responsible for making the system easy to use. The retrieval system chosen was IBM's STAIRS system. STAIRS is the ancestor of many of today's retrieval systems. It provides free-text retrieval on any word in a database, with the usual Boolean operations. Mark Kibbey, then Assistant Director of Automation, and Greg Diskin, Systems Designer, designed a user interface to STAIRS that has proved easy to use without training.

The first database to be installed was the online catalog. In October 1985, a test database of the catalog was created. A tape of MARC records was produced from the LS/2000 system and loaded on the IBM mainframe. The catalog records were indexed within STAIRS. For the next six months, the user interface and retrieval system were refined and tested. In March 1986, the first version of the Library Information System (LIS) was introduced to the public. As well as the online catalog, it contained acquisition order records and several local test files. The catalog, a duplicate of the data maintained on the LS/2000, is kept up to date by copying all changes in the master catalog from the LS/2000 to the retrieval system once a week.

New databases have been added steadily to the system. At first, acquiring them was not easy. Negotiations were protracted and difficult, since the publishers were unfamiliar with the concept of licensing tapes to libraries and inexperienced in pricing those tapes. Two publishers were chosen for final negotiations: the Information Access Company and Grolier. The IAC family of bibliographic databases that index articles in current publications (Magazine Index, National Newspaper Index, The Computer Database, Management Contents, and Trade and Industry) and the Grolier Academic American Encyclopedia were made available to the campus in the fall of 1986.

With the installation of the encyclopedia, the concept of providing a set of basic reference tools took shape, and, in 1987, the American Heritage Dictionary was added. The Inter-University Consortium for Political and Social Research's Guide to Resources and Services was added later in the year. Bibliographies prepared by library staff on various topics have been loaded, as well as an index to architectural illustrations in books from the collection. In the fall of 1988, the serials holdings list of the University Libraries was added as a database separate from the online catalog.

The key to the success of this system is that all services are reached through a single user interface. Whatever the format in which the data is received, it is converted into a standard format, and a computer index is generated. The user interface is a straightforward, menu-driven system that allows the usual Boolean combinations of search terms, provides lists of items that can be sorted in a number of ways, and displays individual records. A more detailed description was published recently in *Reference Services Review*.[5] Figure 12.2 shows an example of the main search screen for the online catalog. The interface design was based on some general guidelines:

- a single interface works for all files;
- screen displays are simple;
- the system is self-documenting;
- online help is available;
- the user gets a result from each command, at the least, a helpful error message;
- the user has a minimum of choices to make; and
- sophisticated search capabilities are available for those who want them.

```
                        CMU Library Catalog
TYPE in up to 4 search keywords OR a Command character.  Then press RETURN.



ADVICE:
1)  Use major keywords and omit short words like 'and', 'the', 'of',
    'his', 'for', etc.
2)  Use $ for truncation.  (school$ = school, schools, schooling ...)
3)  To enter a more complex search, choose option 3.
4)  Always press RETURN after entering data or a menu character.
5)  The DELETE key operates on the character UNDER the cursor.  To correct
    typos, move the cursor backwards with the back-arrow key and
    type over the error.
6)  Send comments and bug reports to diskin+ or call x3692.
-----------------------------------------------------------------------------
COMMAND MENU:
? = HELP                    1 = Scan Index         4 = Author Search
Q = QUIT and logoff         2 = Change Database
                            3 = Command Search
```

Figure 12.2 An example of the main search screen for the online catalog.

Response time is excellent, and the users are happy. Figure 12.3 shows the searches by database in October 1988. It is important to remember that, within the library, the LS/2000 system, which also provides circulation status, remains the principal searching mechanism for the catalog. During the same month, 49,516 catalog searches were conducted on the LS/2000 system, in addition to the 31,597 searches using LIS. More than half of the LIS searches in October were across the network, from outside the library.

The usage figures suggest that the more specialized databases are used more lightly, as might be expected. The value of these databases will need to be weighed against their costs as the libraries develop and refine policies for electronic collections and services. On the other hand, the use of the encyclopedia and the dictionary is gratifying.

We are beginning to see the impact of access to bibliographic databases on other library services. The number of requests to borrow journal articles by interlibrary loan rose from 1,403 in 1985/86 to 2,402 in 1987/88, an increase of over 70 percent. Students and faculty have equal access without charge to interlibrary loan services, and there have been no changes in policy to account for this significant increase.

Another major impact has been on the usage of the microforms collection, as measured by pages printed from the microform readers. When the IAC index databases were added to LIS, the collections were

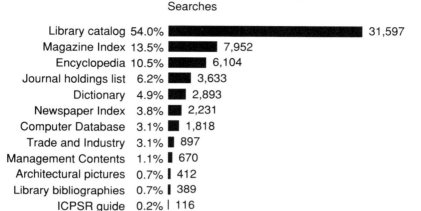

Figure 12.3 **Searches by database in the Library Information System, October 1988.**

reviewed to determine the overlap with the sources referenced in the indexes. Rather than expand the print collection, we acquired a second microfilm support product from IAC. The Magazine Collection and The Business Collection contain the filmed pages of many of the journals indexed in The Magazine Index and Trade and Industry. Identification numbers for film cartridges and frames are shown as part of the citations in LIS. Users print out or jot down these numbers, then visit the Image Resources Center in the library to display and/or print out the articles. For printed pages, the charging system is the same as for photocopies. When ABI/INFORM, which indexes business periodicals, was acquired as a CD-ROM database, the library acquired a number of corresponding journals in microform. A comparison between the number of microform copies made between July and December 1987 (44,413) and the same period in 1988 (63,863) shows a 44 percent increase. The linkage is clear: access to bibliographic information on journal articles, whether on CD-ROM or online, increases journal usage.

Network Support for the Library Information System
The success of the library information system in bringing information to the faculty and students would not have been possible without the enormous number of terminals and personal computers on campus, as well as a campuswide communications network that links them together. The existence of the ubiquitous campus network is very important in planning for library services—they can be built knowing that all computers are connected.

Today, the campus network supports connections at speeds high enough that full pages of documents or high-resolution facsimile images can be moved around the network as needed. Because the information system was developed at a time of transition in campus computing, when the high-speed network was still under development, it does not make full use of the speed of the network and the capacities of personal computers. Almost any terminal or personal computer can use the information service, but no advantage is taken of the power of this modern equipment.

The Library Information System II

The formation in 1986 of the Academic Services Division led to a renewed burst of planning. Much of this was done jointly with the Office of Research at OCLC. One of the surprising conclusions of this planning has been a decision to replace LIS with a different computer system in order to make better use of the power available on personal computers at Carnegie Mellon. The fundamental change is from time-sharing to distributed processing. To understand this movement, it is necessary to describe the new campus computing environment.

Campus Computing in 1988

The Andrew project with IBM has been the catalyst for a campuswide movement from time-shared computing to a network of personal computers. Figure 12.4 shows the basic configuration of campus computing at the end of 1988. The diagram shows no central computers. This is an oversimplification: general-purpose time-sharing services have been withdrawn, but the university still has several large computers, including the mainframe used by the libraries. Carnegie Mellon is also a partner in the Pittsburgh Supercomputing Center. However, the vast majority of computing takes place without the user logging on to any central computer. Whereas a few years ago, thousands of terminals were connected to time-shared computers, today, it is rare to see a terminal. Everybody uses personal computers, and it is estimated that there are as many personal computers at Carnegie Mellon as there are people. Many of them are powerful UNIX workstations with large high-resolution displays.

A fully networked personal computer offers the user a range of services, some provided locally by the user's own computer and others over the network. When the personal computer requires a network service, it sends out a message, waits for the response, and then continues with the task. For example, the message might be a file to be stored, a document to be printed or mailed, or a request for information. Users of network

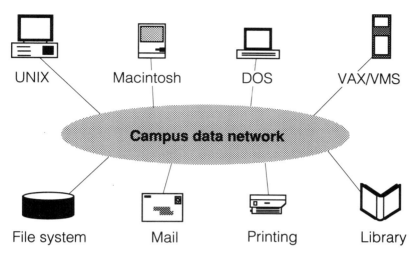

UNIX　　　　Macintosh　　　　DOS　　　　VAX/VMS

Campus data network

File system　　　　Mail　　　　Printing　　　　Library

Figure 12.4　Overview of the campus computing environment at Carnegie Mellon.

services have to be authenticated, but in no case does the user log on to a time-shared computer.

The communications network is described in detail in *Campus Networking Strategies,* the previous volume in this series.[6] By 1988, the network was essentially complete: computer systems that require reliable, high-speed communications between any two points on campus can be introduced. Over 12,000 outlets have been installed, with at least one outlet in every room on campus. Each outlet can be configured for Token Ring, Ethernet, or AppleTalk. By fall 1988, all network types were available in every room, except that Ethernet service was not yet available in dormitories. The university network is connected to all leading national networks and is one of the hubs of the new NSFNET, which provides a high-speed, nationwide backbone.

Four types of network services are shown in Figure 12.4: the file system, electronic mail, printing, and the library information system. The Andrew file system is perhaps the most important, because it is the basis for so many other services. Network mail, bulletin boards, and printing depend on this large, distributed file system. It provides the file storage and data sharing for users of personal computers that central time-shared computers used to provide. To the user, it appears to be one giant file system, but it actually consists of numerous server computers, managed by several groups on campus. Experiments have even demonstrated the technical feasibility of distributing parts of a single logical file system between Carnegie Mellon and MIT over the NSFNET. The experience gained through building and maintaining this file system is important to the plans to build an electronic library, because the information in the electronic library will also be distributed over many computers.

Whereas the communications network on campus is now nearly complete, the network services are in various stages of completion. Since the Andrew project is based on UNIX, the network services provide excellent support for UNIX workstations but are less convenient from other types of computer. One of the major challenges at present is to provide the same level of service to other personal computers, particularly the very popular Macintoshes.

The Second Generation of the Library Information System

The distributed computing environment is being used to build a distributed library information system. Library databases will be stored on information servers, database engines that provide the essential functions for storing and retrieving information. The software that provides the user interface will run on the user's personal computer. The user will not need to know which server holds the information needed; the new system will appear as unified as the current one. The advantages of the new system are: information can be stored in many places on various types of media; the power of personal computers can be used to build a better user interface; and the system will be used to store full documents, not simply text.

In December 1988, the Pew Memorial Trust provided $1.2 million for a three-year project to implement this second-generation information system. The major items to be funded by the grant are:

- expansion of electronic resources;

- facilities for storage and display of the full text of documents;

- the development of a convenient, flexible user interface;

- integration with word processors and personal bibliographies;

- the use of inexpensive distributed file servers in place of large, central mainframe computers; and

- the systematic enhancement of bibliographic records to improve access to information.

Information Servers

For the second-generation library information system, databases eventually will be stored on several types of computers, and some may be

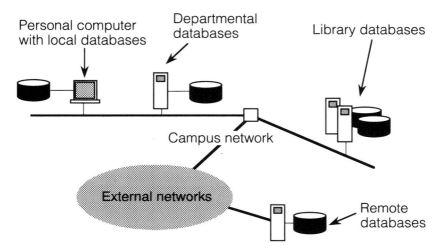

Figure 12.5 The hierarchy of information servers in the new library information system.

maintained by individuals, departments, or remote organizations. Figure 12.5 shows schematically how information servers of various types will be linked to the campus network. For the first stage, Digital VAX 6200 computers running the UNIX operating system are being used, and the databases will be maintained by the library.

Beyond the hardware and the communications support of the campus network, an information server needs database software. Few software packages are suitable for information retrieval from full-text databases in a distributed computing environment. OCLC, however, recently has developed a new database system for its own use that the university will run on the VAX computers. The software will store a great variety of types of information, from catalog records to full documents. As well as text, it can handle graphics, mathematics, and other formats. We expect significant improvements in search capabilities over the current system.

For distributed computing, the format and sequence of messages sent between the personal computer and a server computer on a network must follow a carefully designed specification, known as a protocol. The protocol that appears to be emerging for information retrieval is a national standard with the totally unmemorable name of Z39.50. This standard was developed during the first phase of the Linked Systems Project, for locating and exchanging records among the large bibliographic databases of the Library of Congress, the Research Libraries Group, and OCLC. OCLC is providing Carnegie Mellon with an implementation of Z39.50.

Table 12.2   Databases under Consideration for Library Information System II

Currently licensed	Under consideration
General	
Academic American Encyclopedia[1]	Almanac
American Heritage Dictionary[1]	Thesaurus
Dissertation Abstracts[2]	University information
Magazine Index (IAC)[1]	Oxford Companion Series
National Newspaper Index (IAC)[1]	Oxford English Dictionary
	U.S. GPO Monthly Catalog
	MENU International Software Database
Humanities/Fine Arts	
	Architecture database
	Arts & Humanities Citation Index
	International Bibliography of the Theatre
	Modern Language Association Bibliography
	RILA (art)
	RILM (music)
Social Sciences/Public Policy	
ERIC (education)[2]	America: History and Life
PsycLIT (psychology)[2]	American Statistics Index
	Congressional Information Service
	Historical Abstracts
	Public Affairs Information Service
	Social Science Citation Index
Business/Management	
ABI/INFORM[2]	COMPUSTAT
Corporate & Industrial Research Reports (CIRR)[1]	Economic Literature Index
Management Contents[2]	Working paper abstracts
Trade & Industry Index (IAC)[1]	

Table 12.2   (continued)

Currently licensed	Under consideration
Pure and Applied Sciences	
Kirk-Othmer Encyclopedia[2]	Encyclopedia of Polymer Science
The Computer Database(IAC)[1]	INSPEC (engineering)
	MATHSCI (mathematics)
	NTIS (technical reports)
	Science Citation Index
	Science/technology dictionary

1. Currently licensed on tape
2. Currently licensed on CD-ROM

Databases

An important aspect of the new computing environment is that it supports very large amounts of online storage. An early objective is to license and install a wide range of secondary services. Table 12-2 lists the services currently under consideration. The databases listed cover almost all of the main disciplines at Carnegie Mellon and will go far toward achieving the long-term goal of bringing library resources to everybody's desk.

Enhanced Catalog Records

The plan to enhance current catalog records is a response to the growing realization that traditional MARC records are not ideal for locating items in an online catalog. Because of current cataloging practices, the information found in electronic bibliographic records is limited to author name, title, date and place of publication, and a few subject headings. Sometimes, the information is exactly what the user needs, but, in many cases, it is not sufficient. Experience with the full-text retrieval of bibliographic records in the Library Information System suggests that expanding and enhancing catalog records will provide students and scholars with a greater depth of information, and the utilization of our resources will improve.

The plan is to put into the catalog record the following types of information:

- titles of plays in collections;
- individual papers contained in scientific and technical conference proceedings;
- illustrations in architectural collections; and,
- individually authored chapters of collected books.

Installation

Installation of this new system was under way at the end of 1988. The first VAX server had been installed, and early versions of the OCLC software are being tested. The first new databases will be mounted during 1989.

The Mercury Electronic Library

The second-generation library information system is a very exciting project of immediate value to faculty and students, but it is only a building block in the actualization of the long-term vision of a true electronic library, one that brings to the scholar's desk all of the information needed for research. In particular, the aim is to provide the full text of documents, such as journal articles, in a form so easy to find and to read on the computer screen that scholars will choose to work with them directly on the computer. Achieving this objective requires a blending of computer science research with current library computing experience.

Computer Science Research

It is not surprising that computer science, the discipline in which computers are used most intensively, has come up with the most sophisticated ways to use computing to find and to deliver information. Two areas in which computer scientists are active are particularly important in the building of an electronic library: networks for delivering information from disparate sources and techniques for processing the full text of electronic documents.

The principal network used for computer science research is the ARPANET. Since its introduction in the 1960s, it has created a new way for computer science researchers to exchange information—through electronic mail and bulletin boards. For many purposes, this has proved more effective than traditional forms of communication. Working papers are distributed informally over the network years before the same material is published in journals. A search for information is more likely to be carried out by posting a message on an electronic bulletin board than by visiting a library. For many years, the computer science librarian at Carnegie Mellon has considered electronic information to be a key part of her job. She monitors information on ARPANET bulletin boards and uses electronic mail to copy items to faculty and students. Many faculty members who rarely visit the library and have never met the librarian speak warmly of these services. In this area, at least, librarianship is a changed discipline. And, while computer science is not typical, it is reasonable to speculate that, when researchers in other disciplines are as well equipped with computers, they, too, will work in much the same way.

Techniques for processing complex electronic documents are an active area of research. In 1986, Carnegie Mellon was one of two universities funded by the National Science Foundation EXPRES project on electronic document exchange. (The other was the University of Michigan.) The immediate aim of EXPRES is to create and submit NSF proposals by computer, but the long-term aim is more general: the exchange of scientific information by computer. Documents may include information in many formats, such as text, tables, illustrations, or mathematics. Today, the exchange of formatted text between word processors is feasible, if often cumbersome. The exchange of documents with embedded graphics still presents many technical problems. For preparing documents for the EXPRES project, Carnegie Mellon is using the Andrew Tool Kit; Michigan is using the Diamond system developed by Bolt Beranek and Newman. Much of the challenge of the EXPRES project derives from the difficulties inherent in exchanging complex documents between these totally different architectures.

The Andrew and EXPRES projects have given the university invaluable experience in creating, storing, and displaying full documents by computer. One very important discovery is that, when documents are formatted really well on high-resolution displays, user resistance to reading documents directly from a screen begins to disappear. (As a simple example, the printed version of the help documentation for the Andrew system has been abandoned completely in favor of the online version.) A computer screen is not yet as convenient to read as a well-printed page, but, for works of reference, such as encyclopedias, computers have many advantages. Looking up a cross-reference by computer takes a tiny amount of time compared to that required to do the same task with books; indexes can be much more complete; and, if rapidly changing information is delivered across a network, it can be kept up to date centrally in a way that is impossible with printed materials.

The Mercury Plan
Until a few years ago, these developments in computer science and library automation followed independent paths at Carnegie Mellon (and almost everywhere else). But the formation of the Academic Services division created a climate for cooperation. In the fall of 1987, a proposal was made to build a large-scale electronic library. This library will be called "Mercury." The core planning team included the two authors of this chapter; computer science faculty members James H. Morris and Dana S. Scott; Mark Kibbey, the librarian in charge of library automation; and

Marvin Sirbu, a faculty member from the department of engineering and public policy. Members of the Office of Research at OCLC also have been partners in much of the planning. Digital Equipment Corporation has been a generous supporter, providing several cash grants and equipment valued at $1.25 million that will be used for both Mercury and the new library information system.

Mercury has several aims. The first is to demonstrate that a large-scale distributed library can be built with today's technology. For this purpose, it will function as an actual research library that will contain a large percentage of the information required by a group of scholars and deliver it to them at their desks. It also will be a laboratory for a wide array of studies and experiments in handling information electronically. Finally, the Mercury project will shed more light on two important nontechnical areas: issues of copyright and intellectual property and questions about cost.

The electronic library is not a new vision. However, previous attempts to achieve it, such as MIT's Project Intrex in the 1960s, were too early. They ran into difficulties at every turn: computing equipment was too primitive and too expensive; documents were on paper or microform, not in electronic form; relevant software tools and networks did not exist; the publishing industry and the library users were not prepared to leap so far so quickly. The excitement of planning for Mercury is due to the realization that these barriers are rapidly disappearing.

We believe that it is possible to build, with today's technology, a prototype for a distributed electronic library that could exist on a full-fledged national level ten years from now. Already, high-resolution computer displays and fast networks are widely available. The amalgamation of text with graphics and mathematics is becoming routine. The Andrew file system provides many of the techniques needed to store and retrieve huge numbers of items stored on many different computers.

Computer science has been chosen as the first discipline to use the library. This choice is pragmatic. At present, many of the techniques that will be used to build Mercury are still experimental. The American Association for Artificial Intelligence (AAAI) has been an early supporter of Mercury. With their encouragement, collecting materials in artificial intelligence will be an early priority, as will experiments in computational linguistics and natural language research. Computer scientists already have the equipment on their desks, connected to campus and national networks. Powerful workstations are an integral part of their everyday academic life. They are ready for Mercury.

Design Considerations

Work on Mercury is just beginning, but many of the key design considerations are becoming clear. The overall computing architecture for the second-generation library information system that was illustrated in Figure 12-5 is also intended for storing complete documents. The major computing challenges come from the volume of storage that Mercury requires, the performance of the networks, and the resolution of the displays on the personal computers. Mercury is being built around personal computers with displays of 1,000 by 1,000 pixels and linked by networks with speeds of 1M to 10M bits/second. The second-generation library information system will use conventional magnetic disks; a very impressive system can be built with 50 gigabytes of online storage, as long as all information is stored as ASCII characters. For storing full documents with graphics, much larger storage will eventually be needed. At present, optical disks appear to offer the best promise for building these very large stores, but the technology is still very new. As for speed, the Carnegie Mellon campus network is just fast enough to deliver a full graphic screen, in black and white, from a server computer to a scholar's personal computer in a few seconds. Higher-resolution displays with gray scales and color will need faster networks, but, for the time being, the campus network is fast enough. The NSFNET between research universities is slightly slower but is still fast enough for many purposes.

Perhaps the most important set of early decisions involves the choice of formats for storing complex documents. The challenge is twofold. First, the formats must be technically suitable for what is a very challenging task. Second, there is the issue of standards. An operational electronic library needs to involve many groups of people from a great variety of organizations. Standards are often critical to making rapid progress. Without them, all that can be built is an independent system, incompatible with others, and vulnerable to obsolescence. Yet, early adherence to standards that are technically weak is equally dangerous.

A number of options have been proposed for storing electronic documents. One is to store the documents as scanned images, for instance, in the format used for facsimile transmission. At least one commercial company is busily scanning large numbers of academic documents into this format. The company's first product will be documents on CD-ROM, but the same data formats can be used for Mercury.

Scanned images have some serious disadvantages, however. One problem is the amount of storage required, about 100,000 bytes per page; by comparison, a typical page of unformatted ASCII text requires less than 5,000 bytes of storage. Another problem is that the electronic image will inevitably be of lower quality than the paper image, since resolution is lost in scanning. Finally, information in a scanned image is merely a set of dots, which restricts its usefulness. It can be read but cannot be used to build an index nor can sections be extracted from the whole. As part of Mercury, both OCLC and Carnegie Mellon are conducting experiments in interpreting scanned images by optical character recognition, which would allow the scanned image to be used to build an index. Nobody is yet confident of achieving the accuracy needed for a good index; meanwhile, indexes to retrieve scanned images must continue to be created separately.

Today, almost every document originates on a word processor. There is something very frustrating about taking the electronic format from the word processor, printing it on a page, and then scanning the printed page. The long-term objective is to capture the document in its original machine-readable form. Yet, while this is an attractive goal, the practical difficulties are huge.

When a machine-readable version of a document is available, it can be stored in several ways. The publishing industry is moving steadily toward using a markup language, such as Standard Generalized Markup Language (SGML), as an intermediate step in generating printed documents. For example, a computer version of the entire Oxford English Dictionary has been tagged with SGML markup. The markup language describes the structure of the document, but not how it is to be displayed on a page. To produce a printed copy, design specifications are needed to prescribe how tagged items, such as the body of the text, quoted paragraphs, enumerated lists, and headings of various types, should be laid out.

Storing documents in SGML format has advantages and disadvantages. It is very suitable for a dictionary, since the same material undoubtedly will be used in many products, with different layouts. It also is useful for generating an index, because the structural information can be used to generate multilevel index terms. It also works for some types of computer display, since it is possible to reformat a document as it is being displayed to fit into a window of a specific size or to incorporate an excerpt in some other document. The disadvantage is that the design of the document is lost. As yet, there is no standard way of combining layout design with SGML documents for rapid display on a screen.

The EXPRES project is concentrating on a slightly different strategy, using the draft international standard Office Document Architecture (ODA). Since the ODA standard includes layout information, in theory, it could solve all the problems, but it suffers from the difficulties common with international standards. It is huge and complex, and publishers may never use it. Ideally, it should be possible to display documents exactly as the author or publisher specifies, but the state of development of markup languages and layout specification has not yet reached the point where documents as displayed are necessarily laid out exactly as the designer intended. The initial Mercury plan is to use a combination of SGML and ODA, but this is likely to be modified with time.

Another option has been used for many of the reports generated by the EXPRES project. They are stored in PostScript format. PostScript is a page-description language that gives a complete graphical representation of how a document will appear, whether on the screen or printed on paper. The image can be displayed to the highest resolution that the screen or printer supports, and the storage required for a page of formatted text is not much greater than that needed for the bare ASCII text. Unfortunately, a document represented in PostScript loses structural information, and, sometimes, it even can be difficult to reconstruct the words of the text. Nor can the PostScript representation be easily used to build an index. Nevertheless, reports and communications generated by the Mercury project may be stored and distributed in PostScript format.

Short-Term Plans

Mercury and the second-generation library information system are being built by a single team. The early stages of development are the same for both projects, in particular, the development of the distributed computing environment on the Digital computers. The library information system then will concentrate on acquiring large volumes of textual information, with an emphasis on secondary information, such as abstracts and indexes, while Mercury will begin to capture complete documents (the primary information). Several related research projects already are under way, and a timetable for the full project is being developed. By fall 1989, the Mercury project expects to be able to demonstrate the delivery of the full text of a body of documents in the field of artificial intelligence over the NSFNET.

Conclusion

The rate of progress in library computing at Carnegie Mellon has been remarkable. The work began only in 1981, yet, eight years later, we see no serious technical barriers to building a true electronic library.

The university's joint venture with IBM included a research component to study the social impacts of computing technology. In early 1983, the

University Libraries volunteered for a study of library staff and library user attitudes to be conducted by the Committee on Social Research in Computing. The introduction of central computing and its impact on staff was documented in a survey in the spring of 1983 and a follow-up survey in the spring of 1985.

In their report of that study, the researchers state:

> Computing was to be the solution to the library problem at CMU. At the close of the 1970s, CMU was changing from a regional to a national university. It was attracting more top students and faculty from across the country. The Library, however, had a small and inadequate collection, and its services were too limited for a major research institution. Computers would turn a backwards CMU Library into "the electronic library of the future." They would put CMU "in the forefront of library automation in the country" and "far ahead of any comparable library in the country." Within the library people were told that computerizing library work would demonstrate to the world that the library was participating in the CMU electronic community. It would make the library more popular with students, because CMU students were predisposed to use computers. It would raise the status of library workers with faculty, who already used computers in their everyday work. It would generate more attention and financial support from the university administration. It would enhance the external prestige and job mobility of librarians. Finally, the administrators hoped that by introducing the new technology across the whole library the relatively autonomous departments would be brought closer together.[7]

This rosy picture of only a few years ago concentrated on the automation of traditional library functions. Within five years, most of these objectives had been achieved. As work begins on Mercury, everybody is wondering whether the electronic library will be an adjunct to today's paper-based library or whether it will become the main library service in some disciplines. Nobody on the Mercury team is prepared even to guess at the answer to this question.

Mercury is funded entirely from grant money, and this will continue for the foreseeable future. No traditional library service has been reduced in any way. But, at some stage, the grant funding will run out, and the university will be faced with the dilemma of making trade-offs. Meanwhile, we feel strongly that the only way to discover the value of an electronic library is to build one and to learn by experience.

References

1. Morris, James H., et al. "Andrew: A Distributed Computing Environment." *Communications of the ACM* 29, no. 3 (March 1986): 184–210.

2. Diskin, Gregory M., and Thomas J. Michalak. "Beyond the Online Catalog: Utilizing the OPAC for Library Information." *Library Hi Tech* 2, no. 9 (1985): 71–77.

3. Michalak, Thomas J. "The Application of Centralized Text Editing and Electronic Mail Systems in Libraries: The CMU Experience." *Library Hi Tech* 1, no. 4 (1984): 35–41.

4. Pisciotta, Henry, Nancy Evans, and Marilyn Albright. "Search Helper: Sancho Panza or Mephistopheles?" *Library Hi Tech* 2, no. 3 (1984): 25–32.

5. Evans, Nancy, and Thomas J. Michalak. "Delivering Reference Information through a Campus Network: Carnegie Mellon's Library Information System." *Reference Services Review* 15, no. 4 (Winter 1987): 7–13.

6. Arms, William Y., and John Leong. "Carnegie Mellon University." In *Campus Networking Strategies,* ed. Caroline Arms, EDUCOM Strategies Series on Information Technology (Bedford, Mass.: Digital Press, 1988), pp. 67–89.

7. Kiesler, Sara, Scott Obrosky, and Felicia Pratto. "Automating a University Library: Some Effects on Work and Workers." In *Computing and Change on Campus,* ed. Sara Kiesler and Lee Sproull (Cambridge, England, and New York: Cambridge University Press, 1987), pp. 131–149.

Chapter 13

Johns Hopkins University, Welch Medical Library

Nina W. Matheson

Richard E. Lucier

Robert E. Reynolds

Karen A. Butter

n 1984, the William H. Welch Medical Library at the Johns Hopkins University formally defined its mission and strategies for fully integrating its functions with those of the academic health center. The center's goal is to advance science and health through research, education and training, and health care services. The library's goal is parallel: to advance science and health through services, education and training, and information research. Its service and training components are provided through storage, retrieval, and transfer functions for data, information, and knowledge; its research program focuses on academic knowledge management in medicine and biological sciences.

Overview of the Johns Hopkins Institutions

The Johns Hopkins University (JHU), the Johns Hopkins Health System (JHHS), and the Johns Hopkins Bayview Research Campus make up the Johns Hopkins Institutions (JHI), a highly decentralized and geographically dispersed organization heavily oriented toward research and graduate education.

The Johns Hopkins University, founded in 1876 and privately endowed, is a relatively small but unusually diverse coeducational institution. The School of Arts and Sciences, the School of Engineering, and the university administration are on the main Homewood Campus in North Baltimore. The academic health center, including the Welch Library, is in East Baltimore. Other schools and affiliated institutes are located elsewhere in Baltimore, around Maryland, and in Washington, D.C.

The Johns Hopkins Health System, created as a holding company in 1986, consists of the Johns Hopkins Hospital (JHH), the Francis Scott Key (FSK) Medical Center, the Homewood Hospital Center, and the Johns Hopkins Health Plan, a health maintenance organization with an enrollment of over forty thousand.

The most recently formed of the three elements of the JHI, the Johns Hopkins Bayview Research Campus is a life sciences center located on 130 acres in southeast Baltimore, developed in partnership with the city of Baltimore.

The JHI Communications and Network Strategy

The computing and networking environment of the Johns Hopkins Institutions also is functionally and administratively decentralized and distributed, but networks on the main campus and at the academic health center are interconnected. For the university, the Homewood Computing

Facilities (HCF) furnish centralized time-sharing services, network management, and user support to the Homewood campus, providing access to computer systems from a variety of vendors, among them, AT&T, IBM, and Digital Equipment Corporation.

The Johns Hopkins University objectives for intercampus networking are to provide

- an infrastructure for evolving a medium-speed, multiapplication, multi-vendor data network,
- all users with potential communications access to all available resources, assuming proper authorization,
- dedicated networks for users with similar needs,
- network account security (a backbone accessible to everyone, but dedicated networks requiring authorization), and
- provisions for redundancy, physical security, and survivability.

The strategy for achieving these goals includes:

- medium- to high-speed data transfer over a hierarchical system of baseband Ethernet networks;
- independent support for different higher-level communications protocols, such as DECnet and TCP/IP, in the early stages, with "transparent" network gateways between supported protocols in the longer term;
- network access for lower-speed terminal devices through data switches or digital telephone exchanges;
- hierarchy of networks organized by academic discipline rather than geography whenever possible;
- data, voice, and video transported via complementary but discrete networks;
- data and video services connected between campuses by the institutional microwave system;
- intercampus network links managed centrally whenever possible; and
- access to external networks, supercomputers, and other special-purpose computing facilities provided through centralized Hopkins facilities.

Currently, five interconnected, Ethernet-based networks link the humanities, engineering, basic and social sciences, central administration, and the space telescope and astrophysics network. A total of 1,500 network access points are planned; of the 650 now in use, over half are

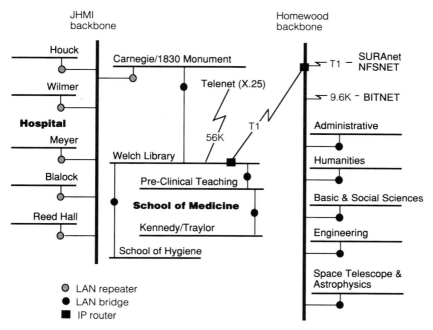

Figure 13.1 The JHMI/Homewood Ethernet network topology.

asynchronous, terminal-to-host connections using terminal servers based on DECnet and/or TCP/IP. This network and the academic health center network are depicted in Figure 13.1.

The Academic Health Center

Clustered in East Baltimore, the School of Medicine, School of Nursing, School of Hygiene and Public Health, the William H. Welch Medical Library, and the Johns Hopkins Hospital are known as the Johns Hopkins Medical Institutions (JHMI). The Johns Hopkins School of Medicine is a research-intensive institution that ranks among the top three institutions funded for biomedical research by the National Institutes of Health. The School of Hygiene and Public Health is known internationally for its specialized academic programs in environmental health sciences, health policy and management, international health, and population dynamics. The School of Nursing offers a two-year, upper-division baccalaureate program and a master's program in affiliation with three Baltimore hospitals.

All physicians at the hospital and the FSK Medical Center hold faculty appointments at the medical school. There are approximately thirteen thousand academic faculty, students, house staff, and support staff within the medical institutions and the health system. It is to this extensive medical community affiliated with the university that the William H. Welch Medical Library provides information services.

The Changing Academic Health Center Environment

Academic health centers are working within an increasingly competitive environment where information strategies take on new significance. Competition is particularly intense in research. Schools are looking beyond funding from the National Institutes of Health to the commercial sector. In addition to expanding the health care system, the university and the hospital have created a for-profit corporation called Dome. As well as operating several profitable services, the Dome Corporation is developing a venture capital subsidiary that will facilitate the marketing of outcomes from faculty research. In such a market-oriented environment, information support takes on a different cast. The pressures for libraries to provide information products and services in a market-oriented mode are beginning to intensify.

The traditional structure of medical education is also changing. Typically, the third and fourth years of medical school are given over to clerkships in hospital wards; at the graduate level, internships and residencies are three- to five-year programs in teaching hospitals. Now, because of federal and state cost-containment regulations, inpatient stays are being curtailed drastically in favor of increased ambulatory care. More and more learning must take place in smaller, widely distributed sites, and the opportunities to observe patients closely over a period of time are lost. Better means must be found to deliver information for clinical learning and decision making to remote sites.

Influences on Medical Information Management Strategies

Equally influential is the impact of several national organizations on the information technology strategies of academic health centers. These organizations are the Association of American Medical Colleges (AAMC), the Association of Academic Health Centers (AAHC), the National Library of Medicine (NLM) and the National Board of Medical Examiners (NBME). Between 1982 and 1986, these associations issued five reports, proposing new directions for information technology management and medical informatics applications. (Medical informatics, broadly defined, combines medical science with technologies and disciplines in the information and computer sciences to provide methodologies for the management of information to support medical research, education, and patient care.)

Concerned with the issues of resource management raised by the new information technologies, AAMC published two crucial studies in 1982. The first reviewed the policy considerations of information management in academic medicine; its major objective was "to stimulate the leaders of medical schools or academic health centers to plan vigorously for the information management future of their institutions."[1] The second study considered potential roles for the library in information management.[2] It proposed that institutional networks link a technologically sophisticated library with intra- and extramural information systems to create an integrated academic information system to support the education, research, and patient care missions of academic health centers. Two years later, the AAHC reinforced these messages by issuing a call for commitment at the highest administrative levels to strategic management of the medical computing environment.[3]

No academic health center can plan its computing and information strategies for the 1990s without defining the place of medical informatics in its medical education, health care, and research programs. This is true, in part, because computers are so basic to modern medical practice. But, more importantly, the academic leadership in medicine has recognized the need explicitly.

Two AAMC publications address the place of medical informatics in medical education. Published in 1984, *Physicians for the Twenty-First Century* grew out of a three-year nationwide study of the professional education of physicians. Aimed at reorienting the emphases in medical education, a critical recommendation calls for medical schools to "designate an academic unit for institutional leadership in the application of information sciences and computer technology to the general professional education of physicians and promote their effective use."[4] The following year, the AAMC sponsored a symposium on medical informatics, entitled Medical Education in the Information Age, to assist academic health centers "to develop a new consensus...concerning the contributions of medical information science and related technologies in meeting the goals of our medical centers."[5] The proceedings describe the state of the art and an agenda of activities that will foster the development of medical informatics. As expressed in the foreword:

> The Association believes that the knowledge explosion which is occurring in medicine and the basic biomedical sciences, coupled with the physician's responsibility for lifelong learning, dictates that medical students and physicians learn to use new strategies for managing the information and knowledge available to them for the treatment of patients. It is necessary for

Table 13.1   Academic Health Centers with NLM Grants for Planning or Modeling Integrated Academic Information Management Systems

American College of Obstetricians & Gynecologists	Harvard University
	Johns Hopkins University
Baylor College of Medicine	University of Maryland
University of Cincinnati	University of Michigan
Columbia University	University of Pittsburgh
Dartmouth College	Rhode Island Hospital
Duke University	University of Utah
Georgetown University	

> our medical schools to change the process of education to de-emphasize the acquisition of knowledge and emphasize information-organizing and problem-solving. Medical information sciences, computers, and new understanding about the processes of clinical decision-making can be powerful factors in education and in information management and analysis.[6]

Another motivation for change in medical education is supplied by the National Board of Medical Examiners, which constructs and supervises examinations required for graduation from most U.S. medical schools. Beginning in 1990, the board will initiate problem-oriented, interactive, computer-based testing.

The National Library of Medicine has provided unwavering leadership and support in this arena for many years. Its training grant programs, initiated in 1972, supported exposure to medical information science for physicians. Presently, postdoctoral training is offered to further research careers in medical informatics. A small but significant grant program has supported research in and development of expert systems.

In 1983, the NLM implemented one of the major AAMC study recommendations, initiating a grant program aimed at developing several prototype Integrated Academic Information Management Systems (IAIMS). The goal is to provide professionals in health sciences institutions with convenient access to an integrated and comprehensive electronic network of data, information, and knowledge, whenever and wherever needed. Each IAIMS prototype is expected to evolve through three phases. The first phase is a one- to two-year strategic planning process. In the second phase, the plan is modeled and tested for two to three years. Institutionwide implementation of the model takes place in a third phase, over an initial five-year period. This NLM program has generated much interest, and its progress is well documented.[7] So far,

Table 13.2   Major Time-Sharing Hosts on the JHMI Ethernet

Location	Computer	Operating System	Use
Johns Hopkins Hospital	IBM 3081	VM/CMS	Administrative
	IBM 3083	VM/CMS	Administrative
	Pyramid 98x (5)	UNIX	Administrative/clinical
	PDP 11/70 (3)	MUMPS	Clinical
	VAX 11/750	UNIX	Research
	PDP 11/84 (2)	MUMPS	Clinical/research
School of Hygiene and Public Health	IBM 4341	VM/CMS	Academic/research
	VAX 11/780 (2)	UNIX	Academic/research
School of Medicine	Harris HCX-9	UNIX	Academic/research
	PDP 11/70 (2)	MUMPS	Administrative
	VAX 8500	VMS	Research
Welch Medical Library	Data General MV-8000	MIIS/MUMPS	Academic
	Sun 4/280	UNIX	Research

thirteen academic health centers and one medical specialty society, listed in Table 13.1, have received support for strategic planning and modeling of prototypes.

Computing strategies for academic health centers differ from general university approaches in several striking ways. Through leadership from associations like AAMC and federal agencies like the NLM, a strategic view of medical knowledge management has been articulated, some approaches have been defined, and the means to model and test these approaches have been made available. Most remarkably, libraries' roles are expected to extend far beyond traditional on-site storage, retrieval, and dissemination of biomedical information.

Computing Strategies for the JHMI

At the Johns Hopkins Medical Institutions, computers are used intensively to support the clinical, administrative, and research missions of the health center. Major time-sharing computers currently in use are listed in Table 13.2. Consistent long-term approaches to data-communications needs date from 1984, when an Ethernet local area network was installed. As

depicted in Figure 13.1, the network has ten major segments, all connected to a backbone segment by protocol-independent bridges and
repeaters. Although physically one network, it is organized logically into
four subnets, for the Schools of Hygiene and Medicine, the hospital, and
the Welch Library. In early 1990, these subnets will be separated physically through the installation of IP routers, which will improve performance
by confining most traffic within the individual subnets but also supporting
TCP/IP protocols across the entire network.

The network provides both high-speed, host-to-host and low-speed,
terminal-to-host services. Most high-speed services are based on TCP/IP
protocols, as well as a small amount of DECnet traffic. Low-speed service
presently is handled by terminal servers using XNS protocols; these
devices are scheduled to be replaced by TCP/IP terminal servers in late
1989. Since 1986, a data-over-voice service offered by the local
telephone company (Central Office LAN) has provided access to the
network for terminal users who are not close to a network segment.
Currently, over one hundred users have signed up for this service. In late
1988, T1 service was established between the JHMI internet and the
Homewood internet. This provides JHMI users with easy access to
SURAnet and national networks.

The JHMI network development was spearheaded by Robert E.
Reynolds, the Associate Dean for Administration and Hospital Affairs at
the medical school. Network operations are coordinated by a group that
is part of the Information Systems Department at the hospital. Network
development and planning are coordinated by a committee consisting of
senior representatives from all parts of the academic health center and
the Homewood campus. Particular operational and development issues
being addressed currently are shown in Table 13.3. The objective is to
extend network access, to provide integrated network services, and to
increase capacity for the growing demand.

The School of Medicine Integrated Academic Information Management Strategy

In 1985, the School of Medicine and the Welch Library jointly received a
one-year grant from the NLM for planning an Integrated Academic Information Management System (IAIMS). This focused attention on future
information needs and emerging technologies in medicine and science.
It also provided the framework, possibly the "skunkworks," to accelerate
the maturation of several nascent ideas.

The planning process involved three broadly representative faculty
committees: the Communications Network Committee, the Bibliographic

Table 13.3   Critical Networking Issues Being Addressed at JHMI

- Development of a JHMI Premises Distribution Plan for wiring to ensure orderly and timely network growth and development
- A link between the Ethernet and the JHMI ISDN Digital Centrex telephone system, based on the ISO standard X.25 network protocol, by early 1990
- Development of a JHMI Integrated Electronic Messaging solution by 1989. As currently envisioned, the ISO X.400 standard mail protocol will be employed to integrate the various messaging systems currently in use (e.g., UNIX Sendmail, Digital's All-in-One and VMSmail, and IBM's PROFS)
- Replacement of the 10M bits/second, coaxial JHMI Ethernet backbone with a 100M bits/second, Fiber Distributed Data Interface (FDDI) backbone by 1991
- Migration from TCP/IP to ISO/OSI protocols by 1993

Database Committee, and the Knowledge Representation Committee. The outcome of their deliberations is a working document that articulates a long-range vision and a set of pragmatic strategies to realize it; these are being implemented in an evolutionary and task-oriented fashion. The network strategy outlined above was the first result. A recommendation to create a Division of Medical Informatics in the School of Medicine was explored both informally and formally within the JHU Medical Advisory Board and is still under study. The Welch Library was given a mandate to manage, develop, and improve access to academic databases through research, education programs, and service initiatives.

The Long-Term Vision: A Knowledge Management Environment
Within the next decade, JHMI workers will meet the majority of their information needs through a hierarchical network of local and remote electronic databases. They will use multipurpose desktop workstations on local communications networks to access a larger internet of national and international networks. Heavily used literature databases and operational clinical systems will be available on local computers, with transparent links to less frequently accessed databases on remote computers. Workers will be able to move easily between clinical and literature databases to retrieve facts, refresh their memories, record relevant data in patients' management records, make decisions about treatments and procedures, access online texts and reference works, review the literature, prepare and administer examinations, compose book chapters, develop and maintain a knowledge base, and communicate with colleagues. Improved software for literature searches, full-text retrieval, and support of the authoring process will respond flexibly to everyday working

needs. For maximum effectiveness, the interface between the system and worker will simulate a desktop and contain a set of online tools as simple to use as a pencil. Initially text oriented, the environment eventually will support voice and image processing. The distant goal is a knowledge management environment, a network of databases that individuals will be able to tap as they do their own memories.

Strategies toward the Future—Multiple Prototype Development

The JHMI strategy is to work toward the knowledge management environment by developing two prototypes, the clinical workstation and the IAIMS workstation. For the clinical workstation, design specifications and requirements were established in early 1984. A team in the hospital is deploying prototypes in selected JHH inpatient nursing stations during the first half of 1989. This project is intended to provide tools to support access to data from multiple distributed databases, to integrate information in formats that can be applied directly to clinical decision making, and to provide the most efficient management of services to patients. In addition to clinical and administrative data, the workstation will provide access to reference sources for medicinal drugs and databases of medical literature. Users will be the faculty clinicians, postgraduate fellows, residents, interns, nurses, and others involved in patient care. The vehicle selected for development is the Sun Microsystems workstation, a UNIX-based, multiuser, multiwindowed environment with a high-resolution, bit-mapped display.

The IAIMS workstation is being developed within the Welch Library in the Laboratory for Applied Research in Academic Information. Its focus is utilization of bibliographic and full-text literature files for study, instruction, research, clinical decision making, and authorship. The development work (discussed in more detail later) will be on both Sun and Apple Macintosh II workstations. The software environment will be based on Brown University's Intermedia software and the IRX search software developed at the National Library of Medicine.

The concurrent development of the two workstations acknowledges common goals while recognizing several fundamental differences between operational clinical databases and scholarly academic databases. The character, presentation, and format of information differ in these two types of databases; the manipulation tools necessary will vary according to time, place, problem, and user class. The convergence of these complementary prototypes, when both are robust, will result in a multi-dimensional knowledge management environment. This approach mirrors the strategy of independent but linked networks for the hospital and academic communities and follows the usual pattern of diversity in the Johns Hopkins community.

The Welch Medical Library—An Overview

At its formal dedication in 1929, the William H. Welch Medical Library consisted of approximately 77,000 volumes of books and periodicals brought together from the hospital, the School of Medicine, and the School of Hygiene and Public Health. An additional 18,000 volumes in rare books and special collections represented gifts from and purchases by the School of Medicine's founding fathers and distinguished early faculty.

Today, the Welch Library is a network of storage and service sites supported by a growing base of information made available across a series of interlinked networks. The entire JHU academic community has access to the Welch Library, as well as to four small satellite libraries. Three of these satellites serve the special information needs in oncology, psychiatry/neurology, and nursing; the fourth is an information resource center for medical students. The combined collections number more than 377,000 volumes. Approximately 70 percent of the monograph collection (nearly all pre-1970 publications) and 15 percent of the journal collection, are shelved in an easily accessible off-campus annex.

The 1988/89 total operating budget for resources and services is $2,852,546. Of 127 academic health center libraries in the United States and Canada, the Welch library ranks sixth in total expenditures and seventh in the number of primary clients.

Administrative Relationships

The Welch Library is one of six independently administered libraries serving the Johns Hopkins Institutions. The six directors form the University Library Council, which meets quarterly to exchange information and consider overarching policy concerns.

The Welch Library is deemed a unit of the School of Medicine, and the director reports to the Vice President for Medicine and the Dean of the Medical Faculty through the Associate Dean for Academic Affairs. The director also is advised by the Welch Information Services subcommittee of the JHMI Joint Administrative Committee, which consists of the executive officers of the JHMI and JHU and is concerned with intercampus issues such as parking, security, facilities development and new initiatives.

Organization

The Welch Library has seventy-six full-time employees, organized into four divisions. Resources Management, with a staff of twenty-eight, is responsible for the facilities and administrative services, stacks management, and collection development and processing, including electronic database resources. Information System Services performs classic reference services, provides interlibrary loan, document delivery, and photocopy services, carries out online searching, and offers instruction in database use and personal information management. This division of thirty-eight staffs a small microcomputer center and four remote service centers in addition to the Welch Library. The Laboratory for Applied Research in Academic Information (known as the Lab) focuses on developing tools for knowledge management. Its staff of eight is primarily supported through grants and contracts. The Welch Library Computer Systems Office is the fourth division; it manages the library's production systems and their connection to the JHMI network. The staff of five maintains and enhances hardware and software for the library's online system of databases and supports its office automation network and the Welch interface to the JHMI network.

Computing Resources

The library's production systems and services run on a Data General computer with eighty communication ports. These services utilize public domain software enhanced by staff programmers. The Integrated Library System (ILS), developed at NLM, supports ordering, cataloging, and circulation of all books, audiovisuals, and microcomputer software, as well as serials check-in, binding information, and billing functions for most library services. Also installed is WELMED, the library's newly developed software for local database management, based on NLM's TOXNET software. Both systems are written and run in the MIIS (Meditech Interpretive Information System), a dialect of the ANSI standard MUMPS, a high-level programming language widely used in academic health centers. The Welch Library is one of two academic health center libraries that develop and manage their own system hardware, software, and databases. Systems development is on a Digital PDP 11/44.

Research and development in the Lab is supported by a Sun Microsystems 4/280, a network of five Sun workstations for development, a network of three Suns for testing, and twenty Macintosh II workstations in test sites. There are more than fifteen public access terminals in the reading rooms and reference areas. A small public microcomputer center provides access to three Macintosh SEs and three IBM PCs networked to a laser printer.

For office automation, the library is migrating from IBM PCs to an AppleTalk network of Macintoshes. The network provides access to three laser printers and a modem. Approximately sixty of the staff are individually equipped with microcomputers. The Welch Library electronic mail system supports the majority of internal communications.

Philosophy and Strategy for Welch Library Services

While the medical institutions as a whole established a plan for an integrated information management system, the Welch Library implemented its own extensive internal operational planning process. Achievement of the long-range vision described earlier requires the design and delivery of new information services, tools, and products. Reallocation of existing resources, including personnel, is necessary, so it is crucial that the library staff understand and accept the strategic vision.

Over the winter and spring of 1984/85, the library management developed a five-year plan and a set of strategies. We began with the premise that the Welch Library should follow the Hopkins clinical departmental model, in which service, research, and education are seen as interlocking functions, each extending and amplifying the others and aimed at advancing scientific and medical knowledge. We identified the library's mission as the management of information and knowledge by means of a highly distributed, high-performance information-transfer system. This requires us to transform the library from a physical facility for storage and retrieval into an academic unit with service responsibilities. To move toward that goal we must

- manage and control our system design and development,
- build tools, interfaces, and databases,
- provide access to essential databases—bibliographic, numeric, and textual,
- teach information and knowledge management, and
- conduct research in medical information science.

The strategies chosen to fulfill this mission were to make basic services (finding, getting, and photocopying books and journals) as efficient and free from criticism as possible, to give expressed user needs the highest priority, to build incrementally and opportunistically on each achievement, to work on parallel, complementary, and convergent functions, and to secure extramural funding for new research ventures. We acquire the materials that have the greatest utility for the largest number of users and provide catalog and indexing access without cost. The resources of other libraries are considered extensions of the Welch collections, and we provide free access to them through routine procedures such as inter-library loan. Access to remote information resources and services also is available through Welch systems, but the costs are assumed by the requester.

Consensus Development

The Welch management group drafted documents laying out the philosophy and strategies. We shared these with a small ad hoc committee consisting of the JHMI administrative officers and a few faculty. We also gave them a list of new services, such as the introduction of various databases, and asked them to judge their desirability and priority. Their advice was to cut out the jargon and explain the outcomes and benefits to the users in simple terms. After several meetings, we had reduced these process and procedure documents to two lists: a year-by-year scenario of new Welch Library systems and services (see Table 13.4) and a list of the steps required to meet that schedule. Most aspects of this scenario have been realized; those that remain are still valid but not yet attainable.

Having secured explicit support from the JHMI leadership, we drafted a detailed five-year management plan and began a series of meetings to introduce the concepts and strategies to library staff. We then assembled a core planning group of thirteen library staff. The Core Group consists of the five senior library administrators (also called the Key Group) and eight individuals selected because of their strategic functions, rather than their professional degrees or administrative responsibilities. These include the personnel administrator, the interlibrary loan supervisor, the stacks and shelving manager, a satellite library manager, the database development coordinator, bibliographic database services librarian, education program librarian, and reference services coordinator.

Using the management plan as a background, the Core Group started over and devised the mission statement and operating plan now in use. The mission is to advance science and health through information. The goal is to develop an electronic environment for effective information transfer and knowledge management to support excellence in research, patient care, and education. This requires a set of tools for accessing, maintaining, and organizing databases that support clinical decision making and the knowledge base of the published literature. The Key Group provides strategic direction; the Core Group, which meets at least monthly, is responsible for overseeing the development of action plans to implement decisions. New ideas and opportunities are discussed by these groups before being incorporated into the planning. Senior

Table 13.4   Summary Projections Made in 1985 of Future Systems and Services

1985   Users of the library's automated system can search the online catalog of the books in the Welch collections published since 1970. Users
also may search a file of journal citations, called JHMI miniMEDLINE,
representing 425 biomedical journal titles covering a three-year
period. Access to the library's system is via terminals in the Welch
library and its satellites. Individuals also may use a terminal or microcomputer to call up the library's system from their offices or homes
twenty-four hours a day. Remote access to library services and
resources is provided through four satellite library operations and
other locations throughout JHMI.

1986   Users have access to expanded information as the online catalog
includes records for the library's journal holdings and items in the
History of Medicine collection, and the JHMI miniMEDLINE file
doubles in size to include eight hundred biomedical journal titles.
Users may place requests for photocopies, books, and computer
searches via the library's electronic mail system. Requests for
reference information and consulting services also are made via the
electronic mail system. A new database consisting of answers to the
most-often-asked reference questions, called Quick/Fact Answer, is
operational in a test mode. The library's computer systems are
nodes on the JHMI Ethernet, providing network access to all JHMI
users. Librarians work with the faculty to maintain course syllabi,
lecture notes, and reading lists online. The Microcomputer Lab is a
repository and distribution site for public domain software as well as
the center for micro-based, computer-assisted instruction programs.

1987   Users may create a search profile that is matched automatically
against the monthly updates to the JHMI miniMEDLINE and online
catalog files. The results of these automatic updates are available to
the user online or via printouts. The JHMI miniMEDLINE file is
expanded to include abstracts of the articles (as well as relevant information from commercial systems such as BIOSIS and Chemical
Abstracts Online). Users may make online requests for books and
journal articles cited in either the online catalog or the JHMI
miniMEDLINE system. Faculty and students have access to library-
sponsored formal instruction and consultation in personal information
management. Interested students will work with the library to evaluate
alternative personal database management (PDM) models as part of
a research effort to develop a prototype PDM. The library's satellite
network is expanded to additional remote locations with Lilienfeld
Library (in the School of Public Health), and all satellites are linked
electronically to the Welch Library and each other. Access to the
university's Milton S. Eisenhower Library catalog is available through
linkages of the JHMI and Homewood data-communications networks.
The library is involved with faculty members in electronic publication.

Table 13.4   (continued)

1988   Users have access, through the online catalog, to the collections of the major JHMI departmental libraries. The JHMI MEDLINE file is expanded to include all journal titles held within JHMI. In light of new technologies, the library examines its hardware/software configurations with particular attention to the distribution of its databases and processing capabilities. The full text of needed documents can be transferred electronically directly to the user's or department's microcomputer. The Microcomputer Laboratory is used by faculty and students to test the application of new technologies in a variety of educational, research, and clinical applications.

1989   Technological advances allow the library to distribute, in compact disk format, copies of all or part of its databases for use by individuals or departments on their microcomputer(s). Voice recognition and translation technologies allow users to make verbal queries and entries to the files. The JHMI departments utilize micro-based file-management systems, which are updated regularly from the Welch information system.

---

management takes responsibility for relating the Welch Library's strategies to the JHMI IAIMS strategies. The associate and assistant directors serve on the appropriate networking, database, and informatics research committees.

The Welch Library Role in the JHMI IAIMS

The technical elements of a knowledge management environment are networks, databases, and workstations. The Welch Library's contribution to the JHMI Integrated Academic Information Management System is twofold. The Welch Library online information-transfer system provides the network component, while the Laboratory for Applied Research in Academic Information is developing the technical and educational components of a knowledge workstation.

The Welch Library Online Information Transfer System
In the first phase of technology adoption, new technologies simply do what always has needed to be done, only faster and better. Replacing our old methods with new has absorbed our attention for the past five years.

Online Databases
The Welch Library made its first online database, a public access catalog, available in 1983. The database included records for the most heavily

used materials—post-1970 books. In 1985, a circulation subsystem was added, allowing users searching the catalog to check whether materials listed were available. By 1986, all pre-1950 titles were incorporated, and the system was open to remote dial-up access. In 1987, library users were offered online access to holdings information for the collection of nearly 5,000 serials. By the end of 1989, the JHMI Online Catalog will include more than 156,000 monographic titles.

It was not until late 1985 that the second database was introduced. Journal literature is of considerable value to scientific researchers, since the half-life of scientific information can be as short as six months. While the library staff performed close to three thousand online searches a year, patrons made it clear that they would welcome the ability to search for journal citations on their own—in fact, after two months of active solicitation, representatives of BRS boasted of selling several hundred passwords in the Department of Medicine alone. Therefore, as soon as the National Library of Medicine authorized libraries to lease all or part of the MEDLARS file, we leased the Georgetown Medical Center Library's pioneering MiniMEDLINE software. In December 1985, we made Welch MEDLINE 500 available for free searching in the library, offering indexes to the 455 most heavily used journal titles in JHMI collections. Initially, the coverage extended back three years. (At the time, this was the largest file mounted on a local system under MiniMEDLINE software.) Responding to popular demand, we added abstracts to the files; in mid-1987, network access became available. Use continues to expand; during 1987/88, 45,261 searches were performed, an increase of 17 percent over the previous year.

Anecdotal evidence suggests interesting benefits to faculty. One is improved online searching of commercial systems. Users who subscribe to BRS want access to the largest databases possible in order to find even the most obscure references. These users develop and hone their queries on our smaller MEDLINE 500 database until they are satisfied with the search criteria; then they dial the commercial service for the most efficient search possible. One scientist now logs on to MEDLINE 500 before he starts an experiment. This way, he can easily search for related information if he observes something unexpected or explore new ideas as they occur to him. Another faculty member says that he can satisfy his curiosity or test a hypothesis so easily in MEDLINE 500 that he no longer puts off searching.

We plan to extend coverage and comparability of these two databases. In the catalog, we will provide index access to the contents of some monographs that are collections of individually authored chapters; we also will explore the feasibility of including book reviews. And we plan to extend the MEDLINE 500 database in several ways. Many users say that they prefer to search a larger file, not because of the breadth of journal titles or the number of years covered, but because they want to search for review articles. We will augment the file with review articles that extend beyond the four-year range of the database. It is our intent to expand the database to include all scholarly journal titles for which we maintain subscriptions.

The third file was added in late 1987. The Blades Center for Clinical Practice, Teaching and Research in Alcoholism offers an alcohol information service. An important feature of this service is WELCORK, a file produced at the Dartmouth Medical School as part of Project Cork. It contains more than 7,300 references to books, journal articles, conferences, and technical reports on alcohol and related drugs. Originating in 1978 as a four-year program to develop a medical school curriculum dealing with the effects of alcohol and the treatment of related problems, the Project Cork Institute now develops resources to support education on alcohol across the entire medical community. The Blades Center pays for the lease of the file, but the Welch Library makes it available to all JHMI users.

The next extension in bibliographic access, online Current Contents, required a different strategy. MEDLINE 500 was no risk; users had more than ten years experience with MEDLINE and knew its benefits. The Current Contents database contains limited but very current information, indexing articles in selected journals published during the previous three months by words in titles, but without abstracts or subject headings. We wanted to test demand and benefits before committing resources to computing support and tape leases. We learned that the University of Maryland Health Sciences Library was in the same situation. After nine months of discussions, we agreed to split database costs and explore interinstitutional networking issues. On June 15, 1988, the Current Contents file at Maryland was opened to free dial-up access by registered JHU faculty. In the first five months, the number of users tripled, and the number of logged hours more than doubled. Interinstitutional network access is anticipated in the second quarter of 1989.

WELMED

WELMED is the name the Welch Library uses for a family of databases searched under an enhanced version of NLM's TOXNET software. Our goal is to provide a common user interface, with a single set of commands and display features, for all Welch Library bibliographic databases.

The WELMED software is a result of collaboration among the Welch Library, the NLM's Division of Specialized Information Services, and the

University of Maryland Health Sciences Library. All three use the MIIS-MUMPS operating system and had something to gain from enhancing TOXNET. An agreement was concluded in late 1986; by June 1988, all Welch Library databases became available under WELMED. Access is through on-site terminals, via telephone dial-up, or across the JHMI Ethernet. After logging on, the user encounters a menu enumerating the databases. Searches on all databases, except for the catalog, are conducted in a uniform fashion: commands operate in the same way but the detailed search options vary. In addition to author, keyword, and title searches (and Boolean combinations), MEDLINE 500 options include a MeSH subject·heading search option, while WELCORK allows searches by terms in the "WELCORK" thesaurus. The user may customize the display and print features: citations can be in either chronological or reverse chronological order; journal titles can be full or abbreviated; subject headings and abstracts can be suppressed or included. Searches can be saved from session to session. In the future, users will be able to search across databases without having to leave one and enter another.

WELMED allows us to offer several new services online. In the MED-LINE 500 file, pressing a single key initiates a photocopy order in the library's document delivery service unit. Book delivery and interlibrary loan request processing eventually will be handled in a similar fashion. In addition, we will develop automatic gateways to commercial databases. With appropriate software controls at our end, we should be able to negotiate a favorable institutional rate.

The alternative to in-depth searching on remote services is access to full files on compact disks; PsycLIT and MEDLARS are now available for use in the Welch Library. However, if demand arises for local online access to these full files, we will develop a prototype rapidly, installing test files and monitoring use before committing ourselves fully.

The WELMED system requires all users to enter personal user numbers and hence provides some useful controls that allow us to study use patterns for collection management purposes. Usage measurements also permit more precise allocation of operating costs.

WELMED supports the local development of databases. Library staff worked with Academic Affairs staff in the School of Medicine to develop a curriculum information database, indexed by keywords describing the content of lectures. Among other uses, this database permits deans and course directors to identify lacunae and redundancies in the curriculum. Another specialized database is the Psychiatry/Neurology Core Concept Database, representing the core materials that support clinical education in the fields of psychiatry, behavioral sciences, neurology, and neurosurgery. Materials cited are selected and annotated by faculty. Initially composed of citations and brief annotations, the file eventually may be expanded to include large text segments. Both of these databases are in prototype stages.

Training and Technology Diffusion
In the 1970s, libraries established audiovisual centers to accommodate new instructional formats. The need quickly emerged for technical staff to maintain and troubleshoot equipment. In the 1980s, libraries have established microcomputer labs to accommodate new formats for information and knowledge management. While a need for technical expertise has emerged, this is not a case of "déjà vu all over again"; we cannot stop after showing people how to turn on machines and which way to insert diskettes. Another order of expertise is needed. Hardware and software are unstable and likely to remain so for several more years. The structure of the databases themselves, particularly full-text files, is equally dynamic. Furthermore, using these technologies is far from an intuitive process. It has become apparent in the last four years that the educational responsibilities of librarians must encompass tutorials in software use, ranging from communications to database searching techniques. It appears to us that the need for this kind of user support will intensify until a workstation with a comprehensive set of tools for knowledge management is developed.

Laboratory for Applied Research in Academic Information
Just as better tools are needed to create and use databases, new approaches to the online representation of text need to be explored. We have begun the second phase of technology adoption: using new technologies to do different things.

The long-term goal of the Laboratory for Applied Research in Academic Information is to develop a knowledge management environment. We define knowledge management as the application of research from the computer, information, and behavioral sciences to the creation, representation, storage, dissemination, and use of the knowledge base. The Lab is assembling an interdisciplinary team with expertise in these areas to pursue that goal through software development, education, partnerships with scientists and scholars, and assessment. Our implementation strategy is twofold: to create prototypes of new tools and to adapt and improve existing ones.

This approach has led to collaboration with three organizations. The first is the NLM. Under contracts with the Information Technology Branch (ITB) of Lister Hill National Center for Biomedical Communications (LHC) at the NLM, the Lab is involved in the implementation and testing of IRX (Information Retrieval Experiment). IRX is experimental UNIX-based retrieval software developed by LHC and available to biomedical institutions on a collaborative basis for biotechnology and information technology research. There are plans to make it available through the National Technical Information Service at some future date. The second collaboration is through an interinstitutional agreement with the Institute for Research in Information and Scholarship (IRIS) at Brown University for the testing and extension of IRIS's hypermedia system, Intermedia. Third, a research memorandum with Apple Computer provides an equipment grant of Macintosh II workstations for research in knowledge management and a consulting liaison from Apple's Advanced Technology Division.

Our work with two text databases illustrates the content and process of the Lab's work. The first is directed to the creation of an environment for scientific research, while the second is primarily concerned with issues of knowledge management in clinical decision making and graduate medical education.

Knowledge Management in Human Genetics

In 1985, the Welch Library had the good fortune to begin a unique collaboration with the LHC's ITB and with Dr. Victor A. McKusick, author of *Mendelian Inheritance in Man* and then chairman of the Department of Medicine.[8] All of us had our separate objectives. ITB was interested in developing a new program to support the creation of online reference works in medicine and in the further development of IRX. Dr. McKusick was looking for better ways to keep his book up-to-date and easier to publish; he was intrigued by the idea of making the book available online to his colleagues and of enhancing the text through graphic images of disorders. For the Welch Library, it was an opportunity to begin a research program that would test IAIMS concepts. The idea is to provide complete electronic support for a scholarly cycle—from searching the literature, through creating new knowledge, to publishing and distributing the information.

Mendelian Inheritance in Man is recognized internationally as a unique and important source of medical genetic information. It catalogs all human traits and disorders that are inherited in a Mendelian manner. The sixth edition, published by the Johns Hopkins University Press in 1983, consisted of about thirty-four hundred entries and eighteen thousand literature references on 1,738 tightly printed pages. About five hundred changes were made to entries each month; these were gathered together every two to four years into a new edition. Each entry consists of a unique identifying number and the name of the disorder, followed by a narrative that includes a description of the phenotype, the nature of the basic defect, and a review of the literature to date. The references are the sources of the information in the narrative. Two important appendixes augment the text: the Human Gene Map and Molecular Defects in Mendelian Disorders. The text is indexed by the names of the disorders and the names of authors who have published on the disorders.

Dr. McKusick's staff already maintained the text in machine-readable form. The first step for the project was to make this available for online searching under IRX. IRX accepts natural-language terms and Boolean combinations of terms and provides a ranked output of search results to the user. Between 1985 and 1988, staff at ITB worked on technical software developments and designed the online version. The Welch Library staff coordinated the project on site at the hospital, working with ITB staff, users, expert consultants, and the author (1) to identify information needs; (2) to introduce the online system; (3) to assess the features of the IRX search software; (4) to develop a thesaurus; and (5) to create a video disk of related photographs and radiographs. We also investigated the feasibility of creating a family of linked human genetics textbooks online.

In September 1986, the project expanded. As a result of support from the Howard Hughes Medical Institute, Online Mendelian Inheritance in Man ceased to be an experimental file for NLM and JHH. It is now available without charge to the scientific community across Telenet and the international packet-switching network. In the first ten months, more than seven hundred users made nearly three thousand database accesses. The average search time is fifteen minutes and more than 20 percent of queries come from outside the United States.

The Lab provides full educational and technical support for Online Mendelian Inheritance in Man, including working with the JHU Press to produce the printed version. We also plan to conduct a study of users and how they integrate use of the online text into their daily work.

With the formal establishment of the Lab in December 1987, we extended our research efforts in software design and implementation. Online Mendelian Inheritance in Man is already an extremely valuable reference work, but, to make it even more useful, we are exploring how to relate it to files with different kinds of information, such as images and biochemical data. We are currently investigating the possibility of linking it to molecular and cell tissue data from two other sites. Because this work will require significant expertise in the subject, we have added a human geneticist with library science education to the Lab staff.

Knowledge Management in Clinical Decision Making

Knowledge management applications must go beyond the research environment to support clinical decision making and medical education. To that end, we have begun to work with a text that is hierarchically structured into chapters and sections, as are most general textbooks and with the more typical situation of several authors and editors. We have selected internal medicine as the subject and the second edition of the *Principles of Ambulatory Medicine* as the text for our initial research in this second area.[9] Reviews and user evaluations suggest that the book is highly respected, and the potential audience is large. Its content is particularly appropriate to the changing health care delivery system and the need to educate doctors in ambulatory settings. The three editors and most of the seventy-six authors and contributors are Hopkins faculty, thus making the text easier to update and maintain. Having seen our success with *Mendelian Inheritance in Man,* the publisher, Williams & Wilkins, is pleased to participate in testing a new way of producing the book. Most importantly, the editors are committed to exploring innovative ways to deliver knowledge in clinical settings. They now are beginning to prepare the text for the third print edition and will create an online version for their own use in graduate medical education.

NLM will provide partial support for one phase of our work in this arena, under the LHC Information Technology Branch's program for Online Reference Works in Medicine. We have mounted the text under IRX on the Lab's research minicomputer. The editors and their clerical staff can access it, other Welch databases, and remote databases such as MED-LINE using Macintosh II workstations provided by the Lab. Lab staff are providing personalized education to the editors and their staff.

Several specific research-and-development aims and activities have been defined for the project through 1989. First, the retrieval capabilities of IRX will be extended to handle the hierarchical structure of a general text. Second, we will develop a prototype manuscript preparation system that supports several authors and editors. Third, we will design and test a "base-level" knowledge management environment that integrates the preparation and retrieval modules in a consistent interface. Beyond 1989, we hope to add artificial intelligence and facilities for incorporating nontext materials.

With partial support from the JHU School of Medicine and Apple Computer, we will use high-level abstractions of the information in *Principles of Ambulatory Medicine* to provide the core of an Electronic Sourcebook of Hopkins Medicine, the initial test database for our work with Intermedia. Intermedia, an object-oriented hypermedia system with an associated framework for developing applications, closely follows the paradigm of our knowledge workstation, a consistent graphics-based interface with online user tools. The tools allow the integration of different types of "objects," such as text, graphics, sound, and animation, into a single knowledge base. The hypermedia knowledge base is organized through links, which can be created between different objects by an author. A link is followed easily by pointing to an icon on the screen; the user need not consult an index or construct a query. For example, if a paragraph on heart disease discusses arrhythmias, an icon associated with the term may point to a typical EKG representation that can be displayed in a window on the screen. Another icon could invoke the particular heart sounds, and a third might bring to the screen a moving image of the heart from different angles. Working with IRIS at Brown, we will add tools for searching databases. This Sourcebook of Hopkins Medicine will be tested in clinical settings, and great care will be taken to link the authors and users through online communications.

Opportunities
Much valuable experience and many new insights already have emerged from our research. For Dr. McKusick, Online Mendelian Inheritance in Man has become more than an electronic version of his text. The ability to search for keywords across the full text has allowed researchers to do studies that were not possible with the printed version. An online annotation feature allows users to send Dr. McKusick corrections, add new information, or make general comments. In September 1987, Dr. McKusick and Welch Library staff took a Sun workstation to an international workshop in Paris. Daily proceedings were used to update and regenerate Online Mendelian Inheritance in Man each evening. Every morning, Dr. McKusick and the conferees had fresh files to consult. This information became available worldwide as soon as the team returned from France. Normally, the results from these workshops take several months to organize and disseminate.

We are only beginning to define the difference between simply putting a textbook online and creating a functional online information resource. Our approach now is to concentrate on the beginning of the knowledge management cycle, collaborating closely with authors and publishers to create online texts. The first step is to put the textbook online so that it can be authored and published more efficiently. The next step is to work with the authors to restructure texts for effective use in an online environment.

We have worked through the first step successfully once and are replicating the process with *Principles of Ambulatory Medicine*. For the production of the eighth printed edition of *Mendelian Inheritance in Man,* we, as the online database manager, were the logical center of work involving author, publisher, and printer, from the preparation of the intellectual content to the production of a magnetic tape for direct photocomposition. This points to an important new role that libraries can assume if they choose.

It is increasingly clear that the testing and refinement of ideas must be done in the field; this demands close ties to groups of scholars in their actual work settings, as well as an ability to respond quickly to their changing needs as they begin to use and understand technology. It is also painfully clear to us that existing education programs and conventional libraries do not prepare people for this work; a crucial issue facing us is to cultivate new researchers in this area. To meet this need, over the next six to eight years, we hope to develop the Lab into a formal academic division. The Dean of the School of Medicine has agreed in principle to this goal. To move effectively in this direction, we must strengthen our research program to include the study of human factors in information systems design and develop a professional training program, beginning with continuing education seminars and summer institutes.

We believe the Lab's work may provide a useful model for other academic libraries that want to explore collaboration with scholars in the production, dissemination, and use of knowledge. The Council on Library Resources recently made a three-year grant to the Lab to build a human factors component into the software development process, to facilitate a debate in the broader academic community on the Lab's knowledge management model, and to test the diffusion of that model in a comprehensive university setting.

Management and Organizational Issues

As the Welch Library pursues its strategic vision, immediate organizational issues have emerged, some internal to the library and others related to the interrelationships of the institutions within JHMI. Management of new interinstitutional facilities like networks remains a problem. Progress is made by committee and by self-interest, which can be slow. To a significant extent, the more useful the Welch Library's database and services system becomes, the more rapidly the East Baltimore network will grow in size and strength. There are now several incentives, beyond using the Welch system, for joining the network and supporting a particular architecture. One is the need to access clinical laboratory information from remote sites. Another is the need of the basic science departments to have effective access to national networks like NSFNET.

Connecting to the network, however, is not a simple process. No centralized academic computer center now provides computing or network support services for the East Baltimore campus, nor is one likely to be formed. We are beginning to provide some of these computing support services as a natural extension of the Welch Library's role.

The greatest managerial difficulty for many libraries lies in getting beyond the first stage of automation—using technology to do fundamentally the same jobs that used to be performed manually. Often, this has as much to do with the inertia inherent in the scale of a library's operations as with its perception of appropriate roles. If speed in achieving new functionality for transferring information is important, a strong case can be made for disaggregating university library systems and allowing branch libraries or even individual departments to develop systems that respond to users' needs rapidly, as long as these can be linked logically in the future. For patient care and life sciences research, time is of the essence. The major organizational issue for us is to keep functional development closely tied to our users' productivity. If what we do in the Welch Library does not improve the quality of the work and efficiency of faculty, staff, and students, we should do something else.

The management issues internal to the Welch Library revolve around the high standards that we have set for our services and systems. Constantly changing technologies require more self-education and continual upgrading of skills. In addition, we must meet expanding and changing demands by reallocating existing resources and discovering new ones. This has meant discarding some established practices and drastically revising others. The most far-reaching change has been to begin training technical staff to undertake tasks previously assumed solely by librarians with professional degrees. Professional librarians are expected to participate, instead, in systems and services development and research work.

Costs

A philosophy of prudent autonomy and evolutionary growth is reflected in Welch Library's expenditures for technical development. The capital cost of equipment over the past five years has been approximately $383,830. Initial acquisition costs of software for library automation (ILS) and online information transfer (WELMED) systems was $36,400. Estimated annual operating costs of the Welch Library multiuser systems are shown in Table 13.5. We believe that these costs are modest. Our operating budget has increased by approximately 10 percent annually since 1984.

Table 13.5 Estimated Operating Costs of Welch Multiuser Systems for Fiscal Year 1988/89

	WELMED Development	WELMED Production	ILS Development	ILS Production	Other*	Totals
Equipment & Supplies						
Contract maintenance	$4,469	$6,791	$1,375	$3,704	$2,884	$19,224
Other maintenance	0	1,980	0	1,080	540	3,600
Utilities	780	990	240	540	450	3,000
Communications	234	3,604	72	1,966	1,037	6,912
Supplies	1,249	2,480	15	1,080	551	5,375
Personnel						
Systems staff	24,936	19,936	16,981	22,989	20,860	105,702
Reference staff	39,320	12,700				52,020
Software						
Contract maintenance	1,260	3,300	180	2,100	960	7,800
Contract prog.	5,000	625				5,625
Databases						
MEDLINE		12,000				12,000
WELCORK		1,800				1,800
Total	$77,248	$66,206	$18,863	$33,459	$27,282	$223,058

*Includes development and production of serials subsystem, electronic mail, and billing systems

The Laboratory for Applied Research in Academic Information is funded largely by grants and contracts. The budget for full support of Online Mendelian Inheritance in Man in 1988/89 is $500,000, of which close to $300,000 is for personnel. This covers editorial development of the content, maintenance of the database, technical support, and marketing the database through exhibits, demonstrations, and training programs. The Welch Library contribution to the Lab includes physical facilities, a portion of the director's salary, and support from other library divisions as useful and appropriate.

Evaluation and Future Plans

The School of Medicine's support for new Welch Library leadership and the IAIMS concept in 1984 was, admittedly, an act of faith. Considerable progress has been made toward the vision proposed by the IAIMS planners. How pervasive that vision is within the Johns Hopkins Medical Institutions, the health system, and the university is uncertain. To pragmatic tool users and tool builders, concepts such as IAIMS or a "knowledge management environment" have precious little reality. These concepts, however, can take on organizational identity. For a library, which, by tradition, has been devoted solely to service, these concepts are powerfully enabling. They provide a context and rationale for devising the methods and securing the means to respond to new needs emerging from the newer information technologies. At the JHMI, the commitment to these concepts is due to the energies of the authors of this paper. It is too early to tell whether they are sufficiently institutionalized to survive a change in leadership.

The Welch Library has sought grant support from the NLM and other agencies and foundations for its model development phase. If forthcoming, these resources of approximately $440,000 per year over three years will support the IAIMS workstation development.

We do not know how online versions of textbooks such as *Principles of Ambulatory Medicine* will prove useful in the medical center environment. We do know that unexpected uses present themselves once online textbooks exist. And we know that the process can change behaviors happily. Dr. McKusick did not expect to become a computer user, but he ended up bending the tool to his uses as he has changed the way he looks upon his book.

Patricia Battin has posed a hypothesis that we are in a position to test. She proposes that the university become the primary publisher in the scholarly communication process. As she says,

At the present time, we are in the untenable position of generating knowledge, giving it away to the commercial publisher, and then buying it back for our scholars at increasingly prohibitive prices.... The electronic revolution provides the potential for developing university-controlled publishing enterprises through scholarly networks supported either by individual institutions or by consortia. The lacking ingredient is the organized capacity for online refereeing, editing, and distribution....[10]

Many publishers are not prepared to take on the tasks of online editing and distribution because so many of the tools needed to put the process into full production are missing. We believe that the traditional refereeing role may need to change for online texts. We have found that the online work becomes more dynamic and interactive with time, as the author receives constant and immediate feedback from users. The Welch Library has begun to function as the primary publisher for Online Mendelian Inheritance in Man. We are not sure that libraries should assume this role beyond the experimental stage, but we know that no other organization in the university is equipped to take on these tasks at this time.

The costs are not insignificant, but we do not have enough information about the costs of present modes of scholarly composition and book production to make a full comparison. This period of exploration needs careful, patient, and steady work. With funding from the Council on Library Resources, we are in a position to test some of our assumptions about knowledge management processes and the Battin hypothesis.

Looking back on the distance traveled over the past four years, we conclude that the effort has been worthwhile. Looking ahead, we believe we are on the right trajectory.

Acknowledgments

The work described is supported in part by National Library of Medicine contracts N01-LM-5-3512 and N01-LM-6-3513, the Howard Hughes Medical Institute, Apple Computer, Inc., and the Council on Library Resources. Thanks go to David J. Binko, Valerie E. Florance, Charles M. Goldstein, Gary G. Moore, and Gretchen L. Ruch for their assistance in preparing the manuscript.

References

1. Wilson, M. P. *The Management of Information in Academic Medicine,* 2 vols. (Washington, D.C.: Association of American Medical Colleges, 1982).

2. Matheson, N. W., and J. A. D. Cooper. "Academic Information in the Academic Health Sciences Center: Roles for the Library in Information Management." *Journal of Medical Education* 57, no.10, part 2 (1982): 1–93.

3. Association of Academic Health Centers. *Executive Management of Computer Resources in the Academic Health Center* (Washington, D.C.: Association of Academic Health Centers, 1984).

4. *Physicians for the Twenty-First Century: The GPEP Report.* Report of the Panel on the General Professional Education of the Physician and College Preparation for Medicine (Washington, D.C.: Association of American Medical Colleges, 1984), p. 14.

5. *Medical Education in the Information Age.* Proceedings of the "Symposium on Medical Informatics" (Washington, D.C.: Association of American Medical Colleges, 1986), p. vi.

6. Ibid.

7. *Planning for Integrated Academic Information Management Systems.* Proceedings of a symposium sponsored by the National Library of Medicine, October 17, 1984 (Bethesda, Md.: The Library, 1985).

   Broering, Naomi C., ed. "Symposium on Integrated Academic Information Management Systems." *Bulletin of the Medical Library Association* 74, no. 3 (July 1986): 234–60.

   IAIMS and Health Sciences Education. Proceedings of a symposium sponsored by the National Library of Medicine, March 12, 1986 (Bethesda, Md.: The Library, 1987).

   Matheson, Nina W., ed. "Symposium on Integrated Academic Information Management System (IAIMS) Model Development." *Bulletin of the Medical Library Association* 76, no. 3 (July 1988): 221–67.

8. McKusick, Victor A. *Mendelian Inheritance in Man,* 8th ed. (Baltimore, Md.: Johns Hopkins University Press, 1988).

9. Barker, Randall, John Burton, and Philip Zieve, eds. *Principles of Ambulatory Medicine,* 2nd ed. (Baltimore, Md.: Williams & Wilkins, 1986).

10. Battin, Patricia. "The Library: Centre of the Restructured University." *Current Issues in Higher Education* 84, no. 1 (1983): 25–31.

Chapter 14

Other Projects and Progress

Caroline Arms

All of the institutions that have contributed to this volume have been pioneers in one way or another, making progress toward a shared vision of access from the scholar's desktop to information resources of many types and in many places. But the contributors are not the only pioneers among libraries, and some steps toward the same vision are being taken outside libraries. This chapter introduces some other projects that may be shaping the library of the future. Much of the information is based on personal communications rather than on published articles. These projects relate specifically to the delivery of information in electronic form to the scholar or student; not included are the myriad projects for linking libraries in networks or using facsimile transmission to support the traditional operations of interlibrary loan and delivery of printed documents. The intention is to offer an informal sampling, not a comprehensive survey.

Online Access to Bibliographic Information beyond the Catalog

The most widespread development is the provision of online access to bibliographic databases other than the library catalog, principally to details of articles in periodicals. Some of the contributing institutions have acquired search software such as BRS/Search that allows them to mount on a local shared computer a variety of indexing or abstracting services, often including the catalog, in a common framework. Enthusiasm for such services has been marked, and usage high. Several other institutions also have taken this path, among them, the University of Pennsylvania, Dartmouth College, and Lehigh University. Some databases have been created locally, such as bibliographies in particular subjects and holdings of serials or special collections; others have been acquired from outside.

The choice of databases available to academic libraries has been limited; many vendors have been hesitant to cut into their existing market for print and online services and either have refused to license their databases or have set unreasonable prices. Government agencies are less concerned with revenues and more concerned with the dissemination of knowledge, and bibliographic databases such as AGRICOLA (from the National Agricultural Library) and MEDLINE (from the National Library of Medicine) have been mounted at many libraries that serve the relevant disciplines. The Information Access Company was one of the few commercial vendors prepared to experiment with the new market, and some of its indexing services, such as the Magazine Index and the Trade and Industry Index, have been licensed by a number of institutions.

Recognizing the trend in academic libraries toward mounting databases locally instead of using remote online services, other vendors now are prepared to discuss licensing arrangements. Software designed to handle bibliographic records usually can handle other structured collections of fairly short text records that can be identified by one or more heading fields. Examples are encyclopedias, dictionaries, and other reference works. A number of libraries have mounted the Academic American Encyclopedia—again, because the vendor, Grolier Electronic Publishing, was prepared to license it at reasonable cost.

Other institutions have taken a slightly different tack, expanding online catalog systems to handle additional bibliographic databases. The Colorado Alliance of Research Libraries (CARL) has developed a shared library automation system that supports acquisitions, cataloging, and circulation. The system has been licensed by five other libraries and consortia, including Arizona State University. CARL has six primary members: five universities and the Denver Public Library. A number of community colleges and other libraries also participate. Recently, a serials management module has been added, with the unusual feature that citations and abstracts for individual articles can be entered as part of the check-in process when a periodical is received. Rather than acquiring indexing services from elsewhere, CARL is compiling its own, related directly to the collection. CARL also has mounted some nonbibliographic files, among them, the Academic American Encyclopedia and tables of statistics on the Denver area.

Vanderbilt University has been working with NOTIS Systems to extend NOTIS to handle bibliographic databases beyond the catalog. The first database added to their online system comprised abstracts from recent medical literature from the MEDLINE database and covers all medical journals in all languages. The next database will combine three indexing services from H. W. Wilson: the General Science Index, the Social Sciences Index, and the Humanities Index. Vanderbilt staff helped specify the system and design the screen displays, while the programming was done at NOTIS Systems, which expects to release this extension as a product.

The University of California has incorporated MEDLINE into the MEL-VYL system, which is an online union catalog for holdings in over a hundred libraries on the university's nine campuses. Plans to incorporate the Current Contents service from the Institute for Scientific Information (ISI) into MELVYL are well advanced.

BRS/Search and STAIRS are systems for storing, indexing, and retrieving information. They are not ideal for compiling and manipulating databases. Files of records usually are prepared elsewhere or using another software package and imported when complete. Correcting individual records or deleting duplicates can be cumbersome. SPIRES (Stanford Public Information Retrieval System) is a more general database management system that has features not usually found in commercial database management systems, which are intended primarily for routine business applications such as accounting or inventory control. SPIRES is designed to handle textual information of variable length, in addition to the numeric, coded, and fixed-length items of information that constitute most business databases. It provides a powerful framework both for creating databases interactively and importing files prepared elsewhere. Like database systems used for business applications, SPIRES includes tools for creating and updating records, as well as a language for building free-standing applications. Roughly forty institutions license the SPIRES software through the SPIRES consortium. The software runs on large IBM or IBM-compatible mainframes and is used for both administrative and bibliographic applications.

In 1982, SPIRES was adopted as the principal database management system for general administrative applications at Stanford University. It has also been used for building library automation applications. The databases that are the basis for the services offered through RLIN by the Research Libraries Group are managed using SPIRES, and, at Rensselaer Polytechnic Institute, SPIRES has been used to develop an integrated library automation system, including acquisitions, circulation, and an online information system. The catalog is one component of the information system; others are library news, a database of uncataloged materials available to support homework (such as lecture notes, answer sheets, and practice exams), and a database of citations and abstracts for articles from journals published by the Institute of Electrical and Electronics Engineers (IEEE).

Several other institutions use SPIRES to provide information services, making information of all kinds available online over campus networks, and sometimes beyond. In some cases, this effort is coordinated by the library; in others, by a computing organization. The University of Alberta has at least thirty public databases accessible, including Webster's Dictionary and the Educational Resources Information Center (ERIC) database, which indexes journals of relevance to education. One of the most widely used SPIRES databases is a bibliographic database of reports and articles in the field of high energy physics. This database is maintained by the Stanford Linear Accelerator Center and used by physicists around the world; the database and SPIRES software have been mounted in research institutions in Europe and Japan. Several years ago, the University of Waterloo began to prepare its own database of abstracts of articles about microcomputers; copies of this database now are used at other universities. Known as Folio, Stanford University's own information system includes a wide variety of local information, including the library catalog (Socrates); a directory of students, faculty, and staff; postings for internships and research opportunities available to students; the catalog of books at the college bookstore; and a variety of other local information. Syracuse University makes a number of local databases available and has also mounted licensed databases, such as the ERIC database and the COMPUSTAT database of twenty years of numerical data from the financial statements of about twenty-five hundred corporations. As well as displaying the raw COMPUSTAT values, SPIRES provides the ability to manipulate the numbers. The system can present formatted income statements and balance sheets and calculate the financial ratios commonly used to assess the financial position of a company.

Different Types of Information

Numerical Data Online
Access to numerical data online is hardly new—the early academic applications of computing were concerned mainly with numerical computations. What is new is the involvement of libraries in providing access to numerical data online, rather than in print. Until recently, central support for general access to numerical data almost always was through the computing service organization or, often, through departmental groups that supported access to data relevant to a particular discipline. Departmental groups also frequently have provided services to those outside the immediate department. For example, a database maintained by an economics department might be used in the sociology department and the business school. In a few cases, these groups have developed into formal organizations that compile and maintain databases and disseminate them widely. One example is the Inter-University Consortium for Political and Social Research (ICPSR). From this group at the University of Michigan a large number of databases, many built as part of research studies or surveys, are available on tape. Another example is the Center for Research into Security Prices (CRSP) at the University of Chicago. This organization is the standard source for historical data on stock prices.

In many cases, however, departmental support groups have not publicized their data resources, because they lack the means to support a campuswide service. Frequently, data files have been acquired for a particular project, with no attempt made to share them. Indeed, it often is very difficult for researchers to find out what data already is available on campus. Recently, several academic libraries have responded to this problem by starting to catalog machine-readable data files on campus; a union catalog of such files is available to the members of the Research Libraries Group. Others have not attempted to catalog files on campus because there are no mechanisms for keeping the information current and accurate, since the materials are controlled by other departments. Another approach taken by some libraries is to provide information about data files maintained by outside sources such as ICPSR and guidance as to how the files can be acquired or accessed.

When a library helps a scholar identify a relevant textual source of information, the process of transferring that information to the scholar is straightforward and well established: once the article or volume is obtained, the scholar studies it. But the conversion of numerical data into useful information involves manipulation with tools other than the scholar's eyes and brain. Identifying and obtaining the files that contain the appropriate data are only the first steps in deriving useful information. The particular data items needed must be selected, an analysis technique chosen, and the analysis performed. Specifications for data selection may be simple: for example, a list of monthly values for the Consumer Price Index between 1965 and 1980. Or they may be complex: for example, given a list of companies and the dates at which changes in dividends were announced, to extract stock prices for each company's common stock for a period running from ten days before the announcement until ten days afterward. The analysis can be simple, such as calculating averages or plotting values over time, or involve complex statistical techniques. Supporting the full range of these activities requires skills and experience not usually found in librarians.

Computer centers have struggled with providing this type of support. When all computer users were expected to be programmers, it was sufficient to tell the user where to find the data and perhaps give him or her a sample program that could be modified to extract the particular values needed and analyze them. Indeed, for the generation of faculty that learned to program out of necessity, this often is still the preferred way of working because it provides total flexibility. But this approach was hardly ideal for undergraduate coursework and for the many faculty members who resisted the pressure to become programmers. Yet developing general services for extracting, storing, and analyzing numerical data demanded resources that often could not be justified except at the largest research universities, because each source of data and each discipline had different characteristics and requirements.

The emergence of departmental support groups was quite natural. The task was to satisfy the fairly homogeneous needs of a single discipline, and the technical staff could develop experience relevant to the particular academic field. In some instances, this merely involved hiring a programmer to service faculty requests for analyses or to extract and format data in preparation for analysis using a standard statistical package. In others, software was developed to provide general facilities for extracting subsets from a body of data and sometimes for performing standard analyses. Around 1970, Project IMPRESS (Interdisciplinary Machine Processing for Research and Education in the Social Sciences) at Dartmouth College developed an interactive analysis system that provided access to a variety of data, including survey results and historical economic and census data. It incorporated simple analysis techniques and the ability to store subsets for analysis with other software.

But the costs of maintaining such a system for a single institution and upgrading it to reflect technological developments and the expectations of faculty and students are high. Unless these costs can be covered by a permanent source of revenue (perhaps by providing services beyond the institution, as CRSP and ICPSR do), such projects typically have relied heavily on the efforts of a few individuals for whom they are a sideline rather than an official responsibility. Some libraries, such as the Mann Library at Cornell (supporting agriculture and the biological sciences), now are starting to help users locate, extract, and analyze numerical data, as part of their mission to provide a gateway to information resources of all types. Just as the pattern in the past has been for departments to provide support within their particular disciplines, it may prove easier for specialized libraries serving a community with specific needs to assume this responsibility than it is for a general research library.

To transform raw data into real information, yet another level of support may be needed. The ability to extract data, prepare it for analysis, and perform the analysis does not guarantee that the results have any value. To select the appropriate analysis technique and ensure that the assumptions behind the technique are valid for the particular set of data may require the assistance of a professional statistician. Many academic computing organizations, particularly in large research institutions, provide this type of support. If libraries are to take an active role in supporting access to numerical data, they will have to determine at which of three levels they want to adopt responsibilities: they may limit their activities to assistance with locating data or providing a gateway through a common online information system; they also may provide support for extracting the data and the mechanics of using a statistical package; they even may extend their services to include professional statistical guidance. Whichever level they choose, close cooperation with other services on campus is essential.

The Mann Library at Cornell has taken on at least the first two levels of service and has introduced the position of "computing statistician." The University of Florida Libraries for some years have taken responsibility for numeric databases acquired on tape, including registration with the computer center and providing access to documentation in the library's reference area. Expert users access the tapes directly, but, for a fee, which varies with the programming effort required and type of user (usually under $100 for a faculty member), the library's programming staff will extract sets of data and format them ready for analysis. For statistical guidance, users are referred to the Center for Instructional and Research Computing Activities.

However, many libraries feel that the first level of service is appropriate because other groups on campus already provide support at the other levels. At Dartmouth College, plans for an extended online information system include gateways to information resources developed by other departments. Among these is CLASS (Computerized Local Archive for the Social Sciences), an easy-to-use interface (on the Apple Macintosh) for selecting data and prescribing simple analyses. CLASS was developed by the social science computing group as the successor to IMPRESS. Unlike IMPRESS, CLASS uses standard software on a mainframe for storing, manipulating, and analyzing the data, but users need not even be aware that they are accessing remote facilities over the campus network. Extracted datasets also can be stored easily on a time-sharing host or downloaded to the Macintosh for further analysis. At Carnegie Mellon, the catalog of ICPSR tapes is online as part of the library information system; displayed with the catalog are names and electronic mail addresses for sources of support on campus for acquisition, retrieval, and analysis.

Images Online

Delivering images online poses a different set of challenges. As with text, the eyes and brain are the primary tools for using images, but there are additional technological problems. Images in high resolution require vast amounts of storage and very high speed networks. A black-and-white image that fills a high-quality display on a personal computer requires an effective transfer speed of nearly 1M bits/second to be displayed in a second over a digital network. Color images require many times that speed, depending on the quality of the color.

At the Massachusetts Institute of Technology, the library has experimented with delivering images to powerful UNIX workstations that can display several independent windows on high-resolution screens. The project, supported by the Council on Library Resources, has developed a distributed alternative to a physical collection of slides that supports coursework in architecture. The collection of seven thousand images of Boston (including photographs, maps, and drawings) has been transferred to videodisk, and a detailed catalog compiled. Specially equipped workstations are attached both to the campus digital computing network and, through a digitizing board, to the broadband cable network used for video transmission. In one window on the screen, using the digital network link, the catalog can be searched, and an image requested. The image is delivered over the broadband cable and displayed in a separate window. Images can be enlarged or reduced on the screen, and the system is being enhanced so that several images can be displayed simultaneously. The images also can be transmitted to television monitors.

This combined use of a computing network and a video network is unusual. Most current applications that store images on CD-ROM or videodisk are designed as stand-alone systems or for networks with only a few workstations. Even with compression, delivering images could absorb an unreasonable proportion of a computing network's capacity, since most of today's high-speed campus networks operate at 10M bits/second or less and that capacity must be shared by many users. If compressed images are transferred, workstations must include hardware or software to decompress the image for display.

The MIT project replaces a service previously available only at the library with an equivalent online service, a simple extension of the traditional library's role. Another type of project integrates access to images with specialized software designed to instruct or support skilled tasks such as medical diagnosis or machine repairs. Hundreds of such applications, often using videodisk, are being developed at academic institutions and by commercial organizations, far too many for mention here. Whether a library should support instructional applications depends on how active a role it has decided or is expected to take in supporting the instructional process. At the University of Southern California, the planned Teaching Library will incorporate such support, but, at many universities, instructional applications of computing are supported through other channels. This is yet another area where the academic community will benefit from close cooperation between library and computing services on campus.

Full Text Online

The vision of the electronic library certainly includes online access to the full text of books and articles (primary information), not just to bibliographic information (secondary information or "information about information.") The commercial legal services, LEXIS and WESTLAW, and news services such as NEXIS are based on the full text of documents. In recent years, many of the commercial online services have added other full-text databases, such as the Harvard Business Review. Search options on these services have been extended to provide some facilities that apply particularly to longer documents, for example, limiting a search for keywords to the first paragraph of an article. Once identified, either the bibliographic information alone or the full text can be displayed on the screen.

Features to support scanning or reading the document online usually are limited, for instance, to requesting the next page or the previous page and locating the occurrences of the search term. The documents usually are fairly short, and, because there are communications charges, the reader is not necessarily expected to study the document online. If the search is to identify relevant sources rather than to find the answer to a particular question, the user might scan the first few paragraphs to confirm that the document is worth further perusal and then print the whole document for later use. The major benefit to the user is the ability to search for terms in the body of the document, not only in the title and abstract.

In the academic context, several projects have involved compiling bodies of text in machine-readable form, usually to support detailed linguistic and textual analysis rather than general reading. Examples are the Thesaurus Linguae Graecae (TLG), a database of classic Greek texts maintained at the University of California at Irvine under the direction of Theodore Brunner, and the database for American and French Research on the Treasury of the French Language (ARTFL), maintained at the University of Chicago by Robert Morrissey. A database of the text of Dante's *Divine Comedy* and sixty commentaries dating from the fourteenth century to the 1980s is being compiled as part of the Dartmouth Dante Project.

The Dante database is accessible over the campus network and from around the country. Like the TLG and ARTFL databases, it is seen as a research tool for Dante scholars everywhere, not merely as an instructional resource for the Dartmouth community. The database is indexed using BRS/Search software, and primary access is by keywords or line number, with limits by canto, language, or commentary. Scholars normally would not expect to read the original text online, because they own printed copies; as a result, no attempt has been made to support convenient reading or browsing of the poem online. The poem's text is divided into segments of three lines according to its *terza rima* form, and the commentary notes are divided and indexed by the lines to which they refer.

This type of access to full text is what literature scholars need for textual analysis, but it is not appropriate for faculty and students who just want to be able to read a book or article without taking a trip to the library. A project of a different type is under way at Stevens Institute. For a course entitled Galileo and the Scientific Revolution, the complete text of the eight books used in the course has been entered into a database.[1] As was the case before the database was available, students are expected to buy three of the texts; the other five are on reserve in the library. The database is maintained using Personal Librarian from Personal Library Software. This software supports normal keyword searches with Boolean operations but has other features as well. If a keyword search identifies a large number of occurrences of the word, the user can request a list of terms that might be related to the topic and would serve to make the search more specific. The list of terms is not based on a prestored thesaurus but on the co-occurrence of words in the database. As an example, the word "fire" occurs 155 times in the database; among the terms that occur most frequently in conjunction with "fire" are "friction," "rub," "burn," "corpuscle," "pore," "hard," and "breeze." By picking one of the unexpected, but specific, terms, "corpuscle" or "pore," the student would be led immediately to discussions of Galileo's theory of heat. Once a relevant section of text has been found, it is easy to browse through the text before and after the section actually retrieved.

Currently, the database can be used on two public IBM-compatible personal computers in the library, but, since the software also runs on a variety of larger computers, similar services could be made available over the campus network. The course first was taught using the database as a resource in the spring semester of 1988. Students used the database for specific homework assignments and general browsing, and at least three-quarters of them also used it as they were preparing their final essays. A survey showed that the students found that the system was easy to use and saved time. Most importantly, the ability to locate relevant material quickly was of pedagogical value. James E. McLellan, the professor who taught the course, found that student reports showed less superficiality than in the past, that students were not drawn, as some had feared, into technical minutiae, and that, in class discussions, they "were able to comment more critically and help guide their classmates more than I have found previously."

While some students read through long passages on the screen, many preferred to identify a list of references and then read from the printed copy. For one focused homework assignment, half the class was asked to use the electronic database, while the others used only the printed texts. For a second assignment, the groups were interchanged. The grader did not know which student was in which group. Students appeared to fall into two distinct sets: those who performed well using the database did not do as well when they used the printed texts, and vice versa. The project leaders plan to follow up this interesting finding with further study and also to experiment with using the system in different contexts. In 1989, the Galileo material will be used at Stevens in a one-week segment of a general course on the history of science (as opposed to throughout a course devoted to Galileo). It also will be used at a liberal arts college, where students may have more inhibitions about using computers than do students at a technical institution where they all have their own. Meanwhile, the software is being upgraded, and when the course is taught next, the database will incorporate graphics and other enhancements.

Features that support convenient study of the complete text of long documents online are not necessarily simple variations of techniques used for displaying bibliographic records. Once users locate long documents using the traditional bibliographic tools, ideally, they should have more sophisticated browsing tools than the simple ability to turn the pages (sequential browsing). On picking up an article, a reader often will skim through it to get an idea of the topics covered and possibly look at figures or citations before starting to read. On the screen, a user should be able to call up an outline of the document, such as a list of chapter or section headings, and choose to look at a particular section or, inversely, having located an interesting paragraph, move easily to the beginning of the section (structural browsing). This requires, not only that new software be developed, but that indicators of the document structure be stored with the text. Rebuilding existing databases to support structural browsing will be expensive, which suggests that commercial services may not move quickly in this direction. But experimental systems on campuses will be able to take advantage of new developments. The Graph-Text software developed recently by OCLC is a prototype full-text display system that supports structural browsing, and other examples can be expected to emerge soon.

Hypertext and Hypermedia

Recently, the terms "hypertext" and "hypermedia" have become common in discussions of applications of technology on campus. The term "hypertext" was coined by Ted Nelson in the 1960s to describe an environment that supports nonsequential writing and reading; special markings in the text (perhaps a highlighted word or phrase or a special symbol) indicate a link to related information. The relationship can take many forms: a definition of a term, an expansion of a summary, a discussion of a related topic, or an annotation. Footnotes are an example of a hypertext mechanism in print, but the term usually is reserved for computerized systems. "Hypermedia" extends the concept of hypertext to include links to nontext materials, such as diagrams, photographic images, or sounds. Systems that support hypertext allow an author to structure material flexibly, without the restrictions imposed by the linear nature of a printed document. However, just as privileges convey responsibilities, this flexibility puts a burden on the author to prevent the reader from getting lost in a maze of links. When writing a book, an author can assume that readers will start at the beginning and read through to the end, making use of traditional tools such as an index or glossary where needed. If they dip into the book and get confused, they know that they should turn to the beginning. When readers finish the last page, they know that they have covered all the material in the book. Readers naturally turn to the beginning of a book to find a table of contents and to the end to find an index and can use those tools whichever page they currently are reading. A bookmark or a pencil will mark the current place if necessary. In time, similar conventions may develop for hypertext; for the time being, however, the hypertext author is responsible for structuring the material appropriately and providing the reader with a sense of the structure through a combination of consistent appearance and explicit navigational tools.

Applications of hypertext and hypermedia fall into three distinct categories. The first category is "published" compilations of information: all links are established by the author, and readers use the finished product very much as they would a printed work. Since following cross-references is much simpler in hypertext than in printed material, obvious candidates for publication in hypertext form are encyclopedias and reference manuals. Such applications may become standard as reference services, combining hypertext links with conventional indexing.

By its very name, Hyperties (The Interactive Encyclopedia System) implies that it was designed with this type of application in mind. Developed by Professor Ben Schneidermann at the University of

Maryland in the mid-1980s, Hyperties is now available as a commercial product from Cognetics Corporation. The system emphasizes simplicity for author and user. In one early application outside the university, it replaced printed displays describing museum exhibits. With a screen that responds to the touch of a finger, the novice user does not even have to use the keyboard. Creating a database of text segments and illustrations also is simple. At a seminar in May 1988, Dr. Catherine Plaisant, an associate of Dr. Schneidermann, described some of the early experience gained with authors of Hyperties applications.[2] Creating links between individual items is easy; the most difficult task for most authors is providing the conceptual overview to guide the user. Hypertext systems need to have built-in tools that encourage and assist authors in this area, as well as navigational tools for the user. New navigational features have been added to later versions of Hyperties.

The second category of hypermedia application, one that is attracting attention in the educational field, takes advantage of the fact that hypertext can be, not just interactive, but active. Intermedia, the hypermedia system developed at Brown University's Institute for Research in Information and Scholarship uses powerful networked workstations to provide shared access to a body of material relevant to a course.[3] The system has been used initially to develop materials to support courses in English literature from 1700 to the present and in plant cell biology. The materials are not just a background resource; they constitute an integral part of the course. Students are expected to add their own annotations and personal links to those that are presented originally. They can thus construct hypertext "essays" and contribute new material and ideas to the database. Intermedia links are not simple pointers but have associated characteristics. One characteristic is the identity of a link's creator; links created by one student are not seen by other students.

The professors who designed and teach these courses have found that student essays and class discussions have improved through access to this material in a flexible form. They also believe that the students develop a better appreciation of the relationships among different topics covered in a course. A Victorian poet may not necessarily be influenced most by an immediate predecessor, who was covered the previous week, but by earlier authors. Biology students expected to write substantial term papers are able to pick appropriate topics early in the term because they can traverse the course material quickly, identifying areas of interest, and understanding how they fit into the syllabus.

The pedagogical success of such active uses of hypertext ensures that more applications will be developed. However, the expense of preparing a body of materials cannot be justified for a single course, or even a single institution. It compares to the effort involved in preparing a major textbook in a field like biology, where hundreds of illustrations and full-color photographs are integrated into the text. Whether a commercial publishing industry emerges for this type of hypertext application remains to be seen. Libraries that have chosen to take an active role in supporting instructional applications of technology certainly must follow developments in this area.

Even for less active applications of hypertext, the experience at Intermedia with developing navigational tools for users is relevant. Unlike some hypertext systems, all Intermedia links are automatically bidirectional; you always can retrace your steps. Another feature is that associated with each link is a one-line "explainer," a phrase explaining the relationship represented by the link, for instance, "Religion and philosophy—Utilitarianism." At any point, the user can call up an automatically generated local map that shows the links from the current document to others, with the links indicated by their explainers. In addition to these automatic navigational tools, the prepared materials include many overview documents. As an example, for each author in the literature database, an overview document contains a portrait and a listing of dates and major works and, in diagrammatic form, links to other files in the database that relate to the author. Intermedia documents are stored in individual files; this allows users to locate and open files directly from file directories without having to follow a sequence of links from a master document. Files can be grouped logically into subdirectories, known as "folders." Again using the literature database as an example, a reader interested in Tennyson could simply select the folder for Tennyson and then open the Tennyson overview file.

Yet further enhancements to navigation were planned after initial experiences with the system. The first is to make the automatic map of local links active, so that links shown on the map can be followed. The second is to add the pathway of items through which the user reached the current item to the map of local links. The third enhancement is to add keywords to links (in addition to the explainers) and allow keyword searches to identify links of possible interest. What is clear is that when users are free to traverse the material in their own way, no one can predict how they will use it, and an array of navigational aids is needed to support different approaches.

Hypermedia applications of the types just described are complete in themselves, and their focus is on the information stored within the hypertext system. The third category departs from the underlying concept, partly because of features beyond hypertext built in to Apple Computer's HyperCard, which is distributed with each Macintosh computer. Since for many, experience with hypertext is limited to HyperCard, there is a misleading tendency to assume that any application of HyperCard is an implementation of hypertext. As well as supporting links between documents (in HyperCard known as "cards") and tools for creating cards, HyperCard also provides mechanisms for activating other software. Although it cannot support large, complex bodies of data, HyperCard can be used to build a consistent, attractive interface for other applications with less effort and less programming experience than usually is necessary. As a result, many HyperCard applications have little to do with hypertext and relationships between pieces of text or pictures; rather, HyperCard has been used as a convenient programming language.

Applications of this type can be relevant to libraries, however, because they can be used as interfaces to online information resources. At the Mann Library at Cornell, an interface to the university's NOTIS catalog is being developed. The University of Southern California has introduced a HyperCard interface to its ORION online catalog. The Perseus project in the Classics Department at Harvard University is using HyperCard for an interface to a prototype library for classicists. Like the Intermedia project at Brown, the Perseus project has received funding from the Annenberg/CPB Project. Classical texts and commentaries on those texts are being stored using database software on a Macintosh II computer. Photographs, drawings, and site plans of classical sites are stored on videodisk. By 1993, the Perseus project hopes to have amassed fifty million characters of text and commentary and five to ten thousand pictures, which will form a valuable resource for research as well as instruction.

HyperCard is not used to manage the Perseus database but to provide access to it. But, in addition to allowing users to retrieve texts and pictures, the HyperCard framework allows students to write commentaries and essays or to draw diagrams showing the action in Greek comedies with links to the relevant images and passages of text. An early version with a partial database already has been used in classes at Harvard and Bowdoin. Greg Crane, the project's director, uses the system heavily in class to show students how a researcher can use the material. He has found that, while some students have responded to the prototype system with enthusiasm and used it effectively, others have found it frustrating. This dichotomy is reminiscent of the finding at Stevens in the Galileo course.

That the examples presented of these three types of hypermedia applications were developed with three different software products should not be interpreted as an indication that each product is only appropriate for one type of application. Many active educational applications have been developed with HyperCard, and any of the products could be used to develop a complete, published hypertext work. Hypermedia is in its infancy. Early hypermedia products (as opposed to systems for developing products) are likely to be derived from established products: training materials will evolve from experience using film, audio, and printed materials; reference works will evolve from printed or online versions.

Interfaces to Online Information Systems

When access to online information services was primarily through terminals, any enhancements to the user interface were likely to increase the computing load on the central computer, so command languages adopted for information retrieval systems were terse and, therefore, often cryptic. For commercial services, most related documentation was in printed form, because customers did not want to run up communications charges unnecessarily. Once personal computers became common, however, attempts were made to make life easier (and cheaper) for the users, and a variety of "front ends" became available. Front-end software that runs on a personal computer can take on some of the information-seeking task, preparing queries for submission to the remote computer and managing the information that is returned.

The list below shows some of the variety of functions that front-end software can serve. The functions are listed roughly in the chronological order in which software implementing the functions first appeared. As personal computers become more powerful, front ends that embrace all the functions will become commonplace.

1. It can minimize connection charges by allowing users to prepare a set of queries offline, submit them in a batch, and store for repeated use.
2. It can check queries for valid syntax.
3. It can prepare queries automatically from choices presented to the user in an attractive and intuitive fashion—a sequence of helpful prompts, a menu of options, or terms entered into a form displayed on the screen.
4. It can display help online when needed.
5. It can support selection of segments of text for integration into a word processor or electronic mail.

6. It can supply a mechanism for downloading bibliographic information and storing it in a personal database in a structured form that can be manipulated.

7. It can provide a consistent, integrated interface to a disparate set of information services.

8. It can modify search strategies if too many or no items are located or on the basis of user feedback.

9. It can integrate access to a thesaurus or knowledge base related to the database being searched in order to identify correct usage and suggest possible synonyms or related topics based on terms entered by the user.

10. It can interpret queries presented in natural language and translate them into formal searches.

11. It can incorporate personal "filters" to screen information, without explicit inclusion in every search—for instance, to exclude material written by the user.

Front ends have been developed by a large number of commercial organizations and academic groups; only a few can be mentioned here. The commercial products tend to support dial-up connections to commercial or standard services and to emphasize controlling charges or manipulating personal bibliographic databases. Front ends developed on campuses tend to be tailored to the particular institution and may emphasize integration with the rest of the academic computing environment.

As mentioned above, several libraries have been experimenting with using HyperCard to improve interfaces to their online catalogs. At Dartmouth, the library and computer center are collaborating to develop a unified network interface to resources (text and numerical) available on a variety of central computers stored using a variety of database packages. The initial implementation will use a Macintosh computer as a front end and provide access to campus information, the online catalog, the American Academic Encyclopedia, a subset of the MEDLINE database, and to the locally developed CLASS archive of numerical data for social scientists. "Cut-and-paste" from the screen into electronic mail messages, word-processing files, and personal bibliographic databases will be supported. The interface described in the chapter from the University of Illinois in this volume incorporates techniques for revising unsuccessful searches. Formerly a link only to the online catalog/circulation system, it has been extended to allow access to remote information services, electronic mail, and files stored on a personal computer.

The application of artificial intelligence to information retrieval has been an active area for research for computer and information scientists over many years; progress has been slow because the problems are complex. Over the last twenty years, there have been continual predictions that effective systems are only a few years away. Front ends for information retrieval that provide the "intelligent" features appearing at the end of the list above still are confined largely to experimental systems, but a few examples are in operation. The successful ones are limited in scope, at least for now. A recent survey by Donald T. Hawkins identified about half-a-dozen examples.[4] For example, at the National Agriculture Library, an expert system, known as Answerman, can lead a user to sources of facts in agricultural reference books and, in some cases, to the facts themselves through access to CD-ROM systems or remote online databases. Another expert system, CANSEARCH, supports searches of MEDLINE on the subject of cancer therapy, using a touchscreen, rather than a keyboard, to lead users through a sequence of questions and choices. In the library at the University of Waterloo, an Online Reference Assistance system has been under test; incorporating descriptions and details of coverage for a wide array of reference works, it guides users to likely sources of information. At the National Library of Medicine, the CITE interface to the online catalog allows the user to express the search topic in natural English.

CITE does not actually interpret the meanings of queries; it simply works intelligently with the words and phrases given to avoid the rigidity of a system based on strict matches. CITE extends the search to include stem variants—for example, automatically including "treat" and "treating" as search terms when a user types "treatment." CITE also maps words into the controlled vocabulary of MeSH (Medical Subject Headings), which is used to index the collection. The authorized MeSH synonym for "treatment" is "therapy," and this term also would be added to the list of search terms. The search identifies records that match at least one of the terms and presents them to the user in ranked order, with the records that match the largest number of terms first. Implementing this type of support for users as an integrated part of a central online catalog would impose unreasonable processing demands on the computer system, but now that most access is from personal computers that can handle some of the processing load, the potential for such enhancements is great.

Recent developments in a related area, front ends to electronic mail systems, also may be relevant to libraries. Systems that screen mail messages have reached the stage of prototype use in small communities. Examples are Information Lens, developed by a team led by Thomas Malone at the Massachusetts Institute of Technology, and ISCREEN, developed by Stephen Pollock of Bell-Northern Research in Toronto.[5] Both systems provide the user with convenient tools to specify rules for dealing with an incoming message, such as

- If it is from my manager, file it in my "urgent" box.
- If it is a meeting announcement, forward it to my secretary.
- If it includes the name of a project in the subject field, file it in the corresponding mailbox.
- If it is a company news bulletin but is not described as urgent, delete it.

Combined with a bulletin board service, this type of system could allow libraries to provide individualized current-awareness services inexpensively. Posting records of all new acquisitions on a bulletin board would be a fairly simple procedure to initiate; indexing records for journals also could be posted as they were loaded onto an online information system. However, even if the bulletin board were divided by discipline, scholars typically would have to scan many irrelevant records to find a useful one. ISCREEN or the Information Lens would support selective, automatic access using rules generated by the user. A scholar could specify that he or she wanted to see details for any new books within certain call number ranges and for all articles that had a certain term in the title or as a subject keyword. Moreover, it would be possible to add and delete rules at will without putting a burden on library staff.

It is clear that increasingly intelligent front ends to information resources will be developed over the coming years and that this is yet another area where coordination with computer services organizations is essential. Libraries also should seek the active involvement of computer scientists to help develop systems that bring into operational use the advances made in experimental systems.

Artificial Intelligence Applied to Indexing

At the other end of the chain from information retrieval is the indexing process, in many ways the inverse of retrieval. From the natural language of a document, the indexer (whether human or automated) must determine the key topics and subject areas that characterize this document, so that a reader interested in these topics will be led to the document.

Whether the records include only a title or add an abstract or even the full text of an article, today's text databases tend to provide two sources of support for searching for material on a topic. The simplest to implement is through a blanket index on every nontrivial word in the records. Any set of text records can be indexed automatically without human intervention. However, this requires a user to try (and try to remember) every term that might be used to describe the topic. For example, "information retrieval" as a search term might fail to identify an article entitled "The Design of Systems for Document Retrieval." Articles on "French novels" would not be retrieved when searching for information in the more general area of "European novels." This is clearly unsatisfactory.

The second source of support is through the application of index terms: words and phrases that describe both the general subject area and distinguishing topics. Journal indexing services not only compile the information from the tables of contents but also add indexing terms, which then are included with the database records and can be searched. Like cataloging, indexing is an expensive operation: professional indexers read the articles and assign the terms. In some cases, the allowed vocabulary for index terms is controlled closely through a thesaurus and indexing rules; in others, it is more flexible. Examples of controlled vocabularies are the subject headings used by the Library of Congress and the MeSH subject headings used by the National Library of Medicine (NLM). Because controlled vocabularies limit the scope of the problem, practical applications of natural language processing for interpreting queries and automatic indexing support are likely to emerge first in areas where strict indexing procedures already exist.

For the most efficient searching of a database with a controlled vocabulary, familiarity with the thesaurus is an advantage. However, few end users have the motivation to explore the intricacies of a complex thesaurus, unless they know that they will need to make frequent searches of a very similar nature. Automatic reference to a thesaurus to find synonymous search terms, as implemented in the CITE interface to the NLM catalog, is a first step. However, rather than a straightforward hierarchical list of terms and synonyms, a thesaurus can serve as the starting point for a knowledge base that "understands" the different relationships among terms. For instance, the knowledge base might recognize that "measles" is an example of "disease," that a "finger" is a part of a "hand," and that "sports" and "athletic injuries" are related topics.

The creation and manipulation of knowledge bases has been the subject of much recent research in artificial intelligence, and practical uses are emerging. Advanced applications of natural language processing, such as machine translation, require semantic understanding of text, not merely syntactic parsing of sentences. It now is understood that this cannot be achieved without the incorporation of background knowledge about the subject matter at hand.

Prototype systems that incorporate knowledge bases for specific subject areas have been developed to provide automatic indexing support. At the National Library of Medicine, the Indexing Aid System is aimed primarily at improving the consistency of human journal indexers.[6] The indexer enters specific terms from the title and abstract. The system maps the terms into the MeSH vocabulary and uses the knowledge base to add more general descriptors as prescribed by the indexing rules. For instance, if "lymphadenectomy" and "irradiation" are entered as treatments, the system not only will generate "lymph node excision" and "radiotherapy" but also will add "surgery" and "combined modality therapy." The first two terms are simple synonyms, but the other terms require the structural understanding that lymphadenectomy is an example of a surgical procedure and that surgery and radiotherapy are different modes of therapy. At BIOSIS, publishers of Biological Abstracts, an experimental system was developed to explore the potential for automatic preliminary indexing from the titles (in natural language) of journal articles as an aid to human indexers.[7] Again, a controlled vocabulary of "concept headings" is used for indexing. A study showed that 75 percent of the primary and secondary subject headings assigned by human indexers could be generated automatically from titles alone. This is achieved using a knowledge base that relates approximately fifteen thousand biological terms, all of which occurred ten or more times in titles indexed at BIOSIS over a one-year period. Such knowledge bases are of enormous potential value for retrieval, as well as for indexing.

Knowledge bases are very expensive to build, and require expert sources of information. In the examples above, the controlled vocabulary provided a valuable initial structure for the knowledge base. Building a knowledge base from scratch for a general area is an enormous task. One experimental retrieval system, I^3R, includes the attractive ability to supplement its knowledge base through interactions with the end user.[8] Systems that can interact intelligently with users, taking advantage of the experience that they bring to the search task, hold great promise for the electronic library.

The National Libraries

Unlike many countries, the United States does not have a National Library. Although the Library of Congress is seen as the premier library and a national resource, it is, as its name implies, the library of the government, not of the nation. It is *the* library for legislators and their staff; requests for information from this community are serviced by a Congressional

Research Staff of more than eight hundred employees. Two other national libraries also serve particular communities, but of a different nature: the National Agriculture Library and the National Library of Medicine. All three have taken the lead in certain aspects of applying technology to the storage, preservation, and dissemination of information.

Throughout this century, the Library of Congress (LC) has been the primary source of high-quality cataloging by subject experts. Initially, catalog records were distributed on cards, encouraging the standardization of card catalogs. After automated processes were introduced, distribution of records on magnetic tape became common, and the MARC (MAchine-Readable Cataloging) record developed at LC was adopted as the basis for national and international standards for bibliographic records. Recently, LC has been a force behind the Linked Systems Project, which supports the sharing of records over computer networks through direct links between libraries' automated systems. Yet more standards have emerged from this project, for automated network protocols to support interlibrary loan and information retrieval. At the earlier stages, the establishment of standards provided a focus for new developments by libraries and commercial vendors. The standard information retrieval protocol, described in more detail in the final chapter, may serve the same role, stimulating progress toward uniform access for scholars to a wide array of remote information resources.

The National Agriculture Library (NAL) is a branch of the U. S. Department of Agriculture. For some years, it has maintained a bibliographic database online, as well as producing printed indexing publications. AGRICOLA (Agricultural Online Access) now contains over two million bibliographic records, primarily to journal articles. Recently, NAL embarked on a cooperative project with forty-two libraries at land grant universities. The full text of journals will be captured in digital form and distributed on CD-ROM disks. Four different sets of material will be generated initially, and four different retrieval packages will be evaluated. As mentioned above, NAL also has experimented with an intelligent retrieval system for locating factual information.

Of the three national libraries, the programs of the National Library of Medicine are most active in spurring movement toward the vision of electronic libraries and integration with other information resources and analytic tools. From the early days of computing, NLM has been a pioneer in the application of computers to library services. It offered early automated information retrieval services in MEDLARS and was again in the vanguard with its online version, MEDLINE. The integrated library system now marketed by OCLC originated in a project at NLM. The IRX text retrieval software in use at Johns Hopkins for the online versions of *Mendelian Inheritance in Man* and *Principles of Ambulatory Medicine* also was developed at NLM.

NLM also has taken an active role in promoting ambitious programs in medical libraries around the country. As recounted by Nina Matheson and her coauthors in the chapter from the Welch Medical Library at Johns Hopkins University, NLM currently is sponsoring the planning and development of Integrated Academic Information Management Systems (IAIMS) at fourteen medical libraries. All but one are at universities. To quote from the foreword to the proceedings of an NLM symposium on the IAIMS program:

> The IAIMS concept is to use computer and communications technologies to bring together a health institution's various information resources into a unified, easily accessible system. The goal is to integrate library systems with the multitude of individual and institutional working information files, such as clinical, administrative, research, and educational databases.[9]

Medical libraries are somewhat different from other academic libraries, in that they support practicing professionals in hospitals in addition to researchers, teachers, and students. Both the literature and the clientele are more homogeneous than they are for a general research library. Nevertheless, the IAIMS concept clearly is related closely to the vision, shared by all of the contributors to this volume, of access for scholars to an array of information resources from their desktops, in a form that they can conveniently manipulate and analyze. The libraries that have embarked on these projects are developing valuable experience on which other libraries can build.

The NLM support can contribute to all aspects of such a project, from planning and installing computer networks, to developing state-of-the-art retrieval systems and professional workstations. IAIMS projects are expected to have three phases: planning, development, and implementation. Of the contributors to this volume, both Columbia and Johns Hopkins, early recipients of planning grants, are proceeding with ambitious plans to provide integrated access to information resources for both scholars and clinicians. Also among the first to receive IAIMS grants were the Dahlgren Memorial Library at Georgetown University Medical Center, under the leadership of Naomi Broering, and the Health Sciences Library at the University of Maryland at Baltimore, whose director is Cyril Feng. Both these libraries have established themselves as groundbreakers.

At the University of Maryland, the Integrated Library Information System (ILIS) provides access to a subset of MEDLINE (MaryMED) and to Current Contents in addition to the catalog. ILIS also includes online forms for users to request interlibrary loans, journal photocopies, and literature searches by a reference librarian. It provides a seamless link to the electronic mail and conferencing system supported by the university, and new book records are posted on the conferencing system daily. In conjunction with the Welch Library at Johns Hopkins and NLM, the TOXNET retrieval software is being enhanced to map subject terms entered by users into the MeSH controlled vocabulary. Since the user will be informed of the mappings, this enhancement also will serve an educational purpose.

For some years, the library information system at the Dahlgren Memorial Library at Georgetown University Medical Center has provided access to a subset of the MEDLINE database, using locally developed software known as MiniMEDLINE. Selections from Current Contents also are available online through software developed locally. The first stage of an intelligent retrieval interface known as BioSYNTHESIS provides a single interface to these bibliographic databases and provides support for selecting search terms. More recently, factual and diagnostic resources have been made available online, including databases of information on drugs and cancer treatment protocols and RECONSIDER, a clinical diagnostic prompting program developed at the University of California at San Francisco. RECONSIDER is used in a course on clinical problem solving and by students on clinical rotations to solve diagnostic problems assigned by faculty and resident doctors. The Medical Center Librarian also is Director of the Biomedical Information Resources Center (BIRC), a modern computer facility with a public cluster of personal computers and a computer classroom. BIRC staff provide training to faculty and staff and are available to assist faculty develop new systems and teaching programs.

The Dahlgren Library recently was awarded NLM funding for the third phase of its IAIMS project, based on the prototypes developed and the infrastructure established in the earlier phases. Plans for this phase are ambitious and too wide ranging to cover fully here. Online resources will be extended, including the full text of journal articles and added factual and diagnostic resources, such as radiology images. BioSYNTHESIS will be enhanced to include access to nonbibliographic resources and to help the user identify which database contains the specific information requested. Workstation systems that integrate relevant tools for accessing and manipulating textual and numerical information will be developed for students, faculty, researchers, and practitioners. Prototypes already developed include a "practitioner workstation," which combines access to the library information system with a database application for managing patient treatment, and a "student workstation," which includes software designed to supplement clinical experience in recording patient histories. The first practitioner workstation was tailored for neurologists. In the new phase of the IAIMS project, variations will be developed to support other clinical areas, and integrated links to the hospital information system for direct access to laboratory reports will be added. Another aspect of the IAIMS project at Georgetown is collaboration and cooperation with other institutions, particularly the medical centers at Johns Hopkins and the University of Maryland. For participants in the IAIMS program to share experiences and resources is an important goal of the National Library of Medicine.

Conclusion

Steps are being taken on many campuses to realize the vision of easy access to a variety of information resources for scholars and students. In a few cases, daring leaps have been attempted, many of them successful. More and more faculty and students routinely use computers, not for their own sake, but as tools to perform specific tasks. They will expect access to information resources to be integrated conveniently with every other task for which they use their computers, be it word processing or analysis of numerical data. General research libraries may not get as closely involved in the development of specialized workstations as will the medical centers that serve practitioners, but they will need to be conscious of the changing computing environment on campuses. The interdependence between computing services and libraries is growing, and cooperative relationships will be essential to take advantage of the potential that technological developments hold. Not every campus will want to accept the risks and burden of being a pioneer, but no library will be able to ignore the developments stimulated by the more adventurous institutions.

References

1. Friedman, Edward A., James E. McLellan, and Arthur Shapiro. "Introducing Undergraduate Students to Automated Text Retrieval in a Humanities Course" (Paper presented at the Conference of the Association for Computers and the Humanities on Teaching Computers and the Humanities Courses at Oberlin College, Oberlin, Ohio, June 17, 1988).
2. Plaisant, Catherine. Presentation at "The Coming of Age of Electronic Text," a seminar of the Study Group on the Structure of

Electronic Text (SGSET), Carnegie Mellon University, Pittsburgh, Penn., May 23–24, 1988.

3. Yankelovich, Nicola, Bernard J. Haan, Norman K. Meyrowitz, and Steven M. Drucker. "Intermedia: The Concept and the Construction of a Seamless Information Environment." *Computer* 21, no. 1 (January 1988): 81–96.

   Landow, George P. "Hypertext in Literary Education, Criticism, and Scholarship." *Computers and the Humanities* 23 (1989): 173–198.

4. Hawkins, Donald T. "Applications of Artificial Intelligence (AI) and Expert Systems for Online Searching." *ONLINE* 12, no. 1 (January 1988): 31–43.

5. Malone, Thomas W., Kenneth R. Grant, Franklyn A. Turbak, Stephen A. Brobst, and Michael D. Cohen. "Intelligent Information-Sharing Systems." *Communications of the ACM* 30, no. 5 (May 1987): 390–402.

   Pollock, Stephen. "A Rule-Based Message Filtering System." *ACM Transactions on Office Information Systems* 6, no. 30 (July 1988): 232–254.

6. Humphrey, Suzanne M., and Nancy E. Miller. "Knowledge-Based Indexing of the Medical Literature: The Indexing Aid Project." *Journal for the American Society for Information Science* 38, no. 3 (May 1987): 184–196.

7. Vieduts-Stokolov, Natasha. "Concept Recognition in an Automatic Text-Processing System for the Life Sciences." *Journal for the American Society for Information Science* 38, no. 4 (July 1987): 269–287.

8. Croft, W. B., and R. H. Thompson. "I^{3}R: A New Approach to the Design of Document Retrieval Systems." *Journal for the American Society for Information Science* 38, no. 6 (November 1987): 389–404.

9. U.S. Department of Health and Human Services. *IAIMS and Health Sciences Education: Proceedings of a Symposium Sponsored by The National Library of Medicine, March 12, 1986* (Washington, D.C.: U.S. Department of Health and Human Services, 1986), p. 1.

Chapter 15

The Context for the Future

Caroline Arms

An earlier chapter helped set the stage for the tales told in the case studies, but it would be misleading to imply that the technological context for the future will be the same. This chapter looks at some of the factors that libraries will have to address over the next few years, as they make further advances toward the goal of access to an array of information resources from scholars' desktops. On the desktops will be ever more powerful personal computers linked to higher-speed networks. Emerging standards for representing the structure of documents will support the coherent development of services to deliver the full text of works online. Communications standards for remote information retrieval will promote convenient access for end users to distant information resources over national computer networks.

How quickly the technological potential is exploited for the benefit of scholarship will depend on some nontechnological factors. One is the general need to modify procedures and organizations to manage the new technology. The traditional publishing industry has found that the technical problems involved in adopting new technology for preparing, editing, composing, and printing books are relatively simple to solve, given enough financial resources; developing new management structures and integrating them into the existing organization represent the real challenge. Also important is the general issue of intellectual property and the protection of copyright. Finally, the pattern of consolidation of the industry, and its effect on innovation, will shape the development of commercial electronic publishing. (For example, both DIALOG and BRS Information Technologies recently have been taken over and will be absorbed into large publishing empires.)

All these issues are too complex to treat in a few paragraphs and will not be covered here. This should not deter academic institutions from starting to build the electronic library. Without operating prototypes, the likelihood of resolving the nontechnological issues will be small, and some form of resolution certainly will be needed before the vision of integrated access to information from all sources can be achieved.

More Powerful Personal Computers

Most information retrieval services in use today assume that the student or scholar has access to a terminal or to a personal computer that emulates the functions of a terminal. Personal computers have the potential to act as intelligent and friendly interfaces, but those on most desks today have limits that make them unlikely candidates to serve as the workstations of the future. Some of the limitations are in the hardware, such as the insufficient speed of the processor or the inadequate size and resolution of the display; others are in the operating-system software, such as the ability to handle only one task at a time and the lack of software tools to build applications that integrate easily with other applications and present a consistent, intuitive interface. It is clear, both from the patterns of computer purchases on campuses and developments in the market, that the emerging scholar's workstation will have a graphical interface that represents applications and other objects by symbols (often called "icons"), rather than always by using words, and allows the user to perform routine operations by pointing at items on the screen rather than by typing commands. Another common feature will be the ability to display several "windows" on the screen simultaneously, just as a variety of books, papers, and tools can be spread out on a desk. And just as scholars can rearrange the items on their desks to suit the task at hand, so they will be able to reposition the windows on the screen—and to change the sizes of the windows as well.

The programming task to develop such an interface from scratch is immense. What is needed is either a toolkit of parts that can be fitted together to construct the user interface or a prefabricated structure within which an application can be built. The HyperCard system developed by Apple Computer for the Macintosh has proved an appealing tool for developing interfaces to information services because it provides a structure for developing applications that integrate with other Macintosh software, allowing nonprogrammers to build useful applications. However, HyperCard is only a beginning; it demonstrates enormous potential but is limited by pragmatic decisions made by the implementers, particularly in relation to the characteristics of the underlying computer. New and more powerful products will emerge based on experience and different expectations of the underlying hardware and operating system.

In today's universities, particularly in departments of engineering and science, an increasing number of students and faculty have access to more powerful personal computing devices. These are known commonly as "workstations," to distinguish them from less powerful personal computers. Typically, they have large, high-resolution displays (1,000 by 1,000 pixels), powerful processors (capable of handling a few million instructions per second), and several megabytes of memory, and run a multitasking operating system, usually a variant of UNIX. Whether the term "workstation" is used in this specific sense or in the more general sense of denoting any device that gives a user access to networked resources (hence including terminals, regular personal computers, and more advanced devices) is usually apparent from the context. While the more general sense is commonly used by librarians, here, and in most discussions of academic computing in the late 1980s, the term is used in the more specific sense.

Around 1982, ambitious projects to develop the distributed academic computing environment of the future were established at a number of universities, notably Brown, MIT, and Carnegie Mellon. The projects had different emphases, with Carnegie Mellon building the underlying components of a distributed environment, while the others put primary emphasis on developing applications to support the curriculum. All were based on the premise that a workstation with a graphical user interface, a multitasking operating system, and built-in networking capabilities would be available at reasonable cost by the end of the decade. The most optimistic hopes were for a workstation appropriate for student use to be ready by the late 1980s at a price of $3,000 (at academic discounts). These hopes have not been realized for two reasons: first, although prices for processing power, memory, and disk storage have fallen rapidly, the cost of a high-resolution display that can show a page at full size has not fallen as fast as hoped; second, the requirements in memory and processing power to support graphical interfaces and multitasking operating systems are higher than expected. These misjudgments are not confined to the academic world. The new OS/2 operating system, from Microsoft and IBM, is proving to require a larger, faster computer than predicted to support the Presentation Manager, its graphical interface. The workstation announced by NeXT, Inc., in October 1988 is priced at $6,500 for the academic market, although the goal was a price of $5,000.

Even if workstations are not yet on every desktop, these projects have changed the shape of campus computing services. They prove the feasibility of a campuswide computing environment that distributes resources throughout a high-speed network instead of focusing them on a single time-sharing system, combining the flexibility and response of personal computers with convenient access to shared resources. Whatever the exact form of the computer on the scholar's desk, university libraries will be operating in a decentralized environment in which individuals have simultaneous access to personal, departmental, campuswide, and national resources.

From these ambitious projects have come, not only important technical advances, but valuable experience. It has become obvious that no academic institution can expect to develop all the software required for a complete academic computing environment. The cost is too high. When the early academic time-sharing systems were developed in the mid-1960s, these endeavors were realistic and even necessary, since the commercial marketplace offered no alternative to faculty and students.

Now, the expectations of users have been raised by the availability of excellent commercial software for general applications—word processors, spreadsheets, and packages for graphics and statistics. The academic computing environment must satisfy these demands through compatibility with commercial developments; it is not enough to supply specific applications that support the curriculum directly and the underlying tools from which new applications can be built. Even if an ideal academic environment is designed and the underlying tools generated, only the most dedicated faculty will wish to develop applications that can never be used elsewhere; neither will commercial software companies want to modify general applications to run in a unique environment. The same pressures apply to small companies building workstations for the commercial market; customers are unwilling to commit to a proprietary technology that is not firmly established. Industry standards, whether official or *de facto,* are important for academic computing environments. Currently the basis for advanced computing services on most campuses is a high-speed network supporting the TCP/IP family of protocols—until recently, the only option for a high-speed network meant to support equipment from a variety of manufacturers. As products that support the ISO protocols emerge, campus networks gradually will migrate to the new international standard, but the conversion may take many years. Most advanced workstations, including those used in the projects at Brown, MIT, and Carnegie Mellon, use the UNIX operating system.

Among academics and many manufacturers, there is currently a drive to adopt a standard set of tools for building applications for UNIX workstations, to assure that software developed for one workstation can be converted easily to run on another. A number of vendors have formed a consortium known as the Open Software Foundation. In January 1989, they announced that their selection for interface standards had the "look-and-feel" characteristics of Microsoft's Windows and the Presentation Manager. This part of the standard defines how the size and position of windows can be changed and how menus of options and commands are presented to the user. The user interface will be known as Motif. For managing windows on the screen, it will rely on an underlying package (called X) that was developed at MIT; the interface toolkit will combine elements from Digital Equipment Corporation and Hewlett-Packard Corporation. However, in this field, as in networking, it is likely that the well-established vendors will develop their own proprietary toolkits, while others cooperate to specify a standard. Among the proprietary interfaces is Open Look from AT&T, which developed the original version of UNIX at its research center, Bell Laboratories. Politics and timing will be as important as technical quality in determining what survives in the marketplace in the longer term.

The scholar's workstation of the future is likely to share many features with the computer introduced in late 1988 by NeXT, Inc., which was designed specifically with the requirements of the academic marketplace in mind. This workstation has been greeted enthusiastically by many of the leaders in academic computing organizations as the first computer that combines an interface as comprehensive and intuitive as that of Apple's Macintosh, the power and flexibility of the UNIX operating system, a toolkit for building applications, and the potential to establish a market that will motivate both faculty and commercial software companies to develop applications. Its initial price is higher than had been hoped but is certainly reasonable in comparison with offerings from other manufacturers, particularly since it includes hardware and software chosen for the market, such as a built-in connector for an Ethernet network and software support for the TCP/IP network protocols. Several general applications are included with the computer, including a word processor and a simple free-text information retrieval system that will index documents by every word. The computer comes with copies on disk of the *New Collegiate Dictionary from Merriam-Webster, The Oxford Dictionary of Quotations,* and *William Shakespeare: The Complete Works,* also from Oxford University Press. NeXT has put the power of an engineering workstation in a package aimed at the general academic community and set a challenge to other computer manufacturers.

There is no doubt that, within a few years, a substantial proportion of the clientele of academic libraries will have on their desktops workstations with graphical interfaces that support capabilities beyond those of today's personal computers: display of the full text of documents on the screen in a resolution that is comfortable to read directly from the screen; flexible integration of network access to remote database servers with local operations such as word processing or managing personal files of information; and support of heavier requirements for computing power, such as those involved in the application of artificial intelligence techniques to information management.

Yet More Storage Options

The trend for heavily used databases to be duplicated and stored closer to the end user will continue. Many libraries already have embraced CD-ROM as an alternative to printed information resources or remote commercial services online. Others, particularly state and public libraries with many dispersed branches and no existing computing network, are publishing union catalogs on CD-ROM, an alternative that allows much more flexible searching than print or microform. Several government agencies, such as the Patent Office and the Post Office, already are using CD-ROM to distribute centrally maintained information, reducing the demand for online access to their databases. As more databases are published on CD-ROM, individuals and departments will begin to acquire CD-ROM readers: as the market expands, the cost of commercial products will drop. Personal libraries of information on CD-ROM may become commonplace. As well as providing reference services on CD-ROM, libraries may need to support CD-ROM products in the same ways that they support software, perhaps providing lending services for occasional use or for trying products out before purchase.

Two closely related optical-disk technologies share many characteristics with CD-ROM and also may be valuable for delivering information in electronic form: WORM (write-once-read-many) disks and erasable optical disks. Both provide inexpensive, compact ways to store large volumes of information, but access is slower than for magnetic disks. WORM disks have been available from several vendors for some years and are used primarily for archiving information that needs to be kept for a historical record but never will need to be changed. CD-ROMs are created from a master that is generated in a single operation, but data can be added to WORM disks gradually. "Jukeboxes" of WORM disks can provide online but relatively slow access to vast quantities of data. When WORM disks holding hundreds of megabytes of data first were introduced, it was suggested that they could be used like floppy disks, with the space gradually being used up as files were copied to new, unused space each time they were modified; however, this use has not established itself in the market. One area for which WORM disks do hold particular promise is office automation, where they can be used to hold corporate files of correspondence, reports, and contracts. In an academic library, this form of storage might be particularly appropriate for storing working papers and technical reports.

More recently, erasable optical disks have been introduced, and a drive for such disks is standard equipment on the NeXT computer. These can serve as alternatives to the magnetic disks currently used on personal computers, providing a medium that is inexpensive and removable like a floppy disk and able to store much more information than the typical hard disk. A disk can store 256 megabytes on one side (some products use both sides of the disk, but the disk must usually be turned over by the user), and suggested prices range from $50 to $250. Prices for drives for the disks currently vary widely, from $1,500 to $5,000. Meanwhile, the price for storage on more conventional magnetic disks continues to drop and performance to improve.

The recent rapid growth in the CD-ROM market for bibliographic, numeric, and full-text databases is due largely to the establishment of the High Sierra standard for storing information on the disks. Accepted standards also will be needed to establish a market for erasable optical disks and for WORM. One reason why WORM technology has not been adopted more widely already is the lack of such a standard; so far, each application has been tied to a particular vendor's equipment. The potential for using optical disks to store moving video images also is hampered by the lack of a standard. Three rival systems now provide for data, audio, and video to be stored on a single CD-ROM disk, each designed for a somewhat different market. The CD-I (the "I" stands for Interactive) system developed by Sony and Philips is a consumer product with a special-purpose player, which would compete with videocassette players and video-game systems. CD-ROM XA ("XA" stands for eXtended Architecture) is an extension to the High Sierra standard, designed for control by a general-purpose computer and supported by Microsoft, Sony, and Philips. Both these systems are inexpensive but suffer from relatively low video quality because of the slow speed at which the images can be retrieved from the disk. DVI (Digital Video Interactive) addresses this problem by using very advanced techniques for compressing the data. The hardware needed to support DVI on a personal computer is much more expensive, currently requiring three separate boards. The DVI technology was developed by engineers at RCA before its takeover by General Electric; recently, the technology and the development team were sold to Intel Corporation, which has announced aggressive plans to develop special chips to bring the cost down. Some libraries will experiment with these new media immediately, while others will wait for the market to develop and standards to emerge before adopting them for routine services.

Standards for Representing and Retrieving Information

The library and computing communities are also aware of the importance of standards as a basis for cooperative ventures. The development of the MARC (MAchine-Readable Cataloging) standard for catalog records by the Library of Congress provided the means to establish bibliographic utilities to support shared cataloging, to combine the catalogs of a group of libraries into a union catalog, and to exchange bibliographic records among libraries. In 1966, the Library of Congress was well placed to propose a standard format, since it was the major producer and distributor of cataloging records—on cards that themselves corresponded to a standard that defines the size, thickness, and placement of holes to allow any card to fit into any catalog drawer. Progressive libraries recognized that distribution of the same information in machine-readable form would be essential for the effective application of computers to library processes and that the time was ripe. The MARC format was refined after two years of experimental exchange of records among a few leading libraries, and the general record structure on which it is based was proposed as a standard. With no commercial or vested interests involved, the general format for bibliographic interchange was adopted as Z39.2 by the American National Standards Institute (ANSI) in 1971 and as ISO 2709 by the International Standards Organization (ISO) in 1972. MARC had no rival as a format for bibliographic interchange, was flexible enough to support local variations, and provided an important impetus to progress in library automation.

Not all standards are so timely or so universally accepted. A standard that is too restrictive and ratified too early in the technical development of a field may hold back progress by inhibiting innovation. Fear of locking into old technology provokes resistance to standardization unless developers find it essential for establishing an initial market. In complex areas, such as computer networking, where several competing participants already have invested heavily in development, the standardization process may be bitter and drawn out, and the incorporation of standards into products delayed. In other areas, the benefits of standardization may be relatively small, and the potential beneficiaries of standardization unable to influence its acceptance. Authors and librarians might be grateful if publishers adopted the ANSI standard (Z39.29-1977) for citations in footnotes and bibliographies, but, since readers—the paying customers—are unlikely to care about standardization, there is little motivation for publishers to change their practices. Some standards emerge through market acceptance or demand rather than through ratification by an official body—witness the markets for IBM-compatible PCs and telecommunications software that emulates the VT100 terminal from Digital Equipment Corporation. Nor is official adoption a guarantee that a standard will be accepted and used. An ANSI standard for the programming language BASIC exists, but, in the personal computer market, Microsoft's dialect of the language dominates. If U.S. government agencies adopt an official standard and build it in to procurement policies, however, the chances of commercial acceptance increase. Several recent standards that have been endorsed officially could be important for libraries delivering information to desktops.

The American National Standards Institute does not develop standards itself. It approves standards developed by other bodies, which must follow ANSI guidelines for developing, documenting, and obtaining consensus for standards. Some of these standards bodies began as ANSI committees but have become independent in the 1980s. The two accredited standards organizations that deal with matters directly relevant to libraries are the National Information Standards Organization (NISO, formerly ANSI Committee Z39) and Accredited Standards Committee X3 (formerly ANSI Committee X3). NISO develops and promotes standards for libraries, information science, and related publishing practices; its members are primarily associations and consortia of libraries and publishers. X3 deals with standards for information-processing systems, and its members are mainly corporations and professional associations, including the American Library Association (ALA) and the Institute of Electrical and Electronics Engineers (IEEE). IEEE is an accredited standards organization in its own right and has taken on a particularly important role in establishing standards for computer networking. For a thorough and readable discussion of standards relevant to libraries and the development process, see *Technical Standards: An Introduction for Librarians,* by Walt Crawford.[1]

Information Retrieval
A standard protocol for information retrieval was approved recently by NISO and ANSI and is now American National Standard Z39.50/1988; the same protocol is being proposed internationally as ISO 10162 and 10163. This protocol was based on one developed as part of the first phase of the Linked Systems Project, which established techniques and procedures for sharing records directly among databases at the Library of Congress, OCLC, and RLG. The protocol defines the format and sequence of messages and responses between the user's application and a remote database server or "search engine." As well as defining procedures for sending search requests and returning results, the information retrieval protocol also provides for servers to require authentication of the user or to send an interim status report before a search is completed.

Figure 15.1 represents, in natural English, a sequence of messages that might be used during a simple search. One general query type (Type-1) has been specified in the standard, but the structure allows for additional query types to be used, either by adding them to the standard or by mutual agreement between parties using the protocol. A Type-1

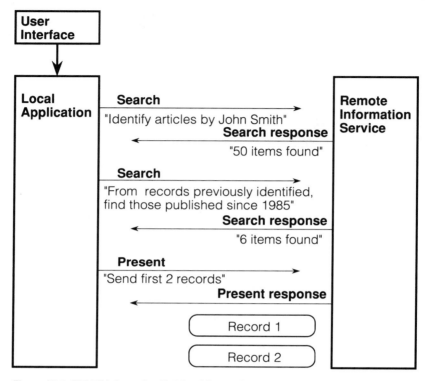

Figure 15.1 Z39.50 Information Retrieval Protocol: a sample sequence of messages.

query has a general form that covers a wide variety of complex searches: in its most straightforward form, it will locate records with specified words or phrases in certain fields (such as author or title) and allow for Boolean combinations of criteria (using "and," "or," or "not"). Additional types of queries might allow for browsing or for requesting information as to which fields are available for searching. The protocol has been described in some detail by Ray Denenberg, one of its key designers, and the formal standard was published in early 1989.[2]

Like other networking protocols, Z39.50 specifies the underlying function but does not restrict the user interface. For example, a protocol for electronic mail specifies underlying functions (e.g., conventions for addresses) and the identification of header fields (e.g., the sender's address to be used for a reply), but the mail interface seen by the user can take a variety of forms and provide local features such as the ability to file mail in different folders according to topic or sender. The user's information retrieval application may require the user to type in search commands explicitly, though not necessarily in exactly the syntax used in Z39.50, or it may construct the query for the user on the basis of menu choices or helpful prompts. The user's application would translate a query in the local syntax into the common syntax of the protocol before passing it to a remote database server. (An important advantage of an accepted standard would be for linking a user to several different databases, some local and others remote, through a common search interface.) The user's application also might include local features, such as tools for compiling personal bibliographies. If adopted widely, Z39.50 could be a key building block in the distributed electronic library of the future.

Until recently, the information retrieval protocol was only in use by the three active participants in the first phase of the Linked Systems Project; the project now is expanding to involve some of the major research libraries. A new phase is the National Coordinated Cataloging Program, in which eight research libraries will work with the Library of Congress to spread the cataloging load while still providing records to the highest standards. Use of the protocol in other contexts is just beginning, including its use over networks using the TCP/IP family of protocols rather than the ISO/OSI protocols used by the Linked Systems Project. With sponsorship from OCLC, the New York State Education and Research Network (NYSERNet) has developed an information retrieval gateway between the two types of network that will allow users connected to NYSERNet to search OCLC's bibliographic database. The Library of Congress and the University of Maryland are investigating the possibility of retrieving and exchanging records over NSFNET. The University of California is planning to use the protocol to link its union catalog MELVYL with library automation systems on individual campuses. Carnegie Mellon plans to use it for its new distributed library information system.

NISO has been developing another standard that is related to the information retrieval protocol for networking: a common command language for online interactive information retrieval. For several years, users of online information services have been frustrated by the differences in conventions and command languages among systems. Many users take advantage of simpler interfaces that provide menus or prompts to construct straightforward queries, but specifying precise searches still often requires the underlying command language. Some examples of commands on different systems to search for books by John Brown would include:

- SS AU=brown, john   (DIALOG)
- brown.au. adj john   (BRS or STAIRS)

- A=brown, john   (NOTIS)
- FIND PA john brown   (MELVYL, University of California)
- /AU=brown, john   (LS/2000)

For complex queries, the differences are much greater.

The draft standard for a common command language, Z39.58, has been through several cycles of drafting and revision. It covers a set of functions usually provided on online systems, including searching in specified fields for keywords and browsing through a list of indexed terms. Keywords can be required to appear adjacent or close to each other or specified in Boolean combinations. Among other features are the ability to choose databases for searching, to sort retrieved items, and to save and refine search strategies. Commands for obtaining online assistance on specific topics or with the current task are also specified.

Z39.58 is not intended to preclude interfaces using menus or prompts, nor to require that every information retrieval system support a command interface. Nor is it intended to inhibit the provision of additional features or types of search. The aim is simply to provide a basic set of commands that a user faced with an unfamiliar information retrieval system supporting a command language should be able to use without confusion. A system that conformed to the standard would not have to provide every function in the standard; however, if the function corresponding to a standard command were not available, the system should be designed to respond with a clear and helpful message to that effect, not with "Unrecognized command" or "Syntax error." Whether such a standard will be accepted widely remains to be seen. If some of the major commercial online services adopt it rapidly, customers may put pressure on the smaller services to conform; without such market pressure, there will be little motivation to take on the effort and expense of modification and customer education.

Representation of Documents

The electronic library will need a standard (or a small set of standards) for representing general documents. Otherwise, the chore of converting documents from many different sources will discourage the creation of large full-text databases.

Information retrieval systems that provide access to the full text of documents can be of two fundamentally different types, although hybrids are possible. To understand the distinctions, consider the example of systems that provide access to the text of journal articles. In the first type, documents are stored as images, and retrieval is based on a separately constructed bibliographic file, which may contain abstracts as well as the usual fields for author, title, publication details, and subject headings. The search system is identical to those with which librarians are already familiar for indexing or abstracting services, with the additional feature that once a relevant article has been identified, its text can be displayed immediately on the screen. As when recorded on microform, the article can be read or printed, but no searching for terms is possible within the article, nor can portions of text be extracted for inclusion in other documents. For this type of system, all that is needed is images of the pages of a printed document. IEEE, in association with University Microfilms International, is taking this approach in preparing a set of CD-ROMs for back issues of its publications. The database will consist of images scanned from the printed journals, combined with indexing and abstracts from the INSPEC database.

In the second type of system, the document is held primarily as sequences of characters (usually coded according to the American Standard Code for Information Interchange, ASCII), so that words within the text can be indexed. This type of system holds enormous potential for more intelligent searching, since not only the words but also the structure of articles could be used to guide the search. The possibilities are many: the occurrence of terms in headings could be given more weight than occurrences within paragraphs; once a relevant section has been located, the system could display an outline of the document to provide a context; and searches for figures or photographs would be possible. For this type of system, the document must be represented in a form that holds the text as characters, as in a word processor, and also indicates the document's structure, identifying its different components, such as sections, footnotes, figures, and appendices.

For the first type of system, an appropriate standard from another context is being adopted for storing text as images. Standards have been developed by the International Telegraph and Telephone Consultative Committee (CCITT) for facsimile transmission. The Group III standard that is most commonly used for transmission over regular telephone lines uses a resolution of roughly 200 dots per inch. The Group IV standard, designed for high-speed digital transmission, uses 300 dots per inch, as do the laser printers in common use today. At this resolution, raw images of text would require two hundred times the storage needed to hold the text in ASCII characters, but the fax standards use compression techniques to reduce the storage required (and the time to transmit an image).

The Group IV fax standard is being used for storing images in a number of pilot projects, including one at the National Agriculture Library that will test a variety of indexing and retrieval systems.[3]

Like microfilming, scanning pages to generate images in digitized form is a straightforward process, taking two or three seconds per page, that can be applied to large volumes of print materials in a routine fashion. The process is the same whether pages present graphics or text; the image as stored contains no information beyond defining where black dots should be printed on paper or displayed on the screen. A second process can be applied to the images of text in order to interpret the individual characters; known as "optical character recognition" (OCR), this process is much less routine. Accuracy depends on typeface, font size, and the quality of the original. In practice, even the best systems average several incorrect characters per page, which is almost certainly unacceptable for automatic indexing without additional quality control. In a project at the U.S. Nuclear Regulatory Commission, an operator spent an average of two minutes per page reviewing the results using a spelling checker.[4] In this project, as well as in the text digitizing project at the National Agricultural Library, the text will be stored both as unformatted characters (for full-text retrieval and rapid browsing) and as images (for full representation in original layout and fonts and including graphics). This duplication is an interim solution until systems that can handle the structure of documents are developed; however, for documents that are available only in printed form, it is a convenient approach.

Most text prepared today starts life on a word processor and also exists in a machine-readable form that incorporates specifications for its final layout. In building an electronic library, it obviously would be better to capture documents directly rather than submitting printed versions to the expensive and error-prone process of scanning and character recognition. Ideally, not only the raw characters but also the structure of the document should be captured in a form that could be useful for intelligent information retrieval. Unfortunately, each system for word processing and page composition uses a different system of "tags" for marking up documents, and, on most systems, the tags merely indicate how a document should be printed, not how it is structured. A few words at the beginning of a document may be tagged to print centered on a line and in boldface, but do they constitute the title or the author's name? Just as the MARC standard provides a common format for the exchange of catalog records, a standard that represents the structure of documents would provide a basis for exchanging complete and complex documents. In fact, two such standards now exist; how widely and rapidly they are adopted will be an important factor controlling progress toward the electronic library.

SGML (Standard Generalized Markup Language)

This standard, adopted by ISO in 1986, prescribes a very flexible, general format for adding tags to a document to describe its structure. Designed to be machine independent, SGML uses tags that can be interpreted easily by humans as well as machines and consist of markers at the beginning and end of text segments known as "entities." Examples of entities are paragraphs, emphasized phrases, headings, chapters, or appendices. SGML also provides for rules that specify how the entities should be related and what entities a particular type of document should have. As an oversimplified example, rules could be established to define the structure of a book as consisting of chapters, each chapter having a title and being divided into sections, each with a heading and a number of paragraphs. The SGML standard defines a conceptual framework for tags and types of documents but does not specify instances: any practical use of SGML demands a set of "document type definitions." Through its Electronic Manuscript Project, the Association of American Publishers has compiled a set of definitions as its AAP Standard for Electronic Manuscript Preparation and Markup, now adopted by ANSI as Z39.59/1988. Several major publishers, including McGraw-Hill and IEEE, were involved in the project and have announced their intention to adopt the standard for internal use.

That documents in SGML format could be used as the basis for retrieving and delivering information online is not necessarily the only motivation for publishers to adopt the standard; it provides advantages in their more traditional business. SGML is concerned only with document structure, not with layout, but documents stored in SGML format can be used as the basis for conventional typesetting, if design specifications are associated with the tags. However, since the structural description is isolated from the design specifications, the document in SGML format is also an excellent base for derivative publications such as chapter reprints or anthologies or for publishing the same work in a variety of media and formats.

A second set of document type definitions has been developed as part of a Defense Department project for Computer-aided Acquisitions and Logistics Support (CALS). This project aims to streamline procedures for supporting equipment and services purchased by the armed services. The first phase has been to establish standards for documentation for projects and products. The CALS standards use SGML for text, but, since

SGML includes no treatment of graphics beyond a general mechanism for referring to entities to be incorporated from elsewhere, a separate standard for graphics was needed. The Initial Graphics Exchange Specification (IGES), developed by the National Institute for Standards and Technology (NIST, formerly the National Bureau of Standards), has been chosen: it is appropriate for engineering drawings, being capable of representing parts of a structured diagram as individual entities. The CALS standards, which include twenty-five generic types of document, already are being written into procurement specifications by the Department of Defense for new systems. Manuals need not be created originally in an SGML format; in many cases, a translation program will be used. The conversion of documentation for existing systems, or those which are in an advanced stage of development, is being considered case by case. In some cases, the documentation will be converted using automatic tools; in others, it will be revised and recreated totally. Official adoption of SGML by the Department of Defense will catalyze commercial development of hardware and software to support the creation, storage, and distribution of documents based on SGML, making it easier for smaller publishers to adopt the standard. Libraries will be able to take advantage of this process.

Indications of support for SGML already are appearing in many areas. At least one text-preparation system supporting the direct creation of documents that conform to the definition of an SGML document type is now available for a personal computer. IBM has introduced an SGML translator for its mainframe document composition system. As part of a project at Ohio State University, programs have been developed to convert documents between the format defined by the AAP/SGML standard for an article and formats for popular mainframe text-processing systems used by academics, such as Scribe. At the Open University in the United Kingdom, course materials created with Microsoft Word using prescribed document templates can be converted to and from SGML automatically. Avalanche Development Company is working on recognition software that uses artificial intelligence techniques to take scanned document images and not only identify the characters of the text but also mark it up with SGML tags by taking account of layout, changes in font, and particular words (such as "note" or "To:"). This project is spurred by the expected need by government agencies and suppliers to convert many existing documents to the CALS standards.

Oxford University Press has recently converted the Oxford English Dictionary to SGML format. This operation was particularly complex because dictionary entries contain a great deal of information communicated through the use of varied faces, sizes, and weights of type and because the formatting conventions had varied over the years. Since the automatic recognition task was beyond the capability of current systems, the dictionary entries were typed from the printed text and indicators of the format changes were included by the typists. Artificial intelligence techniques were used to interpret the format changes and assign tags to the various parts of the entries. Any entries that could not be tagged unambiguously using the automatic method were stored separately for final editing by lexicographers, who used a special editor that recognized the tags and used colors to display the entries for easy checking. This single form of the dictionary will serve as the basis for printed editions of various sizes and completeness, as well as for electronic versions, such as the CD-ROM version already available.

ODA (Office Document Architecture)

In Europe and Japan, another standard for representing text is becoming established, and it, too, has been approved by ISO. The Office Document Architecture (ODA) is a much fuller standard than SGML, including representation of layout, as well as logical structure, and explicit treatment of graphics, tables, and other components of complex documents. With support from a cooperative research program of the Europe Economic Community, known as ESPRIT (European Strategic Programme for Research in Information Technologies), many European vendors (including subsidiaries of U.S. firms) are developing software to create and organize documents in this form. Their emphasis is on filing and retrieving documents in an office or business environment, but many aspects of these efforts will be immediately relevant to information retrieval in the context of an academic community.

In the United States, ODA does not appear to be gaining immediate acceptance, but it has been used as part of the EXPRES project, which is sponsored by the National Science Foundation with the aim of providing a mechanism for the exchange and review of complex scientific documents. As part of the project, translation programs have been written at Carnegie Mellon and the University of Michigan between ODA and the formats used by a number of systems that handle complex documents, such as Interleaf, Diamond (from Bolt Beranek and Newman), and troff (which runs on most UNIX computers).

The wide acceptance of either SGML or ODA for representing structured documents would further the development of software products that support the exchange, retrieval, and display of documents in full text. Word processors would provide features to support the standard representation, conversion utilities would appear as commercial products, and it would be easy to load documents from a variety of sources into an integrated information retrieval system. Without a standard, independent systems would be incompatible.

National Computing Networks

The vision of the electronic library of the future is based on easy access to information resources across campus, across the nation, and even across the world. The last few years have seen an enormous development in general-purpose computer networks that link academic institutions around the United States and the world. Several different networks have evolved from different origins, but efforts to develop a coherent strategy for the future are under way. (For a more detailed description of these networks, see *Campus Networking Strategies,* an earlier volume in this series.)[5] The national network that probably will be the most important in the long term for delivering electronic information to the academic community is the Internet, which supports high speeds and powerful services. BITNET is a less powerful and less expensive network; it reaches many smaller institutions that have not been able to justify the higher budgetary commitment (for equipment and staff support) to connect to the Internet because their campus networks are not immediately compatible. The number of institutions connected to both networks has been growing rapidly, and mechanisms are in place to maintain and upgrade services, speed, and reliability. Networks are now part of the academic infrastructure, general-purpose highways for transporting data.

The Internet

The Internet is not a single network; it incorporates the ARPANET, NSFNET, and many regional networks, which operate using the same family of communications protocols. Although it comprises networks administered by a variety of organizations, it appears to the user as an integrated whole. Just as anyone with a telephone can dial a friend anywhere in the country regardless of which local or long-distance telephone companies own the lines along which the signals travel, a computer connected to the Internet can communicate with any other computer on the Internet. The number of universities with access to this network has been growing fast since the National Science Foundation introduced NSFNET to provide researchers with high-speed access to supercomputer centers. In early 1989, it reached around three hundred academic institutions; at many of these, any computer or terminal attached to the campus network also has access to the larger network. The Internet supports a wide variety of network services: the most commonly used are electronic mail, transfer of files between computers, and the ability to link to a remote computer as if one were at a terminal connected to it directly. However, the network is designed to support the much more sophisticated functions that will be necessary to achieve the vision of transparent access to remote resources. A single logical database may be distributed over several machines, and software running on a user's workstation can refer to files stored on a computer across the country just as if they were stored on the workstation. These advanced network applications are emerging only now from the experimental stage; currently, most network use is still conscious—researchers send messages to colleagues using their network addresses or log on to remote computers.

Several institutions have made their online information systems or databases accessible to remote users who log in over the Internet. For instance, the CARL system in Colorado, the Dante database at Dartmouth, and RPI's information system all can be reached over the Internet. To protect copyright, the tradition of free, open access to all information held by libraries sometimes has to be compromised to comply with restrictions incorporated into licenses by the owners of databases. For instance, the MELVYL online catalog is accessible over the Internet, but access to MEDLINE is restricted to users on the University of California campuses. Other institutions require passwords or have restricted remote access over the Internet entirely, even when it is technically simple. This conflict will have to be resolved before a global information environment can be established, but such resolution will not come without substantial experiments that allow the players in the information industry—authors, publishers, librarians, and scholars—to work together to establish new ground rules on the basis of evidence rather than hypothesis.

In some disciplines, mainly technical fields such as computer science or engineering, access to the Internet is vital to keeping up with developments. Electronic mail is used much more heavily than paper for communicating with colleagues around the world, and the mail system supports an enormous number of mailing lists that function as bulletin boards on various topics. A wide variety of information, including working papers, reports, software, and documentation, is accessible over the Internet through an informal distribution scheme based on a file transfer facility known as "anonymous FTP." FTP (File Transfer Protocol) allows a user to transfer files from one computer to another. Normally, the user needs to sign on to an authorized computer account on both computers. However, all those who have files or documents that they wish to make publicly accessible can store them so that they can be accessed by others who sign on as "anonymous." Once signed on, remote users can look at a list of available files and request that some be transferred to their own computers. This facility provides a primitive form of networked information server. A flaw in the system is that there is no bibliographic control over the materials available—a list of filenames, often cryptic, is not a catalog. At best, one of the files accessible from a certain network address is a list of the other files stored in the same location. There is also no network directory or union catalog. The only way to find out what information of interest is available and where it is stored is through the grapevine or postings on electronic bulletin boards. For example, some months ago, a message on a bulletin board dealing with campus networks announced the availability of a description of the scheme used at the Massachusetts Institute of Technology to ensure that access to network services is authorized. The name of the file and the network address at which it was stored were given; within a few minutes, interested parties could have transferred the report to their own computers to read through at leisure and print copies as needed. But only subscribers to certain bulletin boards would have known of its existence.

At least one individual has attempted to compile an informal list of sources on the Internet, complete with brief descriptions of the types of information available. Librarians hardly would consider it a catalog, but it is certainly better than nothing. However, there is a major problem: the list is itself stored ready for access by anonymous FTP, but, of course, only by those who know of its existence. Even so, whatever the limitations of informal mechanisms for distributing information over the Internet, its widespread use in technical disciplines proves that some members of the academic community are prepared to tolerate systems that are far from ideal if it allows them to access information from their desktops.

BITNET

Whereas the Internet grew from the ARPANET, which supported advanced technical research, BITNET developed to allow any member of the academic community to communicate with colleagues elsewhere. Roughly 450 institutions in the United States are now members of BITNET, and the network is linked directly to counterparts in Canada, Europe, and Japan. Its main services are electronic mail and file transfer. Mail can be exchanged between BITNET and the Internet, as well as several other networks. Like the Internet, BITNET supports mailing lists; some lists are common to the two networks. Some are open to anyone who wishes to subscribe; others are restricted. Many are valuable sources of advice on using particular software packages (there is one for NOTIS); others are nontechnical, discussing campus policies or issues specific to an academic discipline.

BITNET does not allow users to log in to remote computers, but it does support interactive messages between users who are logged on. This feature has been used to support another primitive form of information server. One common use for this capability is to store archives of messages posted on a bulletin board. Typically, messages for a certain period—say, a month—are stored in a file, and people with related problems can transfer copies of the file to their own machines and browse through the file to see if the topic has been discussed. The information server is a database system that is set up to respond to search queries that are sent as messages across the network. For users, this is very different from logging into a database system, whether by dialing up or over a network. Users never see screen displays from the remote system; they merely type commands as messages and dispatch them. Sometime later, a response will come as electronic mail, but, in the meantime, they can continue with other tasks. Help with using the system also may be sought by sending messages. A similar system allows the Stanford Linear Accelerator Center (SLAC) to provide network access to its database of citations for articles on high energy physics. SLAC has added to SPIRES a feature known as Remote SPIRES that allows a SPIRES system to respond over BITNET to messages containing search requests.

The potential of networks for accumulating and distributing information in specialized areas is demonstrated by an example from the University of Delaware. With support from the Delaware Institute for Medical Education and Research, Dr. Borgaonkar of the Medical Center of Delaware maintains two databases that support both research and practice in cytogenetics, the study of heredity through genetic means and the analysis of cells. The first, Chromosomal Variation in Man—A Catalog of Chromosomal Variants and Anomalies, is a bibliographic database containing citations to relevant material scattered in the literature. The second, International Registry of Abnormal Karyotypes—Repository of Human Chromosomal Variants and Anomalies, holds unpublished data on about 350,000 chromosomal analyses, including 65,000 abnormalities. The information is submitted in personal communications, often over BITNET, by over 300 practitioners and researchers around the world. The databases are published in printed form, but there is a four-year interval between editions of the catalog and a two-year gap between editions of the registry. The field is developing rapidly, and online access is essential for locating recent data. Currently, most remote users send requests by electronic mail. Searches are performed locally by Dr. Borgaonkar or his staff, and the results are returned by electronic mail. The university's support group for academic computing expects more demand for direct online access in the future, and the computer on which the database is stored already is accessible from the Internet, BITNET, and commercial packet-switched networks.

A Proposal for a Digital Library

Robert E. Kahn and Vinton G. Cerf of the Corporation for National Research Initiatives recently shared with me a draft proposal for a national information infrastructure, which they call the "digital library system." In the proposal, they look ahead to what might be feasible in fifteen or twenty years, identifying tools that will be needed and problems that will have to be solved before the vision of a world of information resources accessible from the scholar's desktop can be achieved. Kahn and Cerf are no strangers to ambitious, long-term projects, having been instrumental in the establishment of the pioneering ARPANET and its successor, the Internet, and the development of the underlying communication protocols that now form the basis for the NSFNET and many regional and campus networks. In keeping with the distributed model that is guiding most computing developments today, their design assumes that the user will have a powerful workstation that communicates with a variety of "servers" over a high-speed network. It also is assumed that, on this workstation, the user will have a "personal library system," an integrated extension of today's tools for creating, storing, and retrieving information (word processor, spreadsheet, graphics software, and so on).

An intriguing part of the proposal is that communications among components of the system will not be through passive messages; instead, Kahn and Cerf envisage active entities that they call "knowledge robots," or "knowbots." These would be programs that can replicate themselves, create new knowbots, or transfer themselves to another computer. Similar processes already are used in some distributed computing environments, for instance, for mail delivery. A very simple example keeps track of users' unsatisfied requests for online help about the Andrew computing environment at Carnegie Mellon. If a user at a workstation types "help NSFNET" but no help is available on that topic, his or her workstation starts a process that runs a program on a remote computer to put "NSFNET" on a list of unsatisfied requests (or to add "1" to a counter if the topic is already on the list). User services staff review the list regularly to identify the need for changes to the online help system. The Digital Library System would include many types of knowbot, which would operate together to perform particular tasks, such as helping users locate information. Some would be responsible for the user interface, for tasks such as interpreting queries in natural language or incorporating discipline-specific

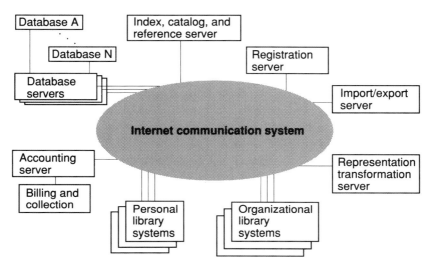

Figure 15.2 Proposed structure for a digital library system.

knowledge and the user's individual preferences in order to formulate a search strategy. Others could retrieve information simultaneously from a variety of sources and choose which to present to the user.

As shown in Figure 15.2, the design includes many types of servers beyond the database servers that actually hold the information and deliver documents or data in response to requests. These additional servers communicate with each other, and perhaps with human administrators, to perform logistic functions. As an example, consider a document that is to be stored in the library system. It would be sent initially to an "import/export server," which would determine whether the document was in a standard form ready for storage. If, for instance, the document was in the format of a particular word processor, the import/export server would enlist the aid of a "representation transformation server," which would convert the document to a standard internal representation. The document would then be passed to the "registration server," which would call on the "index, catalog, and reference server" to determine where it should be stored. The registration server also would pass information on to the "accounting server" on how users should be charged and providers compensated for use of the item.

Kahn and Cerf share a belief with the contributors to this book: that the time is ripe for experimenting and developing prototypes. A common vision of an information network based on powerful personal computers, high-speed communications, and shared resources is emerging. The institutions represented here have described the excitement of being among the pioneers who are taking the first important steps toward this vision. They do not expect an immediate revolution, but all recognize that visions are not achieved without action.

References

1. Crawford, Walt. *Technical Standards: An Introduction for Librarians* (White Plains, N.Y.: Knowledge Industry Publications, 1986).
2. Denenberg, Ray. "NISO Draft Standard Z39.50: Information Retrieval Protocol." *Library Hi Tech News* 39 (June 1987): 1, 7–8.

   ———. "Standard Networking Interconnection Protocols." In *The Linked Systems Project: A Networking Tool for Libraries,* ed. Judith G. Fenly and Beacher Wiggins (Dublin, Ohio: OCLC, 1988).

   National Information Standards Organization. *American National Standard Information Retrieval Service Definition and Protocol Specification for Library Applications, ANSI/NISO Z39.50/1988* (New Brunswick, N.J.: Transaction Publishers, 1989).
3. Andre, Pamela Q. J., and Nancy L. Eaton. "National Agricultural Text Digitizing Project." *Library Hi Tech* 6, no. 3 (1988): 61–66.
4. Bender, Avi. "An Optical Disk–Based Information Retrieval System." *Library Hi Tech* 6, no. 3 (1988): 81–85.
5. Arms, Caroline. *Campus Networking Strategies,* EDUCOM Strategies Series on Information Technology (Bedford, Mass.: Digital Press, 1988).

Glossary

This glossary provides general descriptions of some of the acronyms and more technical terms used in this book. The descriptions are not necessarily formal definitions. Words or phrases in boldface in a description themselves appear as items in the glossary.

Access point A term, usually in a **bibliographic record**, by which a record may be searched and identified. In traditional card catalogs, the usual access points are author, title, and subject. But automated systems also may allow access through other terms (often called **indexes**), such as publication date.

Acquisitions The department or function within a library that handles the purchase and receipt of books and other materials. **Periodicals** and other **serials** usually are processed separately (see **serials control**), since different procedures are required for subscriptions and multiple issues.

AGRICOLA Agricultural Online Access. This bibliographic database maintained by the National Agriculture Library contains over two million bibliographic records, of which roughly 90 percent are to journal articles.

ANSI American National Standards Institute. This body approves U.S. standards for many areas, including libraries, information technology, and communications. It is a member of the International Standards Organization, **ISO.**

AppleTalk A proprietary network architecture from Apple Computer, Inc.

Application protocol A protocol in the uppermost layer (layer 7) of the **OSI** Basic Reference Model for network architectures. The user interacts with this layer when using network services for particular tasks, such as reading or sending mail or accessing a remote database. Examples are the **X.400** protocol that supports electronic mail and the **Z39.50** protocol that supports information retrieval.

ARPANET An experimental network, linking universities and other organizations involved in networking research. Part of the unclassified segment of the Defense Data Network, it was established under the auspices of the Defense Advanced Research Projects Agency (DARPA), which provides basic research, development, and technology transfer for the Department of Defense. An important family of higher-level networking protocols, based on **TCP/IP** (Transmission Control Protocol/Internet Protocol) and adopted widely on national and campus networks, was developed on the ARPANET. Several networks managed by different agencies are linked together, using the same protocols and sharing a common addressing convention. Collectively, these networks are known as the ARPA Internet or simply as the **Internet.**

ASCII American Standard Code for Information Interchange. Established by the American National Standards Institute (**ANSI**), this coding scheme uses the numbers from 0 to 127 (7 bits) to represent the standard typewriter characters and some communication control signals. Most personal computers and non-IBM terminals and mainframes use ASCII for representing and communicating characters.

Asynchronous communication Communication in which streams of characters are sent in sequence but at no particular time intervals. Most of the common non-IBM terminals use asynchronous communication, at speeds up to 19.2K bits/second. This is also the standard form of communication supported on most personal computers.

Authority control The process by which the authoritative forms of names, subject headings, and so on, used in a file of bibliographic records are applied and maintained consistently.

Authority record A record that shows a name or subject heading in the form established for use in a file of bibliographic records and lists alternative forms that should refer to this heading. A full authority record also cites sources consulted in establishing the heading and used to justify the chosen form.

Beta test The final stage of testing a product before it is released. During this stage, the product is tested by potential customers in operational use.

Bibliographic access The means to locate a document or work through a compilation of **bibliographic information,** such as a catalog or index.

Bibliographic control A term that describes the activities through which bibliographic information on items is recorded and published in catalogs or indexes so that readers can locate and gain access to those items. It provides **bibliographic access.**

Bibliographic information Information describing a book, article, or other item, including such elements as title, author, publisher, date of publication, and physical description. Other elements that help in identifying or locating works often are categorized loosely as bibliographic information, including **subject headings,** location, and **call number.**

Bibliographic record A record containing **bibliographic information** about an item. Examples of bibliographic records are catalog cards and entries in **indexes** of journal articles.

Bibliographic search The process of identifying a work or document through a systematic search of compilations of **bibliographic information,** such as catalogs and indexes.

Bibliographic utility An organization that maintains bibliographic databases, enabling it to offer computer-based support to libraries for shared cataloging, interlibrary loan, and other library operations. There are four major bibliographic utilities serving libraries in North America, each with its own distinct mission and characteristics: **OCLC, RLG, UTLAS,** and **WLN.**

Bit A binary unit of information that can take the value 1 or 0. It is the fundamental unit of digital communication. Information is transmitted over networks as streams of bits.

Bit-mapped display A computer display for which each pixel (dot on the screen that can be lit or unlit) can be controlled individually by mapping a set of bits in the computer's memory to the set of pixels on the screen. Such displays can represent arbitrary images, whereas the displays used with many earlier personal computers or terminals can represent only characters from a predefined set. Bit-mapped displays require more memory and higher-speed communications than do character displays.

BITNET Because It's Time NETwork. A cooperative academic network providing mail, information, and file-transfer services among 435 member institutions, with links to similar networks in Canada, Europe, the Far East, and South America.

Boolean logic A form of symbolic logic developed by George Boole (1815–1864), an English mathematician. Terms expressing logical conditions can be combined using the Boolean operators: "and," "or," and "not." An example of an expression in Boolean logic is: (Title = "Biology") and (Author = "Camp"). Using a card catalog, a reader would perform her or his search in two stages, first finding "Biology" in the title catalog and then leafing through cards to locate the work by the particular author (or, alternatively, finding "Camp" in the author catalog and then searching for the individual work). Online catalogs and indexing services that support Boolean logic can combine the two stages into a single operation.

Bridge A link that joins two physical local networks into a single communications subnet, overcoming the physical constraints that limit a single physical network. (For instance, an Ethernet or AppleTalk bus is limited to a certain length because signals attenuate over distance.) A bridge is a link at the second level (data link layer) of the **OSI** Basic Reference Model for network architectures. Many bridges act as filters, passing only the traffic that needs to move across the physical boundary and thus reducing unnecessary traffic. **Routers** provide more isolation between linked networks.

Broadband A transmission system with a wide frequency range, in which many different sets of signals (channels) are on the transmission medium simultaneously. Each set of signals is translated to a particular frequency range. An example is cable television, where many channels are broadcast at once on a single cable. A broadband local area network uses hardware developed for the cable television industry and may handle video distribution, as well as a diversity of data services.

Browsing An informal searching technique by which the user scans information in a relevant area by first locating a title or keyword that is of interest and then looking at titles or text that are "close." In the library stacks, this corresponds to finding an interesting title and looking on the neighboring shelves; since volumes in open stacks normally are shelved by call numbers established through a classification system based on subject area, this is a long-established approach to finding relevant works. Online catalogs often support searches by call number, thus providing an exactly equivalent process. They also may support browsing through other indexes, such as author or subject heading, thus supporting the same capability as leafing through catalog cards. For full-text material, the term is used to describe informal scanning of a book or article; in this case, browsing through a work may be sequential ("turning pages") or structural (skimming chapter headings, looking at figures, and so on).

BRS Information Technologies Originally Bibliographic Retrieval Service, BRS Information Technologies provides one of the major online information services. The company also markets its search software, BRS/Search. In late 1988, the company was acquired by Macmillan Inc., which was acquired in turn by Maxwell Communication Corp.

Bulletin board The electronic equivalent of a board on which anyone (or a certain set of people) can post notices. Many electronic mail systems support electronic bulletin boards: notices are posted and read in the same way that messages are sent between individuals. Electronic **conferences** and mailing lists are other terms used to describe similar capabilities. The distinction among the terms is more administrative than technical, relating to whether participation is open to all or controlled and whether users are notified automatically of new postings or have to make a deliberate choice to check for them.

Call number An identification number that indicates where a volume is shelved in a library. In a library with closed stacks, this is the number by which users can "call" for books to be delivered to the reading room. In most libraries, the call number derives from a subject classification scheme, such as the Dewey Decimal system or the scheme established by the Library of Congress.

CALS Computer-aided Acquisitions and Logistics Support. A project of the Department of Defense to streamline support for weapons systems: the first phase is the specification of standards for documentation that suppliers will be required to provide in machine-readable form. The chosen form for representing formatted text is the **SGML** standard.

CCITT International Telegraph and Telephone Consultative Committee. This group sets international standards for the communications industry. The acronym derives from the French version of the name: Comité Consultatif International Télégraphique et Téléphonique.

CD-I Compact Disc Interactive. A technology (based on compact disks) that would require a special-purpose player and compete with video cassettes and video games as a consumer product.

CD-ROM Compact Disk Read-Only-Memory. A computer storage medium that takes advantage of the same technology used for storing sound in digital form on compact disks. The information is encoded by creating miniscule pits and bumps on a metal-coated plastic disk. It is read by interpreting the reflections of a laser beam from the surface. Disks are copied from a master; each can hold 600 megabytes of data (for example, the text of around four hundred books), which can be read but not modified. The cost of a disk (as opposed to the information on it) is around $3, which makes it a very cheap storage and distribution medium for large volumes of information that do not need constant updating, such as back issues of journals. However, information cannot be retrieved from CD-ROM as quickly as from magnetic hard disks, and the medium is unlikely to be appropriate for storing databases that will be accessed simultaneously by many users. Most CD-ROMs containing textual, graphic, and numeric data are now generated in a standard format developed by the **High Sierra** Group. See chapter 1 for more information.

CD-ROM XA Compact Disk Read-Only-Memory eXtended Architecture. This is an extension to the **High Sierra** standard format for **CD-ROM**; it supports the inclusion of video and sound.

CERFNET California Education and Research Federation Network. A regional network attached to the **NSFNET** and part of the **Internet.**

Charge Check an item out of a library.

CICS Customer Information Control System. Mainframe communications software from IBM that supports terminal access for applications programs that may handle simultaneous transaction requests from many terminals.

Circulation The library operation that supports the borrowing of materials by users. A circulation system must support identification of both users and materials, allow users to **charge** (check out) items, and permit the application of individual library policies on borrowing periods and fines.

CLASS Cooperative (formerly California) Library Authority for Systems and Services. Originally a regional library organization, CLASS now acts as a broker for RLIN services worldwide.

Codex A volume consisting of pages bound between covers. This form of presenting and preserving knowledge had largely replaced the scroll by the fourth century. Until the middle of the twentieth century, the collections of libraries consisted almost entirely of works in this form, but **microform** and electronic resources now offer alternatives.

CompuServe An online information service that also provides gateways to other information resources and a range of services to support **electronic mail, bulletin boards,** and special-interest groups.

Conference A forum for discussing a certain topic or group of topics through electronic messages. Facilities for electronic conferences are provided in conjunction with some **electronic mail** systems and are similar technically to those for electronic **bulletin boards.**

CRIS Current Research Information System. This system supports a database of summaries of research projects in the U.S. Department of Agriculture and cooperating institutions.

Database server A program or dedicated computer that manages a database and can respond to requests over a network for individual items of information from it. A database server is not the same as a file server, which provides access to entire files, but no searching function.

Data switch A device comparable to a telephone exchange but designed to handle data communications rather than voice. The primary functions are to allow many terminals to share a limited number of connections to a host time-sharing computer and to permit the same computer terminal to access several hosts. There is a move toward providing these functions through **terminal servers** on general-purpose high-speed networks, which allow much more powerful forms of communication among computers.

DATEXT An early information service on **CD-ROM,** providing information on corporations from a variety of sources. In 1987, Datext Inc. was acquired by

Lotus Development Corporation, and the information service is now part of the Lotus One Source family of CD-ROM products.

DECnet The proprietary family of networking protocols by Digital Equipment Corporation for its VAX computers. At the lower levels, DECnet can use **Ethernet, X.25,** or a proprietary protocol.

DIALOG One of the major online information services, offering access to more than 250 databases. The system was developed by the Lockheed Corporation, which sold DIALOG Information Services Inc. to Knight-Ridder Inc. in July 1988.

Document type definition A formal description of a class of document using the **SGML** markup language. Examples of document types are books, articles, manuals, and memoranda. Documents consist of components such as chapters, paragraphs, headings of several levels, footnotes, titles, authors, and publication dates. A document type definition describes components (both mandatory and optional) and rules for their relationships (for instance, that a chapter should consist of a chapter heading followed by paragraphs).

DVI Digital Video Interactive. A technology that uses sophisticated compression techniques and special hardware to store and retrieve the vast amounts of data required for video and high quality sound on CD-ROM. The DVI technology was originally developed by engineers at RCA and has been acquired by Intel Corporation. The technology will provide much higher quality than **CD-ROM XA** or **CD-I** but because it will be more expensive, DVI is not expected to be the basis of consumer products until the late 1990s. Sample products are expected in 1991, when chips have been developed to perform the compression and expansion of data.

Electronic mail A facility that permits the exchange of messages between users over computer networks. Some electronic mail systems also support electronic **bulletin boards** or **conferences.**

ERIC Educational Resources Information Center of the National Institute of Education, U.S. Department of Education. ERIC publishes two printed indexing services: Current Index to Journals in Education (CIJE) and Resources in Education (RIE). The combined databases are available on **CD-ROM** and online through several commercial services.

ESPRIT European Strategic Programme for Research in Information Technologies. A program of the European Economic Community that supports advances in the application of information technology through research grants and the establishment of standards.

Ethernet A popular low-level network protocol, developed at Xerox Corporation. Several families of higher-level protocol are compatible with Ethernet, including **TCP/IP.** It also has been adopted as an international standard (**ISO** 802.3).

Facsimile transmission A method for transmitting images by electronic means over telephone lines or computer networks.

Fax Popular abbreviation for **facsimile transmission.**

File server A computer on a network that functions as a store of files that can be accessed over the network as if they were stored locally on the user's own computer. The files may be public files intended for shared access or private files stored on shared hardware for reasons of convenience or economy.

File transfer A network service that allows files to be transmitted from one computer to another.

Free-text retrieval Retrieval of portions of text by searching for occurrences of any word or combination of words in the text itself, as opposed to retrieval based on indexes generated separately.

Front end A combination of hardware and software that functions as an interface to another computer system. The term often has been applied to communications devices attached to mainframe computers to control access from a variety of terminals. More recently, it has been adopted to describe software that runs on a user's personal computer to provide convenient and flexible access to a remote computer, and it is primarily in this sense that the term is used in this book. In both cases, the front end reduces the processing load on the remote system and the variety of tasks that it must perform.

Full-text database A database that holds the complete text of documents, in contrast to a database of **bibliographic records,** which holds information about documents, but not the documents themselves.

High Sierra A format for laying out files on a **CD-ROM,** developed by a group of vendors that met in the High Sierra Casino on Lake Tahoe in 1985. The format was adopted almost unchanged as an ISO standard in 1987. The acceptance of this standard has provided an impetus for the expansion of the market for CD-ROM products.

Hit rate The percentage of records in a file for which successful matches are found in a master file. The term often is used to refer to the proportion of items in a library's collection for which cataloging records are found in the files of a **bibliographic utility,** such as **OCLC** or **RLG.**

Holding symbol A code or symbol in a union catalog indicating that a particular library owns a given cataloged item.

Hypermedia An extension of **hypertext** that incorporates media other than text, such as graphics, sound, and video.

Hypertext A term coined by Ted Nelson in the 1960s to describe "nonsequential writing." A hypertext system (usually computer based) allows authors to link pieces of information, to create paths through a body of material, and to annotate existing texts. Readers can follow trails of footnotes and refer to related materials without losing their original place in the text. In the 1980s, several commercial software products that support hypertext have emerged.

ILLINET Illinois Library Network. A regional library network that acts as broker for OCLC services. The member libraries have also established ILLINET Online, a union catalog of holdings.

Index A tool for locating specific information in a body of material. The term is used in this book to describe three different forms of indexes: conventional indexes to printed volumes; products of indexing services, which typically contain (online or in printed form) bibliographic records for journal articles and support access by author, title, and subject; and indexes to machine-readable databases. These last usually are hidden from the user but nevertheless are the means of access to individual items of information.

INSPEC Information Service for the Physics and Engineering Communities. An abstracting service published by the Institution of Electrical Engineers in Great Britain.

Integrated system In the library field, this is a computer system based on a single central bibliographic database that automates a variety of operational tasks. Integrated systems usually incorporate modules to support **acquisitions, circulation, serials control,** and so on.

Internet A network of linked networks. With the initial **I** capitalized, the term usually refers to the linked networks that currently use the **TCP/IP** networking protocols developed on the **ARPANET** and cooperate to maintain common and compatible conventions and procedures. The Internet includes ARPANET, **NSFNET,** regional networks, and campus networks. Over time, the Internet is expected to migrate to the emerging **ISO** standard networking protocols.

ISO International Standards Organization. This organization, which has national standard-setting bodies as members, establishes international standards in many areas. In the networking area, ISO developed the Open Systems Interconnection (**OSI**) model for networking architectures. Using this layered model as a framework, ISO gradually is adopting one or more standard protocols for each of the layers. In 1989, the ISO family of protocols is not as complete as the **TCP/IP** family of protocols in use on the **Internet.** Among the lower-level protocols adopted as ISO standards are those that form the basis for **Ethernet** and IBM's **Token Ring**, as well as the **X.25** protocol that is widely used for commercial long-distance networks.

LEXIS A **full-text database** from Mead Data Central, Inc., that supports the legal profession. The online service covers federal, state, and foreign law and provides access to case law, statutes, and other sources of legal information.

Library automation The automation of the processes used in libraries to manage the acquisition of and access to library materials. The term often is used in this book to distinguish the automation of traditional procedures from the provision of online access to information for end users.

Linked Systems Project A project that has developed networking protocols to support the direct exchange of records among library database systems. The first implementation was for the exchange of **authority records** among RLIN, OCLC, and the Library of Congress. The project is now expanding to support the exchange of **bibliographic records** among online catalogs. As part of the project, the **Z39.50** protocol for information retrieval was developed.

Local system In the library field, this is a computer system for library automation that is based in an individual library, rather than provided by a **bibliographic utility** for shared access by many libraries.

MARC MAchine-Readable Cataloging. A standard format for exchanging machine-readable catalog records, developed by the Library of Congress in the late 1960s and ratified as a national, and then international, standard in the early 1970s. This standard has been a catalyst for the automation of traditional library processes.

MEDLARS Medical Literature Analysis and Retrieval System. The entire system of databases produced and distributed by the National Library of Medicine.

MEDLINE MEDLARS online. The National Library of Medicine's online bibliographic retrieval system consisting of citations and abstracts from approximately thirty-four hundred biomedical journals indexed during the current and two immediately preceding years.

MeSH Medical Subject Headings. A controlled vocabulary used by the National Library of Medicine to index journal articles included in **MEDLARS** and books included in the **NLM** online catalog.

Microfiche A small sheet of film (usually four by six inches) on which several pages of information can be stored photographically in reduced form and displayed on a special reader for reading or printing.

Microfilm A narrow strip of film on which pages can be stored photographically in reduced form and displayed on a special reader for reading or printing.

Microform A mechanism for storing printed images in reduced, photographic form in order to store or distribute large bodies of information more conveniently than is possible with paper. Microform is used heavily in libraries for storing materials that are easily lost or damaged or take more space than their utility justifies. Examples are past issues of newspapers or magazines, corporate annual reports, and rare, fragile volumes or manuscripts. The most common techniques employ **microfilm** and **microfiche.**

MIIS Meditech Interpretive Information System. A dialect of **MUMPS** that is specific to Data General hardware. Several large library management systems are written in MIIS.

MiniMEDLINE Proprietary bibliographic database searching software developed by the Dahlgren Medical Library of Georgetown University.

Modem A device that converts the digital signals used by computers into analog signals for transmission over conventional telephone lines, and vice versa.

MUMPS Massachusetts General Hospital Utility Multi-Program System. A medical applications software program language, developed by Octo Barnett, Harvard University, that is widely used in academic health centers.

NACO Name Authority Cooperative Project. A project in which a few participating libraries began to submit to the Library of Congress (LC) **authority records** for names not found in the LC authority file. This project was chosen as the first application of the **Linked Systems Project.** It has now been expanded and renamed National Coordinated Cataloging Operations.

NCCP National Coordinated Cataloging Project. A program in which certain research libraries will work with the Library of Congress to contribute **bibliographic records** following LC cataloging practices.

NEXIS A full-text database from Mead Data Central, Inc., that provides online access to articles from major newspapers and magazines.

NISO National Information Standards Organization. This group develops and approves standards that relate to libraries and information services. Formerly the Z39 subcommittee of ANSI, NISO is now part of the National Institute of Standards and Technology (previously the National Bureau of Standards).

NLM National Library of Medicine. A pioneer in the application of technology to library automation and information services.

NOTIS Northwestern Online Totally Integrated System. An **integrated system** for

library automation, developed at Northwestern University and now maintained and distributed by NOTIS Systems, Inc. See chapter 4 for a description of the system and its development.

NSFNET A three-level network sponsored by the National Science Foundation to support research. The NSF is responsible for the operation and management of a high-speed backbone network. Linked to the backbone are mid-level networks, which can be discipline-specific or regional. Campus networks attach in turn to mid-level networks. All these networks currently operate using the **TCP/IP** family of protocols and, with **ARPANET,** form the **Internet.** In time, the NSFNET and related networks will support the emerging **ISO** family of protocols.

NTIS National Technical Information Service (U.S. Department of Commerce). The central source for public sale of U.S. government–sponsored research, development, and engineering reports, as well as computer software, programs, and data files.

Null modem cable A cable used to link two terminals or personal computers that allows the devices to communicate in the same way as they would over a telephone line with modems at both ends.

NYSERNet New York State Education and Research Network. A regional network attached to the **NSFNET** and part of the **Internet.**

OCLC Online Computer Library Center. A nonprofit organization that provides services and products to support library operations. OCLC maintains a **union catalog** of holdings in libraries around the world and serves as a **bibliographic utility.** See chapter 2, which describes OCLC in more detail.

ODA Office Document Architecture. An **ISO** standard for the representation of formatted text, including explicit treatment of graphics and tables. This standard is widely supported in Japan and Europe but has not found much support in the United States. It is cumbersome to implement, but more complete than **SGML.**

OCR Optical character recognition. A process by which the image of a page is automatically converted into codes representing the printed characters, so that the text can be manipulated with a word processor or indexed for retrieval by individual words in the text.

ORBIT Online Retrieval of Bibliographic Information Timeshared. This online information service was acquired by Maxwell Communication Corp. in 1986 and incorporated into the Pergamon ORBIT Infoline service.

Original cataloging Preparation of the bibliographic record for an item without reference to an existing record for it. To avoid this expensive process, most academic libraries subscribe to a **bibliographic utility** that provides access to an online **union catalog** of the holdings of many libraries and supports **shared cataloging.**

OSI Open Systems Interconnection. The Open Systems Interconnection Basic Reference Model for network architectures was developed by the International Standards Organization (**ISO**) in 1978 as a framework for networking standardization. This model has seven layers. In ascending order, these are: physical, data link, network, transport, session, presentation, and application. Each layer has specific functions and relies on the services provided by the layer below it. For example, the physical layer (level 1) provides the mechanical and electrical interface for sending individual bits, while the data link layer (level 2) defines mechanisms for sending groups of bits between two points and checking for transmission errors. The user interacts directly only with **application protocols** (level 7) that support particular tasks. A network architecture that follows the model must define protocols for each layer and for the interfaces between the layers. ISO gradually is defining protocols for each of the layers, but there is not yet as wide a range of OSI application protocols (and hence network services) as is provided in the **TCP/IP** family of protocols or in proprietary network architectures from several manufacturers.

PAIS Public Affairs Information Service. This service indexes journals on public affairs and public policy. The PAIS International database is an online version of two printed indexing services: PAIS Bulletin and PAIS Foreign Language Index.

Periodical A publication appearing at regular or stated intervals, generally more frequently than annually. The term is not normally applied to newspapers.

PLATO Programmed Logic for Automatic Teaching Operations. A computer-aided instruction system originally developed at the University of Illinois and marketed by Control Data Corporation.

PostScript A computer language that describes the appearance of a page, independent of any particular printing device. Developed by Adobe Systems Incorporated, this language has been gaining ground as a format for storing and transmitting formatted documents that can be printed on a variety of equipment.

PsycINFO A bibliographic database that indexes journals in the field of psychology, published by the American Psychological Association.

PsycLIT A subset of **PsycINFO** published as an indexing service on **CD-ROM.**

Public services Those library functions that entail regular, direct contact between library staff and library users, including circulation and reference services. Many libraries divide their operations into two groups: public services and **technical services.**

Reserve collection A portion of the collection that is shelved separately and assigned restrictive borrowing periods to assure greater access to certain user groups. In academic libraries, reserves systems often support reading lists associated with particular courses.

Retrospective conversion The process of converting existing manual records (usual from catalogs) into machine-readable form, as distinct from the adoption of computer-based tools for routine cataloging of new acquisitions. For very large collections, this task is a daunting prospect that may not be economically justifiable.

RILA Repertoire International de la Littérature de l'Art (International Repertory of the Literature of Art). Published by the Getty Art History Information Program, this bibliographic database is generated through the cooperation of an international group of art historians. The main editorial office is at the Clark Art Institute in Williamstown, Massachusetts.

RILM Repertoire International de la Littérature Musicale (International Repertory of Music Literature). This bibliographic database was established by the International Association of Music Libraries and the International Musicological Society and is maintained at the City University of New York.

RLG Research Libraries Group. A nonprofit corporation owned by thirty-six major universities and research institutions. Its primary mission is to improve the management of and access to information resources necessary for the advancement of scholarship. As a basis for the programs that support this mission, RLG has established an online **union catalog** and a computer network through which access is provided. This technical infrastructure is the Research Libraries Information Network (**RLIN**). See chapter 3, which describes the Research Libraries Group in more detail.

RLIN Research Libraries Information Network. The technical infrastructure that supports the programs of the Research Libraries Group (**RLG**).

Router A device, usually implemented on a special-purpose computer, that links local area networks. A router is a link at the third level (network layer) of the **OSI** Basic Reference Model for network architecture and can link networks that use different low-level protocols (such as **Ethernet** and **Token Ring**). A router provides more isolation between networks than a **bridge** does.

SDLC Synchronous Data Link Communications. A protocol in IBM's **SNA** network architecture that corresponds to the second level (data link) layer of the **OSI** Basic Reference Model for network architecture.

SDSCnet San Diego Supercomputer Center Network. A mid-level network attached to the **NSFNET** and part of the **Internet.**

Search engine The component of an information retrieval system that performs the searching function, in contrast to the components that generate indexes or provide the user interface. By separating the search engine from the user interface, it is possible to customize interfaces for individual users without increasing the load on the computer system that acts as the search engine.

Search profile A set of queries customized for a particular user and run routinely to keep a scholar aware of new publications in a particular field.

Sequential browsing Scanning a database or piece of text in a predefined order. In a book, this corresponds to turning the pages; in a card catalog, to leafing through the cards in a drawer. Some online information systems support sequential browsing through indexes, providing an indication of how many times indexed terms appear in the database. Most full-text databases support sequential browsing (screen by screen) through retrieved documents. Few systems currently take advantage of the structure of longer documents to permit **structural browsing,** such as skimming through chapter headings or allowing the reader to skip to the beginning of the section that contains a relevant keyword.

Serial A publication issued in successive parts intended to be continued indefinitely. The term includes **periodicals,** annuals, newspapers, proceedings of societies, and so on.

Serials control The function or department within a library that manages the ordering, receiving, and binding of serials. Because subscriptions and the receipt of many issues against the same purchase order require special treatment, this function usually is handled separately from the **acquisition** of individual items.

Server A program or dedicated computer that provides services to other computers or users on a network. For example, a **file server** provides shared access to a file system, and a **database server** can service requests for individual records from a shared database.

SGML Standard Generalized Markup Language. Adopted as an international standard (**ISO** 8879-1986), this language provides a standard methodology for marking up a document with **tags** that identify its components (such as paragraphs, headings, and footnotes). Unlike the internal formats used by word processors, SGML tags can be read directly by a human (such as an editor or proofreader) as well as by a computer. SGML provides for the definition of types of document and for rules that govern relationships among the constituent components of a given document type. For example, a book can be defined as consisting of chapters, with each chapter having a single heading and any number of paragraphs. A document stored in SGML format can serve as the basis for a printed publication when tags are associated with layout instructions. It also can serve as the basis for an information retrieval system that takes advantage of a document's structure, for instance, by supporting **structural browsing** as well as **sequential browsing.**

Shared cataloging The preparation of bibliographic records for items by referring to existing records for them. The driving force behind the development of **bibliographic utilities** was the potential for savings from shared cataloging through the maintenance of an online **union catalog** of the holdings of many libraries.

Shelflist A file of bibliographic records arranged by call number that functions for library staff as the master inventory of a library's collection. In a manual system, this was separate from the catalogs arranged by author, title, and subject that were intended for public use. In an **integrated system** for **library automation,** a single bibliographic file can serve as catalog and shelflist.

Skunkworks A term initiated by Lockheed California Company and used to denote a highly innovative, fast-moving, and slightly eccentric activity operating at the edges of the corporate world. Popularized in *In Search of Excellence,* by T. J. Peters and R. H. Waterman, Jr. (New York: Warner, 1982).

SNA Systems Network Architecture. IBM's layered architecture of communication protocols.

SOLINET Southeastern Library Network. One of the regional library networks established to broker the services of OCLC.

Source code The programming statements that are used to generate a piece of software. Most software is sold in a form that has been converted into the computer's internal representation and cannot be modified. For crucial, complex software, such as a library automation system, customers with sufficient technical expertise often prefer also to acquire the source code, which gives them flexibility to make local modifications and security against potential problems such as vendor bankruptcy.

SPIRES Stanford Public Information Retrieval System. A database management system developed and maintained at Stanford University. Originally designed to support a bibliographic database for physicists, SPIRES also supports conventional administrative applications.

SQL Structured Query Language. A language for manipulating database records. Developed by IBM, SQL has now been ratified by ANSI as a national standard and is being incorporated into most major database management systems, particularly to support database applications distributed among several computers.

STAIRS Storage And Information Retrieval System. An IBM software product that supports retrieval of information by searching on any word in a body of text.

Stopword A word considered insignificant for indexing or searching, such as "the," "of," and "and."

Structural browsing Scanning a book or document by taking advantage of its structure, as opposed to simply turning the pages (or moving sequentially through screen displays, if online). For example, a scholar often glances at section headings, appendixes, and figures in an article before settling down to read steadily from beginning to end. Or a reader seeking specific information may consult an index to locate a term and then look for the beginning of the section or chapter in which the term is used.

Subject headings Terms that describe the subject areas to which a publication contributes and that can be used to index the item for retrieval by a subject search. To provide effective **bibliographic access** to items, subject headings usually are chosen from a thesaurus or authorized list. The Library of Congress Subject Headings are widely used for general collections, but more specialized systems of subject headings are used in some areas (for example, **MeSH** for medical publications). Subject heading schemes must be maintained and updated to respond to expanding bodies of knowledge.

SURAnet Southeastern Universities Research Association Network. A regional computer network attached to the **NSFNET** and part of the **Internet.**

Synchronous communication Communication in which data is transmitted at a fixed rate with the transmitter and receiver synchronized. By avoiding the need for start and stop elements, higher transmission speeds can be achieved more efficiently than are possible with **asynchronous communication.**

Tags Sequences of codes embedded in text to label parts of a document or to provide formatting instructions to printing equipment. In **SGML** and other markup languages, tags are used to mark the components of a document, such as headings, emphasized phrases, footnotes, and so on. Tags usually have a form that can be read directly by a human proofreader if necessary, as distinct from the internal codes used by most word processors to represent formatting information.

TCP/IP Transmission Control Protocol/Internet Protocol. This pair of mid-level network protocols is the basis for the **ARPANET** family of protocols. It has been widely adopted by government agencies and universities and is supported on many types of equipment. However, most users expect to migrate gradually to the standard protocols adopted by **ISO,** as those standards are developed more fully and supported in commercial products.

Technical services Library functions that support the collection, including acquisitions, cataloging, serials control, and physical processing (such as binding and bar-coding). Another group of library services are the **public services** that support users directly.

Telenet A commercial packet-switching network based on the **X.25** network protocol.

Telnet The protocol in the **ARPANET** family that allows users to log in to a remote computer over a network.

Terminal An input/output device without general-purpose processing capabilities, designed for use with a host computer. A terminal usually consists of a screen display and a keyboard, as well as an interface for connecting to a computer or network.

Terminal emulation A technique for communication between a personal computer and a host time-sharing computer. A program runs in the personal computer, emulating the functions of a particular type of terminal. In addition to possessing the capabilities of a regular terminal, most terminal emulation software provides a file-transfer function. **File transfer** requires a matching program running on the time-sharing computer.

Terminal server A communications device that allows terminals (or personal computers emulating terminals) to link to a high-speed general-purpose computer network for access to time-sharing computers on that network.

Time sharing A method of allowing many people to use a computer simultaneously, by allocating slices of time to each user in turn. If the computer processor is powerful enough and time slices are short and frequent, a user appears to have sole use of the computer.

Token ring A network protocol that uses a special message, known as a "token," to control access to a ring. The IBM Token Ring is an example of a protocol using this technique. An almost identical protocol has been adopted as a national and international standard (**ISO** 802.5 Token Ring). Several families of higher-level protocols are compatible with this token ring protocol, including **TCP/IP,** the higher-level ISO protocols, and IBM's **SNA** protocols.

Union catalog A catalog of the collections of a group of cooperating libraries. **Holding symbols** indicate which libraries hold a particular item.

UTLAS A **bibliographic utility** originally based on a system developed at the University of Toronto to support Canadian libraries. After expanding to provide library support services internationally, UTLAS became a for-profit subsidiary of the International Thomson Organization.

WESTLAW An online information service, published by West Publishing Company. This full-text service provides access to statutes, court proceedings, and a variety of other legal information.

WLN Western Library Network. Originally the Washington Library Network, this **bibliographic utility** assumed a new name when it started to provide services beyond the state of Washington.

X.25 A network interface standard for communicating at 56K bits/second over long-haul networks. Developed by **CCITT,** the standard has been adopted as an **ISO** standard and is widely implemented. It is used by commercial networks such as Telenet and includes protocols for the three lowest layers of the **OSI** model for network architectures.

X.400 A standard **application protocol** for **electronic mail,** ratified as an **ISO** standard and widely adopted in Europe and on international commercial networks. Moves are being made in the academic networking community to support this standard in addition to the SMTP mail protocol that is part of the **TCP/IP** protocol family.

Z39.50 A networking protocol for information retrieval, developed as part of the **Linked Systems Project** but applicable to other distributed information systems.

Bibliography

One of the aims of this volume is to encourage interaction and cooperation between two campus divisions that serve the academic community: the library and the computing services organization. When it comes to suggesting additional reading, the balance of published literature is rather one-sided. Computer services in universities are very different from those in corporate or government settings, because of the traditional independence and autonomy of academic departments and scholars. The primary means of communication among members of the academic computing community is over the networks, through electronic mail and bulletin boards. Academic librarians belong to a wider community; libraries of other types (public, corporate, or school) share many of the same problems. Since the published record is at the core of the librarian's work, it is not surprising that the library literature is extensive. Since their generation is a traditional library service, bibliographies abound, covering all issues and topics that relate to libraries of all varieties. Consequently, this bibliography makes no attempt to be comprehensive. Instead, it emphasizes material accessible to the general reader, suggesting background material and continuing sources of information about progress toward the electronic library.

This volume is the third in the EDUCOM Strategies Series on Information Technology from EDUCOM and Digital Press, in which authors from various institutions describe their plans and planning processes for applying technology in an academic context. The first volume dealt with computing services in general; the second covered computer networks. Since the delivery of electronic information to scholars depends on such networks, the latter volume provides a valuable context for the present work and a nontechnical introduction to the field.

McCredie, John W., ed. *Campus Computing Strategies*. Bedford, Mass.: Digital Press, 1983.

Arms, Caroline R., ed. *Campus Networking Strategies*. Bedford, Mass.: Digital Press, 1988.

This is not the first book to present case studies of libraries adapting to technological change. In the early 1980s, Cline and Sinnott used formal methodologies of social science to examine the effect of automation on the structure and functioning of four academic libraries. A project sponsored by the National Association of College and Business Officers studied management, planning, and the impact of technological change in another four university libraries. In both volumes, the emphasis is on changes within the library resulting from the automation of technical library operations. From the viewpoint of a public library, Dowlin described the ambitious steps taken in the Pikes Peak Library District to develop a community information center.

Cline, Hugh F., and Loraine T. Sinnott. *The Electronic Library: The Impact of Automation on Academic Libraries*. The Lexington Books Special Series in Libraries and Librarianship, ed. Richard D. Johnson. Lexington, Mass.: Lexington Books, 1983.
Dowlin, Kenneth E. *The Electronic Library: The Promise and the Process*. Applications in Information Management and Technology Series, ed. Ching-chih Chen. New York: Neal-Schuman, 1984.
Hyatt, James A., and Aurora A. Santiago. *University Libraries in Transition*. Washington, D.C.: National Association of College and Business Officers, 1987.

The vision of the electronic library is not new. Vannevar Bush's formative description in 1945 of a scholar's workstation is cited frequently. A few years earlier, Ethel Fair had urged librarians to be more adventurous in their use of technology to provide improved service.

Bush, Vannevar. "As We May Think." *Atlantic Monthly* 176, no. 1 (July 1945): 101–8.
Fair, Ethel M. "Inventions and Books—What of the Future?" *The Library Journal* 61 (January 15, 1936): 47–51.

Collections of essays provide valuable summaries of the state of the art and prevailing attitudes, now and in the past. In times of technological pressure, it is illuminating to look back and see both how rapid change has been and how the fundamental issues of scholarship and access to information remain the same.

Benson, Ian, ed. *Intelligent Machinery: Theory and Practice*. Cambridge, England: Cambridge University Press, 1986. This book resulted from a conference to identify opportunities for scientific collaboration. It provides a practical survey of artificial intelligence.

Cole, John Y., ed. *Books in our Future: Perspectives and Proposals*. Washington, D.C.: Library Of Congress, The Center for the Book, 1987. This collection of essays, studies, and reports was prepared as part of a study of "the changing role of the book in the future," authorized by the United States Congress in 1983.

Edelman, Hendrik, ed. *Libraries and Information Science in the Electronic Age*. Philadelphia: ISI Press, 1986. This volume presents twelve lectures given between 1983 and 1985 at American schools of library and information science by prominent scholars and practitioners in the field.

Greenberger, Martin, ed. *Management and the Computer of the Future*. Cambridge, Mass.: MIT Press and John Wiley & Sons, 1962. This book collects a series of lectures presented at the Massachusetts Institute of Technology to celebrate the university's centenary.

Shera, J. H. *Documentation and the Organization of Knowledge*. Hamden, Conn.: Archon Books, 1966. In these essays, a library school dean urges librarians to take advantage of automation, particularly for "documentation," the term then used for the compilation and retrieval of bibliographic information.

As is clear from the case-study chapters in this book, journals provide the primary mechanism for keeping up with new developments in many areas. Of the many journals aimed at the library community, several focus on the application of technology. The three listed here cover all aspects of library operations: traditional processes, clerical and administrative tasks, and information delivery. *Library Hi Tech* is particularly accessible to nonlibrarians.

Information Technology and Libraries. The quarterly journal of the Library and Information Technology Association.

Library Hi Tech. Published quarterly by Pierian Press. C. Edward Wall, the editor and publisher, seeks out articles that expose the issues that he considers to be of primary importance to librarians. Articles include tutorials, historical surveys, essays, and descriptions of operational systems and projects, with an emphasis on the dissemination of practical experience.

Library Technology Reports. Published by the American Library Association. This journal is devoted to reports, reviews, and surveys on automation products and installations.

Other journals and magazines cover more specialized areas. Listed here are a few that often include material particularly relevant to the delivery to end users of information in electronic form.

Inform. Published by the Association of Information and Image Management, this magazine covers topics such as electronic and microform archiving, document scanning, and optical character recognition.

Journal of the American Society for Information Science. Published quarterly, this journal covers the area of information retrieval. Articles range from technical research papers on algorithms for information retrieval to historical surveys and special features on topics such as telecommunications and the National Library of Medicine's IAIMS initiative.

Laserdisk Professional. Published by Pemberton Press. This magazine, introduced in 1988, covers the use of optical media for information systems.

Online. Published bimonthly by Online Inc., this magazine covers the use of online information systems, with topics ranging from economics and industry analysis to the design of user interfaces.

Online Review. Also dealing with issues related to online information systems, this international journal is published six times a year by Learned Information Ltd. in Oxford, England.

In an area of such rapid change, readers may be interested in fuller and continuing coverage of recent developments in particular areas relating to technology in libraries. Bibliographies and annual reviews abound.

ALA Yearbook of Library and Information Services. Chicago: American Library Association. This annual survey of developments in all areas of interest to the library community includes short articles on library automation and information retrieval.

Annual Review of Information Science and Technology. Washington D.C.: American Society for Information Science. This publication, issued annually since 1966, consists of chapters by specialists covering developments in particular areas through reviews of the published literature. Examples of recent chapters are "Artificial Intelligence and Information Retrieval," "Systems that Inform: Emerging Trends in Library Automation and Network Development," and "Economics of Information."

Bowker Annual of Library and Book Trade Information. New York: Bowker. This publication includes bibliographies, directories of organizations, industry statistics, and short reports on a variety of issues, such as standards, copyright, and legislation affecting libraries and publishers.

Library Hi Tech Bibliography, vols. 1, 2, and 3. Ann Arbor, Mich.: Pierian Press. Each of these volumes includes about fifteen annotated bibliographies compiled by contributing librarians. Topics cover all aspects of technology that might be applied to libraries, from "Barcoding Collections" and "Designing High Tech Library Buildings" to "The Library as Local Online Information Utility" and "Graphics Capture, Storage, and Transmission."

Surveys and reviews of different aspects of library automation and library networks serve to provide a fuller background than this volume attempts.

Crawford, Walt. *Current Technologies in the Library: An Informal Overview.* Boston: G. K. Hall, 1988. Crawford's straightforward style provides an overview that is neither superficial nor confused by detail.

Cummings, Martin M. *The Economics of Research Libraries.* Washington, D.C.: Council on Library Resources, 1986.

Hagler, Ronald, and Peter Simmons. *The Bibliographic Record and Information Technology.* Chicago: American Library Association, 1982. This volume, intended as a text for a core-curriculum course in a library school, introduces obsolescent, current, and new bibliographic practices in both manual and automated contexts. An excellent source for the nonlibrarian who wants a thorough understanding of the terminology and practices of catalogers and indexers.

Advances in Library Automation and Networking. Greenwich, Conn.: JAI Press. The first volume of this series was published in 1987. The material is presented from a perspective of a balanced regard for bibliography and traditional library practice in the context of computers and telecommunications.

Hildreth, Charles R. *Library Automation in North America: A Reassessment of the Impact of New Technologies on Networking.* München, West Germany: K. G. Saur, 1987. Prepared for the Commission of the European Communities, this volume focuses on the role of the bibliographic utilities.

Martin, Susan K. *Library Networks, 1986–87: Libraries in Partnership.* Professional Librarian Series. White Plains, N.Y.: Knowledge Industry Publications, 1986. For those familiar with computer networks, this volume presents an excellent picture of how library networks differ from them. Also included is a directory of library networks and members.

Reynolds, Dennis. *Library Automation: Issues and Applications.* New York: Bowker, 1985. A thorough and readable treatment of the automation of traditional library processes, including online catalogs and remote search services.

Rush, James E. "The Library Automation Market: Why Do Vendors Fail? A History of Vendors and their Characteristics." *Library Hi Tech* 6, no. 3 (1988): 7–33.

Saffady, William. "Characteristics and Experiences of Integrated Systems Installations." *Library Technology Reports* 23, no.5: 651–767. This review includes general discussion and specific information such as tables showing the number of installations by vendor for different types, sizes, and locations of libraries.

The surveys in the previous section primarily relate to libraries in general or to traditional library operations. For the reader interested in exploring new areas of library services, here are a few possible starting points.

Benson, James A., and Bella Hass Weinberg, eds.. *Gateway Software and Natural Language Interfaces.* Ann Arbor, Mich.: Pierian Press, 1988.

Chen, Ching-chih, and Peter Hernon, eds. *Numeric Databases.* Norwood, N.J.: Ablex Publishing Corporation, 1984. This is a collection of papers intended to introduce the special characteristics of numeric databases to librarians and to encourage libraries to consider access to numerical information as a service that complements access to bibliographic information.

Conklin, Jeff. "Hypertext: A Survey and Introduction." *IEEE Computer* 20, no. 9 (September 1987): 17–41. This article surveys a number of hypertext systems not mentioned in chapter 14 and describes the "essence of hypertext." However, as the author admits, the article can only "hint at the potential." Hypertext must be experienced to be appreciated.

Desmarais, Norman. *The Librarian's CD-ROM Handbook.* Westport, Conn.: Meckler, 1989. This volume provides a general overview of the technology and a survey of products and services. Although the survey will be out of date soon, its free-form discussion is more readable than a directory in list format.

Fayen, Emily Gallup. "The Answer Machine and Direct Connect: Do-it-yourself Searching in Libraries." *Online* 12, no. 5 (September 1988): 13–21.

Friedman, Edward A. "Word Management Systems: An Introduction." *Inform* 2, no. 5 (May 1988): 12–15. A description of scanning and optical character recognition in the context of making the full text of books available online at Stevens Institute.

Friedman, Edward A. "Word for Word." *Inform* 2, no. 8 (September 1988): 22–24. A sequel to the previous article, emphasizing the characteristics of the retrieval software used for the project.

Helgerson, Linda W. "CD-ROM and Scholarly Research in the Humanities." *Computers and the Humanities* 22 (1988): 111–16.

Rowlands, Ian, ed. *Text Retrieval: An Introduction.* London, England: Taylor Graham, 1987. This slim paperback consists of contributions to a course designed to introduce nonspecialists to the field of online text storage and retrieval. It contains general discussions, comparisons of software products, and case studies from corporate and academic settings.

Weiskel, Timothy C. "University Libraries, Integrated Scholarly Information Systems (ISIS), and the Changing Character of Academic Research." *Library Hi Tech* 6, no. 4 (1988): 7–27. This article challenges libraries to respond to pressure from scholars for library systems that allow them to integrate access to bibliographic information into their developing personal information systems.

The Linked Systems Project, which began in 1980 as an experiment in linking the primary bibliographic databases, has developed networking protocols that can serve as a basis for much wider cooperation and access among libraries. The project and protocols are described in a recent publication from OCLC. Avram, one of the originators of LSP, argues that progress is slow because "there does not exist any effective vehicle for national planning and coordination."

Avram, Henriette. "Toward a Nationwide Library Network." *Journal of Library Administration* 8, no. 3/4 (Fall/Winter 1987): 95–115.

Fenly, Judith G., and Beacher Wiggins, eds. *The Linked Systems Project: A Networking Tool for Libraries.* OCLC Library, Information and Computer Science Series. Dublin, Ohio: OCLC, 1988.

The importance of standards to the information industry is hard to overestimate. Walt Crawford, of the Research Libraries Group, has written widely and with insight and clarity in this area. His book on technical standards does not cover some important standards developed since the book was written in 1986, but his introduction to the field is still valuable. A new edition is under consideration. Crawford is also the current editor of the official publication of the National Information Standards Organization (NISO).

Crawford, Walt. *Technical Standards: An Introduction for Librarians.* Professional Librarian Series. White Plains, N.Y.: Knowledge Industry Publications, 1986. Books in this series are now available through G. K. Hall.
———. "Standards, Innovation and Optical Media." *Laserdisk Professional* 2, no. 1 (January 1989): 31–37.
Information Standards Quarterly. Published by the National Information Standards Organization, this newsletter was formerly *The Voice of Z39.*

Computer networking is a complex technical field and finding an introduction at the right level can be difficult. For some, the ideal is an article that briefly introduces the jargon and conceptual framework, particularly, the OSI Basic Reference Model for network architectures.

Denenberg, Ray. "Open Systems Interconnection." *Library Hi Tech* 3, no. 1 (1985): 15–26.
Barden, Robert A., and Richard Golden. "Networking and Telecommunications on Campus: A Tutorial." *EDUCOM Bulletin* 21, no. 2 (Summer 1986): 18–25. This article gives examples of different types of networks in use on many campuses.
Lefkon, Richard. "A LAN Primer." *Byte* 12, no. 8 (July 1987): 147–154. This article concentrates on the OSI model and the low-level protocol standards for high-speed local area networks.

For others, a topic as complex as computer networking needs to be introduced through a book that goes into more depth.

McNamara, John E. *Local Area Networks: An Introduction to the Technology.* Bedford, Mass.: Digital Press, 1985. An excellent introduction to local area networks for the nontechnical reader.
Tanenbaum, Andrew S. *Computer Networks.* 2nd ed. Englewood Cliffs, N.J.: Prentice-Hall, 1988. This textbook is intended for use in theoretical telecommunications courses but is very readable if one skips the technical sections.

Descriptions of some of the various national and international computer networks and their histories may be of interest. The article by Quarterman and Hoskins is an excellent summary of the variety of networks as they were in 1986. Quarterman has since expanded the article into a book that is a valuable, comprehensive source of information and a contribution to history.

DARPA. *A History of the ARPAnet: The First Decade.* Cambridge, Mass.: Bolt Beranek and Newman, April 1983.

Jennings, Dennis M., et al. "Computer Networking for Scientists." *Science* 231, no. 4741 (February 28, 1986): 943–50. Also reprinted in *EDUCOM Bulletin* 21, no. 2 (Summer 1986): 2–9. A description of the origins of the NSFNET.

Mills, David L., and Hans-Werner Braun. "The NSFNET Backbone Network." *Computer Communications Review* 17, no. 5: 191–96. Special issue of papers presented at the SIGCOMM '87 Workshop on Frontiers in Computer Communications Technology, Stowe, Vermont, August 11–13, 1987, sponsored by ACM SIGCOMM.

Oberst, Daniel J., and Sheldon B. Smith. "BITNET: Past, Present, and Future." *EDUCOM Bulletin* 21, no. 2 (Summer 1986): 10–17.

Quarterman, John S. *The Matrix: Computer Networks and Conferencing Systems Worldwide.* Bedford, Mass.: Digital Press, in press.

Quarterman, John S., and Josiah H. Hoskins. "Notable Computer Networks." *Communications of the ACM* 29, no. 10 (October 1986): 933–71.

The establishment of a unified and comprehensive national network for computing and information access has been a vision for many years, but, recently, prompted in part by programs in Europe and Japan, the possibility is being looked at more closely. A major thrust of EDUCOM's Networking and Telecommunications Task Force (NTTF) is to stimulate discussion in this area and bring the issues to the notice of legislators and government agencies. National Net '88, a conference on national networking that launched the public effort, was held in the spring of 1988 and thirteen of the presentations were published in a double summer/fall issue of the *EDUCOM Bulletin.* Of these, two were directly related to information retrieval and the exchange of bibliographic records over networks, while others addressed the strategic importance of a national network, technological challenges, and issues of funding and the cooperative involvement of the public and private sectors. Only a few of the articles are listed here.

Avram, Henriette D. "LSP and Library Network Services in the Future." *EDUCOM Bulletin* 23, no. 2/3 (Summer/Fall 1988): 52–58.

Fraser, A. G. "Opportunities and Obstacles for a National Research Network." *EDUCOM Bulletin* 23, no. 2/3 (Summer/Fall 1988): 22–31.

Hancock, Ellen M. "The Strategic Importance of a National Network." *EDUCOM Bulletin* 23, no. 2/3 (Summer/Fall 1988): 3–7.

Porter, Donald D. "Information Retrieval for the NSFNET Community." *EDUCOM Bulletin* 23, no. 2/3 (Summer/Fall 1988): 59–62.

Other issues of the *EDUCOM Bulletin* and its successor, the *EDUCOM Review,* have included related articles, and the NTTF has issued policy papers intended to expose the issues to as wide an audience as possible.

Branscomb, Lewis M. "Planning the New National Network." *EDUCOM Review* 24, no. 1 (Spring 1989): 7–10.

EDUCOM Networking and Telecommunications Task Force. "A National Higher Education Network: Issues and Opportunities." EDUCOM, Princeton, N.J., May 1987. Most of the text of this working paper was published under the same title, with Robert Gillespie and Michael M. Roberts as primary authors, in the *EDUCOM Bulletin* 22, no. 4 (Winter 1987): 2–5.

EDUCOM Networking and Telecommunications Task Force. "The National Research and Education Network: A Policy Paper." EDUCOM, Washington, D.C., April 1989.

King, Kenneth M. "In Search of a National Computing, Information Access, and Networking Agenda." *EDUCOM Bulletin* 22, no. 3 (Fall 1987): 2–4.

Roberts, Michael M. "The Need for a Higher Education Computer Network." *EDUCOM Bulletin* 22, no. 1 (Spring 1987): 9–10.

The convergence of interests of libraries and computing organizations on campus has been widely discussed, in this volume and elsewhere. Several articles on the topic are listed at the end of chapter 11. Convergence in the areas of national networking and electronic publishing is also an important issue.

Molholt, Pat. "Library Networking: The Interface of Ideas and Actions." Office of Library Programs, U.S. Department of Education, June 1988. This report is a personal statement that outlines a potential role for the Office of Library Programs in the development of a unified national strategy for library networks, including convergence with computer networks.

OCLC. *Campus of the Future: Conference on Information Resources.* OCLC Library, Information, and Computer Science Series, no. 5. Dublin, Ohio: OCLC, 1987. Senior administrators, computer center directors, and librarians from eight major universities "at the forefront of technical initiative" met to explore issues affecting the adoption of new methods for the publication and distribution of knowledge.

Wall, C. Edward. "The Conference on Information Resources for the Campus of the Future." *Library Hi Tech* 4, no. 4 (Winter 1986): 37–48.

Woodsworth, Anne. "Libraries and the Chief Information Officer: Implications and Trends." *Library Hi Tech* 6, no. 1 (1988): 37–44. Woodsworth summarizes the results of a study of senior academic officers charged with coordinating the implementation and use of information technologies. A monograph based on this study will be published by the American Library Association.

Credits and Trademarks

Photography Credits

Cover
Duke Humfrey's Library, The Bodleian Library, Oxford University   Billett Potter

Introduction
Main reading room, Library of Congress   Library of Congress

The Technological Context
Online catalog terminals at Northwestern   David Delo

OCLC Online Computer Library Center
OCLC headquarters   OCLC
Graph-Text display   OCLC

Research Libraries Group
Closeup of keyboard for Chinese/Japanese/Korean terminal   Research Libraries Group

Northwestern University
Computer room at Northwestern Library   David Delo

Clemson University
Sikes Hall in early spring   Clemson University Communications Center

University of Illinois at Urbana-Champaign
Main library building   University of Illinois

Brigham Young University Law Library
Law student workstations   David A. Thomas

Georgia Institute of Technology
Price Gilbert Memorial Library   Georgia Tech News Bureau

University of Southern California
Doheny Memorial Library   Lois Gervais

Columbia University

Students at library entrance on Broadway   Columbia Public Information Office

Cornell University

Welcome screen for Mann Library's Scholar's Information System   Cornell Media Services

Carnegie Mellon University

Engineering and Science Library   Bill Redic

Johns Hopkins University, Welch Medical Library

Online catalog terminals at Welch Medical Library   Norman Watkins

Other Projects and Progress

Andrew workstations in Hunt Library at Carnegie Mellon   Bill Redic

The Context for the Future

Compact Disk Read-Only Memory   OCLC

Trademarks

The companies listed below hold the following trademarks, or market the following products, mentioned in this book.

3Com   3Com Corporation
America: History and Life, Historical Abstracts   ABC/CLIO
PostScript   Adobe Systems Inc.
Amdahl 5890-300E   Amdahl
Chemical Abstracts Service   American Chemical Society
Economic Literature Index   American Economic Association
MATHSCI   American Mathematical Society
PsycINFO, PsycLIT, Psychological Abstracts   American Psychological Association
AppleTalk, Hypercard, LaserWriter, Lisa, Macintosh, Mac II, Mac SE   Apple
    Computer, Inc.
Open Look, UNIX   AT&T
Model 100 Terminal   Beehive International
BLIS   Bibliotechniques, Inc.
Biological Abstracts, BIOSIS   BIOSIS
Diamond   Bolt Beranek & Newman
BRS/Search   BRS Information Technologies (a subsidiary of Maxwell
    Communication Corp.)
Intermedia   Brown University
Hyperties   Cognetics Corporation
CompuServe   CompuServe
Cyber 990, PLATO   Control Data Corporation
ABI/INFORM   Data Courier Inc. (a division of University Microfims International)

Eclipse, MV-8000   Data General

DIALOG, DIALOG Business Connection   DIALOG Information Services Inc.
(a subsidiary of Knight-Ridder Inc.)

All-in-One, DEC, DECmate, DECnet, DECSYSTEM-20, MicroVAX, PDP 11, TOPS,
ULTRIX, VAX, VAX-11/750, VAX-11/780, VAX 6200, VAX 8500, VAX 8600, VAX
8650, VAX 8810, VAX 8820, VAXcluster, VAXstation, VAX/VMS, VMSmail, VT100
Digital Equipment Corporation

Compact Disclosure   Disclosure Incorporated

Floating Point System T-20 Hypercube   Floating Point Systems Inc.

GEAC   GEAC Computer Corporation Limited

BioSYNTHESIS, MiniMEDLINE   Georgetown University

RILA   Getty Art History Information Program

Harris HCX-9   Harris Corporation

Business Collection, Computer Database, InfoTrac, Magazine Collection, Magazine
Index, Management Contents, National Newspaper Index, Search Helper
Information Access Company

Arts and Humanities Citation Index, Current Contents, Science Citation Index, Social
Science Citation Index, Trade and Industry   Institute for Scientific Information,
Incorporated

INSPEC   Institution for Electrical Engineers

80386   Intel Corporation

Interleaf   Interleaf Inc.

RILM   International Association of Music Libraries

CICS, IBM, IBM 3081, IBM 3083, IBM 3090, IBM 3270, IBM 3705, IBM 3708, IBM
3725, IBM 4331, IBM 4341, IBM 4381, IBM Information Network, IBM PC, IBM
PS/2, IBM Token Ring, MVS, MVS/XA, OS/2, Presentation Manager, PROFS, SNA
STAIRS, VM, VM/CMS, VSE   International Business Machines Corporation

Corporate & Industrial Research Reports , CIRR   JA Micropublishing Inc.

Encyclopedia of Polymer Science & Engineering, Kirk-Othmer Encyclopedia of
Chemical Technology   John Wiley & Sons, Inc.

FastPath   Kinetics (a division of Excelan, Inc.)

Bib-Base/Acq   Library Technologies, Inc.

X Window System   Massachusetts Institute of Technology

ORBIT, Pergamon ORBIT Infoline   Maxwell Communication Corporation

LEXIS, NEXIS   Mead Data Central, Inc.

MIIS   Medical Information Technology Inc.

MENU The International Software Database   MENU The International Software
Database Corp.

MICOM   MICOM Systems, Inc.

Microsoft, Microsoft Windows, Microsoft OS/2 Presentation Manager   Microsoft
Corporation

Modern Language Association Bibliography   Modern Language Association

AGRICOLA, Answerman   National Agriculture Library

IRX, MEDLARS, MEDLINE, MeSH, TOXNET   National Library of Medicine

NeXT   NeXT, Inc.

NOTIS **NOTIS Systems, Inc.**
ACQ350, CAT CD450, Graph-Text, ILS, LS/2000, Newton, OCLC, M300, M310,
    Micro Enhancer, SC350, Search CD450 **Online Computer Library Center, Inc.**
Paradyne 850 **Paradyne Corporation**
Personal Librarian **Personal Library Software**
PAIS **Public Affairs Information Service, Inc.**
ProNET **Proteon, Inc..**
Pyramid 98x **Pyramid Technology Corp**
RLIN **Research Libraries Group**
Scribe **Scribe Systems Inc.**
ADABAS **Software AG**
BALLOTS, SPIRES **Stanford University**
COMPUSTAT **Standard & Poor's Corp.**
Sun 3, Sun 4 **Sun Microsystems**
Easynet **Telebase Systems, Inc.**
GTE/Telenet **Telenet Communications Corporation**
International Bibliography of the Theatre **Theatre Research Data Center**
Tymnet **Tymnet-McDonnell Douglas Network Systems Co.**
UTLAS **Utlas International**
WESTLAW **West Publishing Company**
Applied Science and Technology Index, Art Index, General Science Index,
    Humanities Index, Library Literature, Social Sciences Index, WILSEARCH
    H.W. Wilson Co.
WYSEpc **Wyse Technology**
Ethernet, Sigma 9, XNS **XEROX Corporation**

Index